The Elusive Quest for European Security

St Antony's Series
General Editor: **Eugene Rogan** (1997–), Fellow of St Antony's College, Oxford

Recent titles include:

Carl Aaron
THE POLITICAL ECONOMY OF JAPANESE FOREIGN DIRECT INVESTMENT IN
THE UK AND THE US

Craig Brandist and Galin Tihanov (*editors*)
MATERIALIZING BAKHTIN

Simon Duke
THE ELUSIVE QUEST FOR EUROPEAN SECURITY
From EDC to CFSP

Tim Dunne
INVENTING INTERNATIONAL SOCIETY

Ken Endo
THE PRESIDENCY OF THE EUROPEAN COMMISSION UNDER JACQUES DELORS

Anthony Forster
BRITAIN AND THE MAASTRICHT NEGOTIATIONS

Fernando Guirao
SPAIN AND THE RECONSTRUCTION OF WESTERN EUROPE, 1945–57

Huck-ju Kwon
THE WELFARE STATE IN KOREA

Cécile Laborde
PLURALIST THOUGHT AND THE STATE IN BRITAIN AND FRANCE, 1900–25

C. S. Nicholls
THE HISTORY OF ST ANTONY'S COLLEGE, OXFORD, 1950–2000

Miguel Székely
THE ECONOMICS OF POVERTY AND WEALTH ACCUMULATION IN MEXICO

Steve Tsang and Hung-mao Tien (*editors*)
DEMOCRATIZATION IN TAIWAN

St Antony's Series
Series Standing Order ISBN 0–333–71109–2
(*outside North America only*)

You can receive future titles in this series as they are published by placing a standing order.
Please contact your bookseller or, in case of difficulty, write to us at the address below with
your name and address, the title of the series and the ISBN quoted above.

Customer Services Department, Macmillan Distribution Ltd, Houndmills, Basingstoke,
Hampshire RG21 6XS, England

The Elusive Quest for European Security
From EDC to CFSP

Simon Duke
Associate Professor
European Institute of Public Administration
Maastricht
Netherlands

in association with
ST ANTONY'S COLLEGE, OXFORD

First published in Great Britain 2000 by
MACMILLAN PRESS LTD
Houndmills, Basingstoke, Hampshire RG21 6XS and London
Companies and representatives throughout the world

A catalogue record for this book is available from the British Library.

ISBN 0–333–77798–0

First published in the United States of America 2000 by
ST. MARTIN'S PRESS, INC.,
Scholarly and Reference Division,
175 Fifth Avenue, New York, N.Y. 10010

ISBN 0–312–22402–8

Library of Congress Cataloging-in-Publication Data
Duke, Simon.
The elusive quest for European security : from EDC to CFSP / Simon
Duke.
p. cm. — (St. Antony's series)
Includes bibliographical references and index.
ISBN 0–312–22402–8
1. National security—Europe. 2. Europe—Defenses. 3. European
cooperation. I. Title. II. Series.
UA646.D8697 1999
355'.03304—dc21   99–15389
                                                    CIP

© Simon Duke 2000

This book is printed on paper suitable for recycling and made from fully managed and sustained
forest sources.

10   9   8   7   6   5   4   3   2   1
09 08 07 06 05 04 03 02 01 00

Printed and bound in Great Britain by
Antony Rowe Ltd, Chippenham, Wiltshire

To the memory of Professor Margaret Gowing

Contents

List of Tables

List of Figures

Acknowledgements

The Elusive Quest for European Security developed from an interest in the history of the various attempts to create a security and defence component to the European integration process. I am much indebted to Dr Christopher Seton-Watson for his initial encouragement of my interest as a graduate student in the early 1980s. Although much has been written on the early days of the European Defence Community, European Political Co-operation and the Common Foreign and Security Policy, there appeared to be little offering the general reader, or those new to the field, a *tour d'horizon*. My thanks therefore go to all those who encouraged me in this hopefully useful endeavour.

My thanks go first and foremost to my wife Roberta who not only tolerated my obsession but also did invaluable work in editing and proofing various stages of the manuscript. Her efforts were all the more noble since she was also trying to finish off her own dissertation and cope with the advanced stages of pregnancy.

Various themes in this book have been presented at a number of conferences including most notably the European Community Studies Association's biannual conference, that of the International Studies Association, as well as a number of smaller ones. To all those who listened and made suggestions, I am also indebted. Professor Finn Laursen, Head of the Thorkil Kristensen Institute of the South Jutland University Centre, deserves special mention for inviting me to his institute in November 1996 to explore and crystallise a number of ideas appearing in the book.

Knowledge of other cultures, political systems, and languages is an obvious challenge for any scholar embarking upon a multi-country study. I am no exception and I am accordingly grateful for the insights and observations given to me by numerous people who have a better insight than I do into the workings of a given state. In particular, Albrecht Schnabel, a former colleague now at the United Nations University, Tokyo, was a marvellous critic and guide for all things German. Sophie Vanhoonacker, a colleague at the European Institute of Public Administration, not only read an earlier draft but unselfishly shared her own scholarship examining transatlantic security relations during the Bush years. I am also greatly indebted to her for guiding me (as well as correcting me) on matters Belgian. Jacek Rostowski, Head of

xiii

the Economics Department at the Central European University, Budapest, also provided a most valuable outsider's perspective (often asking the obvious but difficult questions) while also providing insights into Polish perspectives on European security. Ferenc Miszlivetz, of the Magyar Tudományos Akadémia, provided me with many chances to discuss various themes in contemporary European security with Hungarian audiences. I am grateful to him for these opportunities as well as his own observations and friendship. I would also like to add my profound thanks to those anonymous reviewers connected with the St Antony's/Macmillan series and to the General Editor, Eugene Rogan. Their comments and insights have been of immense assistance. My thanks also go to Tim Farmiloe of Macmillan who agreed to publication on what appeared to be the potential of a rather rough manuscript. I hope I have not disappointed with the final product.

Any work addressing European security inevitably has to address the transatlantic aspects. My interest in this aspect of European security was fostered by my years in the United States. Discussions with my mentor at The Ohio State University, the late Joseph Kruzel, and those with my colleagues at the Mershon Center, have proven of immense value over the years. I am also indebted for the observations and encouragement of Professors Edward Keynes and Robert Harkavy of the Department of Political Science at The Pennsylvania State University. Both were highly supportive colleagues and it was always illuminating and entertaining to discuss various ideas, some of which as a consequence do not appear in the book.

Writing comes naturally to some, but I often struggle. At particularly difficult times I appreciated the encouragement of a fellow scholar, Professor Robert Doyle, then at the Université des Sciences Humaines de Strasbourg, who always had faith in my ability to execute the task. His own persistence and positive results in his endeavours provided encouragement when self-doubt crept in.

Lastly, this book is dedicated to Professor Margaret Gowing who was my D.Phil thesis supervisor. Sadly she died as the book was nearing completion. I count as one of her last graduate supervisees before she retired in 1986. She set standards for scholars which, as a student, I could only aspire to. I continue to fall far short but remain privileged to have benefited from the wisdom and humility of a remarkable scholar and person.

In spite of the assistance I have received from numerous sources, any errors or mistakes remain mine alone.

Maastricht   SIMON DUKE

Acronyms, Abbreviations and Conventions

ACE	Allied Command Europe
AFCENT	Allied Forces Central Europe
AFNORTHWEST	Allied Forces North West Europe
AFSOUTH	Allied Forces Southern Europe
ARRC	ACE Rapid Reaction Corps (see ACE)
AWACS	Airborne Warning and Control System
CAP	Common Agricultural Policy
CD	Common Defence
CDP	Common Defence Policy
CDU/CSU	Christian Democratic Union/Christian Social Union (Germany)
CEEC	Central and East European Countries
CEG	Capabilities-Expectations-Gap
CFE	Conventional Armed Forces in Europe (Treaty, 1990)
CFSP	Common Foreign and Security Policy (also 'second pillar')
CIA	Central Intelligence Agency
CINCEUR	Commander-in-Chief Europe (US)
CIS	Commonwealth of Independent States
CJTF	Combined Joint Task Force Concept
C^3I	Command, Control, Communication and Intelligence
COREPER	Committee of Permanent Representatives
COREU	Correspondance Européenne (internal EU communications network)
CNAD	Conference on National Armaments Directors
CRISEX	Crisis (management) exercise
CSCE	Conference on Security and Co-operation in Europe (also see OSCE)
CTEU	Consolidated Treaty on European Union
DoD	Department of Defense (US)
DG	Directorate-General (followed by relevant reference number, e.g. DG1A)
EAA	European Armaments Agency
EADC	European Aerospace and Defence Company
EAPC	Euro-Atlantic Partnership Council (successor to NACC)
EC	European Community
ECMM	European Community Monitoring Mission
ECSC	European Coal and Steel Community
EDC	European Defence Community
EDIG	European Defence Industries Group
EEA	European Armaments Agency (by end of 2001)

EEC	European Economic Community
EFTA	European Free Trade Area
EMU	European Monetary Union
EPC (until 1954)	European Political Community (related to EDC)
EPC (post 1970)	European Political Co-operation
ESDI	European Security and Defence Initiative
FAWEU	Forces Answerable to the WEU
FOTL	Follow-on-to-Lance
FRY	Federal Republic of Yugoslavia
EU	European Union
FCO	Foreign and Commonwealth Office (United Kingdom)
GATT	General Agreement of Tariffs and Trade
HQ	Headquarter
ICRC	International Committee of the Red Cross
ICTY	International Criminal Tribunal (for former Yugoslavia)
IEPG	Independent European Programme Group
IFOR	Intervention Force (precursor to SFOR in Bosnia)
IGC	Intergovernmental Conference
INF	Intermediate-Range Nuclear Forces (Treaty, 1987)
JNA	Yugoslav People's Army
JSTARS	Joint Surveillance and Target Attack Radar System
KLA	Kosovo Liberation Army
MAPE	Multinational Advising Police Element (Albania)
MBFR	Mutual and Balanced Force Reduction
MCG	Mediterranean Co-operation Group
MLF	Multilateral Force
MRP	Mouvement Républicain Populaire (France)
NACC	North Atlantic Co-operation Council (became EAPC)
NAC	North Atlantic Council
NAFTA	North American Free Trade Area
NATO	North Atlantic Treaty Organisation
NBC	Nuclear, Biological and Chemical Weapons (see also WMD)
NNAs	Neutral or Non-Aligned Countries
OCCAR	Organisation for Joint Armaments Co-operation (Germany, France, Italy, and the United Kingdom)
OSCE	Organisation for Security and Co-operation in Europe (formerly CSCE)
PDD-25	Presidential Decision Directive 25 (US)
PfP	Partnership for Peace (NATO)
PHARE	Poland and Hungary Assistance for Economic Restructuring Programme (extended beyond the two named countries)
PPEWU	Policy Planning and Early Warning Unit
QMV	Qualified Majority Vote
RAF	Royal Air Force (UK)
RRF	Rapid Reaction Force
SACEUR	Supreme Allied Commander Europe
SEA	Single European Act
SFOR	Stabilisation Force (Bosnia)
SIPRI	Stockholm International Peace Research Institute

START	Strategic Arms Reduction Treaty
TEU	Treaty on European Union (also known as Maastricht Treaty)
THALES	Technology Arrangements for Laboratories for Defence European Science
UN	United Nations
UNHCR	United Nations High Commissioner for Refugees
UNPREDEP	United Nations Preventive Peacekeeping Mission (Macedonia)
UNPROFOR	United Nations Protection Force
USECOM	US European Command
USIA	United States Information Agency
VOPP	Vance-Owen Peace Plan
WEAG	Western European Armaments Group (succeeded the IEPG in 1992)
WEAO	Western European Armaments Organisation
WEU	Western European Union
WEUCOM	Western European Union Communications Network
WMD	Weapons of Mass Destruction
WTO	World Trade Organisation
WUDO	Western Union Defence Organisation

Introduction

When reviewing the plans for the European Defence Community (EDC), Sir Winston Churchill commented that it was a 'sludgy amalgam'.[1] This vivid image applies with as much force to the Common Foreign and Security Policy (CFSP) in the 1990s as it did to the EDC of the 1950s. The comparison furthermore serves as a reminder that progress towards European economic and political union is an ongoing process that must be put in its historical perspective. Although the context in which decisions are made may have changed, many of the same questions and themes encountered in the attempts to establish a EDC were also encountered later in the European Political Co-operation (EPC) process and, most recently, in the CFSP process. Indeed two issues have dominated the post Second World War security debate in Europe. How should the Europeans keep the US involved in Europe's defence and what should the nature and extent of the European contribution be?

The aim of this book is to provide an overview of the security and defence aspects of European integration in an historical perspective. The book is intended to appeal to the general reader who may be curious about what the second pillar of the European Union is, and how it evolved. It is also hoped that this attempt to present an overview will be of help to students of European studies and maybe even to the more specialist reader. The general books on the EC/EU cannot possibly present details or trace the themes of fifty years of debates on European security. Although the book is confined to the security and defence aspects of European integration, it recognises that it is often impossible to draw a strict line between the foreign, security and defence facets of European integration, especially in post-Cold War Europe. The Cold War preoccupation with the superpower nuclear stand-off did not

1

make the distinction between security and defence significant in the European context, since the latter was largely provided outside the confines of the European Community and the EPC process. Despite this fact, it was evident to the early advocates of European integration that the European Union would be incomplete without a security dimension.

The end of the Cold War changed the context in which the European Communities operated, most notably the dissolution of the distinction between west and east removed many of the difficulties previously encountered in various attempts to incorporate a security component into the integration process. The inclusion of a whole variety of challenges, ranging from the environment to nuclear proliferation to drug trafficking, all under the security rubric, has actually made it easier to agree upon the wisdom of a security dimension to the integration process. Many contemporary security challenges do not require huge manpower or resources but they do require vigilance. Defence, by way of contrast, was and is intimately linked to the ideas of national defence and ultimately to state sovereignty. Historically, defence integration was attempted through the EDC and the associated EPC process. More recent attempts to knit together both the security and defence dimensions in the CFSP framework have again shown the limitations of giving practical effect to 'Euro-options'.

The same question can be applied to the CFSP deliberations – how should the Europeans keep the US involved in Europe's defence and what should the nature and extent of the European contribution be?

Four central areas of enquiry guide the structure of the book. The first is to consider the historical origins of the security dimensions of European integration. An examination of the various attempts to include an explicit or implicit security dimension into the post-war integration process is not merely of idle interest. The history of the EDC and its demise offer many lessons for the contemporary observer. Although the historical parallels can be overdrawn, there is a certain resonance between the questions asked in the 1950s and the 1990s. For example, the questions concerning the role of Germany in European security; the concerns over the ambivalent role of the United States; the problems associated with the cautious approach of France toward European security designs (particularly those not of its own making); the issue of Britain's Atlanticist orientation and its equivocation on its position *vis-à-vis* its role in Europe; and the question of which institutions should incorporate these conflicting tendencies. There are however some important differences that must also be borne in mind, such as the changes in the domestic and foreign priorities of many major powers and the changing nature and understanding of security and, indeed, the concept of 'Europe' without blocs.

The second area of concentration examines a number of flexible arrangements that have been introduced in the 1990s in order to facilitate joint collaboration between the WEU, EU and NATO. However, the extent to which the European Security and Defence Initiative (ESDI) and the CFSP (the second pillar of the EU) are, or can be, integrated is questioned. Special emphasis is placed on the Treaty of Amsterdam, which emerged from the 1996–7 Intergovernmental Conference (IGC), and NATO's historic Madrid summit. Together the Treaty of Amsterdam and the Madrid Summit initiated the process of eastward expansion. Overall, the rapid pace of developments in European security and their subsequent institutional manifestations has been impressive. Yet the question remains – have these multifarious changes actually enhanced European security?

The third area considers the role of the US in current and future European security. The importance of the US to European security designs is built upon the assumption that an active American role in European security issues continues to be beneficial to both parties. Having made this observation, an appropriate role for the US is a matter of considerable disagreement amongst the European allies. Getting the balance right between involving the US in European security, with due regard being paid to the need for more European *responsibility* sharing, will be a delicate task. It is also argued that the security and defence aspects of transatlantic relations cannot be considered in isolation from other components of transatlantic relations nor from US interests in other regions of the world.

Finally, the reader's attention is drawn to a series of problems, which are not exhaustive, but are especially pressing if progress is to be made toward the formulation of a Common Defence Policy (CDP) and a Common Defence (CD). Amongst the problems considered are those of membership of the European security institutions, the state of military preparedness of the distinctly European military apparatus, command and control arrangements, intelligence availability, and the national versus privatised nature of the European and American defence industries respectively.

Making sense of Europe, defence and security

The intellectual discourse surrounding post-Cold War European security has been shaped, some might argue confused, by the introduction of notions of soft or expanded security, incorporating such diverse themes as nationalism and self-determination, migratory movements from North Africa, religious extremism, environmental threats, proliferation of weapons of mass destruction and so forth, into one common understanding of security.[2] *Security*, as a term, has become a far more expansive notion than the Cold War variant, not necessarily because there are new threats, but simply by the fact that many old threats were overshadowed by the spectre of nuclear warfare and have, since the waning of this overarching threat, re-emerged. A further significant change from the Cold War variant of security is the change from inter-state conflict to intra-state conflict. Of the twenty-five major armed conflicts recorded in 1997, all but one (India–Pakistan) were primarily internal.[3] Only one conflict was recorded in Europe in 1997, in Northern Ireland, but the negotiation of a cease-fire and a political settlement in spring 1998 have hopefully removed this from the list. The challenge to Europe's security is therefore primarily from surrounding areas, especially Africa and south-east Europe, where increased conflict is evident. Moreover, the post-Cold War challenges to security do not necessarily require a traditional military response. Instead demands for conflict prevention and a variety of types of peacekeeping will call for flexibility and ever long-term commitments.

The fact that peace and stability rests upon a variety of factors beyond the purely military made the search for 'comprehensive' security a preoccupation amongst the early post-Cold War thinkers. The rejuvenation of the UN and the CSCE (now OSCE) was indicative of the fact that the effects of conflict were widely seen in global terms and demanded increasing commitments of resources and personnel from the developed countries. The expansive nature of comprehensive security has though done little to sharpen thinking about what *security* is. From the perspective of the developed countries the global terms of conflict were far easier to adopt, such as nuclear proliferation or environmental issues. However, whatever enthusiasm existed for utilising a revitalised UN in highly complex internal conflicts soon evaporated. The initial euphoria following *Operation Desert Storm* in 1991, quickly waned in the light of costly failures in Somalia and Bosnia. The global nature of security was further compromised when the bloody conflicts in the Caucasus and Chechnya reminded the UN and regional organisations that parts of the globe were still essentially off bounds.

Within Europe the issue of what is security is no less opaque. Defence organisations, such as NATO or the WEU, have been forced to adopt a bewildering variety of tasks in order to justify their continuing existence. The emphasis accorded to defence, stemming from the

Cold War era treaties establishing the organisations, can be easily changed on paper. Adapting military force structures and, some might argue mindsets, is a far more arduous task as the tragic results in Bosnia have illustrated. The willingness of the EU to embrace, through its second pillar, security tasks has been cautious. In part this is due to legitimate concerns about what security might entail and what it might cost, in human and resource terms.

Defence on the other hand remains a jealously guarded preserve against supranational incursion. The right of self defence is not only a recognised legal right, but the size and qualitative power of the armed forces with which to defend the nation state are often a source of national identity and pride. The logical step of moving from a Common Foreign and Security Policy to a Common Defence Policy, and from there to European Armed Forces, is one that has been firmly resisted. In spite of the fact that none of the EU Member States face a direct military threat, the idea of merging national forces (and, with them, national defence industries) into a regional arrangement remains premature. Moreover, in spite of the progress that has been made in other areas of European integration, such as monetary union, defence integration is coloured by historical suspicions, resentments, and misperceptions that have been held for fifty years or, often, longer.

If the meaning of security has become murky in the post-Cold War world, so too has that of 'Europe'. A restrictive interpretation would suggest that Europe is the fifteen EU members. This is however an interpretation which is wanting for two reasons. First, the overlapping mosaic of security institutions in Europe (the WEU, NATO, OSCE and even the Council of Europe) makes the idea of constricting security considerations to the EU excessively insular. Second, the wide range of challenges which now fall under the 'security' rubric, as discussed above, possess regional and often international dimensions. The problems of the composition of 'security Europe' were tested already in Bosnia, Albania, and at time of writing, in Kosovo. Two relevant observations arise from these events. First, Bosnia's case would suggest that the parameters of European security and defence are not the same. It was recognised at an early stage that the disintegration of Federal Yugoslavia would provide a challenge to European security. As a result of this recognition, the early efforts to address the problems of the disintegrating Yugoslavia were diplomatic, while the use of force to *defend* Europe's security interests was not generally supported. Second, the Albanian crisis emphasised local responsibilities that, in turn, would suggest that there is a strong sub-regional theme to European security (one not limited to the Mediterranean dialogue, or outreach to the Maghreb, but one that also enjoys strong northern support in the Baltic Sea region). What Europe has become, or is in the process of becoming, in security terms is every bit as complicated as defining the nature of security itself. The European security map is further complicated by the ambiguous position occupied by the neutral or non-aligned EU members; while they may be willing to participate in Petersberg-type tasks, their association in other areas may be less discernible.[4]

Perhaps the obvious needs stating by way of summary – 'security' and 'Europe' will not mean the same to all states at any given time and the apparent clarity of both terms, compared to the Cold War, has vanished. As unsatisfactory and messy as this might be, the predicament seems to demand a flexible but structured approach to how security and defence are regarded within the EU, NATO, or the WEU. Circumstances also mean that one should expect that responses to challenges might demand different levels of participation from different states. This simple fact is already reflected in the post-Cold War development of flexible force packages, which can be used in a variety of different ways and locations. Flexibility though can be paralysing too, since it introduces the idea that aside from national defence all other obligations are subjective and elective.

Europeanising security?

In the outpouring of books and articles on European security in the last decade or so there has been an overwhelming concentration, for understandable reasons, on NATO. One can also find a small, but profound, literature on the human rights work of the OSCE and the Council of Europe. Until recently though, relatively little had been written about European security and defence with the WEU or EU in mind.[5] There are some obvious reasons for this such as the fact that the WEU has spent the majority of its life in a deep slumber that it has only recently reawakened from to emerge as the fledgling defence arm of the EU. While the role of the WEU is not, and has not been, to establish 'Euro-alternatives' to the Atlantic Alliance, the question of whether the North American allies will always wish to be intimately involved in Europe's security problems makes the need for a 'Euro option' important. Keeping this in mind, the WEU set itself an historic task in 1995:

It is now time for the WEU states to examine together the new conditions of their security. The aim of this collective endeavour, itself a contribution to the process of integration – one of the cornerstones of peace in Europe – is to identify the common interests of Europeans, the risks and potential threats, but also Europe's new responsibilities in a strategic environment in which Europe's security is not confined to security in Europe, and in which Europe has acquired the capability to make its own contribution to the building of a just and peaceful world order.[6]

The extent to which any other organisation, or member, is in a position to foster and build a European defence identity has often been couched in terms of the European versus Atlanticist debate with, apparently, little middle ground. It appears that since the end of the Cold War a *modus vivendi* between the two approaches has arisen, which rests upon the recognition that it is necessary to have both an active European and a transatlantic component for continued security. The recognition of the significance of both European and transatlantic dimensions to European security is though largely a political construct and, while not totally bereft of military substance, many of the vexatious practical details have yet to be worked out.

It is argued that the political significance attached to the introduction of flexible 'European' options is however hollow without equally flexible military arrangements. In this regard the Combined Joint Task Force (CJTF) concept has been forwarded as the main hope of providing the practical assistance necessary to mount flexible operations, with or without the North American allies. CJTF remains though largely a concept. The test of whether the EU, the WEU (with prime responsibility for the defence implications of the Union), and NATO move beyond designs on paper depends upon further institutional adjustment as well as upon the adoption of streamlined procedures. Above all, it depends up the existence of political will on the part of the EU members to give substance to a European Security and Defence Identity (ESDI). Historically, the EC had the luxury of debating the desirability of a security or defence addition to the Community with a safety net – the US military presence in Europe and the US global nuclear preponderance. The safety net no longer exists in the same sense, yet the current debates have some resonance to those of the European Defence Community debates of the 1950s when, if all else failed, the US would still be there. The EU remains largely unaffected by any sense of urgency to address the pressing problems of providing for Europe's future security in spite of the fact that the US has made its unwillingness to be the global policeman plain.

Aside from developments in the US, it is recognised that those in Russia and the Ukraine will also have a very direct bearing on European security arrangements. It is critical that the Commonwealth of Independent States (CIS) continues to abide by existing arms control agreements, especially those pertaining to weapons of mass destruction (WMD). Compliance with the START II, Conventional Forces in Europe, and Non-Proliferation treaties, to name but a few, will also depend upon civil control of the armed forces. Additionally, questions about effective civil control of the armed forces in the CIS countries raise direct concerns about proliferation and the possibility of elements in CIS militaries fostering nationalist sentiment or forming opposition blocs within countries that have feeble democracies. In recognising the importance of CIS and Russian developments in general, a key issue for European security will be whether the CIS is able to develop into a serious regional actor, as well as a security actor. The chief impediment to closer relations amongst the twelve CIS states remains the sizeable number of potential flashpoints. The treatment and circumstances of Russian minorities throughout the CIS and beyond may also prove a source of instability and a pretext for Russian military intervention.

It is clear that European security, for the foreseeable future, must continue to accommodate the interests of Russia as well as the US and this, in turn, will require adjustment on the EU's part to the post-Cold War security environment. It would be premature to suggest that the necessary accommodation can or cannot be made but what follows will hopefully highlight some of the potential pitfalls as well as some of the progress made along this path.

Putting the EPC/CFSP into the academic context

Prior to the 1991 Maastricht summit, the EC had largely been regarded as a 'civilian power' while the EPC was often seen as, at best, a parallel process. The EPC's general significance was only emphasised when scholars considered its historical role in the European integrative process. Beyond this historical consideration, a rather small group of predominantly European security specialists focussed on the importance of the EPC. The result being that the EPC emerged as an interesting, if quirkish, theme of one or more chapters in the general EC books.[7] The EPC was also normally set in the framework of close Franco–German relations within the EC. This, in turn, gave credence to the idea that some form of transnational 'civilian power' was in the making that would ultimately make military competition and aggression virtually unthinkable. Any security dimension to the EC was therefore subsumed in the idea of the EC as a 'civilian power'. The EPC's low profile also reflected the perception held by a majority of the EC member states that foreign policy remained a matter of national autonomy. The idea of the EC as a 'civilian' actor therefore developed in a foreign and security policy vacuum of the EC's own making. No real attempt was made to link the EC with 'hard' security issues until, at the earliest, the 1980's in the aftermath of NATO's 'Dual-Track' decision.[8] The proposed transition from the European *communities* to European *Union* posed a formidable challenge: for the first time the EC member states had to address in a forthright manner the extent to which their combined unit really was a 'civilian power'. The extent to which the EPC was not a parallel process, but a largely separate one, became apparent during the deliberations of the Intergovernmental Conference (IGC) leading up to the Maastricht summit.

The post-Cold War debate amongst academics, which was marked by a North America resurgence in interest in European studies, contributed little to considerations of the ties between the integration process and security. To realist scholars like John Mearsheimer, the absence of a compelling threat would begin to undo the fabric of this imagined cohesiveness: 'Without a common Soviet threat and without the American night watchman, Western European states will begin viewing each other with greater fear and suspicion, as they did for centuries before the onset of the Cold War.'[9] This line of reasoning and other similar ones rest upon the contention that Europeans are unable to learn from their history and, when left to their own devices, are quite likely to resort to destabilising and antagonistic behaviour. Certainly the observations that the tumultuous events of 1989–91 left Europe dominated by a powerful Germany were often accompanied by a knowing historical wink. A similar refrain, taken up in Europe by François Heisbourg and others, predicted the renationalisation of European defence policies and assets – again, presumably, as a precursor to conflict which European countries were unable to avoid.[10]

While the way forward may not be without considerable ambiguity and may lend credence to realist predictions, the well-developed historical sensitivities of many Europeans need also to be borne in mind. Indeed, neo-realists rejected the overly pessimistic tone of Mearsheimer's prognostications but agreed that there was a need for a continued, albeit downscaled, US military role in Europe. Subsequent calls for an Atlantic Union or a new transatlantic bargain reflected both the belief that the security of Europe was a legitimate concern of North America and that caution was appropriate in allowing European allies to formulate their own designs.

Although it is tempting and perhaps intellectually easiest to interpret the vicissitudes of the EC's collective diplomacy through a realist prism, other paradigms should be considered. Theories of interdependence and regime theory compliment the functionalist and neo-functionalist models, which were periodically used to explain European integration, for example in the 1970s.[11] The two sets of theories have several assumptions in common, the main one being that growing ties between states will form interdependent relationships which, in time, will become more important and prevalent than military power, which is the traditional measure of power and prestige of the unitary state. The functionalist school of technocrats, led by Jean Monnet, found it desirable to embark upon economic integration using supranational institutions. As Ernst Haas commented, 'Converging practical goals provided the leaven out of which the bread of European unity was baked.'[12] But, as Haas also observed, an integration process based on pragmatic expectations is not durable unless backed by vision. Over the years functionalist approaches to European integration have been refined to reflect the fact that there is not only a 'spill-over' process but a 'spill-back' process at work, which may result in an 'integration threshold'. This in turn recognises that the beneficiaries of integrative steps achieved vested positions in the system such that a return to an earlier mode of action is undesirable.[13] Although security was implicitly included in the various theoretical approaches, many theories made an inadequate attempt to explain where security and defence belonged in the integration process and whether the same or different observations to those normally applied in the economic realm were pertinent. Conveniently, the institutional separation between NATO (the 'security community') and the EC (the evolving civilian power) fostered the illusion that security-related issues would be answered in due course with the evolution of the EC along functionalist or regime theory lines.

The dearth of security-oriented literature in the heyday of European integration studies stands in marked contrast to the enormous out-pouring of books and articles in the last half of the 1980s and the first few years of this decade. In general terms, previous work can be divided into four prevalent categories: the group of more prevalent international relations texts which informed the theoretical discussions on European security;[14] those studies addressing the foreign policy aspects of the EU's relations with non-European countries, which tended to be highly detailed case studies;[15] a rapidly growing literature on the EU and central and eastern Europe;[16] and a well-established EU–US literature.[17] There are in addition a great number of books concentrating on institutional aspects of the EU and national positions.[18] Finally, there are a growing number of books dedicated specifically to the security dimensions of European integration.[19]

The resurgence of intellectual interest in the EU, especially from across the Atlantic, poses a number of other problems for the security-oriented scholar. Foremost amongst them is the task of ascertaining the extent to which earlier scholarship from the heyday of the study of European integration, in the 1960s and 1970s, has anything to offer for the contemporary scholar?[20] Was the prevailing international security background so different in the past that there are few lessons to be drawn, for example, from the evolution of the EPC for better understanding the CFSP? Are the academic peg holes of reference, such as federalism, neo-realism or functionalism, too excessively rigid to assist analysis of contemporary European security? It should also be borne in mind that the security-oriented European literature of the Cold War era was necessarily limited by the bipolar structure of the international system. The consequence of this limitation is that 'European' security *per se* did not exist and the study of west European security was largely confined to Europe between the superpowers or to 'Europe's' role in the NATO setting. There are nonetheless important insights from the earlier works that address the EDC and the EPC processes; for example, the societal and institutional memories of such events as the 1966 Luxembourg Compromise or the cruise missile debate, continue to inform and shape the current security dialogue. A better understanding of the EDC and EPC will also enable an assessment to be made on whether the CFSP marks a *saut qualitatif* or whether it is merely an incremental development.

Finally, it may appear somewhat foolhardy to peer into the future, especially considering the snail's pace of CFSP development. The book does not aim to provide prescriptions but it does highlight a number of barriers to progress that can only be overcome by the genuine exercise of a common will. Identification and understanding of the problems or reservations is hopefully the first step on that road.

1
The European Defence Community – Precursor to the CFSP?

Intellectual origins

Ideas of a federal Europe enjoy a long history of intellectual endeavour. The notion of a unified and prosperous Europe is one that came to the fore in the mid-nineteenth century. Federal ideals though remained hostage to the balance of power politics of the day, being first tarnished by the Crimean War and then seemingly smashed by the Franco-Prussian War of 1870 and the collapse of the Concert of Europe. The shock of the First World War, perhaps surprisingly, evoked few suggestions of federal solutions to Europe's parlous security, with the notable exception of the Briand Plan. In this century the federal concept found its most eloquent proponent in Count Richard Coudenhove-Kalegri, whose 1923 calls for European federalism in his 'Manifeste Paneuropéen' struck a chord in post-World War II Europe dominated by the US and the Soviet Union.[1]

The more recent designs for a federal Europe arose as a reaction to fascism during World War II. Prisoner-of-war camps and resistance movements promoted federalist ideas that eventually coalesced in a collection of federalist documents from various resistance movements entitled *Europe de demain* which, in turn, rekindled the idea of continental security rather than that of the individual nation state.[2] For instance, Ernesto Rossi and Altiero Spinelli, both political prisoners on the island of Ventotene, wrote a manifesto (which later assumed the name of the island) calling for the 'abolition of the division of Europe into national sovereign states' based on the recognition that 'it is impossible to maintain a balance between the independent European states'.[3] Following the fall of Mussolini, the European Federalist Movement was established illegally on 27 August 1943 in Milan.

However, it soon moved its base of operations to Geneva where, for the first time, federalist thinkers from several European countries could propagate their federalist ideas. In July 1944 a 'Draft Declaration of European Resistances' was issued which included a call for a Federal Union among the European peoples. Specifically, the federal union was to be endowed with a government 'responsible not to the member-states, but to their peoples', while an 'army [would be] placed under the orders of this government and excluding all national armies'. In addition, a Supreme Court which will judge 'all questions arising from the interpretation of the Federal Constitution', was proposed.[4] The Draft Declaration and a number of conferences drawing together those of federalist persuasion eventually led to the establishment of the Union Européenne des Fédéralistes on 27 August 1947.

Not all agreed though on how a federal Europe should be organised or how to attain a united Europe. Jean Monnet, who is often thought of as the father of European integration, advocated a neofunctional approach to federalism whereby integration could be gradually realised in specific sectors, commencing in areas of lower importance to national sovereignty, and then spilling over into other sectors. An essential element of Monnet's federal Europe was a 'union franco-allemande'.[5] Altiero Spinelli and Ernesto Rossi, supported by many other prominent intellectuals and writers, such as George Orwell and Albert Camus, saw a direct assault on national sovereignty in the immediate aftermath of the war as the best way to attain a federal Europe. Winston Churchill also revived the prospects for a united Europe when he called for the building of 'a kind of United States of Europe' in an historic speech in Zurich in 1946.[6]

The need to build defensive arrangements in Europe became increasingly apparent. The first step in this direction was the Treaty of Dunkirk, signed between France and Britain in March 1947. Although it is difficult to see how Germany could have posed any significant military threat at the time, it nevertheless reassured France. The Dunkirk treaty served as the foundation for a more expansive arrangement, which was agreed to a year later. The *Brussels Treaty of Economic, Social and Cultural Collaboration and Collective Self-Defence*, created a regional defence organisation, the Western Union, involving Belgium, Britain, France, Luxembourg and the Netherlands. The following month, April 1948, the Western Union Defence Organisation (WUDO) was established to enact the defence provisions of the treaty. Field Marshal Montgomery was the first chairman of the new body. It is also worth noting that while the Brussels Treaty is remembered for its defensive provisions, it also recognised that Europe's security could only be provided for by parallel efforts in the economic and social spheres. None of the WUDO members had illusions about the organisation's shortcomings. It was apparent to all, especially Britain, that the continent's defence could only be provided for with American assistance. The US did not need much persuading to furnish this support since the 1948 Berlin blockade, the first real crisis of the Cold War, illustrated the inability of the Europeans to provide for their own defence. Senator Arthur Vandenberg also convinced the US Congress of the need for a transatlantic defence pact. A resolution bearing his name allowed the US, in principle, to adhere to collective defence alliances, in accordance with Article 51 of the UN Charter. Less than two weeks after Vandenberg's resolution the Soviet Union imposed a blockade on Berlin, with the intent of thwarting western defence schemes. The effect was however to accelerate the conclusion of the North Atlantic Treaty, which was signed in Washington on 4 April 1949. Soon after NATO's birth, Field Marshal Montgomery pressed for the incorporation of WUDO into NATO in order to avoid duplication of effort. WUDO duly became the precursor to what later became the 'European pillar'.

The year 1949 marked not only the birth of NATO but also that of the Council of Europe in Strasbourg. The Council soon became the nucleus for discussions on European problems. In spite of the overwhelming difficulties with the very idea of a European army, let alone the practical details, Churchill gave voice to the first coherent postwar expression of a European army in an address to the Assembly of the Council on 11 August 1950:

> We should now send a message of confidence and courage from the House of Europe to the whole world. Not only should we re-affirm, as we have been asked to do, our allegiance to the United Nations, but we should make a gesture of practical and constructive guidance by declaring ourselves in favour of the immediate creation of a European army under a unified command, and in which we should bear a worthy and honourable part.[7]

Churchill was at the time out of power but was nevertheless acutely aware of the need for Europe's leaders to at least appear to be thinking of Europe's future peace and security. By so doing, Churchill surmised that a signal would be sent to the US Congress that the European allies were taking a positive stance on the provision of their own security. It was also clear at that time that the general defences of western Europe and the process of normalising the Federal Republic of Germany meant that the issue of providing for the Federal Republic's defence could not be postponed indefinitely. Several factors made this a matter of some urgency: the dramatic military force disparities between a disarming west and the Soviet Union, the 1948 Berlin blockade and coup in Czechoslovakia and the outbreak of war in Korea on 24 June 1950. Scarcely a month after Churchill's speech the US, through the North Atlantic Council, called for an immediate decision in favour of German rearmament.

Jean Monnet quickly realised that 'stonewalling was not a policy'.[8] Konrad Adenauer, appointed as the Federal Republic's first Chancellor on 15 August 1949, was quick to recognise that any moves towards German rearmament would have to be done with the co-operation of France and, preferably, Britain as well. As a result, Adenauer's proposition of 7 March 1950, to create a political union between Germany and France, placed the onus on France to take the initiative. Monnet recognised only too well in April that the European and international situation required a 'profound action, one that is real, immediate, dramatic, and which changes things'.[9] A partial response to the Federal Republic's wishes to be treated as a 'normal' country was provided by Robert Schuman, the French Foreign Minister, on 9 May 1950. He proposed, on Monnet's initiative, putting coal and steel resources into a common organisation open to all countries of Europe. This proposal neatly avoided addressing the rearmament issue head-on. However the Schuman Plan would also have the intentional effect of monitoring German steel production and thus weapons production, an important subtext. More generally the plan reflected Monnet's belief that rearmament should take place within the NATO context and that it should be a common effort, not a 'juxtaposition' of national ones.[10] The official French position was that Germany should be allowed to contribute materially to its defence, but not to contribute weapons. Two subsequent official French notes to Washington showed support for co-ordinated arms production between the two countries.[11]

Washington undoubtedly influenced the French position on German rearmament when it made clear that any US contribution to the defence of Europe would only be forthcoming if the European allies contributed an adequate amount to the defence against communist aggression. On 22 July 1950 the American Secretary of State, Dean Acheson, asked his European NATO counterparts to indicate by 5 August their proposals for rearmament. In the following month John McCloy, US High Commissioner in Germany, leaked plans for a

West European Army that included ten fully integrated German divisions. Acheson himself made it clear that US assistance to Europe would depend upon the allies equipping sixty divisions, ten of which should be German.

Acheson's insistence that continued US military commitment to Western Europe would be provisional was undermined by the decision of the US Congress on 9 September to commit additional forces to Europe on a semi-permanent basis. On the following day, further undermining Acheson's position, President Harry Truman approved 'substantial increases in the strength of the United States forces to be stationed in Western Europe in the interest of the defence of that area'. Truman's decision was prompted by the earlier outbreak of war in Korea and the realisation that the newly-created NATO was ill-equipped and undermanned to stand up to a similar concerted attack. However, Truman also added that

> a basic element in the implementation of this decision is the degree to which our friends match our actions in this regard. Firm programs for the development of their forces will be expected to keep full step with the dispatch of additional United States forces to Europe. Our plans are based on the sincere expectations that our efforts will be met with similar actions on their part.[12]

Truman's historic announcement set the backdrop for the Foreign Minister's Meeting of 12–14 September 1950, which resulted in the recommendation that some important concessions be made to Germany in the defence arena but stopped short of endorsing German participation in a European army. The ministers did however release a communiqué that the allies would 'treat any attack against the Federal Republic from any quarter as an attack upon themselves'.[13] A simultaneous meeting of the North Atlantic Council on 26 September resulted in a decision to put the unified package proposal 'in suspense with comforting phrases until we could make arrangements with the French in which both of us would yield something'.[14] The comforting phrase concocted by the Council was that the participants agreed to the establishment, as soon as possible, of 'an integrated force under centralised command...to deter aggression and to ensure the defence of Western Europe'.[15] Significantly, it was also agreed that the force would be organised by NATO, under its political and strategic guidance. Overall however the two meetings failed to achieve anything solid; yet they were nevertheless significant since, as Acheson remarked, 'they comprised the first real debate NATO had had about the twin subjects of Germany and European defence and greatly advanced the thinking in all allied countries on both subjects'.[16]

Broadly speaking, Britain, Canada, Italy, the Netherlands and Norway supported the US call for a common European defence with an integrated German component. But the idea was unpalatable to others, especially the French. Schuman held out stoically against German rearmament at the NATO Council meeting in September and when the Defence Ministers met in October, Jules Moch, the French Minister of Defence, restated Schuman's position. In a verbal report of the Foreign Minister's New York conference on 24 September 1950, the French High Commissioner André François-Poncet, reported that the French opposition declared that they were 'not authorised' to discuss Germany's rearmament and that the Socialists in France were bitterly opposed to the remilitarisation of Germany.[17] If Schuman appeared to be an enthusiastic backer of the plan, the possibility that the French Socialists would leave the Cabinet could entail a grave government crisis. François-Poncet also pointed out to Adenauer that the French public 'still had to get used to the notion of German participation … Things had happened somewhat too suddenly.'[18]

The British position, as espoused by the Foreign Secretary, Ernest Bevin, and Secretary of Defence, Emmanuel Shinwell, was in favour of the construction of a common defence force, primarily as a way of securing the US offer of long-term commitments to the defence of Europe made by President Truman. British support for an integrated force, expressed in the Foreign Minister's communiqué of 19 September,[19] was also based on the understanding that the US would not only play a major role but that any entity that emerged would be under the wing of NATO.

For his part, Adenauer understood that, 'There were to be no national armies in addition to the proposed international force, with the exception that France was to be able to keep her army in Indochina under her own command.'[20] While Adenauer was personally a strong backer of a German contribution to a European armed force, not all shared his enthusiasm. Minister of the Interior, Gustav Heinemann, tendered his resignation over precisely this issue. The German Protestant church was also opposed.[21] As Adenauer observed, 'I had now to be very careful to avoid a situation in which [Protestant Church President] Niemüller and Heinemann were publicly represented as the friends of peace and the Federal Government as tending toward warlike solutions.'[22] Fortunately for Adenauer the next initiative was to come from France; Schuman, and Hervé Alphand, the French Ambassador to Washington, concluded at the end of September that there must be a French line of action. Monnet concurred, arguing that France faced three choices: to do nothing; to back German rearmament; or to widen the Schuman Plan to include defence.

The Pleven and Spofford plans

Under Monnet's guidance the French initiative on European defence was to be engineered by Schuman's Chief of Staff, Bernard Clappier, Paul Reuter (a lawyer and consultant to the *Quai d'Orsay*), and Hervé Alphand. The absence of any military personnel on the small committee stemmed from Monnet's view that European defence was 'essentially a political question'.[23] René Pleven, the Prime Minister, from whom the plan would subsequently take its name, presented the scheme to the parliament on 24 October 1950. However, Both Pleven and Monnet held private reservations about it. As François Duchêne makes clear: 'Even Monnet was far from in love with the scheme. Several people working near him at the time had the impression that he regarded the European Army as at best premature.'[24] Despite his reservations, Monnet emphasised that, 'we have little chance of succeeding other than by giving the opposition a positive impression that this is inspired by European unity'.[25]

The Pleven Plan proposed the creation of 'une armée européenne rattachée à des institutions politiques de l'Europe unie'. In addition to elements of their national forces, the participants would pledge to defend Europe under a Supreme Allied Commander in time of conflict (but under national control in all other circumstances). In accordance with this, a European Defence Minister with its own command and staff structure was proposed. The suggested army would be comprised of contributions at the battalion level and would total some one hundred thousand men. The plan also envisaged a European Council of Ministers with a single defence budget and arms procurement process. Finally, the plan contained a number of extremely significant caveats. For example, for all but the West Germans it was to be *an* army not *the* army and other participants could also retain national forces for colonial and other uses. These caveats were important in the plan's approval in the *Assemblée Nationale*, which took place on the afternoon it was introduced in a 349 to 235 vote. Negotiations on the Pleven Plan could not however commence with other countries until the Schuman Plan (for the Coal and Steel Community) had been signed.

The British reaction to the Pleven Plan was that, on paper, there was no difficulty with the idea of a European Defence Community (EDC). As Anthony Eden commented, he never thought that '[Britain] need have any apprehension on account of a closer union between the nations of continental Europe'.[26] Behind closed doors however British concerns were that the plan was too ambitious, especially so soon after a major war. Ernest Bevin was especially critical of the plan on several grounds: it might damage relations with Washington; it was premature without a European budget or a European armaments programme; and it could be interpreted by the USSR as constituting a hostile bloc.[27] Eden's own position was to 'encourage France and Germany to form the European Defence Community and support the Schuman Plan, but that Britain should not participate in them, and should instead persuade the Truman administration that they should both help from without rather than participate from within'.[28]

The reaction from Washington was also critical. Acheson reflected that: 'Aside from the minimal accretion to European defence that the plan offered, the second-class status accorded Germany was all too obvious.'[29] In spite of the public pronouncements that the plan was a 'welcome' initiative, and that it would receive 'sympathetic examination', Acheson's private assessment was that the plan was 'hopeless' – a view that Acheson describes as being 'confirmed' by General Marshall and 'concurred in' by Truman.[30]

West Germany, not yet a member of NATO, was required by the plan to put its forces under a single Supreme Allied Commander. This was generally acceptable to Adenauer, given his refusal to participate in the 'remilitarisation of Germany by the creation of a national army.[31] What was unpalatable however was the blatant second-class status conferred on Germany by the Pleven Plan. The *Bundestag* was quick to attack the plan for being 'discriminatory', denying Germans 'equality', and for being a thinly veiled attempt to create a 'German Foreign Legion under a European coating'.[32] The Social Democrat opposition, through Kurt Schumacher, denounced the plan while Adenauer chose to diplomatically point out to France and others the undesirable and weak position the plan put Germany in. To many Germans the Pleven Plan was also contradictory since, on the one hand, it appeared to offer an even-handed approach when it stated that 'inescapable common duties can be fulfilled only if there exist common organisms' and that an army of a united Europe must involve, 'to the greatest possible degree, a complete fusion of all of its human and material elements under a single European political and military authority'; while, on the other hand, the plan recommended that German troops should be integrated into the European army at the 'lowest level of unit possible'.[33] Furthermore, the stipulation that Germany sign the Schuman Plan, for the creation of a European Coal and Steel Community, as a precondition for German accession to the European Army, heightened German sensitivities. In response to these concerns, the French High Commissioner, François-Poncet, reassured Adenauer that 'any discrimination against Germany was completely out of the question' and that 'under the Pleven Plan Germany was to be completely equal with other partners'. François-Poncet also personally assured Adenauer that the French government believed that the 'problems of Europe could only be solved on the basis of Franco-German understanding'.[34] In spite of the reassurances, Adenauer pointed to the 'psychological situation in the Federal Republic and to the growing sense of insecurity of the people'. He considered 'further delay dangerous.' He also expressed his regret to François-Poncet that the Pleven Plan had 'not made sufficient provision for measures to be taken immediately'.[35]

Although the Pleven Plan carried an unmistakable French *imprimatur*, it was not a French invention. Discussion about a 'European army' had been a matter of political concern in the Council of Europe and national capitals for at least four years prior to the French initiative. Although Adenauer saw the French plan as flawed in many respects, he accepted it as part of his goal of securing European approval of West Germany. Indeed, Adenauer viewed the Pleven plan, alongside the Schuman Plan, as the 'essential foundations of Europe'.[36] However, Adenauer also knew that German public support for the plan depended upon a modification or preferably the abolition of the Occupation Statutes so that Germany could assume an equal role in defence and other matters. At a meeting with the Allied High Commissioners on 16 November 1950, Adenauer argued passionately for the replacement of the Occupation Statutes with a series of agreements and the restoration of German jurisdiction. He also argued for a return to the legal situation of 1933 regarding broadcasting, as he viewed the ability to broadcast as a critical tool for engaging the German people in a campaign for the protection of European freedom. In subsequent meetings British High Commissioner Ivone Kirkpatrick supported Adenauer's position. Serious differences with Schuman and the French commissioner remained though. Predictably the Russian reaction was wholly negative and on 15 December 1950 the French Ambassador in Moscow was informed of a proposal to assemble a foreign ministers conference to address the implementation of the

Potsdam Agreement on the Demilitarisation of Germany. The Russian overture was designed to disrupt the NATO Council meeting of 7 December 1950 where, amongst other topics, the Pleven and the Spofford Plans were to be discussed. The latter, an American backed initiative, modified the Pleven Plan by dropping the French insistence that the Schuman Plan be passed prior to the creation of a European army.

Adenauer's acceptance of the Spofford Plan was based on the proviso that any German contribution would be of completely equal with regard to arms and command authority but not numbers of men. Adenauer reasonably maintained that without heavy weapons the chances of German troops effectively defending themselves would be compromised while without some form of national command authority, such as a High Command, any German military contributions would inevitably be seen as second class with a subsequent loss of morale and effectiveness. In light of these reservations it is not surprising that the German public, government and parliament rejected the Spofford Plan precisely on the grounds that it merely substituted one form of inequality, that of the Pleven Plan, for another.

The rejection of the Spofford Plan and the constant delays in the formulation of a European defence had significant effects on American policy and prompted a debate about America's international role. Several critics of American policy, such as the American Ambassador in London, Joseph P. Kennedy,[37] demanded a withdrawal of US military forces from Korea, Berlin and, more generally, an ungrateful Western Europe. This, combined with criticism of the United Nations, and a growing tide of neo-isolationism and anti-communist hysteria, launched the 'Great Debate' in the Senate between those committed to an active overseas military and foreign policy role and those in favour of a highly restricted one. The details of the debate are covered in admirable detail and clarity elsewhere[38] but several key points of disagreement between arch-isolationist Senator Robert Taft and Acheson deserve highlighting since they resemble Congress's neo-isolationist sentiment during President Clinton's first term in office. The first area of disagreement between Taft and Acheson was on the merits of a broad US internationalist foreign policy and an interventionist security policy. As in the more recent debate, the positions rested upon a restrictive versus an expansive perception of America's vital national interests. The second area of disagreement was the issue of what was required to protect American interests. While Taft recognised that Western Europe was significant to America's interests, he argued that these interests could be primarily defended by air and sea forces. Only when the Europeans had demonstrated their capacity to develop a defence with a good chance of success, would Taft 'not object to committing some limited number of American divisions to work with them in the general spirit of the Atlantic Pact'.[39] Third, Taft and Acheson disagreed on whether the President could legally commit US troops overseas without Congressional permission. Eisenhower, in his role as NATO's first Supreme Allied Command Europe (SACEUR), summarised Acheson's position when he argued that 'in the absence of any other acceptable leader the United States should take the leadership, the American troops in Europe should be increased but that no rigid formula or limit should be laid down'.[40] In opposition to this view the Taft lobby was assisted by current events and, in particular, the US Eighth Army's loss of Seoul and retreat to the Han River. Events in Korea also led to the signature by one hundred and eighteen Republicans of 'A Declaration of Policy', which called for a revision of tragic and costly US foreign programmes.

The 'Great Debate' lasted until April 1951. It concluded with a Senate resolution expressing the sense of the Senate (in other words, it did not enjoy force of law) that no more than four divisions could be deployed to Europe without Congressional approval. It also recommended that the President consult with the Joint Chiefs of Staff and that they, in turn, assure Congress that the allies were making 'full and realistic' contributions to the collective defence. And, finally, that there be consideration of the potential use of the military assets of West Germany and Spain.

The aforementioned Truman announcement of 10 September 1950 and the subsequent debate posed two distinct choices for any potential European defence community. The first version was the *American-NATO solution*, backed enthusiastically by Acheson and Truman in the US and Adenauer and the British in general. It permitted the rearmament of Germany, but no German general staff, within an Atlantic command under an American commander. The extra backing given to this version by the commitment of additional US combat forces, and their explicit presentation as such, made this an attractive option to all but the French. The second and primarily French course proposed *a European Army*, also under Atlantic command, but run by a European minister, which implied not only no German general staff, but no German Defence Ministry and no full German divisions either. As the 'Great Debate' commenced in the US Senate the Allied High Commission began talks in Europe at its Petersberg offices near Bonn on the Atlantic approach. A month later, on 15 February, talks opened in Paris chaired by Hervé Alphand on the French scheme for a European Army drawn from the six Schuman Plan countries.

While the two sets of European negotiations proceeded, the final details were added to the Treaty establishing the ECSC. Representatives from Belgium, France, Italy, Luxembourg, the Netherlands and the Federal Republic of Germany signed the treaty in Paris on 18 April 1951. Although over the years the ECSC has often been portrayed as a somewhat isolated and rather peripheral organisation, 'the founders of the Community thought of it merely as one side of a triangle, the other two sides planned being the EDC and the EPC'.[41] Progress towards the EDC proved however to be slow and contentious. The two sets of negotiations, in Petersberg and the Palais Rose, were eventually reconciled following an initiative from McCloy and David Bruce, the US Ambassador to Paris. On 21 June, Jean Monnet met personally with Eisenhower and insisted that the rearmament issue could only be addressed in a European framework. In the meantime, Bruce proposed an interim report designed, in effect, to serve as a record of progress that had thus far been made. In this report the German Under-Secretary of State, Walter Hallstein, was careful to draw Bruce's attention to the difference between 'the genuinely European Schuman Plan and the Pleven Plan, a largely French concept in origin'.[42] Bruce, for his part, was equally emphatic that nothing should be done that would hinder combining the Atlantic forces under a unified command.

American support for a European Army was underlined on 3 July when Eisenhower publicly endorsed the concept in a speech to the English Speaking Union. The State Department also undertook to support a 'real European federation even though the membership may be restricted and even though there was the possibility that Germany might eventually become … the dominant element'.[43] Some important shifts also occurred in the deliberations on the Pleven Plan that made the reconciliation of the two sets of negotiations feasible. Originally the plan called for the integration of the German armed forces at the smallest level possible, which was assumed to be a reference to combat teams, but gradually this shifted to talk of 'small divisions'. By 24 July 1951 Alphand, as chair of the Pleven Plan Conference, was able to summarise the emerging central theme: 'This integration must be as complete as possible as regards men and material to the extent compatible with military requirements … it is also to represent, in conjunction with the European Coal and Steel Community, a very important stage on the road to the creation of a united Europe.'[44]

Support for the Interim Report was heightened in France by the general elections of 8 August, which resulted in the Socialists, including Jules Moch, leaving the second Pleven government and thus removing a main source of opposition. The one remaining contentious question, over the size of the basic German military contribution, was solved by Eisenhower in October when the word 'groupings' was selected (basically divisions with a sanitised name).

Not all were enraptured with the projected EDC though; most notably the representatives of the smaller countries held reservations. For instance, the Belgian Foreign Minister, Paul van Zeeland, saw the proposed EDC as a means to force the pace 'apparently in hope of achieving European unity by the back door, and loading down the European army proposal with [a] top-heavy superstructure borrowed from the Schuman Plan'.[45] The Benelux countries held a preference for a NATO-style coalition army, contrary to the federalist views of the French, Germans and Italians.[46] Other parts of the Pleven Plan were contentious to select interest groups. For instance, the proposed EDC was also to apply to nuclear materials; this alone almost guaranteed British resistance, as well as that of the French Atomic Energy Commissariat.

Discussion of rearmament, manpower contributions to the common defence and budgetary contributions to the common pool, touched off an early version of what was later to become the familiar NATO burdensharing debate. The key problem was that of how to raise the standard of living in (western) Europe whilst simultaneously rearming it and contributing to a common defence in the making. Dirk Stikker, the Dutch Foreign Minister, pointed out that a lowering of the standard of living would 'endanger the social peace on the home front which is so essential to our defense effort'.[47] Pronouncements such as this gave rise to suspicion by John Snyder, US Treasury Secretary, that the US was supposed to pick up the tab. A resolution to the question of how to share the burdens was given to a twelve-member Temporary Council Committee which, in turn, had the authority to establish a three man working group with instructions to produce a report on this problem by 1 December 1951.

The group suggested by Schuman and René Mayer was comprised of Averell Harriman, Jean Monnet and Sir Edwin Plowden. The mandate of the 'Three Wise Men' committee was to assess realistic force levels that would fit NATO's political, economic and military capabilities. A reassessment was necessary since it had become obvious that the original Pentagon assessments on this matter were clearly exaggerated.

The 'wise men' were to make important contributions to NATO's deliberations but, arguably, their proposals were no more realistic than were those emanating from the Pentagon. Still, the Three Wise Men committee illustrated the immense complexity of working out the details of a common defence, as technicalities played a large part in its deliberations. Issues such as what should be counted as a German defence contribution (i.e. should this include frontier police, the defence of Berlin and veterans' care?) to the EDC took considerable time to resolve.

In the meantime, several developments in the Federal Republic provided the necessary changes in the postwar situation that enabled it to assume a more active role in the projected EDC. First, the revision of the Occupation Statutes of 6 March 1951 allowed the transfer of powers from the occupation forces to the Federal Republic. Revision also gave birth to a national Foreign Office, the establishment of which permitted the Federal Republic to enter directly into negotiations with other governments.[48] In a second significant development, the Committee of Ministers of the Council of Europe accepted the Federal Republic as a full member on 2 May 1951. This marked the most significant membership for Germany of postwar international organisations (the others being the OEEC and the European Payments Union). In a welcoming speech to the Council of Europe the Chairman of the Committee of Ministers, Dutch Foreign Minister Stikker, said that West Germany assumed its 'legitimate place in Western Europe because Western Europe has realised that Europe cannot exist without Germany nor Germany without Europe'.[49] These developments, along with a formal termination of the state of war with Germany, on 9 July 1951, remedied many of the disabilities that Germany had borne since the end of the war.

A subsequent Three Power Conference, on 10 September 1951, attended by Dean Acheson, Herbert Morrison and Robert Schuman, underlined emphatically the American, British and French readiness to let Germany participate in the defence of the West. In a series of discussions with the High Commissioners (McCloy, Kirkpatrick and François-Poncet) two important reservations emerged; the first of which addressed the Federal Republic's ability to produce heavy weapons and atomic energy and the second of which considered whether controls in these areas could exist at the European level. Britain's position was summarised in a series of conversations between Adenauer, Parliamentary Under-Secretary for Foreign Affairs in the FCO Lord Henderson, Foreign Secretary Herbert Morrison and Prime Minister Winston Churchill, held between March and December 1951.[50] The British objected to supra-national authority although some form of loose association along functionalist lines was not excluded. The objections to supranationalism then, as now, rested partially upon the constitutional argument that, unlike many other European countries, Britain's directly elected parliament has considerable power and the government is responsible to the parliament. A more complete rationale may however lie in the tendency to regard the special relationship with the US as a critical aspect of British foreign and security policy.

A sense of urgency was injected into the Three Power Conference by Dean Acheson who pointed out that US presidential elections would take place the following year. Difficulties soon emerged however with the European proceedings on the EDC. In February 1952, open differences emerged between France and Germany over the Saar question and NATO. McCloy, irritated at the developments, wrote to Adenauer expressing his concern that at every important juncture in European history the Saar should resurface.[51] McCloy also believed that the appointment of Gilbert Grandval, formerly French High Commissioner at Saarbrücken, as Ambassador, was the 'volley of certain anti-European French circles against the European idea and certainly against the European Defence Community'.[52] The emergence of the Saar as a critical issue was all the more surprising in light of an exchange of letters between Adenauer and Schuman on 18 April 1951 stating that the final status of the Saar should not be prejudiced by either side.

The link between German membership and the French position on the EDC came to light in January 1952 as a result of statements by the Federal Republic's Under-Secretary of State Walter Hallstein, to the Foreign Minister's Conference in Paris. The French interpretation of the speech was that Germany was using potential NATO membership as a means of putting pressure on France to pass the EDC Treaty. Up to a point the French interpretation was right, the Germans did see a link between the EDC and NATO but this was contained in the General Agreement reached with the Foreign Ministers of France, Britain and the US. The general agreement incorporated a pledge to assist the integration of the Federal Republic into the European Community which 'includes the developing Atlantic Community'.[53] To Adenauer's mind, membership of one involved membership of the other: 'I personally was sure that if we entered the European Defence Community the march of events would quite naturally make us into members of NATO one day. Before we entered the European Defence Community and thereby acquired certain obligations, a connection with NATO had to be established to enable us to influence it in some way.'[54]

With the Saar and NATO issues as backdrop, the debate in the French National Assembly commenced on 11 February 1952. Five days later the French Prime Minister, Edgar Fauré, put a motion to vote, part of which said:

> The National Assembly approves that Germany should not be subjected to discrimination in the integrated organisation. It demands that the contractual agreements which are to replace the occupation regime when the European Defence Community has entered into force must contain the necessary guarantees with respect to arms production, the police force, and the distribution of financial burdens. It further demands that the admission of Germany to the European Defence Community should in no case be connected with her entry into the Atlantic Alliance…The National Assembly enjoins the government…to request the British and American governments to guarantee the commitments entered into towards the European Defence Community in the event of a breach or a violation of the Agreement by a member country and to substantiate this guarantee by an appropriately prolonged stay of sufficiently strong American and British troops on the continent of Europe.[55]

The *Assemblée Nationale* pronounced favour 'd'un pouvoir politique européen supranational' on 19 February. At the same time discussions were taking place in the French parliament, Foreign Ministers Eden, Acheson and Schuman met in London with Adenauer to discuss, amongst other things, the connection between NATO and the EDC. French opposition to the Federal Republic's accession to NATO was based on the observation that, by treaty, NATO is a defensive organisation and Germany could not be admitted while it maintained its claim on particular territories. Although the subsequent NATO Council meeting of 22 February 1952 in Lisbon was concerned mainly with the technical aspects of contributions to a common European defence, it did approve of the establishment of a European Army. The creation of which was solidified in a press conference at which the Canadian chairman of the Council, Lester Pearson, along with Eden and Schuman, publicly endorsed the design.[56] The reaction in Moscow to the progress made in London and Lisbon was sufficiently alarmed to result in the issuance of identical notes to the British, French and US ambassadors in Washington by the Soviet ambassador, Andrei Vishinsky, which called for a peace-treaty to be reached with a new all-German government, the withdrawal of all foreign troops from German soil and the prevention of a German coalition or military alliance against any power whose armed forces had fought in Germany.

Meanwhile the EDC negotiations in Paris continued to have problems. The main obstacle was satisfying demands for guarantees against German secession that had surfaced under the new French government of Antoine Pinay. Nevertheless, by the beginning of May the Bonn contractual negotiations and the Paris negotiations on the EDC had advanced sufficiently to allow for a signature of the respective agreements. The General Agreement, or *The Convention between the three powers and the Federal Republic of Germany*, was signed on 26 May and the treaty establishing the EDC was signed on 27 May 1952 by the foreign ministers of Belgium, France, Germany, Italy, Luxembourg and the Netherlands. This process was not however without upsets; for example, on 22 May the French Cabinet voted to require a guarantee against German secession from the EDC as a precondition to signing the Contractual Agreement. At the suggestion of an American advisor, Philip Jessup, an agreement was reached between the three countries that, '[Accordingly], if any action from whatever quarter threatens the integrity or unity of the Community, the [British and French] governments will regard this as a threat to their own security. They will act in accordance with Article 4 of the North Atlantic Treaty.'[57] (See Appendix 2.)

It should be briefly noted that what eventually emerged in the EDC treaty was different from the Pleven Plan and less supranational than the first plan inspired by Jean Monnet. Overall, the treaty establishing the EDC intended, as its primary aim, to make war between the (west) European powers impossible. In fact, the implications of the treaty certainly suggested that, if ratified, a federal Europe would soon emerge since the transfer of the sovereign right to raise armed forces, arguably the most important state power, to a supranational authority would *ipso facto* be followed by integration in the economic and foreign policy fields. That it marked too radical a transition of powers to a supranational authority was to become evident in the ratification process.

Following the signature of the EDC Treaty a further agreement was signed between the six EDC members and Britain, which reiterated a private agreement reached between Acheson and Eden prior to the NATO Lisbon summit and agreed to by Schuman at the summit. The declaration read:

If at any time, while the United Kingdom is party to the North Atlantic Treaty, any other party to the present Treaty, which is at that time a member of the European Defence Community, or the European Defence Forces, should be the object of an armed attack in Europe, the United Kingdom will, in accordance with Article 51 of the United Nations Charter, afford the Party or Forces so attacked all the military and other aid and assistance in its power.

From conception the EDC was to have a close relationship with NATO and less close, but still palpable, with the UN. The explicit link drawn between NATO and the emergent EDC was established through Article 4 of the North Atlantic Treaty which implied a commitment to consult together when, 'in the opinion of any [NATO] member, the territorial integrity, political independence or security of any is threatened'. 'Consultation' was though much weaker than the more extensive commitments to assist in case of military attack contained in the subsequent article of the North Atlantic Treaty. (See Appendix 2) Moreover, the British guarantee was little more than a reaffirmation of Britain's existing commitments as a UN member, in spite of the apparent comfort that it afforded the French. The EDC Treaty also had conditions attached to it which were to weaken its hand from the outset and strengthen that of NATO. Two weaknesses in particular foreshadowed the EDC's eventual demise. First, Belgian Foreign Minister, Paul van Zeeland, had managed to subject the EDC's finance arrangements to partial national vetoes. And, second, the Pinay government lent its signature to the EDC Treaty on the express condition that no immediate attempt should be made to ratify it.

In spite of its weaknesses, to Adenauer the EDC Treaty marked an enormous step forward in establishing the Federal Republic's place in a Europe where the nation state had 'a past but no future'.[58] He observed:

> The European federation was to begin in the most sensitive area, the military. European wars would be impossible in future. By being made part of the most comprehensive defence system in history we would obtain the greatest imaginable security. We would cease being the mere object of political and strategic calculations and would help determine action ourselves...As long as we were an occupied country, as long as we were not yet part of the Western defence system, we were a no-man's-land between the two big power groups.[59]

The demise of the EDC

Within France the haggling over the details of the EDC and its sister organisation, the EPC, began almost immediately after the Six signed the EDC treaty. The idea of a political community was certainly not new in France and had been seriously entertained since late 1950, when there was an apparent need for a 'constitutional roof' over the prospective ECSC.[60] The scope of this roof varied but at its broadest the Italian Prime Minister, Alcide de Gasperi, proposed that the ECSC/EDC Assembly should prepare a draft European constitution for discussion by European governments. Robert Schuman proposed that the EPC be put on the official agenda in June 1952, which satisfied the dual aims of answering the socialist critics as well as providing the 'communities' with a political framework that they lacked.

Thus, the EPC was born when, on an initiative from Monnet and Schuman, the EDC was hitched to the Common Assembly of the ECSC. At a later date, on 10 September 1952, the Common Assembly was asked to align its numbers with those of the EDC Assembly and to establish itself as an *ad hoc* assembly with the mandate of drawing up a draft EPC Treaty to be presented to the member governments. In spite of possible legal quibbles, the EPC's design was entrusted to a constitutional committee of the *ad hoc* assembly with Heinrich von Brentano in the chair. The committee's resultant proposal, tabled in Strasbourg on 6 March 1953, posited limited political integration. In the security arena the EPC was to 'ensure the co-ordination of foreign policy' but only in those cases 'likely to involve the existence ... security and prosperity of the Community'.[61] The EPC would therefore, according to the constitutional committee of the *ad hoc* assembly, provide the means for co-ordinating diplomatic issues arising from the work of the ECSC and the EDC. The potential role of the EPC, although somewhat limited, nevertheless drew expressions of concern from France regarding the possible effects on overseas territories. To this end, the government of René Mayer demanded in February 1953 that the other five EDC signatories sign a protocol designed to protect the 'the unity and integrity of the French army and that of France'.[62] Mayer's demand needs to be viewed within the context of the ongoing struggles in Indochina, but it nevertheless clearly identified one of the weak aspects of the EDC – how many forces should be retained for the defence of non-European interests? With regard to the EDC, the Socialists in the *Assemblée Nationale* demanded a more democratic structure that included a Parliamentary Assembly elected by universal suffrage.

The details of the fate of the EDC are covered well elsewhere.[63] There are however several puzzling aspects to its stormy passage in the *Assemblée Nationale*. For example, following the signature of the EDC Treaty, Robert Schuman waited almost six months before submitting it to the chamber. When it was eventually submitted, it coincided with the trial of several former Alsatian SS members who were accused of mass murder of civilians in World War II. The obvious negative climate generated by the trial served as a reminder that there were still considerable sensitivities under the surface. An additional oddity was the appointment of Jules Moch, a Socialist, and Pierre Koenig, a Gaullist, as *rapporteurs*. Both were known to be hostile to the EDC and Koenig even subsequently wrote the preface to an anti-EDC pamphlet that appeared in January 1954.

Aside from the above factors, which may have only had an incidental bearing on the outcome of the EDC debates, a series of changes in France and elsewhere during 1953 and the early months of 1954 were to have a more discernible negative effect on the EDC. The departure of Schuman from the *Quai d'Orsay* in January 1953, the death of Stalin in March and the signing of an armistice in Korea on 27 July, helped to defuse the air of crisis in which the EDC had been conceived. A succession of unstable cabinets under Antoine Pinay, René Mayer and Joseph Laniel contributed to the EDC's demotion in urgency, since none of the three premiers wished to stake their political futures on an issue that was known to be highly controversial. The shifts in the international atmosphere also meant that the arguments in favour of the EDC increasingly rested upon the proposition that the EDC alone would guard against German revanchism. This, in turn, provided ammunition for the SPD opposition in the Federal Republic. The presentation of German rearmament as a potential threat also aided critics in the *Assemblée* who saw no point in constraining the French military if this were indeed a threat. The only circumstance in which France could therefore reasonably be expected to participate in the EDC was with the presence of a third (and ideally fourth) major military power in the community. Britain was the obvious but unwilling partner.

On 11 January 1952, Anthony Eden gave an address at Columbia University in which he summarised the central concern of Britain toward European integration:

If you drive a nation to adopt procedures which run counter to its instincts, you weaken and may destroy the motive force of its action … you will realise that I am speaking of the frequent suggestions that the United Kingdom should join a federation on the continent of Europe. This is something which we know, in our bones, we cannot do. We know that if we were to attempt it, we should relax the springs of our action in the Western democratic cause and in the Atlantic association which is the expression of that cause. For Britain's story and her interests lie far beyond the continent of Europe.[64]

Eden's statement answered the general question about the Atlanticist orientation of British foreign and security policy but it did not answer the specifics of Britain's relationship with the EDC. This was an issue that Schuman and Eden worked out on 1 February 1952. Their meeting resulted in an agreement in which Eden promised to make a positive and supportive case for EDC to the House of Commons.[65] In spite of Eden's statement of support there were many political and practical difficulties with the British position. Schuman wanted a formal declaration of British support for the EDC that Eden found difficult and not entirely necessary. In response to Schuman's constant demands for 'automatic' British commitments to the EDC, the British resisted firmly on the grounds that such an assurance was unnecessary since it already existed through NATO. Eden however realised that some formal declaration of association with the EDC was required if Britain was to avoid the blame for the failure of the EDC. Eden also faced pressure from the Netherlands, mainly from Dirk Stikker, to extend the 1948 Brussels Treaty to the EDC members. Eden resisted this however since he was uneasy about committing Britain for a period of at least fifty years, as stipulated in the Brussels Treaty. (See Appendix 1) The much sought after declaration was eventually given in a watered-down form in a supporting tripartite declaration between Britain, France and the United States upon the signature of the EDC Treaty by the six members.

Britain's true attitude toward the more general question of European integration became apparent in the summer of 1952, with the launch of the so-called Eden Plan. The plan, in brief, proposed that the ECSC, the EDC, EPC and any other future organisations, should be subordinated to the Council of Europe's Committee of Ministers and Consultative Assembly. From Eden's point of view this would serve as a 'point of contact with European developments'; it would 'reconcile the aim of the six powers'; and it would 'guide and check' the tendency for Euro-institutions to multiply in 'an unwieldy manner'.[66] To Monnet however this was another British attempt to 'influence the Community without paying the membership fee'.[67]

The death of Stalin offered a chance to explore, once again, the possibility of a four-power settlement in Europe. The shaky regime of

Georgi Malenkov in the Kremlin, accompanied by the dismissal of the Minister of State Security, Lavrenti Beria, seemed to offer a window of opportunity to the British and French to reach a negotiated settlement. With such a settlement in mind, Eden, John Foster Dulles and Georges Bidault held a preparatory meeting to prepare the agenda for a four-power gathering on 2 December in Bermuda.[68] The Bermuda meeting emphasised the degree to which the United States wanted to see the already prolonged ratification process of the EDC Treaty speed up, irrespective of international changes. The extent to which the ratification of the EDC Treaty was seen as important to Congress can be gauged by Dulles's warning to Eden and Bidault that, 'unless there was some positive action towards European unity in the next two to three months, [Congressional] foreign aid appropriations would be so rigid and so qualified that there would be very serious repercussions on the N.A.T.O. programme'. In reference to any possible failure to ratify the EDC Treaty, Dulles warned that 'he could not take the responsibility for saying that Congress would continue their firm and loyal support of N.A.T.O. or pursue the creation of a strong economic and military body on the continent of Europe, if this situation were to drag on much longer'.[69] The Secretary of State's brother, Allen Dulles, also pushed for ratification of the EDC Treaty in his capacity as Director of the CIA. Leonard Mosley claims that, 'from the director's own discretionary fund, he paid one member of the French cabinet $30,000 a year for himself, and, during the French Chamber's discussion of the European Defence Community project, handed him another $500,000 to distribute among his fellow members'.[70] After the Bermuda conference a meeting of the North Atlantic Council in Paris from 14–16 December, under the chairmanship of Bidault, reinforced the American warnings made at Bermuda.[71]

The forthcoming presidential elections in France gave a further sense of urgency to the need to speed up the EDC ratification process. In spite of the air of urgency, Eden recalls that 'the French seemed impervious either to cajolery or to the prospects of dire alternatives'. He therefore suggested to Dulles the possibility of 'strengthening the N.A.T.O. obligations and machinery, and thus control Germany ourselves within N.A.T.O'. Eden added that these thoughts should of course be kept strictly between the two, 'as we must give no hint to the French that there was an acceptable alternative to the E.D.C'.[72]

Laniel's re-election as Prime Minister on 7 January 1954 strengthened the French position in the forthcoming Four Power Berlin summit. The approval of the EDC Treaty by the Dutch First Chamber on

20 January also provided a note of optimism for the forthcoming summit. The Four Power (France, the Soviet Union, the United States and the United Kingdom) conference held from 25 January to 18 February was, as Eden noted, a 'conference about Europe, in Europe'. Despite the optimistic note, none of the issues on the Berlin conference agenda (the questions of reducing tension in international affairs, the convening of a five-power meeting, the German question and European security and the Austrian State Treaty) were resolved. The only constructive outcome was the agreement to hold a further meeting in Geneva to discuss Korea and the restoration of peace to Indo-China.

In the Federal Republic, the *Bundestag* and *Bundesrat* passed the EDC Treaty in 1953, but without French approval it was generally understood that the community was as good as dead. The Netherlands and Belgium ratified the EDC Treaty by mid-March 1954 followed, shortly thereafter, by Luxembourg in April. In Italy though the EDC ratification process was deadlocked in a stand-off between the Christian Democrats, who wanted to move ahead speedily on the EDC ratification process, and the Socialists, who preferred a more cautious approach determined largely by the outcome of the French ratification debate. The French Socialists wanted to see the creation of a European Political Authority (EPA), while the Gaullists ardently opposed the supranational aspects of the EDC as well as talk of an EPA. Only the *Mouvement Républicain Populaire* (MRP) wholeheartedly supported the EDC.

Throughout all of the ratification debates, Washington remained keenly interested. It moved in close tandem with London and was gratified when, on 13 April 1954, the British signed an association agreement with the six EDC members that restated their intention to keep their forces in Europe. Three days later President Eisenhower personally supported this initiative by restating his commitment to maintain forces on the continent.

On 12 June 1954, the wavering support of the French took a turn for the worse when the Laniel government fell, as a result of the worsening situation in Indo-China and the fall of Dien Bien Phu. The new government under Pierre Mendès-France assumed power on 18 June with the ambitious goal of settling the quagmire in Indo-China within thirty-two days. The pressure to do so inevitably placed the EDC on the backburner.[73] Aside from the situation in Asia, open questions concerning the EDC still existed which, it was feared, would create an army that would leave the bulk of France's forces organised into division-size units only, with the higher levels of command embedded in a supra-national structure. In an aspect of the EDC debate that is often overlooked, the French atomic researcher Bertrand Goldschmidt and General Charles Ailleret were involved in a bid for French membership of the nuclear club and by May 1953, Pleven was informed of the feasibility of France's nuclear aspirations. The EDC treaty however stipulated in Article 107 that the six members may not dispose of any more than 500 grammes of plutonium without permission from the supranational Commissariat. This, in effect, rendered inexecutable the secret programme of the *Commissariat à l'énergie atomique.*[74]

Mendès-France's thirty-two day promise was maintained by a general settlement in Geneva on 21 July, complete with an agreement to establish the South East Asian Treaty Organisation (SEATO). The resolution of this question left Mendès-France free to turn his attention to the EDC before the summer recess of the *Assemblée.* On 19 August 1954, he proposed the indefinite postponement of plans to standardise the armed forces, the deferment for a minimum of eight years when a supranational court might begin functioning and veto power for any member over EDC actions. The Brussels Conference of the six EDC countries quite naturally refused to consider these modifications which changed the tone and meaning of the EDC substantially. Despite the entreaties of Eden and Dulles, the deathblow was dealt by the *Assemblée* a week later in an unspectacular motion (passed by 319 to 264 votes, with 43 abstentions) to 'move to other business'. The EDC was dead without, as Major-General Edward Fursdon observed, 'ever having been accorded the honour or the dignity of a funeral oration'.[75]

Ernst Haas wrote that: 'Reasons of national preoccupation clearly swayed most of those who opposed EDC, while equally clear considerations of national preoccupations have made this party a champion of further supranational integration for coal and steel.' Haas attributed the divisive debate over the EDC, as opposed to the smooth passage of the ECSC, to the contents of what was on the table:

EDC brought to the fore passions in French political life whose demonstration has seen no precedent since the Dreyfus Affair. It pitted advocates of direct negotiations with the Soviet Union against supporters of NATO and against third forcists. It opened up the Pandora's Box of the role of Germany in East–West relations. And it forced dedicated 'Europeans' to come to grips with politicians merely concerned about the least dangerous way of rearming Germany. Compared to this maelstrom, the debate over ECSC had been quiet and rational.[76]

The demise of the EDC certainly did not demote the importance of security but, rather, it illustrated that the road to a federal Europe would not be traversed by direct appeal for European security arrangements. As Simon Nuttall has commented, 'The failure of the Defence Community, and with it the Political Community, meant that the high road to European unification was barred. The low road of functional integration was now tried with greater success.'[77] Henceforth, the security issues would be addressed either tangentially, through economics, or in fora that went beyond the EDC powers to include, above all, the United States.

The aftermath – thoughts in the bath

News of the EDC's rejection was a crushing blow for Adenauer who had fought significant domestic opposition to ensure its ratification.[78] With its defeat the dream of full German sovereignty appeared to vanish, as did the possibility that the Bonn Contractual Agreement and the EPC would be ratified, since both were dependent upon the passage of the EDC Treaty. At the Brussels Conference, of 19 August, Mendès-France had conceded that, should the EDC fail to be ratified in the *Assemblée*, 'some other solution of the German problem must be found, with or without France, without delay'.[79] Eden had already instructed the FCO to design alternatives should the EDC fail to be ratified by France. One alternative forwarded by the FCO was a 'diluted E.D.C., within the framework of N.A.T.O., to which the United Kingdom would belong'.[80] Although this design would hold considerable appeal for the French, there was little hope of attracting other EDC powers. Eden's preference, and that of the FCO, was to bring Germany into NATO under various safeguards that were 'effective but not blatant'. It was with this understanding that Eden commenced discussions with Adenauer and his American counterparts.

Eisenhower's perspective was summarised in a message on 3 September sent to Bedell Smith, who was Acting Secretary of State (Dulles was in Manila participating in the signing of the SEATO treaty).[81] In the message he outlined three substitutes for the EDC: first, a revised version of the EDC with the concerned countries; second, NATO with German accession as a full member and; three, a series of unilateral agreements between European and Atlantic countries with a goal of providing for the security of the Federal Republic. Dulles subsequently boiled the alternatives down to two: *either* bring Germany into NATO with the Federal government agreeing voluntarily to limit its arms *or*, if the French should object, to go ahead with a defence agreement without the co-operation of the French. Eden was broadly in agreement and, according to his memoirs, it was 'in the bath on Sunday morning' in early September that it 'suddenly occurred to me that I might use the Brussels Treaty' as a solution to the impasse.[82] Eden subsequently called for a nine-power meeting in London involving the five Brussels Treaty powers, plus Italy, Germany, Canada and the United States, with the express purpose of agreeing on a solution to the German problem. Even if Eden's thoughts in the bath were not entirely original, the idea of incorporating Germany into the Brussels treaty was a stroke of genius.[83]

Why was the Brussels Treaty seen as a suitable vehicle for the reinvigoration of Europe's defences? From Eden's perspective, the treaty contained several advantages. First, it provided a new political framework for Europe, without discrimination, and it could readily be transformed into a mutual defence pact of the Locarno type. Second, the supranational aspects of the EDC, which had provided the ostensible grounds for Britain's non-participation, would not be present. Third, the Brussels Treaty had a duration of at least fifty years, compared to NATO's (initial) twenty. For these reasons a reshaped Brussels Treaty appeared ideal for the task of incorporating and 'normalising' Germany (and Italy).

The London and Paris conferences

The Nine-Power conference commenced on 28 September 1954 in a strained atmosphere, largely due to the 'defensive attitude' of Mendès-France.[84] In particular, relations between France and Germany were tense as a result of statements made by General Rocquencourt six days before the meeting, when he snapped that in order to meet the French demands for elaborate controls and checks on Germany, a 'super police state' would be necessary in which 'inspectors could constantly check up on baby carriage factories to make certain that they were not manufacturing guided missiles in secret'.[85] Eden, noting the difficult atmosphere, decided at an early stage to appraise Dulles of the nature of an 'unprecedented' commitment that he was willing to offer. In return Dulles was willing to offer a matching US pledge if progress was made toward European unity. It was decided that, at an appropriate moment, Dulles would make a statement along these lines and Eden, in response, would make his offer.

On cue, the end of Dulles speech gave Eden the perfect platform:

> if the hopes that were tied into the European Defence Community
> treaty can reasonably be transferred into the arrangements which
> will be the outgrowth of this meeting, then I would certainly be dis-
> posed to recommend to the President that he should renew a pledge
> comparable to that which was offered in connection with the
> European Defence Community treaty.[86]

Eden was then able to offer Britain's commitment to maintain four
divisions and the Tactical Air Force on the continent for as long as a
majority of the signatories to the Brussels Treaty desired it. In one of
his most memorable speeches Eden said:

> My colleagues will realise that what I have announced is for us a
> very formidable step to take. You all know that ours is above all an
> island story. We are still an island people in thought and tradition,
> whatever the modern facts of weapons and strategy may compel.
> And it has been not without considerable reflection that the
> Government which I represent here has decided that this statement
> could be made to you this afternoon.[87]

The reaction to Eden's statement was 'electric' although, curiously,
some interpreted Eden's statement as a victory for Mendès-France.[88] In
one sense it was a victory for France since it had finally attained assurances from Britain that it would never be left alone with a rearmed
Germany. Still, the conference could also be portrayed as a French concession since, as Dulles pointed out, 'I think [Mendès-France] feels that
[the American and British] statements, and notably the British statement, create a situation which makes it almost impossible for France to
reject a reasonable settlement of the conditions which would make
possible the admission of Germany to NATO and the creation of
European unity with some supranational features on the basis of the
Brussels treaty.'[89]

In practical terms the Nine-Power conference achieved the following:

- A Committee of the Big Three (France, Great Britain and the US)
  agreed to arrange the end of German occupation;
- West Germany was to be invited to accede to the Washington Treaty,
  to contribute the same forces as in the EDC Agreement (that is,
  twelve divisions and an air force of around one thousand aircraft)

and the powers of SACEUR were to be extended to prevent the independent deployment of these armed forces;

- West Germany and Italy were to accede to the Brussels Treaty organisation which would establish the minimum size of their respective contributions to NATO and control the manufacture of certain weapons; and
- West Germany was prohibited from the manufacture of atomic, biological or chemical weapons.[90]

The conferees reconvened in Paris on 21 October to sign an agreement confirming all of the above undertakings as well as to establish the Western European Union (WEU). *The Protocols to the Brussels Treaty, Modifying and Completing the Brussels Treaty* were signed in Paris on 23 October 1954. (See Appendix 3) With the addition of Germany and Italy, for the first time since the Second World War, countries who had been on opposing sides were brought together in the Western European Union.[91] The WEU was, to use Alfred Cahen's memorable phrase, 'born at the cross-roads of European construction and Atlantic solidarity'.[92] Almost from the outset the WEU was viewed with suspicion. It was not the supranational foundation for European unity that the EDC could have been, nor did it entirely escape federalist leanings. It was not a defensive alliance in the traditional sense since it lacked any integrated military structures, it had no common defence budget, no integrated licensing and letting of arms contracts and no European defence minister or ministry. Integration of military units would take place only at the army group level and defence policy formulation and implementation remained unambiguously a matter of national jurisdiction. The WEU was therefore destined to be NATO's junior sibling from conception. Article IV of the Protocol amending and modifying the Brussels Treaty even stated as much – 'the Council and its Agency will rely upon the appropriate military authorities of NATO for information and advice on military matters'. Eden echoed this when he commented that the WEU was 'accepted by the North Atlantic Council *as part of* the NATO defence system'.[93]

In some important regards the Modified Brussels Treaty went beyond the Washington Treaty establishing NATO. (See Appendices 1 and 3) For instance, it provided for a greater degree of commitment to its Member States and stronger guarantees that military aid would be provided for a Member State under attack, than the NATO Treaty does. Article V of the Modified Brussels Treaty commits members, in the event of an armed attack, to 'afford the Party so attacked all the military and other aid and assistance in their power' in accordance with the provisions of Article 51 of the UN Charter. In spite of the Article V commitments, the Modified Brussels Treaty's real accomplishment was one that Wyn Rees has described as 'one of reassurance and maintaining accountability over Germany'.[94]

Aside from the relationship between the WEU and NATO, the Paris Agreements also addressed the status of Germany and that of the Saar. As a consequence, Germany was admitted as a full member to NATO and, at the same time, the occupation of Germany was formally terminated. In a declaration by the Federal Government, appended to the Modified Brussels Treaty, it was agreed by the governments of France, the United Kingdom and the United States, that the Federal Republic would not engage in any action 'inconsistent' with the defensive nature of the NATO and the Brussels Treaties. In particular, it would not resort to force to reunify Germany or to modify its current boundaries. In return, the three governments recognised the Federal government as the only 'freely and legitimately constituted' German government. They also pledged to defend Berlin as well as support the resolution of the reunification issue by a negotiated peace settlement resulting in a free and unified Germany. Agreement was also reached on the size, nature and role of allied defence forces to be stationed on the territory of the Federal Republic. In response to French concerns that NATO safeguards be introduced in the event of German membership, it was recommended that the Alliance be reinforced in several areas to include command and control, logistics and levels of forces. It was also agreed, again in response to French anxieties, that the Washington Treaty should be considered of indefinite duration.[95] On the Saar issue a Franco-German agreement was signed in Paris which suggested giving the Saar the opportunity of autonomy within the framework of the WEU, with a referendum to determine the final status of the territory. The 'Europeanisation' solution was rejected by the Saarlanders in 1955 by 423 000 to 202 000 when they opted in a referendum for a return to Germany; a wish that was made effective on 1 January 1957 following elections organised under the auspices of the WEU. As Alfred Cahen, former Secretary-General of the WEU, has written: 'The settlement of the Saar problem was one of the most important political achievements of the WEU during the first phase of its existence.'[96]

The London and Paris conferences elicited positive responses from other regional organisations, such as NATO and the Council of Europe. Resolution 66, adopted by the Consultative Assembly of the Council of Europe on 11 December 1954, welcomed the results of both conferences but, in particular, the British undertaking to maintain forces on the continent indefinitely. Resolution 67 made recommendations for a closer association amongst the WEU and the Council of Europe and the ECSC, as well as between the WEU Assembly and the Consultative Assembly.

As with the EDC, signing a treaty was only the first step. On 24 December the *Assemblée* defeated the ratification bill by 280 to 258 votes. However, the defeat was to be short-lived as four days later the result was reversed and France joined the WEU following a decision by Mendès-France to make the question of ratification one of the survival of his government.

Predictably the Soviet Union was immediately critical of the treaty's ratification. In response, the Soviet Union renounced a number of bilateral treaties including the 1942 treaty with Britain and the 1944 one with France. On 14 May 1955, five days after the first NATO Council meeting with the Federal Republic as a full member, the Soviet Union and seven satellites signed a defensive treaty and, with this, the Warsaw Treaty Organisation (WTO) was born. The alliance structures that dominated European security for the remainder of the Cold War were thus established.

2
The Rebirth of European Security

From the Fouchet plan to European political co-operation

Once born, the formal division of Europe into two heavily armed camps quickly overshadowed the WEU. In terms of armed strength and support it was apparent that NATO was very much the larger and more important structure. The WEU was further marginalised by the fact that the potentially important role of the quasi-supranational Armaments Control Agency (ACA) was never fulfilled, in part because the necessary economic integration needed to provide the infrastructure was not in place. Since the armaments control aspects of the WEU could not serve as its *raison d'être*, the WEU was left with its defensive role – one in which NATO was more proficient. The meeting of the six ECSC foreign ministers at Messina in May 1955 reflected the larger powers' awareness that in defence and security matters NATO was undeniably the focus of west European efforts.

At a North Atlantic Council Ministerial session, held on 10 May 1955, the Belgian Foreign Minister, Paul-Henri Spaak, observed that 'there was not such a thing as "European defence"' and that the 'European idea was necessarily a limited concept'.[1] Spaak articulated the evident tension between the European ideal and the historical disadvantages of being a small state sandwiched between larger states. He spoke of the possibility of a 'Atlantic Commonwealth analogous to the British Commonwealth' that might better address the smaller states' needs. Spaak's French, Italian and British counterparts[2] supported his position but Halvard Lange, Norway's Foreign Minister, argued that the Norwegian public was worried that the WEU might create an 'inner circle' within NATO from which Norway would be excluded. The Portuguese representative, Paulo Cunha, echoed Lange's reservations.

In Germany's case, Adenauer supported the notion that NATO was the 'proper place to discuss major international problems', however he also adamantly pointed out that the functions of the WEU and NATO were different.[3]

Despite the widespread recognition of NATO's importance as well as the WEU's destiny to play second fiddle, concern about American dominance of NATO kept alive the perceived need for some type of European security framework. Occasionally, but rarely, such notions found a public forum. The overwhelming weight of the US in European security affairs was, unsurprisingly, felt most keenly by Germany. For instance, in 1956, in a speech advocating European federation in Brussels, Adenauer spoke of the unhealthy nature of the fundamental imbalance of power within the Alliance:

> in the long run the European allies cannot fully develop their entire strength for their own benefit and that of mankind if they continue to find their salvation and their security exclusively under the patronage of the United States.
>
> This cannot and must not become a permanent condition, since in time it would cause the energies of Europe to wither, and also because surely the United States will not be inclined to give Europe an unreasonable amount of assistance permanently. The vital necessities of European countries need not always be identical with the vital necessities of the United States and vice versa; from this situation could ensue diverging political convictions which, in turn, could lead to independent political action ... [4]

The same idea was expressed in 1957 by the WEU's General Affairs Committee:

> It is a fact that NATO is under American leadership and from this there results a moral and political unbalance which is harmful to the efficiency of the Organisation. But the necessary balance can only be established if the principal powers of Western Europe transcend their differences – I shall not call them antagonisms – and unite, finally, to achieve European integration.[5]

The timing of the above statements reflects the trauma of the 1956 Suez debacle, which underlined the need for less dependence on the US. The year was also notable for the Venice conference amongst the Six where the main item on the agenda was a report by Spaak to create a European Economic Community. In security terms the Soviet intervention in Hungary, on 23 October 1956, drove home the realities of divided Europe. Washington's reaction to the launch of Sputnik the following year also appeared to indicate that the US was less obviously able to defend Europe's interests. General Charles de Gaulle, in whom the concerns of US dominance of the Alliance found a mouthpiece, would take up the refrain with much more vigour and effect in 1958.

The Treaty of Rome establishing the European Economic Community (EEC) was signed on 27 March 1957 between six countries – Belgium, the Federal Republic of Germany, France, Italy, Luxembourg and the Netherlands. The Treaty established both the EEC and the European Atomic Energy Community (Euratom) as well as a convention on the workings of certain common institutions. The EEC, as its title suggested, was functionally broader than the European Coal and Steel Community but was limited to economics, social policy, monetary policy and commercial policy. In spite of the absence of any mention of foreign, let alone security policy, in the treaty, it nevertheless was viewed as the foundation for political integration.

In the FRG's case, in the aftermath of the failure of the EDC, the Federal Republic's Foreign Ministry 'remained firm in its determination to pursue integration as a matter of policy'.[6] Max Ophuels, Director of the Office of International and Supranational Affairs in the German Foreign Office, saw the need for Europe to move beyond co-operation arrangements to Federal institutions, with the necessary transfer of sovereign power.[7] The Foreign Ministry attributed delay on progress towards integration to the French although 'some internal resistance' in the West German government was acknowledged. The US State Department wished to encourage and support Germans and other Europeans, 'without giving the impression of US initiative or pressure'.[8] Confidentially, the US also considered that 'France had been laggard' in its support of movements towards integration.[9] The British position, summarised in a meeting of senior officials in Washington, which included Sir Roger Makins, the British Ambassador to the US, was that membership of Euratom and the projected EEC would 'conflict with the interests of the Commonwealth association... The government had therefore made the decision not to join'.[10] The Italian government, on the other hand, expressed its support for the moves towards European integration. In the French case Christian Pineau, the French Foreign Minister, made it clear that France could not be a part of the Common Market 'without a great deal of prior negotiations, and also a great deal of education in France'.[11] However, it was de Gaulle's implacable opposition to supranationalism that caused a fundamental reassessment of the aims and objectives of integration.

A British 'grand design', forwarded by David Ormsby-Gore to the Consultative Assembly of the Council of Europe on 1 May 1957[12], attempted to break down some of the emerging institutional duplication and barriers by proposing that the Council's Assembly open up direct relations with all of the other European intergovernmental organisations. With the Eden Plan in mind, the Ormsby-Gore design was received with suspicion since it was unclear to what extent Britain was championing Europe and to what extent it was promoting support for the Atlantic Union. A clear answer appeared to be given when Britain rejected participation in the EEC in favour of the looser trade-only European Free Trade Area (EFTA), which it formed with six other countries in May 1960.[13]

De Gaulle's accession to power on 1 June 1958 did not suit the newly founded EEC's low-key approach to addressing external questions. The only 'external' provisions of the previous year's Treaty of Rome were those concerning the gradual transfer of trade policy to the community, but a careful reading of the treaty will show that in this realm the Community had ambitions to play an active international role.[14] All other aspects of external relations remained firmly in the hands of the six members, including national arms production.[15] De Gaulle nevertheless believed that France was the only power who could stand up to 'les Etats-soi-disant unis' (the so-called United States) and lead Europe. He also believed that foreign policy could not be exercised through a supranational body but that it had to remain the preserve of the state, for only in this manner could a common conception of a European role in international affairs be realised.[16]

In a memorandum of 17 September 1958 de Gaulle expressed his concern that the security of western Europe was not adequately provided for by the existing arrangements.[17] He proposed to his British and American counterparts, Prime Minister Harold Macmillan and President Dwight Eisenhower, that a 'directoire à trois' be established to address questions of international politics and strategy. The response was predictably unenthusiastic and rested upon objections to de Gaulle's transparent desire to place France on a par with the US or Britain. West Germany therefore became the natural partner for France's desire to shape the future of the integration process. During Adenauer's visit to France in September 1958, the chancellor made clear his desire for the formulation of long-term ties with France on international issues. These ties were later to solidify into the 1963 Elysée Treaty. Adenauer, however, shared the British concern about the extent to which de Gaulle's policies could be construed as anti-American and anti-NATO.[18] The Dutch were understandably wary of a Franco-German consortium on foreign policy issues especially in the absence of Britain as a balancing factor. Italy remained cautious and insisted that any development of external policy within the community must include the Six.

It soon became clear that de Gaulle's objective was not limited to questions of security but also applied to the Community itself. As Simon Nuttall observed, his intent was, 'To provide a higher authority through which the sovereign Member States would be able to exercise political control over the activities of the Community institutions.'[19] In June and again in September 1959, de Gaulle proposed extensive discussions on all external matters, including NATO issues, and that these talks would exclude the Commission. In June, a Franco-Italian proposal envisaged quarterly meetings of the Foreign Ministers of the Six to discuss international developments. However, the Benelux countries soon raised concerns with the French approach; namely on the non-role of Britain, on the effects it would have upon NATO, and on its potential for alienating Brussels. The resistance of the Benelux countries led to a compromise on 23 November 1959, whereby the Foreign Ministers would hold quarterly discussions. Furthermore it was stipulated that the EEC's Council be informed of the substance of deliberations and be invited to participate when the substance touched upon Community competence. Finally, it was agreed that discussion should not prejudice the work of either NATO or the WEU.

With the help of such compromises, de Gaulle secured Adenauer's support by the end of July 1960. The latter being prompted by Eisenhower's apparent lack of resolve in the face of Soviet demands on Berlin to design more formal structures for external co-operation amongst the Six. On 5 September 1960 de Gaulle again called for regular co-operation amongst the west European states. The agenda and necessary background papers for meetings to address co-operation were to be prepared by four committees of national civil servants dealing, respectively, with political, cultural, economic and defence affairs. The latter, in particular, was intended to place the 'Atlantic Alliance on a new basis to be proposed by Europe'.[20]

At the level of the Six, a summit was held in Paris on 10–11 February 1961 to discuss more concretely the idea of creating a European Political Community. The Netherlands, as Dutch Foreign Minister Joseph Luns made clear, was opposed to any political union without British participation. However, Spaak's reappointment as Belgium's

Foreign Minister in March 1961, following his four year appointment as NATO's Secretary-General, appeared to offset the Dutch intransigence since Spaak was a well-known supporter of political union (having presided over the ill-fated EPC talks in 1952–3). Still, Spaak was also a dedicated supranationalist and the political union de Gaulle had in mind could only be attained through an intergovernmental process.[21] Ultimately de Gaulle was triumphant: on 28 June 1961 the Assembly of the Community passed a resolution in favour of political co-operation between the Six. A second meeting of the Six in Bonn, on 18 July 1961, resulted in the acceptance, in principle, of the need for periodic meetings between the heads of state or government. The resultant Bad–Godesberg Declaration included vague wording in favour of the creation of a Union amongst the European states as well as for the need for the Community to reinforce the goals of the Atlantic Alliance. The French president of the negotiating committee, Christian Fouchet, was charged with the mandate to draw up the general framework for a treaty on political union based on the input from the four committees mentioned above. The committee was soon deluged with proposals from Belgium, Germany, Italy and Luxembourg, in addition to de Gaulle's own. The Netherlands alone declined to submit a draft.

The first of two Fouchet committee drafts was presented on 19 October 1961. It incorporated many of the ideas appearing in various meetings since January 1960. Under the draft of what became known as 'Fouchet I' a common foreign and defence policy was to be established with other 'free nations'. A Council, consisting of the Heads of Government, would meet every quarter of a year, as would the Foreign Ministers. The draft also proposed that a Political Committee, composed of senior Foreign Ministry representatives of the Six, would meet in Paris to implement the Council's decisions. In the meantime, Britain made it apparent, through a conversation between Spaak and Lord Alec Douglas Home at the end of November 1961, that it wanted to be informed of developments in the negotiations.

On 13 January 1962, the *Quai d'Orsay* drew up the revised Fouchet Plan, which attempted to take into account the various objections to the first drafts. In particular, it was recognised that the common defence of a confederated Europe should result in '*strengthening the Atlantic Alliance*' – a phrase inserted at the express insistence of several leaders, including Adenauer.[22] The modified document was intended to be the basis for the next meeting of the Fouchet Committee, to be held on 18 January 1962. However, prior to the meeting, de Gaulle carefully removed the four words referring to the Atlantic Alliance from the

draft as well as any references to new members, much to the consternation of the other partners involved. De Gaulle's revised draft was gradually re-amended in the committee until, by the time the Foreign
Ministers' meeting of 20 March 1962 took place in Luxembourg, it
resembled the original draft. The damage though had been done since
there was now the perception that de Gaulle's motives were not
entirely transparent and that, when it suited the President, he would
amend and even misrepresent the wishes not only of the *Quai d'Orsay*
but those of the fellow members of the committee.

The Luxembourg meeting also saw a number of divergent positions
emerge on several fundamental issues, such as the relations of the proposed Union with the Atlantic Alliance and the provisions for revising
treaties. A week prior to the Luxembourg meeting Edward Heath had
given an address to the WEU's Assembly expressing his hope that
Britain could play a role in the discussions on the future political structure of Europe. This *préamble anglais* polarised the discussions between
France, on the one hand, and Belgium and the Netherlands on the
other. Spaak and Luns subsequently made their refusal to sign any
treaty establishing political union without British participation very
clear at the Foreign Minister's meeting in Paris on 17 April 1962.[23] As a
result, the Paris gathering ended without further scheduling of meetings on political union and in spite of Spaak's efforts to revive the dialogue, de Gaulle dealt the *coup de grâce* on 14 January 1963 when he
vetoed Britain's application to join the EEC. Political union, and with it
foreign or security union, was not seriously discussed for the next
seven years.

The attempt by the Fouchet drafting Committee, largely at de
Gaulle's behest, to impose an institutional superstructure on the EEC
not only created fertile ground for institutional power struggles (culmi-
nating in the 1966 Luxembourg Compromise) but also made accommodation with NATO all the more difficult. A looser, consultative body
might have made compromise possible, as the Davignon Plan was later
to illustrate. More than anything else then, the debate over the
Fouchet Plans marks a case study in the now familiar European versus
Atlanticist dispute. Indeed, the French proposals and the stalwart
British 'outside' defence of Europe's transatlantic ties proved to be the
undoing of the Fouchet schemes. As one Dutch commentator wrote:

> The French proposals of 1961–2 for foreign policy cooperation
> contained certainly unacceptable implications for the supranational
> character of the EC, but the Atlantic implications caused the most

alarm as became clear from the predominant role which the famous *préamble anglais* played in torpedoing the project.[24]

The European versus Atlanticist strains left some in an uncomfortable position of sitting between the two camps. For instance, the West German Defence Minister, Franz-Josef Strauss, during a speech to the WEU Assembly in May 1960, argued that

> [The Atlantic Alliance] must be based on two pillars. It must have two functioning reliable components, the North American component and the Western European component ... It is not only a question of the division of military tasks; it is primarily a question of political insight, that of the recognition of reciprocal tasks.[25]

The first few years of the 1960s also witnessed the WEU slide inexorably towards slumber. Those aspects of the WEU's work for which it had sole responsibility, such as the Saar question and control of armaments, soon fell into disuse when the Saar plebiscite was held and it became apparent that the maximum level of armaments was in no danger of being violated. It was evident to Sir Robert Boothby, with characteristic bluntness, that the WEU had 'outlived its usefulness'. It was, he observed, 'set up in frantic haste, following the collapse of the E.D.C., to deal with two problems – the problem of the European Army and the problem of the Saar. The problem of the Saar has been settled, and the only reality in defence is surely N.A.T.O.'[26]

The special relationship and European defence

Although stalwart British backing of transatlantic ties had been key to undoing French plans for the creation of European political union, the relationship between the US and Britain was not without difficulties. The Kennedy–McNamara decision to cancel all work on the Skybolt air-to-ground missile system, the growing US preoccupation with Indo-China and Cuba and open doubts within the US administration about the need for, and wisdom of, a British deterrent force, culminated in a crisis in Anglo-American relations. It was the cancellation of Skybolt however that produced the biggest rift, ultimately illustrating the lack of communication between the two countries.[27] Theodore Sorensen, special counsel to Kennedy, reflected on the British reaction as follows:

> British press and politicians complained with some justification that the Americans had been tactless, heavy-handed and abrupt, that the US was revealing either an insensitivity to an ally's pride and

security concerns or a desire to push her out of the nuclear business. Latent resentment of Kennedy's refusal to consult more on the Cuban missile crisis boiled to the top. Some charged that the Skybolt system was not really a failure, and that the US was threatening cancellation to force Britain to fulfil its troop quota in Western Europe.[28]

The crisis was eventually defused in December 1962 at a meeting between Kennedy and Macmillan in Nassau. Their personal relationship made some kind of offer in lieu of Skybolt possible. As a result, the Nassau agreement was announced in a communiqué in December 1962. The agreement had two components. First, British Polaris submarines were to be assigned to NATO command unless 'supreme national interests' were at stake, in which case they would operate solely under British command. Second, a 'mixed-manned' multinational NATO seaborne deterrent force (known as the Multilateral Force or MLF) was proposed. The MLF was designed to be the centrepiece of Kennedy's 'Atlantic partnership' but France interpreted the MLF as further evidence of preferential treatment of the British by Washington. George Ball, US Secretary of State during the Nassau meeting, who was aware of the potential for third party misinterpretation, cautioned that any deal outside of the NATO multilateral network would be regarded not only as pro-British discrimination but also as 'indifference to nuclear proliferation'.[29] Despite Ball's warnings, Kennedy went ahead with his version of the MLF. The Nassau agreement should also be viewed in the context of Kennedy's 1961 decision not to assist the French bid for an independent nuclear deterrent as well as his decision not to give medium-range, land-based, missiles to NATO.

Because of its confusing underlying purpose, the proposed MLF had little support from NATO members with the exception of Germany, who was an enthusiastic backer. But not only did the MLF prove unable to win support, in many respects the Nassau agreement failed in all of its main objectives. Namely, it failed to incorporate West Germany unobtrusively into a nuclear relationship within the Alliance; it failed to dispel the impression of preferential British treatment; it failed to change the impression that the US retained a decisive nuclear monopoly, particularly over command and control arrangements; and it failed to dampen the French desire for an independent nuclear force and may have even strengthened De Gaulle's resolve. Perhaps the most revealing commentary on the entire Skybolt–Nassau–MLF affair was provided by Richard Neustadt when he commented that: 'There is no "Europe"... What one man is it to be shared with – De Gaulle,

Adenauer, Macmillan? None of them can speak for Europe.'[30] With Britain as the 'outsider' there would inevitably be tension between the inclusion of a security or defence element into any suggested EPC and the preferences of the smaller EEC members, who sought security assurances through the Atlantic Alliance. As a potential member of the EEC Britain could bolster the prospects for political union precisely by emphasising its close relations with Washington and providing the required assurances to the smaller members. This, of course, is exactly what de Gaulle opposed.

What was though less perceptible about Britain was that, in spite of French protestations of Anglo-Saxon collusion, Britain had in fact begun a slow process of reorienting, beginning in 1956 in the aftermath of Suez, towards a European destiny. A combination of factors served to direct this orientation: the Suez debacle itself; the spectacular economic growth being attained by the EEC countries (especially when compared to the economic decline under Harold Wilson's governments); the accession of a younger generation to power on both sides of the Atlantic who were less Atlanticist in orientation; and the growing preoccupation of Washington with south-east Asia and the subsequent decline in Anglo-American relations in light of allied failure to back the US in the region. While the shift in Britain's foreign and security interests was also part of a wider reorientation of its post-colonial priorities, it also reflected a more general shift amongst the Six.

The fields of Elysée

Relations between France and the US, especially between Eisenhower and de Gaulle, were extremely problematic in the face of suspicions that Washington retained a preference for relations with London over the more general European–US partnership. To Eisenhower and Macmillan it was evident that the European community should be developed '*within* the Atlantic community'.[31] Both were fond of reiterating that the report of the Three Wise Man, had stressed that: 'The moves towards Atlantic co-operation and European unity should be parallel and complementary, not competitive or conflicting.'[32] De Gaulle's perspective was coloured not only by his wartime experience but also by a deep mistrust of the US going back to American (and British) obstruction of the French occupation of the Ruhr in 1923. French relations with NATO deteriorated when, as a reaction to the Nassau agreement and the proposed MLF, de Gaulle insisted on an independent *force de frappe* and announced unilateral cuts in the

French troop contributions to NATO. Thus, distrust of the US, accompanied by suspicions held toward Britain that it was America's Trojan Horse in Europe, led to the obvious conclusion that French designs for Europe could best be attained with Germany's support. Differences between France and the Benelux countries, which had become evident during the Fouchet negotiations, also left de Gaulle with the prospect of negotiating arrangements for political co-operation with only Italy and Germany. Negotiations with the former quickly broke down on the grounds that Italy did not wish to be put in a position of 'permanent weakness'.[33] It was therefore to Germany that de Gaulle turned.

Relations between France and Germany, at least on paper, as illustrated by the signature of the Franco-German (Elysée) Treaty on 22 January 1963, were becoming stronger. Amongst other things, the treaty provided for the eventual harmonization of military doctrine, the establishment of combined operational research, military exchanges, joint armament projects and an examination of the potential for Franco-German collaboration in the civil defence area. Under the terms of the agreement, the heads of government would meet twice yearly while the respective foreign ministers would meet quarterly to discuss co-operation on foreign policy, defence and politics. The treaty was however interpreted as an attempt by Paris to snatch away Germany from American influence, just as the Nassau meeting was perceived as snatching Britain away from offers of collaboration with France. Since the signing of the Elysée treaty followed close on the heels of de Gaulle's rejection of Britain's EEC application, the impression that any future European integration would be subject to Franco-German approval was reinforced.

However, the treaty, at the insistence of the *Bundestag*, included assurances that the common defence network of the Atlantic Alliance would be strengthened. These guarantees, alongside the replacement of Adenauer as chancellor by Ludwig Erhard, proved to be further obstacles to the attainment of de Gaulle's vision of a confederal Europe. In spite of the added pro-Alliance tone of the treaty, American irritation was evident. According to a conversation between Kennedy and Maurice Couve de Murville, French Foreign Minister, in October 1963, US irritation stemmed from the fact that the US was also trying to attach the Federal Republic to western institutions.[34] To Couve de Murville, however, the future role of the Federal Republic was one of 'European construction' and although the link of the Atlantic Alliance had 'certainly existed between the European states, it did not take the place of everything for ever'.[35]

Over the course of the next few years three successive French-inspired crises were to challenge the very future of European integration, including the prospects for European security integration.

De Gaulle's three impediments

The first crisis was provoked by the deterioration of Franco-American relations throughout the 1960s that gave rise to the more general issue of the future of France's association with NATO. In a press conference in May 1965 de Gaulle made his feelings plain:

> NATO will disappear as far as we're concerned in 1969. We shall announce this at the beginning of next year in order to give the time necessary for the indispensable arrangements to be taken, for, after that date, there will be no more foreign forces on French territory, apart from those that we will want to have and they must be under our supervision ... [The Atlantic Treaty] will be replaced, if our partners so wish, with bilateral agreements: thus we shall also be able to conclude one with the United States, one with Britain, one with Germany.[36]

Hervé Alphand, the French Ambassador in Washington, immediately realised that this would not only mean the end of any friendship with the United States but also the end of the Europe of the Six. But de Gaulle's announcement was prompted not so much by anti-Americanism but more by the sense that, on important matters of security, Washington was ignoring its European allies. For instance, the shift of US strategy away from Dulles's doctrine of massive nuclear retaliation to McNamara's flexible response strategy, stressing a graduated mix of conventional and nuclear responses and which was gradually put into operation in 1961 and eventually adopted as official NATO doctrine in 1965. Not only did the European allies have very little say in this process but they feared the strategy would open the possibility of limited nuclear war on European soil with the US as the main decision-maker.[37] For France it was also a question of a perceived infringement of French sovereignty and, by expelling NATO forces (mainly US) from French soil, the entire exercise of sovereignty would be recovered. De Gaulle warned that: 'France intends to recover, in her territory, the full exercise of sovereignty, now impaired by the permanent presence of allied military elements or by the habitual use of its airspace.'[38] Accordingly, in compliance with de Gaulle's wishes, representatives of France left the military bodies of NATO on 1 July 1966 but maintained representation in the Alliance Council. All American and Canadian bases on French territory were to be withdrawn by 1 April 1967.

These years were all the more traumatic since they came hot on the heels of an equally grave second crisis in the EEC provoked by de Gaulle. The Community's crisis was prompted by the French concern that it was becoming too federalist and that the Commission, under Walter Hallstein, was pushing for too many powers for itself. The catalyst for the crisis was a dispute over the 31 March 1965 proposals by the Commission to finance the common agricultural policy (CAP) of the EEC through levies on agricultural imports and duties on industrial imports. Following the transitional period for the implementation of CAP, ending in 1970, these funds would effectively be the Commission's resources. The proposal would also have significantly extended the European Parliament's control over the budgetary process. The withdrawal of the French Permanent Representative, Couve de Murville, on 30 June, effectively paralysed the EEC in its ability to conduct anything other than routine business and also threatened the Community with the prospect of entering a fiscal year with no approved budget. The 'empty chair crisis', as it became known, was resolved at a meeting of the Foreign Ministers of the Six on 28–9 January 1966. The resolution became known as the Luxembourg compromise.[39] Although the Luxembourg compromise marked an 'agreement not to agree' for the Six and a victory of sorts for de Gaulle, it also marked the decline of unequivocal French direction of European integration.

The third impediment to European integration was de Gaulle's second rejection of British membership of the EEC within a week of its 10 May 1967 application by Harold Wilson's Labour government. The rejection prompted Britain to press for admittance to the EEC through the WEU in July 1967. De Gaulle however pronounced on 29 November that he still did not see Britain as ready to join the European Community. The Labour government left its application on the table in the WEU but it was obvious that there would be no progress until de Gaulle left office – this was not to occur until 1969. Thus the demise of the Fouchet Plan and the 1965 'empty chair' crisis were both significant impediments to the integration process, as was de Gaulle's preoccupation with the Anglo-Saxon challenge. In the end, however, de Gaulle's visions for Europe were to be frustrated by neither Britain nor the US, but by the unravelling of his domestic leadership precipitated by the May 1968 riots and the Soviet-led invasion of Czechoslovakia. Together, these events thwarted de Gaulle's designs for a *rapprochement* with Russia and his personal ambitions to be the architect of a new Europe.

The WEU's decline and the Eurogroup's rise

With the seccession of de Gaulle's longest-serving Prime Minister, Georges Pompidou, as the new French Premier on 15 June 1969, the way was finally opened for British membership of the EEC. The essential details of British membership were agreed to by mid-1970, although formal membership was not to take place for another three years. The middle of the decade also witnessed the Labour party's surprise loss in the general election to what was to prove to be Britain's most pro-European postwar government under Edward Heath.

As has been observed, the British employed the WEU as a conduit to the Six during its membership negotiations. By so doing, Britain inadvertently contributed to the WEU's eventual marginalisation since its bid for EEC membership only provoked a boycott of the WEU by France. The Harmel plan of 3 October 1968, to relaunch European co-operation through the WEU, was also promptly rejected by France at the Rome meeting of the WEU Council on 21 October. Additionally, the WEU Council decided to halt the exercise of its economic activities and, alongside this, Council members also stopped meeting before sessions of other international organisations, such as the UN. According to Alfred Cahen, ex-Secretary General of the WEU: 'Ministers then deserted the Council, which held virtually no more meetings at that level until 1984.'[40] Although the WEU Assembly, consisting of parliamentarians from the member states, continued to meet from 1973 until the organisation's rejuvenation in 1984, it was also essentially in hibernation.

The focus of European security collaboration, such as it was, shifted from the WEU to NATO with the founding of the Eurogroup in 1968 immediately prior to a meeting of all of the NATO Defence Ministers.[41] The objective of the Eurogroup was firstly to demonstrate greater European unity and, secondly, to provide a second tier of communication for Britain with the Six, this time within the NATO context. The emphasis of the Eurogroup's discussions tended to be on practical co-operation; to facilitate this a number of technical sub-groups were created.[42] The Defence Ministers of the Eurogroup countries met every six months to direct the activities of the sub-groups and to discuss major developments in European security. An additional purpose of the Eurogroup was to improve relations with the US, which was then enveloped in the growing storm clouds of the burdensharing debate.[43]

The election of Richard Nixon as President of the United States on 5 November 1968 was to herald a series of initiatives emanating from Washington to shape a more coherent European defence effort. The

prime instrument in this regard was the Nixon doctrine, which her-
alded the 'one-and-a-half' war strategy[44] combined with a concerted
attempt by Washington to persuade its European allies to improve
their defence effort within the Alliance. In a speech to the North
Atlantic Council in Brussels in December 1970 Nixon warned in
Dullesian fashion: 'NATO's conventional forces must not only be maintained, but in certain key areas strengthened. Given a similar approach
by our allies, the United States will maintain and improve its own
forces in Europe and will not reduce them unless there is reciprocal
action from our adversaries.'[45] The intention behind the Nixon initiative was to encourage defence collaboration between the US and
its European allies as well as a more efficient use of resources. The
Eurogroup played an instrumental role in both these aims, acting as
the prime defence-planning group within NATO and promoting
European input to the planning process. The biggest constraint to
Nixon's initiatives was without doubt the refusal of France to participate in the group. France believed the Eurogroup to be too closely associated with NATO's Defence Planning Committee and it also objected
to the stated aim of increasing European contributions to the common
defence. There were initially other Eurogroup skeptics, such as Portugal
who was preoccupied with Africa, and Canada who feared that the
group would weaken not strengthen the two pillars. Both Britain and
Germany were enthusiastic supporters. A later French attempt in 1973
by French Foreign Minister, Michel Jobert, to promote the WEU as an
alternative to NATO's Eurogroup met with little interest and served to
underline French isolation and sensitivities.

European political co-operation – the Hague summit

With the advent of the 1970s the EEC still lacked an external political
persona with the possible exception of the second Yaoundé Convention, which was signed on 29 July 1969.[46] The EEC remained, as the
organisation's initials suggest, for the most part an *economic* community. The question of repairing the damage of the 1966 Luxembourg
compromise and of making the Community something more than
economic was raised on 22–3 July at a meeting of the Council of
(Foreign) Ministers of the Six by Maurice Schumann. He proposed a
conference on the subject of a greater role for the EEC to be held at the
end of the year. The Hague summit of the Heads of Government was
scheduled to meet on 1–2 December 1969 and had on its schedule
enlargement (from six to nine), as well as the prospects for economic,

monetary and political union. In retrospect, the timing of the meeting was propitious since serious reservations about US involvement in Vietnam and the growing use of superpower summitry, such as the opening of the SALT talks between the US and the USSR in Helsinki on 17 November 1969, were once again giving credence to the idea of European co-operation (EPC) on external issues.

The Hague Summit proved to be a significant landmark since it not only launched the enlargement process and monetary unification but, at the instigation of the recently elected Chancellor of the Federal Republic, Willy Brandt, foreign ministers were called on to consider strategies for political unification.[47] Since the request was directed to foreign ministers, the assumption was that the primary emphasis should be upon foreign policy co-operation. The mechanisms to be used were initially deliberately informal but, with the passage of time, it was hoped they could be formalised. The summit called for no less than a 'united Europe' which would make an international contribution 'commensurate with its role and mission'. Almost a year later the report called for by Chancellor Brandt was unveiled. Since Belgium held the Presidency for the first half of 1970, the report was named after Étienne Davignon, a Belgian diplomat and future Commissioner.

The Davignon report marked the launching of the EPC process. It called for a series of regular meetings between foreign ministers and senior foreign affairs ministry officials so that the world might know that 'Europe has a political vocation'.[48] A final version of the report was submitted to the Council in May 1970 and eventually adopted by the Conference of Foreign Ministers meeting in Luxembourg on 27 October 1970 – which is why the report is also commonly referred to as the Luxembourg Report. The Council of Ministers endorsed the report and initiated a regular series of meetings; a process that occurred *outside* the Treaty of Rome but in tandem with it.[49] Although the spirit of the Fouchet Committee's earlier deliberations coloured the report, it was far less extensive in scope and it excluded formal arrangements in favour of the responsibility of the host country (whoever happened to be holding the EEC Presidency) to make the 'necessary arrangements'. Moreover, co-operation was confined to the 'field of foreign policy'. Defence was not discussed in the report because of the earlier sensitivities shown by the Benelux countries towards anything that may appear to damage NATO and transatlantic security links.[50]

The mechanism for attaining mutual understanding and solidarity in major issues of international politics consisted of twice yearly meetings of the Foreign Ministers, hosted and chaired by the country holding the Community Presidency. The meetings would be prepared by a committee of Directors of Political Affairs, known as the Political Committee, which met four times per year. In the course of its preparation the committee was authorised to form working groups and consult experts as needed. A Conference of the Heads of State or Government could be held instead of the ministerial meetings if the Foreign Ministers considered a situation serious enough to warrant it. In terms of scope, the governments could consult on 'all major questions of foreign policy' while Member States could 'propose any subjects they wish for political consultation'.[51]

The first meeting of the Foreign Ministers in their EPC guise was held under German chairmanship on 19 November 1970. The chair, Walter Scheel, was anxious to impress upon his colleagues the potential for the EPC to make a valuable contribution to détente in Europe as well as to extend Germany's *Ostpolitik* to a community-wide enterprise.[52]

The Copenhagen report to Tindemans: the decline of EPC

The Luxembourg Report also called for a second report in two years time 'to ensure continuity on the task embarked on'.[53] By that time, Denmark, Ireland, Norway and the United Kingdom had signed treaties of accession to the European Communities – thus making ten.[54] Brandt and Pompidou had also in the meantime met in Paris and on 11 February 1972 called for a summit of the Ten[55] to examine the possibilities for the creation of a permanent secretariat for political co-operation.

The Paris Summit, of 19–20 October 1972, discussed political union and other Community-pertinent topics. Following the meeting, the Heads of State and Government 'expressed their satisfaction at the results obtained since the political cooperation machinery was formally set up on the basis of the texts of 27 October 1970'. However, further intergovernmentalism of the EPC process was resisted by the smaller member states because they feared the imminent enlargement of the community and a potential Paris-Bonn-London triangle. Thus, the Summit merely instructed the Foreign Ministers to prepare another report by the end of June 1973 on ways to improve political co-operation 'in accordance with the Luxembourg Report'.[56]

The second report was delivered at the Foreign Minister's Copenhagen meeting of 23 July 1973. In compliance with their task, the nine ministers[57] elaborated upon the Luxembourg report rather than replacing it. The ministers called for 'co-operation', not a 'community', which implied that the process would be related to the EEC but not an integral component of it. The agreement to 'consult' on important questions of foreign policy made in the earlier Luxembourg Report was reiterated. The report claimed that the consultative habits initiated by the Hague Summit had led 'to the "reflex" of co-ordination amongst the Member States which had profoundly affected the relations between each other and with third countries'.[58] Moreover the 'characteristically pragmatic mechanisms set up by the Luxembourg Report' had led to 'a new procedure in international relations and an original European contribution to the technique of arriving at concerted action'. Since both the Communities and the EPC process had as their eventual aim European unification, the report also elaborated upon the need for co-ordination. The EPC's machinery was described as 'distinct from and additional to the activities of the institutions of the Community which are based on the juridicial commitments undertaken by the Member States in the Treaty of Rome'.[59] Two methods of improving upon consistency were suggested. First, the Council, through the President of the Committee of Permanent Representatives, should be 'informed by the Presidency of the agreed conclusions which result from the work of the Political Cooperation machinery, *to the extent that these conclusions have an interest for the work of the Community'*. Second, the Ministers should be able, *'if it so desired*, to instruct the political cooperation machinery to prepare studies on certain political aspects of problems under examination in the framework of the Community'.[60]

Finally, the Report included some adjustments to co-operational procedures. For example, the number of meetings of Foreign Ministers was raised to four times per year while the restriction on the number of meetings of the Political Committee, specified as four per annum in the Luxembourg Report, was lifted (the committee had in any case met nine times in the previous twelve months). The Luxembourg Report had also stipulated that each Member State could send a 'correspondent' from its Foreign Ministry, who should liase with his or her opposite numbers. Under the Copenhagen Report this allowance was formalised into the 'Group of Correspondents' which was charged with the responsibility of following and studying the problems of political co-operation.

In the Summit of the Heads of State and Government in Copenhagen, on 14 December, the *Document on European Identity* stressed the importance of co-ordinating foreign and security issues for a more united Europe. Furthermore, it provided for a dialogue structure on these issues, aided by the installation of a Telex network (COREU) between the Foreign Ministries. Since the Federal Republic of Germany joined the UN as a full member on 18 September 1973 the importance of reaching common positions within the UN was given special emphasis. As Peter Brückner observed: 'Ever since, the Member States have progressively developed disciplines, in written and unwritten rules and procedures, with a view to improving their cohesion in the UN through the various modes of political expression, in particular joint statements, voting, and common explanations of vote.'[61] The main task of the *Document on European Identity* was to assess progress towards the eventual goal of political union and to underline the importance of unity and Europe's common goals. Based on the assertion of the need to adopt a more distinct European identity the Europeans, led by France, announced their intention of pursuing an independent policy in the Middle East – an area in which the US had hoped for allied support. Henry Kissinger reflected that: 'Europe, it emerged increasingly, wanted the option to conduct a policy separate from the United States and in the case of the Middle East objectively in conflict with us.'[62]

In addition to being the year in which the FRG joined the UN, 1973 was also the year that the Mutual and Balanced Force Reduction (MBFR) talks commenced in Vienna, the year that Kissinger (in retrospect, unfortunately) dubbed the 'Year of Europe', and the year in which transatlantic relations were put to the test. The catalyst for troubled transatlantic relations was the Brezhnev–Nixon Summit. Michel Jobert was suspicious that the proposed New Atlantic Charter, a key part of the 'Year of Europe', was an attempt by Washington to damage French interests and promote those of the Atlantic Alliance. Kissinger reflected upon Jobert's sensitivities in his memoirs:

> If we were planning to work through NATO, the Year of Europe might turn into a device to pressure France to resume full participation; if the European Community was to be our counterpart, the practical consequence would be an American attempt to lobby the other members, hence diluting (if not worse) any leadership of France.[63]

The centrepiece of the 'Year of Europe' was supposed to be the US proposal for an Atlantic Declaration which, in part, was designed to inspire confidence in the Alliance amongst the postwar generation. As Kissinger notes, America's allies were preoccupied, 'they used our initiative for an Atlantic Declaration as the anvil for forging their own emergent institutions. They were less interested in a new basis for Atlantic unity, some considering it an interruption – perhaps even intentional – of their dominant preoccupation'.[64] The effect would appear to have been quite the opposite from that intended. One of the unintended effects of the 'Year of Europe' was to push France to promote more EPC involvement at the highest level.

President Pompidou called on 28 March 1974 for the initiation of regular meetings of the Nine at the level of Heads of State or Government. At the same time Pompidou warned of the dangers of America's *'accord préable'*. Pompidou's initiative was supported by his British and German counterparts, Edward Heath and Willy Brandt, respectively. The designs for the shape and competence of the European Council, which was the name given to the meetings of the Nine at Head of State or Government level, was a task that was to fall to others, since all three were replaced over the next few months. James Callaghan replaced Heath in February, Giscard d'Estaing replaced Pompidou in May, and Helmut Schmidt replaced Brandt also in May. Details were discussed prior to the Paris summit, but formalised at a 9–10 December 1974 summit. It was agreed that the Heads of State or Government accompanied by their Foreign Ministers should meet three times a year under the EPC flag, and that the European Parliament should be elected by direct universal suffrage. As a further effort to boost progress towards political union, the Belgian Prime Minister, Leo Tindemans, was commissioned to write a report on the Community's progress towards European Union.

The 1975 Tindemans Report explicitly recognised that 'European Union' would be incomplete without a common security policy. Yet, Tindeman's ideas were far too radical and federal in their approach to stand any chance of support. For example, Tindemans suggested that actions of the community should, *'devenir commune dans tous les domaines essentiels (des) relations extérieures, qu'il s'agisse de politique étrangère, de sécurité, de relations économiques, de coopération'.*[65] According to one account, whilst touring Europe to prepare his report on European integration, Tindemans discovered that 'common action in the field of foreign policy had become the single most frequently quoted justification of the integration process'.[66] Although the report served as the basis for discussion at a subsequent European Council meeting, it had little impact. Soon thereafter the drafting of reports was to become a formality, in 1976 it was agreed that the Commission and the Foreign Ministers should present annual reports assessing progress towards European Union.

In his authoritative work on EPC Simon Nuttall notes that by 1977 EPC had reached a 'plateau' where the Nine could continue as they had been but could not do much more. Nuttall suggests a number of reasons for this:[67]

- The lack of 'institutional underpinning' with the result that effectiveness depended heavily on a 'climate of optimism' amongst those participating;
- The absence of 'internal dynamism' meant that many crucial questions were not addressed, such as East–West relations in Europe;
- The lack of international crises to which the Six/Nine would feel obliged to react; and
- Following Pompidou's interest in EPC, Giscard's 'restrictive line' dampened any enthusiasm to work through the EPC.

Of the reasons identified by Nuttall, the last is the most influential. As a result, the decade drew to a close with the failure of the EPC to react in a timely fashion to the Christmas Eve 1979 invasion of Afghanistan by the Soviet Union, apart from a condemnation by the Nine on 15 January 1980. This obvious ineffectiveness could have sounded the death knell for EPC. Instead, it seems to have acted as a spur to action, at least in the rhetorical sense.

From London to the Single European Act

François Mitterrand's accession to power on 10 May 1981 and his appointment of Claude Cheysson as Foreign Minister removed the main impediment to the growth of the EPC, which had centred on Pompidou's refusal to allow the Commission to associate itself fully with political co-operation. However any chance of developing a security dimension to the EPC was firmly blocked by the neutral Irish. Following practical calls from Douglas Hurd, the British Foreign Secretary, for support for the EPC process and the creation of automatic crisis-reaction mechanisms, a flood of proposals ensued, most notably from the Federal Republic's Foreign Minister, Hans-Dietrich Genscher, whose ideas were to reappear more formally in the Genscher–Colombo plan later on in 1981.

The various proposals were to surface in the London Report, the third in the series of reports shaping the EPC prior to the Single European Act. The essential details of the 13 October 1981 London Report had already been worked out at prior high-level meetings. The report claimed that political cooperation had become a 'central element in the foreign policies of all Member States' and that the Community was 'increasingly seen by third countries as a coherent force in international relations'.[68] The Foreign Ministers of the Ten[69] maintained that 'significant progress' had been made in political co-operation since the Luxembourg Report, noting that EPC had 'steadily intensified' and that its scope had 'continually broadened'. They also noted though that in spite of achievements in this area, 'the Ten are still far from playing a role in the world appropriate to their combined influence'.

Perhaps more significantly the London Report sought to enhance EPC by urging that the Ten strive not only for 'common attitude' but 'joint action'. In order to attain this a number of practical improvements were suggested. Amongst the suggestions was the dual use of formal meetings that should henceforth include 'only items of major importance', as well as the use of informal 'Gymnich-type meetings' that would have no formal agenda and which should be confidential.[70] Structurally, a few modifications were also suggested. For instance, the considerable burdens incumbent upon the Presidency were noted (as in the Copenhagen Report) and it was suggested that additional operational support could be provided without 'reducing the direct contact pragmatism and economy that are among the chief virtues of the present arrangements'.[71] The report also advocated a strengthened commitment to consult the full association of the Commission within the EPC process 'at all levels'. Additionally it proposed the creation of a 'small team' of officials drawn from the previous and succeeding Presidencies to assist the Presidency. The team, soon dubbed the Troika Secretariat, proved to be an important mechanism for ensuring some consistency in the EPC's activities. In a further development the mandate of the EPC was extended to 'foreign policy questions bearing on the political aspects of security'.[72] Precisely what 'political aspects of security' constituted was deliberately not spelt out, yet it was clearly as far as Ireland was willing to go whilst retaining its neutral status. Mention of the political aspects of security did not go unnoticed. The London Report was invoked a few years later in a European Parliamentary resolution, adopted on 14 February 1984 and penned by Altiero Spinelli, stressing the importance of including security issues in any plans for European union.

The Genscher–Colombo Plan of 12 November 1981, mentioned briefly above, is also worthy of note since it marks the first time that an initiative within the political sphere carried a German and not a French *imprimatur*.[73] A number of factors account for this, amongst them being the perceived need for a *Westpolitik* to balance Germany's *Ostpolitik*. In essence, Genscher's design was intended to reinforce EPC while at the same time addressing defence problems and boosting the appeal of his Free Democratic Party (FDP). Since the plan emanated from Genscher and the FDP it did not have the backing of the Federal government and therefore required an outside sponsor. Genscher found this in the Italian Foreign Minister, Emilio Colombo. Somewhat ambitiously, the plan proposed a scheme to overcome the Luxembourg compromise (which had instituted a seemingly endless succession of national vetoes), to strengthen EC institutions, and enhance security co-operation. In short, it advocated a direct linkage between the economic and political aspects of the EC's work. Predictably, Paris was adamantly against any such linkage. The Irish were again opposed to the mention of co-operation in security matters. The Danes and Greeks also shared concerns in this regard. Agreement on the various drafts of the plan was elusive under the Belgian and Danish Presidencies. It was only when Germany assumed the Presidency, at the beginning of 1983, that a sufficiently watered-down version could be agreed upon in the form of the June 1983 *Solemn Declaration on European Union.*

The Solemn Declaration managed to expand upon the London Report's 'political aspects of security' to include economic ones. It also strengthened the hand of the European Council, by giving it the task of issuing general guidelines for the EPC, and the Presidency of the European Council, by requiring it to present a report to the European Parliament. The Solemn Declaration further stressed the London Report's newfound emphasis on security, claiming that 'by speaking with a single voice in foreign policy, including the political aspects of security, Europe can contribute to the maintenance of peace'. Finally, the declaration established the link between political co-operation and the 'co-ordination of positions of member states on the political and economic aspects of security, so as to promote and facilitate the progressive development of such positions ... in a growing number of foreign policy fields'.[74]

In spite of the seemingly optimistic tone engendered by the Solemn Declaration, security remained largely a marginal element of the EPC. Although the amount of co-ordination between the EC foreign offices increased enormously the mechanisms for overview and information dissemination were either absent or a matter of executive privilege in many countries. Reports and declarations were numerous, but what they amounted to in practical terms was often obscure. The outbreak of the 1973 oil crisis, which led to the French-backed Euro-Arab dialogue in December, also illustrated the increasing difficulties (and artificiality) of dividing the economic from the political spheres of the

EC's work. In practical terms the early record of EPC was not impressive. For example, attempts to co-ordinate EC actions with regard to sanctions against South Africa met with resistance and actions that were undertaken with regard to Arab–Israeli relations appeared to have no perceptible effect. Anglo-French differences hindered progress in general, as did persistent unilateral actions on the part of Greece. The EPC's low point was reached with its confused and piecemeal response to the Soviet invasion of Afghanistan in 1979. The early 1980s declaration of martial law in Poland, followed by the invasion of the Falkland Islands by Argentina, and the invasion of Lebanon by Israel, all demanded a concerted response. Responses tended to take the form of economic sanctions, as in for example, those imposed on Argentina, which more often than not merely illustrated that the Community was unable to muster the necessary collaboration to effectively enforce them.[75] Whatever its faults, the EPC process did at least encourage the habit of regular dialogue, even if this meant regular disagreement, and a regular flow of information between foreign ministries.

The 1970s, and much of the following decade, were however marked by a number of negative developments in US–European relations, especially those between America and Germany. The 1977 'neutron bomb' debate between Germany and the Carter administration marked an especially low point in relations between the two. According to a top advisor to Schmidt at the time: 'This incident is what convinced us to move closer to the French and to make the European pillar stronger – so that we could become real partners and would not be told by the Americans what to do.'[76] A second instance of inadequate consultation on the part of Washington occurred during the Reagan presidency. In this case, the seeds of German discontent were planted by frequent assurances given to Bonn that bilateral US–Soviet arms control negotiations on intermediate-range nuclear (INF) missiles would not result in the dismantling of 72 Pershing 1A missiles without Bonn's consent. However, putting these assurances aside, the bilateral negotiations resulted in the agreement to dismantle *all* intermediate-range nuclear forces. In December 1987, as negotiations neared completion, Bonn was faced with what amounted to a *fait accompli* since, although the missiles were technically German, the warheads were American, and the missiles were obviously useless without the all-important warhead. The Pershing missiles also had been a CDU symbol of close US–German relations. In the aftermath of the INF debacle, when the Bush administration proposed deploying new short-range FOTL (Follow-on-to-Lance) missiles on German soil, all German political parties were opposed. More generally, the period from 1979, and NATO's 'dual-track' decision, until the INF Treaty in 1987 was marked by considerable activism amongst the west European publics against missile deployments. The missiles became a potent symbol of anti-American sentiment and provided a context for discussions about an enhanced west European role in security affairs. Despite the fact that the 1979–87 period saw some of the worst postwar differences between Washington and the west European capitals, the EPC process remained frustratingly incoherent and on many issues failed to find one voice.

The post-Genscher–Colombo Plan advancement of the EC into the political realm can be attributed to President François Mitterrand. During a speech to the European parliament, on 24 May 1984, he called for an intergovernmental conference (IGC) with the goal of establishing a new Treaty 'which must not of course, be a substitute for existing Treaties, but an extension of them in fields they do not currently cover. This is the case of the European political community'.[77] At the 25–6 June 1984 Fontainebleau meeting of the European Council, Mitterrand appealed again for a relaunch of the EPC. The committee established at Fontainebleau soon found itself divided along the familiar lines of the Genscher–Colombo Plan. It did though agree to the establishment of an *ad hoc* committee consisting of selected representatives of Heads of State and Government who could suggest improvements to the co-operation between the Community and any other field of concern, including EPC. The *ad hoc* committee, chaired by Senator James Dooge, a former Irish Foreign Minister, produced a draft report bearing the chair's name in December 1984 and a final report in March 1985. The latter concerned itself mainly with internal aspects of the Community's work, with occasional reference to the external aspects. In so far as the EPC featured in the final report, it served to produce the same reservations and positions engendered three years earlier by the Genscher–Colombo Plan. Broadly speaking, Denmark held serious reservations about extending the EPC's mandate beyond the political and economic aspects of security; Greece expressed concern that further expansion into security issues might damage relations with NATO (not to mention its own substantial US military assistance); Senator Dooge expressed the predictable reservations regarding security on behalf of Ireland; while the original Six plus Britain remained committed to extending the association between the Community and the EPC. Perhaps as a sign of this belief in the need for enhanced European security and defence collaboration, an agreement was signed on 9 July 1984 by the Defence Ministers of the

Federal Republic, France, Italy, Spain and the United Kingdom, to construct a common combat aircraft. For some this first step was to become a symbol of the profound difficulties of creating a common European security and defence.

The Single European Act and Title III

In a now familiar pattern, the period preceding the IGC saw a flurry of activity. It was in the lead up to the European Council's meeting in Milan in June 1985 that Geoffrey Howe, British Forign Secretary, recalls '[Britain] incorporated foreign-policy provisions in a treaty text for the first time...' The genesis of this incorporation is curious and affords an interesting glimpse into the complex relations between the three major European actors. Howe wrote:

> Margaret Thatcher invited Chancellor Kohl to Chequers in May 1985, on his own, and there handed him this draft text with a view to it being used as a joint Anglo-German initiative...There was a silence from Bonn for the next couple of weeks. Then, suddenly, about eleven days before the Milan Summit in June, a Franco-German text using the same material appeared in almost the same words. It was that which became in due course incorporated as Title III...I tell that story because I never understood how it happened... and it is an illustration of the realities of trying to conduct business and negotiate treaties in Europe.[78]

Whatever the origins of the texts, the two differed in some important regards.[79] For instance, the British text advocated, at best, the *status quo*. It might even be considered a step back from the London Report since it envisaged EPC remaining a parallel process with the Commission playing a limited role. The Franco-German 'Draft Treaty on European Union' was more extensive in design. It aimed for the formation of a European Union, and included EPC as an integral component. The Franco-German Draft Treaty also proposed a Secretariat General of the Council of the EU under the direction of the Secretary-General of the EU, which was to be responsible for EPC. The French and Germans obtained good mileage out of their text since virtually the same text was to appear verbatim in Chancellor Kohl's and President Mitterrand's later appeals for political union in April 1990.

Because of the differences between the texts, the lead-up to the Milan summit did not bode well. It was more than likely that summit discussions would be polarised between the British text on the one hand and the Franco-German version on the other. However, several important changes occurred before the Milan summit that modified the context of the discussions and avoided a re-run of the earlier Genscher–Colombo impasse. On 14 June 1984 the transmission by the Commission to the Council of a 'White Paper' on the achievement of a Common Market by 1992, had the effect of putting pressure on the Member States to move forward on political union. Then on 19 July 1984 Jacques Delors was designated to assume the Presidency of the Commission from the Luxembourger Gaston Thorn. Delors' appointment gave the integration movement a vocal advocate while his close relationship with Mitterrand gave French initiatives added weight. But by far the most important change affecting the external environment was Mikhail Gorbachev's assumption of the leadership of the Soviet Union in March 1985. This had the almost immediate effect of transforming the East–West dialogue but, just as significantly, it also transformed the West–West discourse by opening up the possibility that Europe might no longer find itself the object of a prolonged superpower struggle.

The European Council's June meeting on 28–9 June 1985 in Milan did not resolve the differences between the Franco-German and British visions but the changed environment created sufficient support for the call for an IGC. The IGC had three objectives: to form a single market, to formulate a common foreign and security policy on the basis of the British and Franco-German texts, and to extend EEC activity into other areas. Foreign Ministers opened the subsequent IGC on 9 September 1985 and over the course of the next three months they met six times. In between their six meetings the ministers addressed the daunting task of finding ways to implement the IGS's three objectives. The undertaking was divided between a committee under Luxembourg (Presidency) chairmanship, with primary responsibility for deliberating upon treaty revisions, and a Political Committee, with the trust of considering ways of enhancing EPC.

Work proceeded apace in both committees under the clear understanding, stemming from the Milan Council decisions, that the eventual design would be a single framework with pillars. The task was supposed to be concluded by the end of 1985 but the European Council's meeting of 2–3 December failed to resolve several outstanding issues. The meeting, with Jacques Santer of Luxembourg as President-in-Office, did however produce a text of a draft Treaty on European Cooperation in Foreign Policy. The draft included some old issues (security remained restricted to political and economic aspects) but also some new (the recognition that the development of closer cooperation on security issues would contribute to the formation of a European identity and the determination of the Member States to maintain the technological and industrial resources necessary for their security). Santer nevertheless wished that the European Council would have 'gone further in the matter of security policy'.[80]

The following Foreign Minister's meeting of 16–17 December did manage to bring agreement a step nearer, but Denmark and Italy continued to hold reservations over institutional issues – the former objecting that institutional reforms went too far and the latter objecting that they did not go far enough. The mid December meeting also produced a Declaration of the Ten, including Spain and Portugal, on East–West relations. The final compromises were reached at the final ministerial session in Luxembourg on 27 January 1986. Nine Member States signed the Single Euroopean Act (SEA) on 18 February and the remaining three (Denmark, Greece and Italy) eventually signed on 28 February. (See Appendix 4.)

Title I of the SEA, concerning the common provisions, stipulated that the objective of the European Communities and the EPC was 'to contribute together to [make] concrete progress towards European unity'.[81] The SEA also noted the 'responsibility incumbent upon Europe to aim at speaking with one voice and to act with consistency and solidarity in order more effectively to protect its common interests and independence'. The SEA formally established the European Political Co-operation process as part of the EC under Title III 'Provisions on European Cooperation in the Sphere of Foreign Policy'. Title III defines the overall objective of EPC as the formulation and implementation of a 'European foreign policy'.[82]

Under Article 30 of the SEA, the parties agreed to 'inform and consult each other on *any foreign policy matters of general interest* so as to ensure that their combined influence is exercised as effectively as possible through co-ordination, the convergence of their positions and the implementation of joint action'.[83] Thus, compared to the London Report, the SEA represents a significant change: while the earlier report had restricted co-operation to 'important foreign policy questions' of relevance to the Ten, the SEA declared that the 'determination of common positions shall constitute a point of reference for the policies of the High Contracting Parties'.[84] However, in the debates prior to the SEA, both Britain and France refused to be bound to the EPC in their capacity as Security Council members. Article 30(7) (b) of the SEA commits those who participate in international institutions and international conferences in which not all of the parties participate, to 'take

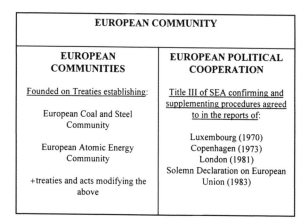

EUROPEAN COMMUNITY	
EUROPEAN COMMUNITIES	**EUROPEAN POLITICAL COOPERATION**
Founded on Treaties establishing:	Title III of SEA confirming and supplementing procedures agreed to in the reports of:
European Coal and Steel Community	Luxembourg (1970)
European Atomic Energy Community	Copenhagen (1973) London (1981)
+treaties and acts modifying the above	Solemn Declaration on European Union (1983)

Figure 2.1   The Single European Act and the European Community.

full account of the positions agreed in European Political Cooperation'. In spite of British and French insistence that the Security Council obliged them to present their national positions only, there is also the more general stipulation that all parties shall 'endeavour to adopt common positions on the subjects covered by this Title' in international institutions and conferences. The final phrase, 'in this Title', meant that EPC competence could not be extended to the external activities of the Community, such as international trade or finance.

In so far as institutions are concerned, the developments were modest. The signatories were required to 'endeavour to avoid any action or position which impairs their effectiveness as a cohesive force in international relations or within international organizations'.[85] External policies were to 'be consistent' and the Presidency and Commission were given 'special responsibility' in this regard.[86] There were however no enforcement procedures – Article 31 makes it clear that the jurisdiction of the Court of Justice does not extend to Title III. With reference to earlier complaints from the European Parliament (EP) during the IGC, Title III provided that the European Parliament should be 'closely associated' with the EPC process. In order to facilitate this the Presidency should 'regularly inform' the EP of the foreign policy issues being examined in the EPC framework and in turn the views of the EP are 'duly taken into consideration'.[87] The Commission was also to be 'fully associated' with the proceedings of EPC. A modest EPC secretariat of five officials plus support staff[88] was established in Brussels, which was separate from the Council Secretariat, with the task of 'assist[ing] the Presidency in preparing and implementing' the activities of EPC.[89] By limiting the power of the secretariat severely, Paris hoped to ensure the intergovernmental character of political co-operation and stymie any hope for autonomous development. The earlier British suggestion for some form of rapid reaction mechanism was also included. The Political Committee, or a ministerial meeting if need be, could be convened within forty-eight hours at the request of at least three Member States.

With regard to the security aspects of the SEA, it was recognised that 'closer co-operation on questions of European security would contribute in an *essential way* to the development of a European identity in external policy matters'.[90] The signatories were ready to co-ordinate their positions more closely on the 'political and economic aspects of security'. Such mention of 'economic' aspects of security appeared to challenge Article 223 of the Rome Treaty, which specifically excluded armaments from the Common Market.[91] However, the signatories expressed their determination to 'maintain the technological and industrial conditions necessary for their security'.[92] Finally, with due deference to Atlanticist sensitivities, the SEA specified that: 'Nothing in this Title shall impede closer co-operation in the field of security between certain of the High Contracting Parties within the framework of the Western European Union or the Atlantic Alliance.'[93]

Although EPC was to remain primarily a parallel process to the Communities, a stipulation was made in the SEA that the 'external policies of the European Community and the policies agreed in the European Political Cooperation must be consistent'.[94] At the end of the British Presidency, Sir Geoffrey Howe, as President-in-Office of the Council, stressed the 'considerable success' the Presidency had had in ensuring consistency between EPC and Community activity. Howe warned that 'arbitrary distinctions in the external relations of the Community make no sense, least of all of course for the countries with which we are dealing' – Japan and the US were mentioned specifically.[95] The absence of any formal bridging structures, the lack of any legal enforcement mechanisms, and the 'parallel' nature of the EPC process meant that in practical terms it was virtually impossible to ensure consistency or coherence between the activities of the Community and EPC.

Overall, the SEA marked something far removed from a federal foreign policy of the type recommended by the Tindemans Report and, in particular, the stipulations on security were notably cautious. Moreover, there was no specific mention of defence. Title III of the SEA did however give shape to the Maastricht Treaty and later to the Treaty of Amsterdam. Panayiotis Ifestos's conclusions regarding the SEA are worth quoting with this observation in mind:

> The Single European Act did not fundamentally change European Political Cooperation. It innovated considerably by putting 'Davignon machinery' in a treaty form, thereby ending its precarious status, but it left unchanged its character, its working methods, and its legal and institutional separation from the EEC institutions. Taking into account that the Single European Act was preceded throughout the 1970s and 1908s by debates, proposals, initiatives, and the work of the Intergovernmental Conference, it follows that the arrangement reached in 1986 will form the basis for the Community's diplomatic cooperation for many years ahead, possibly for the remainder of this century.[96]

In spite of the apparently modest aspirations of the security element of the SEA, the fact that it was mentioned at all is noteworthy. That it merited mention might owe something to the reactivation of the WEU which, to some, opened up the possibility that the WEU would gradually become the security arm of the EC. To pessimists, the WEU's inherent weaknesses and lack of a clear role provided the ideal means to bury the EC's security dimension.

The reawakening

If NATO had proven that, at least from 1973 on, it was the only serious European security actor, why then was the WEU aroused from its slumber?[97] Superficially, the decision to reawaken the WEU was surprising, given that at the time of its new start the WEU Assembly had dispensed with many of the organisation's original tasks. See Table 2.1 for the WEU components that were transferred. Many of the transferrals of competence to other organisations stemmed from the Assembly's wish to avoid the duplication of tasks and not so much from the inability of the WEU to assume its various mandates. This said, there would appear to be five inter-related contributory factors that explain the WEU's resuscitation.

First, successive reports from the 1970 Luxembourg Report on were marked by an implicit and, on occasion explicit, recognition of the fact that European integration could not be complete without a security dimension. Furthermore, the EPC process expanded in scope with crises (such as those in the Middle East, South Africa, Cyprus, and Portugal) that demanded some coherent Community response. In spite

Table 2.1   Transferral of WEU responsibilities

WEU Agency/ committee	Transferred to	Date
Social/cultural (Arts. II–III of Modified Brussels Treaty)	Council of Europe	14 Sept. 1970
Political consultation within WEU Council	EPC	24 May 1972
Agency for the Control of Armaments	Phased out*	27 June 1984
Standing Armaments Committee	NATO/IEPG	13 Nov. 1989

*Although it remained responsible for monitoring non-production of chemical weapons in Germany.

of the appearance of coherence symbolised by the signing of the Helsinki Final Act in July 1975 under the Italian Presidency, the danger that the EPC process would be overwhelmed by a never ending series of problems was still present.

Second, a series of disputes between the US and its allies encouraged greater exploration of European security co-operation. For example, differences in Middle East policy between the US and the Nine came to the fore as early as 1973 and resulted in the launch of the Euro-Arab dialogue the following year. Differences were also exposed following the Arab Summit in Rabat on 25 October 1974, where the decision was made to offer the Palestinians, represented by the PLO, an observer seat in the General Committee. Immediate rifts became evident between the more pro-Arab sentiments of the French and the Italians and the more pro-Israeli leanings of the Germans (with memories of the Munich Olympics only three years old) and America. As has already been mentioned, a further serious rift between the US and its European allies came as the result of the North Atlantic Council's 1979 Dual-Track decision. The increasing willingness of the Reagan administration to engage in far-reaching defensive programmes without allied consultation, such as the unveiling of the Strategic Defense Initiative (SDI) on 23 March 1983, had the effect of further distancing the US from its European partners.[98] Other causes of disagreement between the US and its allies ranged from the inadequate consultation surrounding the Gorbachev–Reagan deal at a summit in Reykjavik in 1986 (to cut the number of their strategic nuclear weapons by fifty percent) to differences over the April 1986 air strike against Libya carried out by

US forces operating from bases in Britain. Disagreements featured in other non-security areas of transatlantic relations as well, such as the GATT Uruguay Round. Prime Minister Thatcher's relations with Presidents Reagan and Bush though were a notable exception throughout many of the disagreements mentioned.

The third major reason for the WEU's resuscitation was France's unique predicament in Europe. Since the French decision to leave the integrated military command of NATO in 1966, France had been left with an ill-defined and increasingly anachronistic position in Europe. Thus, to the government of François Mitterrand, the prospect of a French-led European security initiative was an attractive policy option. France was further motivated by, in roughly equal measures, resistance to US leadership in the security realm, concern over West Germany's increasingly independent policy towards central and eastern Europe, and Britain's close relations with Washington. Evidence of strains between the US and Germany, the former's principal security partner in Europe, also opened the door for a French initiative. The initiative came in the form of French proposals for trilateral security discussions between France, Britain and Germany. The prospect of a trilateral dialogue that might exclude the other nations of Europe, understandably led the smaller European powers to voice concern. Belgium and Luxembourg forwarded their own proposal that the WEU would be the appropriate venue for Euro-security discussions. Not all were enthusiastic about the prospect of a revived WEU however. Germany saw the Modified Brussels Treaty, which curtailed German arms production in certain key areas, as a reminder of its inferior status[99] while, for Britain and the Netherlands, a revitalised WEU was viewed as a potential challenge to NATO.

The fourth reason for the WEU's revitalisation is that by the mid-1980s it was apparent that security, as a concept, had moved beyond its purely military context, most notably with the addition of the Helsinki process and the inclusion of a strong human rights dimension to the European security dialogue. The need for a broader, Europe-oriented, security platform outside the Atlantic Alliance was arguably in evidence by 1984 and became increasingly obvious as the decade drew to a close.

The fifth, and final, reason for the reawakening of the WEU was the continuing disputes within NATO over burdensharing. These disputes resulted in a number of attempts to redress the balance with the US generally arguing that it should pay less while the European allies continued to complain of the 'one way' street in defence purchases from across the Atlantic. It was not a debate that would be easily settled and, alongside the other tensions, it provided the catalyst to revive the

WEU. As Wyn Rees has noted though, 'Tensions in US–European relations and the progress in European integration provided the necessary motivation', but the objective was not the 'replacement of the Alliance'.[100] Rather the aim was to provide a European forum in which these issues could be discussed and since the forum included stalwart Atlanticists, there was little danger of the WEU acquiring an anti-Alliance or anti US label.

The actual reawakening of the WEU, an 'act of rebirth' as Alfred Cahen calls it,[101] took place during a series of meetings in 1984–5. The meetings were prompted initially by a French proposal to reactivate the organisation, which was forwarded to WEU members by the French Minister for Foreign Affairs, Claude Cheysson. The French proposal was soon adopted at a meeting of the WEU Ministerial Council on 12 June 1984. At a meeting of the Council in Rome, on 26–7 October 1984, accompanied for the first time by the seven WEU Foreign and Defence Ministers, the ministers reaffirmed their commitment in a declaration to the promotion of progressive unity. They also declared that they 'were conscious of the continuing necessity to strengthen Western security and specifically Western European geographical, political, psychological and military dimensions'. All resolved to make 'better use of the WEU framework in order to increase co-operation between the member states in the fields of security policy', whilst also acknowledging that, 'the Atlantic Alliance ... remains the foundation of Western security'. A number of institutional reforms were also forwarded in the Rome Declaration, which included the 'activation of the Council as a central element in the efforts to make greater use of the [WEU]'.[102] The final meeting in the WEU's 'rebirth' was held, at the same level, in Bonn on 22–3 April 1985.

However the 're-birth' was hampered by three factors. First, the WEU had no intergovernmental organs with which to facilitate joint reflection, let alone action. The innovation of involving Foreign and Defence Ministers in the Rome meeting and onwards partially remedied this deficiency. A number of other intergovernmental bodies were also established, such as the framework that brought together the Political Directors of the Ministries of Foreign Affairs with representatives of equivalent rank from the Ministry of Defence. A Special Working Group comprising the politico-military directors from the Ministries of Foreign Affairs (again with similarly ranked officials from the Ministries of Defence) was also established. *Ad hoc* mechanisms drawing experts together from Ministries of Defence and Foreign Affairs, to discuss special topics, Mediterranean security and the allocation of defence resources, were also instigated. The intergovernmental innovations however also produced fresh problems. As Alfred Cahen recalls: 'It soon became clear that, despite the similarity of political options, the approach to problems could vary quite considerably between Ministers and Ministries of Foreign Affairs on the one hand and Defence on the other, principally because the working methods were not always the same.'[103]

With the rebirth of the WEU firmly in mind, a number of prominent Europeans began to actively promote the WEU. For instance, in a lecture to the Belgian Institute of International Relations in March 1987, the British Foreign Secretary, Geoffrey Howe, called for a revival of the WEU 'as a forum for defining European defence priorities *within NATO*'. He added that 'a better European defence effort, galvanised perhaps through the WEU, can lead to a more substantial European pillar of the Alliance'.[104] The same pro-Atlanticist sympathics were expressed, characteristically more forcefully, the following year by Prime Minister Thatcher in her now infamous Bruges speech to the *Collège d'Europe* when she stressed, 'the great importance of NATO' and warned against 'any development (as a result of Franco-German initiatives) of the Western European Union as an alternative to it'.[105] The Conservative Bow Group called upon the WEU to 'take up the challenge it was created for, namely to be an embryo European Defence Community'.[106]

Jacques Chirac, then Prime Minister of France, appealed to the French parliament, for a 'charter' to define Europe's interests on security matters. For Chirac, the reawakening of the WEU was a means by which France could once again have a decisive voice in security affairs after its self-imposed twenty-year exile. Also of importance to France was the fact that the role of conventional and nuclear armaments would be stressed within the WEU's forthcoming platform, thus underlining the significance of the British and French contributions (and, perhaps, the lack of a German role in this regard). For his part, Chancellor Kohl was willing to put meat onto the bones by proposing the creation of an integrated Franco-German brigade. France accepted this proposal on 19 June 1987. The brigade though was to create a good deal of anxiety, since there was an inherent ambiguity about whether the brigade was to be the nucleus of an independent European defence capability, or whether it was an effort to bolster the European pillar of the Atlantic Alliance. The joint brigade came into being on 22 January 1988, along with a joint Franco-German Security Council.

The appeals from the various national leaders reflected those of Jacques Delors, President of the Commission, who in mid-March forwarded a proposal to convene a meeting of the European Council in order to adopt a European position on the ongoing disarmament negotiations and to 'lay the foundations for a European security policy'. With this in mind, at a press conference on 12 July 1987 Delors called for 'a political institution which would group together all those members of the Community who wish to be associated with it and which, for the time being, would be separate from the European Community'. More controversially, he suggested a theatre nuclear role when he advocated that Europeans 'should equip themselves with a defence institution in the wider conventional field *including theatre nuclear weapons* which belong to them'.[107]

Concern that the WEU relaunch might pose an alternative to NATO (held mainly by Britain and the Netherlands) was partially allayed when, on 27 October 1987, the WEU Council issued its *Platform on European Security Interests*. The Platform emphasised that, 'the security of the Western European countries can only be ensured in close association with our North American allies', and that, 'The security of the Alliance is indivisible'. It also stressed that US conventional and nuclear forces played an 'irreplaceable part in the defence of Europe' and that the nuclear element was capable of confronting a potential aggressor with 'an unacceptable risk'.[108] As reflected in earlier statements, the WEU Council was aware that the process of constructing an integrated Europe would be incomplete so long as it did not include 'security and defence'. Thus, in its three sections the *Platform* attempted to secure and strengthen the transatlantic link, to reinforce European integration including security and defence, and to pursue an active arms control and disarmament policy. The document went to extreme lengths to placate those members who were concerned that an enhanced European security role might be at the expense of ties with the Alliance:

> We recall the fundamental obligation of Article V of the modified Brussels Treaty to provide all the military and other aid and assistance in our power in the event of an armed attack on any one of us. This pledge, which reflects our common destiny, reinforces our commitments under the Atlantic Alliance, to which we all belong, and which we are all resolved to preserve.[109]

Despite the *Platform*'s claim that an integrated Europe would not be completed until security and defence were included, only seven of the Twelve EC members were WEU members and no formal relations between the two organisations existed and no provision existed for holding EPC meetings at the same time as WEU ministerial meetings.[110]

As part of its rebirth, or more accurately because of its rebirth, the WEU also began to assume an active military role, most notably during the Iran–Iraq war. Beginning in August 1987, WEU members began to pay more attention to matters outside the Alliance, thus highlighting one of the important differences between the Modified Brussels Treaty and the Washington Treaty.[111] On 19 April 1988, the WEU Council invoked Article VIII(3) of the Modified Brussels Treaty for the first time, using it for the legal basis for *Operation Cleansweep* – a two year minesweeping operation in the Gulf involving Belgian, British, French, Dutch and Italian forces.[112] It is worth briefly noting that any significant contribution from Germany in the WEU context was held to be contradictory to the Basic Law, although Germany did send ships to the Eastern Mediterranean relieving allied ships en route to the Gulf.[113] The naval contributions to the operation were technically co-ordinated under WEU aegis but command and control, along with the rules of engagement, remained national in all cases except those of Belgium, Britain and the Netherlands. An effective WEU response to the Gulf operations was all the more important since, as Willem van Eekelen (at that time Dutch Minister of Defence) argued, 'Politically, it would be very important to be able to show to the US Congress that the Europeans were taking responsibility "out-of-area" in close coordination with the US.'[114]

With the renewed vigour of the WEU, demands for membership also grew. Portugal and Spain joined on 14 November 1988 following an invitation from the WEU Ministers and, in the same year, Greece and Turkey notified the WEU Council of their interest in joining. *Operation Cleansweep* however also illustrated the limits of WEU military collaboration. The most obvious limitation was the lack of any unified command and control prior to 1 July 1988, after which the common operational command was set up between the contributing forces. Despite the joint command arrangements, vessels from Belgium and the Netherlands co-operated closely through the WEU while France and Italy preferred to stay under national command but exchanged 'tactical information'. Rules of engagement were also determined nationally.[115] However, it was not until Saddam Hussein's invasion of Kuwait in August 1990 that the WEU became, informally, the security arm of the EC.

Not a meeting of minds – towards the 1991 IGC

Although conjecture, it is likely that if the dramatic changes in Europe at the end of the 1980s had *not* occurred, the EPC would in all likelihood have remained a parallel process. These changes, along with

French pressure, demanded an immediate response that guaranteed that foreign and security policy would be included in the purview of the IGC. The inclusion of these aspects was also provoked by Washington's reaction to the end of the Cold War and the announcement of a 'New Transatlantic bargain'. Washingtons's response to the changing institutional parameters of European Security was delivered by US Secretary of State, James Baker III, on 12 December 1989 at the Berlin Press Club. In what soon became a much-quoted speech, Baker appealed:

> Working together, we must design and gradually put into place a new architecture for a new era. This new architecture must have a place for the old foundation and structures that remain valuable – like NATO – while the construction of institutions – like the E.C. – that can help draw together the West while recognizing that they can also serve new collective purposes. The new architecture must continue also serving as an open door to the East. And the new architecture must build up frameworks – like the CSCE process – that can overcome the division in Europe and bridge the Atlantic Ocean.[116]

Appeals were also made amongst the Community members and within the EP for a European security system, but quite different from what James Baker III had in mind. On 21 March 1990, the Belgian government published a memorandum addressing the need for fundamental institutional reform and forwarded a number of proposals to be discussed at the IGC or in a parallel venue.[117] The Belgians noted the 'urgent need' for a 'truly common foreign policy', arguing that the Community should participate as 'a political entity' in discussions on foreign affairs. Their document suggested that the General Affairs Council provide the 'common framework' for Community action. Greater co-operation was also advocated between the Political Committee and Committee of Permanent Representatives (COREPER). The Belgian memorandum, which enjoyed considerable support from other Community members, was to make a valuable contribution to the forthcoming Dublin talks.

A joint letter dated 19 April 1990 from President Mitterrand and Chancellor Kohl to the Irish Presidency of the Council complimented the Belgian proposals. Mitterrand and Kohl's letter called on the Dublin Council to 'initiate preparations for an Inter-Governmental Conference on political union' and to 'define and implement a common foreign and security policy'.[118] When the European Council met in Dublin they recognised the complimentary nature of the two documents and recommended that both should form the basis for any proposed modifications to the SEA. On 7 June 1990, twenty-one members of the EP from centrist parties proposed the adoption of common security policies. They also proposed that the future architecture of European security should be designed, *within the framework of the EPC* and the CSCE.[119]

As a result of the various proposals, the European Council called in Dublin, on 25–6 June, for a common EC foreign and security policy (CFSP) and an IGC on political union to be scheduled for 14 December 1990. The Dublin meeting concluded by agreeing to convene a parallel IGC (to that on Monetary Union) to deal with the possibility of establishing a CFSP.[120] This initiative was followed a month later by an appeal at the London NATO Summit for the adoption of a 'European identity' in the security domain. Hans van den Broek, a member of the European Commission with responsibility for external affairs, captured the spirit of the Dublin meetings when he explained the need for a CFSP as follows:

> First, because our citizens want the Union to play a more active role in international affairs…Second, in most parts of the world the European voice will only be heard if there is a united voice – or it will not be heard at all. Third, the end of the Cold War has dramatically changed the strategic situation of the European Union. The Soviet threat has disappeared, but many new risks have appeared. The US has substantially reduced its presence in Europe and is concentrating on domestic issues. In these changed circumstances, it is clear that Europe will have to take on more responsibility for its own security. With nearly 380 million people, with a combined GDP ahead of the US, with the largest single market in the world, as the most important player in international trade, as the main source of development assistance and humanitarian assistance and humanitarian aid to the third world, the European Union simply cannot avoid taking increased responsibility in world affairs.[121]

It should however be noted that in spite of the prevailing mood of optimism, the Belgian and Franco-German initiatives lacked detail and substance and some potentially serious areas of difference remained. The Dublin Council meeting of June 1990 hinted at the dividing lines that were to appear in the IGC and ultimately in the Treaty on European Union itself. Broadly, Germany was enthusiastic about tying economic and monetary union to political union for several reasons. First, Kohl saw the formation of EMU as a logical part of the progression towards union of which foreign and defence integration would be an integral part. Second, the political union discussion, with Germany at the helm as its most vociferous backer, would help allay fears of the newly unified Germany and any wayward Bismarckian foreign and security policy leanings.[122] However, France and Britain were nervous about the idea of extending formal control over foreign and security policy to the Commission and, to a lesser extent, the EP. This nervousness, alongside the considerable pressure to move towards majority voting on matters of joint action instead of consensus and more amorphous joint decisions, threatened to undo many of the Gaullist tendencies of the parallel (but not integrated) EC–EPC processes. On security issues, the familiar divisions between the Atlanticists, primarily Britain and the Netherlands, and the French, who were pushing for an integrated European defence with a Franco-German partnership at the centre, were also evident. On specifics, Germany was content to sit on the fence: neither opposing the formation of a European security identity, nor wishing to detract from the importance of NATO to Europe's defence.

Having decided on the *grand dessin,* the Dublin meeting delegated responsibility for the details of political union to the respective foreign ministries of the Twelve. The fact that the task did not, as might have been expected, fall to the European Council suggests that political union was still not a burning issue. Moreover, the vagueness of the mandate gave the foreign ministries a horrifically difficult assignment. Predictably, the complexity and sensitivity of the undertaking led it to be delegated to the Permanent Representatives, who ultimately submitted a 'Reflection Document', which merely restated the well-known differences between the national positions on political union. In turn, the platitudes of the Reflection Document were the basis for the European Council's June 1990 decision to hold an IGC on political union in December. The lead up to the European Council's decision accomplished remarkably little and in many ways simply rehearsed the familiar debates prior to the SEA.

While there appeared to be a general will to incorporate EPC into the IGC discussions, there also appeared to be very little agreement on any of the details between the twelve. Public pronouncements on a number of fundamental issues, such as German unification, meant that the forthcoming IGC was primed to commence with profound differences between Britain, France and Germany.[123] Although the rapidly changing events in Europe provided a dynamic context for the IGC, the critical questions remained. Did the EC members really intend to give substance to political union or just produce a face-saving treaty lacking in substance? Would the EC move beyond the EPC's parallel process to create an integrated political and economic union, including foreign and security dimensions? In addition, the question of what kind of association the revived WEU should have with the Community remained.

3
From Political Community to Uncommon Security

The EPC made two highly significant contributions to the IGC process. First, involvement in EPC gave rise to a sense of common values and identity, which in turn underpinned the IGC discussions. Second, the history of EPC illustrated that the CFSP discussions need not be about extremes – federalism or complete national autonomy – but about combining sovereignty with voluntary constraint. Just as it was highly unlikely that Community members would choose to renationalise foreign policy, thus undermining the fruits of EPC collaboration, it was also unrealistic to expect the same competencies of the Community in the economic and monetary realm to be extended to foreign and security policy. The IGC was therefore a search for a balance between national and community interests and, some might argue, the lowest common denominator.

Before moving to an examination of the IGC, the importance of the 1990–1 Gulf War to the IGC needs to be considered. The war is of interest for two prime reasons. First, it emphasised unambiguously how dependent the participating European states were upon the US as well as upon NATO. Second, it underlined the need for the incorporation of a security and defence component to the IGC, as well as helped to overcome doubts held by those who resisted the idea of a security dimension to the IGC. The heavy use of European-based US forces in the Gulf also underscored Europe's importance as a forward base for operations in the Middle East in US strategy.

The Gulf War and political union

Prior to Saddam Hussein's invasion of Kuwait on 2 August 1990 the prospects for anything meaningful arising from the myriad of meetings on political union seemed dim.[1] In fact, the European Council's desire to apparently delegate responsibility to formulate political union suggested that it was a somewhat peripheral concern. The response to the invasion though could not have made a clearer case for the need for political union since the European reaction to a clear and incontrovertible violation of international law was confused. France tried, in vain, to organise a European response while launching its own unilateral diplomatic quest for a withdrawal of Iraqi forces, including last ditch negotiations headed by Roland Dumas, the French Foreign Minister. Germany soon became bogged down in a prolonged debate on the use of German forces out of the NATO area. Britain, characteristically, looked to Washington for initiative and collaboration.

Following the invasion and the passage of UN Security Council resolution 661, calling for an embargo on oil products and the freezing of all overseas Iraqi assets, agreement was reached on 21 August 1990 to co-ordinate any potential European military response through the WEU, including the sharing of all logistics, intelligence and the co-ordination of forces. Any show of solidarity however soon collapsed into disputes about what forces should support any military action. As Pia Wood observed:

> In the initial stages of the crisis, Great Britain sent six warships, France sent the aircraft carrier *Clemenceau* and the Netherlands sent two frigates. In September, the British government, without consulting or informing the other EC members, decided to send 6,000 combat troops to the Gulf, a decision that directly contradicted EC policy of maintaining pressure on Iraq through the embargo and demonstrated the importance Britain placed on the Atlantic link. Eventually each country responded individually.[2]

The formation of a coalition of no less than 31 countries on the night of 16 January 1991 with the mandate of restoring sovereignty to Kuwait, posed an awkward dilemma for Germany. The alleged constitutional restrictions on the ability of German troops to intervene out of the NATO area provided a rather unconvincing, but convenient, pretext for non-action. As Bregor Schöllgen wrote, it was not surprising that the constitutional restrictions were held up, but what was surprising was the fact that 'leading exponents of German policy had nothing to say, temporarily leaving the international image of the Republic in the hands of a noisy minority which was highly critical of the allies'.[3] As Schöllgen and other observers have pointed out, the criticisms voiced against Germany's 'cheque book diplomacy' (summarised by some in the coalition forces as, 'They pay, we die') were not entirely just since Germany did participate in material support, preventative measures in Turkey and, after the end of hostilities, in minesweeping operations in the Gulf. It was though, as Schöllgen again notes, 'indicative of the deep-rooted insecurity of German policy during this crisis that these measures were decided upon and carried out in virtual secrecy, hidden from the public, and in those cases where this was impossible, for example when participation in NATO activities was involved, it gave rise to very unconvincing public debate'.[4]

The French, caught in the obvious bind of not wanting to appear to collaborate too closely with the US, assumed a semi-independent role on the left flank of *Operation Desert Storm*. This suited both their equipment (predominantly lightly armoured vehicles) as well as their political requirements. They were though, like their British counterparts, subordinated to the XVIII (US) Corps. The British assumed a position in the centre of the advance, with the VII (US) Corps, as befitted both their heavy armour and their very close integration with the US at senior planning levels. Operations *Desert Shield* and *Desert Storm* suggest that in a large operation calling for a lead-nation, which it is assumed will be the US in most instances, Anglo-American ties will remain close while, for political appearances, the French will participate in a manner retaining the impression of independence. The important question for the IGC (and beyond) was what roles could be assumed in smaller operations where the US was unwilling to be lead-nation or where an American lead might be inappropriate. As it turned out however, the Gulf War proved to be the exception rather than the rule in post-Cold War security.

The role of the WEU in the Gulf War merits brief consideration. The President of the WEU Assembly, Robert Pontillon, condemned the Iraqi invasion of Kuwait within twenty-four hours and, once again, called for Article VIII (3) of the Modified Brussels Treaty to be activated.[5] The links between various European security organisations became particularly intense during *Operations Desert Shield* and *Desert Storm*, as seen by 'the number of occasions on which foreign ministers went immediately from meetings in one forum to meetings in the other forum as they attempted to show that Europe was a significant element in the international response to events in the Gulf'.[6] The Chiefs of Defence Staff of the WEU met in Paris on 27 August 1990 and established a three-tier control structure. Seven of the nine WEU members agreed to participate in a forty-five vessel WEU naval embargo of Iraq.[7]

The embargo proved extremely divisive with France pushing to co-ordinate the command under the WEU while Britain, mindful of the non-WEU and non-European forces in the embargo operation, pre-ferred to co-ordinate its efforts with the English-speaking forces (notably the US). Criticism of the WEU's failure to establish coherent command and control came not only from outside the organisation but internally as well from the Assembly of the WEU.[8] The advent of *Operation Desert Storm* in January 1991 rendered the WEU all but irrele-vant as the British, French and Italian air and ground deployments fell under a joint US–Saudi command structure, sanctioned by the UN.

The effect of the Gulf War, later reinforced by the unfolding crisis in Yugoslavia, was threefold: first, it moved security and defence to the forefront of the more general questions of European integration; sec-ond, rather that having the luxury of time to dream up new institu-tions or designs, the reform of *both* NATO and the EPC/EC became a complementary, not exclusive, process; and third, the response to the Gulf War underlined the need for armed forces capable of implement-ing Community decisions.

The Luxembourg and Dutch models and the IGC

The 1990–1 IGC on European Union commenced under the Italian Presidency although the bulk of the work took place under the subse-quent Luxembourg and Dutch Presidencies. The job of the Italian Presidency in the second half of 1990, prior to the commencement of the IGC, was to give substance to a variety of initiatives aiming to estab-lish a foreign and security component to the Community. In keeping with the prevailing spirit and following a meeting of the EC Foreign Ministers at Asolo on 6–7 October, the Italian President of the Council, Gianni de Michelis, tabled an ambitious proposal to incorporate all secu-rity aspects into a common foreign and security policy (CFSP), including the transfer of WEU competencies to the EC. The Italian proposal marked one extreme while Britain and Denmark took up the opposite extreme and advocated, in essence, a continuation of the EPC. Germany was close to the Italian position and stressed the need to link the politi-cal with the economic aspects of European union. France was supportive of measures guiding Europe towards a common foreign policy, stipulat-ing that an active role should be played by the European Council, but it was opposed to integration of defence into the Community.

Just prior to the Rome European Council meeting near the conclu-sion of the Italian Presidency, Kohl and Mitterrand wrote a letter, dated

6 December 1990, addressed to the President of the Council. It asserted that 'foreign policy and common security would have the vocation of extending to all areas' and 'that political union should include a true security policy that would in turn lead to a common defence'.[9] Amongst the measures addressed in the letter was that of creating a more concrete relationship between the WEU and political union and the formal creation of a common security policy within the political union. The underlying tension between the French desire to emphasise a distinct European security and defence element and the German concern that any steps toward European security and defence integration should not be at the cost of US exclusion, was apparent. The letter also suggested that: 'The treaty will provide for the possibility of adopting certain decisions at a majority as soon as the new treaty enters into force or within a period of time to be specified.'[10]

The Rome meeting of the European Council on 14–15 December 1990 attempted to draw together the multiple proposals into one coherent plan of action.[11] Space prohibits mention of the details of all of the proposals since by the end of the Italian Presidency there were at least five proposals on the table for CFSP.[12] In light of these many proposals, the Rome European Council agreed that there was a general need for the IGC to discuss political union, including a CFSP. It was also accepted that any common policy would be reached on the basis of vital common interests, that progress towards the CFSP would be a deliberative but gradual process and finally, that there should be coherent institutional procedures. In spite of the Presidency's valiant efforts, the exact shape of the developing CFSP, emerging out of the bilateral and multilateral proposals, remained confusing. Nevertheless, a synthesis of the various proposals suggested that there was common agreement on the need to extend the role of the projected Union in the security realm, and to include questions such as arms control, disarmament, OSCE-related matters, support for UN operations and non-proliferation measures. Defence though remained a tricky area in spite of the fact that the end of the Cold War had removed the strongest objections to the inclusion of defence as a legitimate subject of discussion for the IGC. The main problem concerning the defence aspects was how to reach the desired balance between those who perceived a need for a more active European defence role and those who were reluctant to pursue this for fear of damaging the Atlantic Alliance and transatlantic relations.

Amongst the flurry of paper, the national approaches were reasonably clear. Germany wished to reassure its allies of its strong support for multilateral roles. France, in a fit of pique in 1991, announced its intention to withdraw any remaining troops from German soil (as a result of NATO's revised force structure which appeared to reinforce SACEUR's role), threatened to weaken NATO and attempted to strengthen its bid for European leadership in foreign and security matters. Britain, following a somewhat pragmatic line, advocated maintaining its ties with NATO and its presence in Germany, whilst also expressing interest in strengthening the European pillar of the Alliance. Italy advocated that the 'WEU will be placed under the authority and the aegis of the European Council'.[13]

Discussion of the proposals that had been submitted to the Italian Presidency produced three identifiable groups. The first group, consisting of Belgium, Greece, Italy, Luxembourg, and Spain enthusiastically supported the Franco-German initiatives aimed at establishing a CFSP with a common defence as an integral part of the future union. The second group, consisting of Britain, Denmark, the Netherlands and Portugal, was reluctant to see a CFSP established – all, it should be added, for slightly differing reasons. Concerns were also shared amongst the second group countries about the possible weakening of NATO by the establishment of a CFSP with a European defence component. Finally, the Republic of Ireland, a special case, was concerned that a common foreign policy tied to a common security policy would compromise its neutrality.

By the time the IGC on Political Union commenced, the Luxembourg Presidency accepted in broad terms the British, Danish, French and Portuguese sensitivities to federalist structures and adopted instead a broad 'pillar' approach based on intergovernmentalism.[14] It was to the Luxembourg Presidency during the first half of 1991 that the unenviable task of trying to establish a common ground amongst the Twelve fell. This was initially attempted by means of a questionnaire circulated in January 1991. From the responses, it became apparent that the IGC would have to address issues beyond the CFSP to include a third pillar (justice and home affairs), as well as questions of institutional accountability and reforms. In an attempt to elucidate upon these points, Franco-German thinking was laid down in the Dumas–Genscher *Joint Initiative on Establishing a Common European Foreign and Security Policy*, of 4 February 1991.[15]

The Dumas–Genscher initiative aimed to close the emerging gaps between Paris, Bonn and London. It did this by reaffirming the importance of the Atlantic Alliance, by supporting the preponderant role of the European Council and by endorsing the unanimity voting procedure. CFSP was to be extended to 'all areas of external relations', but the primacy of commitments to the WEU, NATO and the US military presence in Europe was also maintained. The WEU was to become the 'cooperation channel' between Political Union and NATO. The Dumas–Genscher proposals also argued that as a CFSP develops, 'the formal link established between the WEU Treaty and the Alliance should be adopted in accordance'. The proposals further endowed the European Council with the ability to decide (on what basis was unclear) which facets of European security should fall under the CFSP, and moreover suggested a number of suitable issues that might be considered immediately within the Union framework, such as disarmament and control of armaments in Europe, peace-keeping measures in the context of the UN, nuclear non-proliferation and economic aspects of security. It should however be noted that the Dumas–Genscher proposals represented a tempering of French wishes for a more independent European security identity. The plan foresaw 'a WEU that would become the nucleus of a European defence entity but at the same time serve as the European pillar of NATO', and that an 'organic relationship' would be established between the WEU and the EU, ideally one that placed the WEU under the aegis of the European Council.[16] The proposals left open enough room for French notions of a completely restructured NATO while at the same time acknowledging the Kohl government's need to give NATO primacy in Europe's security arrangements.[17]

One result of the Dumas–Genscher Plan was the emergence of an Anglo-German relationship, linked by the common belief in the importance of transatlantic ties and the need to enlarge the Community. The British Foreign Secretary, Douglas Hurd, in a Churchill Memorial Lecture, on 19 February 1991, stressed that: 'The defence of Europe without the United States does not make sense. The common foreign and security policy [of the proposed EU] can include certain general security questions (the CSCE, regulation of armaments and non-proliferation, for example) but it cannot replace the military functions of NATO.'[18]

In an attempt to draw together the various strands, the Luxembourg Presidency produced a 'Non-Paper' on 12 April 1991.[19] The 'Non-Paper' marked an attempt to solve several questions: what was the CFSP's association with the Communities? What was the WEU's role and institutional structure? And what was the WEU's relation to the Communities? On the first point, it was suggested that there should be a separation between the Communities and the CFSP and justice and home affairs (later solidified in the pillar structure) but that they all should be part of the same Union and that, in the long term, the Union should have a common defence policy. The 'Non-Paper' also added that the role of the WEU should be sufficiently flexible to allow association for defensive purposes. Finally, it was suggested that different procedures should be adopted for co-operation and common actions. The former, it was suggested, may be decided upon in the Council by majority (of an unspecified type). The 'Non-Paper' generated heated discussion and resistance, primarily from Belgium, the Netherlands and Italy all of whom had fought hard against an intergovernmental (i.e. 'pillar') approach. Meanwhile, the 'Atlanticists' (primarily Britain) also disliked mention of a common defence policy for the Union.

In response to the criticisms of the 'Non-Paper', the Luxembourg Presidency unveiled its *Concept of Political Union*, to the European Council on 18 June 1991. The full maintenance of the *acquis communautaire* was stressed, as was the desire to 'reinforce the identity and role of the Union as a political entity on the international scene'.[20] It also stated that common foreign and security policy should 'extend to all questions relating to the security of the Union', but that the 'defence identity' of the Union should be decided at the last stage of the IGC, thereby taking into account the 'traditional positions of certain member states'.[21] Ultimately, the Luxembourg Presidency's concept was designed to stimulate thinking and discussion, which it did. But it neglected to consider some of the more controversial topics, such as whether the Council should reach its decisions by qualified majority or unanimously, and what should be the roles of the Commission and the European Parliament. The structure of the political union was therefore no clearer than it had been at the commencement of the IGC although the June document did contain the significant addition that a single institutional framework would be created.

The Dutch Presidency, which took over in July 1991, proved to be an interesting contrast to the previous Presidency because there was more sympathy to a *communautaire* approach. In spite of the fact that the fundamental shape of the CFSP, even if somewhat opaque, had been established by the former Presidency the incoming President of the Council, Hans van den Broek, was convinced that he could muster enough support to overthrown the 'pillar' approach. The Dutch Ministry of Foreign Affairs *Draft Treaty Towards European Union*, tabled on 23 September, called for the community to design and implement a CFSP which should include *all* questions pertaining to security. These in turn, should 'complement' the existing ties to NATO and the WEU, 'which continue to contribute in a significant fashion to security and stability'. Unlike the Luxembourg Presidency's proposals, the Dutch proposal abandoned the pillar concept in favour of an all encompassing umbrella. The abandonment of the pillar approach was almost guaranteed to raise the ire of London since, amongst other things, it implied that the creation of a unified structure would extend the jurisdiction of the Court of Justice to all aspects of the proposed Union, including CFSP. London found allies in Paris who objected to several aspects of the proposals, especially those that would extend the competence of the European Parliament.[22]

It would be an understatement to call the Dutch proposals unpopular (even Bonn declined to support then). Faced with resounding opposition, the 'pillar' approach advocated by the Luxembourg Presidency prevailed. Other Dutch proposals that met with an unenthusiastic response concerned the question of voting (consensus versus majority), the role of the Commission, the European Parliament and the EPC Secretariat, and the relationship between the WEU and the Community. The collapse of the Dutch proposals promised a re-run of the debates that took place under the previous Presidency with, in all likelihood, the same outcome. An initiative was required which would prevent stalemate. This came from two unlikely bedfellows in the form of an Italian–UK *Declaration on European Security and Defence* released on 5 October 1991. The declaration was the result of an Italian leading action designed to 'convince a particularly reticent Member State of the need for a Political Union gradually to include a common foreign and security policy'.[23] It foresaw that the WEU would complement a European defence dimension in two ways: 'as defence component of the (political) Union and as a means of reinforcing the European pillar of the Alliance'. An operational role for the WEU was also proposed with the creation of a European reaction force 'capable of responding flexibly in a range of possible circumstances' in crises occurring beyond NATO's borders. The main point of the declaration was to ensure that the development of a European identity in the field of defence 'will not be contradictory but compatible with a strengthened and reformed NATO'. Douglas Hurd emphasised the need to combine the 'long-term prospect of a European security policy...with the need of not doing anything in the short term which weakens NATO'.[24] The Italian–UK declaration was quickly dismissed by France, Germany and Spain as too 'Atlantic-oriented'. The three countries subsequently invited countries of the 'same wavelength' as themselves to discuss the matter in Paris – much to the annoyance of the Dutch Presidency.

The next initiative was a warmed-up version of the earlier Franco-German proposal on defence and security of 4 February 1991. In a joint letter (11 October 1991) from Chancellor Kohl and President Mitterrand to the Dutch President of the European Council, Ruud Lubbers, the two leaders stressed the importance of Europeans showing clearly, 'by means of specific decisions and institutional measures, that they want to take on greater responsibility in the areas of security and defence'.[25] A draft Franco-German *Treaty on Political Union: Common Foreign and Security Policy,* attached to the joint letter, contained a number of suggestions or initiatives. One of the most notable features of the draft treaty was the central role given to the WEU, which was seen as 'an integral part of the process of European Union'. Indeed, Kohl and Mitterrand proposed that decisions and measures taken by the Union in the CFSP area 'may be developed and implemented entirely or in part by the WEU'.[26] In a section entitled 'Creation of an organic link between the WEU and the Union', the draft treaty suggested, amongst other things, 'The setting up of military units under the WEU'. In their conclusions it was suggested that Franco-German military co-operation would be strengthened 'beyond the present Brigade' and that the enlarged force could then 'serve as the core of a European corps'.

The draft treaty however neglected to address many of the contentious questions that had plagued the deliberations, such as the role of the Commission and the European parliament and the question of qualified majority voting. In terms of substance the draft treaty actually suggested very little that was new; yet in terms of symbolism it accomplished several things. First, with half an eye on the forthcoming NATO summit in Rome, Kohl and Mitterrand reiterated an earlier statement (this one had appeared in their joint letter of 6 December 1990) that WEU–NATO co-operation was a 'matter of strengthening the Atlantic Alliance as a whole by increasing the role and responsibility of Europe and by establishing a European pillar'.[27] It was hoped that such a statement emanating from Paris as well as Bonn would placate London. Second, the initiative in the form of the draft treaty indicated clearly that the engine of the integration process was the relationship between Paris and Bonn. Third, the possibility of using an expanded Franco-German brigade to accomplish NATO out-of-area tasks opened up the potential for an EU–WEU nexus that would not only be the foundation of the European security pillar, but could take over tasks that NATO found difficult to assume.[28] Fourth, the letter and draft treaty bound Paris and Bonn together in three important concessions. Paris conceded to Bonn the idea of a political union, while Bonn backed Paris in its position on NATO's out-of-area disputes in the autumn of 1991 and, more importantly, surrendered its sovereign position on Monetary Union.

The extent however to which the dual letter and draft treaty was more than window-dressing has been questioned. For instance, Panos Tsakaloyannis has commented: 'The proof that the perseverance of the Franco-German amity was more important than results in the IGC is the fact that French and German officials were kept in the dark as to the contents of the initiative.'[29] The British were also critical of the initiative. Defence Minister, Michael King, 'did not see the logic of this new initiative', while Hurd, saw 'no reason to duplicate what NATO is doing, in fact there is a certain danger in this'.[30] British criticism was unsurprising in light of the criticism given to their initiative, which had been launched with Italy earlier the same month.

The Dutch Presidency released a new draft Union Treaty in early November 1991, which was discussed by the EC Foreign Ministers later that month.[31] Although the draft reverted to the pillar structure, it also fudged some important issues. Now only weeks before the summit was due to convene, the Dutch draft Union treaty was added to the myriad of proposals already on the table. There appeared to be little chance of agreement in Maastricht although there was at least agreement, in principle, for the need for a security and defence dimension to the integration process.

The voice from across the Atlantic

In what became a pattern, the US reaction to hints of European security collaboration was mixed. The US had historically supported a stronger role for western Europe within the Alliance but, at the same time, any such moves were interpreted as potentially damaging to NATO and US leadership within it.

From 1989 onwards it was apparent that the Bush administration viewed NATO as a central security organisation, in part as a counterweight to the British and French concerns about German reunification, but also as a means of maintaining influence within Europe. The US conception of post-Cold War Europe was outlined by Secretary of State James A. Baker III, in an address made in December 1989 in which he reiterated President Bush's call for a Europe 'that is whole and free'.[32]

In Baker's description of the 'new security architecture' he stressed the need for 'old foundations' (like NATO) and the need for the construction of new institutions – like the EC and the OSCE process. In an implicit justification for the US role in Europe's security Baker observed that

> hopes for a Europe whole and free are tinged with concern by some that a Europe undivided may not necessarily be a Europe peaceful and prosperous. Many of the guidelines that brought US securely through four sometimes tense and threatening decades are now coming down. Some of the divisive issues that once brought conflict to Europe are reemerging.[33]

The envisaged US role was partly motivated by the concern over the notable absence of either British or French plans for European security post-German reunification. Indeed, the British and French reaction was to work together to hinder or even postpone reunification. In December 1989, Prime Minister Thatcher commented: 'If there was any hope now of stopping or slowing down reunification it would only come from an Anglo-French initiative.'[34] Thus, the role of NATO became, in American eyes, all the more important as a means of ensuring a continued US military presence in Europe (nearly all of it in Germany) to assuage Franco-British concerns about reunification, while at the same time keeping Germany firmly tied to a multilateral framework. What a reunified Germany and a continuing, albeit reduced, US military presence in Europe could not do was to reassure the Soviet Union. If Gorbachev was to be placated, NATO's political role must be stressed while its military aspects must be de-emphasised. Underlining the importance of the CSCE's pan-European security role would also appease Gorbachev.

Following Secretary Baker's December 1989 speech, NATO's *Declaration on a Transformed North Atlantic Alliance* (July 1990) set out to define the shape of Europe's security. The declaration promised to 'enhance the political component of our Alliance'. The progress made 'within the European Community towards political union, including the development of a European identity in the domain of security' was recognised as contributing to 'Atlantic solidarity'. The declaration proposed a 'joint declaration' between the Warsaw Treaty Organisation countries and NATO that 'we are no longer adversaries'. It further invited the countries to 'establish regular diplomatic liaison with NATO', and advocated that the 'CSCE should become more prominent in Europe's future'.[35]

President Mitterrand's personal reaction to German reunification was to resist it, but in the face of Bush's support, the question was not whether unification would occur, but when. Accordingly, Mitterrand sought to expand the EC's role by, first, binding Germany unequivocally to the EMU process and, second, by advocating in April 1990 a second intergovernmental conference on political union, including a common foreign and security policy. Mitterrand had been in favour of greater foreign and security policy integration prior to German reunification, but this support was based on the assumption that France would be able to deal with a divided Germany from a position of strength. German reunification changed the French position radically. What France now sought was a *quid pro quo*; in return for French influence over the German mark, France would sacrifice some autonomy in its foreign and security policy.

Franco-German security integration had in fact been making cautious steps since 1983, but it was not until a joint letter was issued by Kohl and Mitterrand on 14 October 1991, proposing that a European 'force' be built out of the 4200 man Franco-German brigade and that this should eventually constitute a Euro corps, that their common security concerns found a potent symbol.[36] The reaction from the Bush administration to the Franco-German brigade proposal was to reassert NATO's position in European security by reiterating at the June North Atlantic Council meeting in Copenhagen that 'NATO is the essential forum for consultation among the Allies' and that the Alliance provides 'one of the indispensable foundations for a stable security environment in Europe'. He also stressed that: 'NATO embodies the transatlantic link by which the security of North America is permanently tied to the security of Europe.'[37] Despite the Bush administration's concern (shared by Britain) that a European Security and Defence Identity (ESDI) and the proposed 'Eurocorps' could weaken NATO, the *New Strategic Concept* incorporated ESDI by arguing that 'it would have an important role to play in enhancing the Allies' ability to work together in the common defence'.[38]

The British reaction to German reunification and, later, to the Kohl–Mitterrand initiative, was not to attempt to incorporate Germany in a European defence arrangement but to balance Germany (and France) by underlining the importance of not only NATO but also the military role of the US in Europe. The Thatcher government accomplished this through the WEU. Douglas Hurd saw the WEU as a 'bridge' between NATO and the EC and as a 'means of strengthening the European pillar of the Atlantic Alliance'.[39] The WEU also had the inherent advantage, from the British view, of being intimately connected to NATO and (since the Eurocorps was seen as a means of enhancing collaboration between WEU member states) it was not unreasonable to believe that it would strengthen the Alliance's European pillar.

In spite of talk of a 'new security architecture' the essential ambiguity behind the extent to which Washington really wished to encourage a more independent European security and defence identity remained. The underlying ambiguity emerged in spectacular style in the Bartholomew Memorandum of 20 February 1991.[40] The memorandum has had much importance attached to it in the security-related literature in spite of the fact that until recently it was unavailable to the public. Willem van Eeklen first made public the memorandum in his 1998 publication *Debating European Security*.[41] Given the importance attached to the memorandum it is worth quoting from at length:

> In light of the rapidly changing circumstances we all need to be particularly careful to avoid taking positions or making decisions that have unintended consequences. Given the changing situation in the Soviet Union, the US role in the Gulf and the debate over responsibility-sharing, the US–EC economic tensions, this is not a time for Europeans to be sending a message however unintended to the US public suggesting that they want to reduce or marginalize the US role in Europe. We know that this is not the intention of our European allies, but we want to stress the danger that positions which seem to emphasise European over transatlantic solidarity or institutional changes which diminish the centrality of the Alliance could pose for American opinion on and support for the transatlantic partnership.
>
> While we understand that the logic behind political integration leads toward a union that ultimately encompasses security affairs, we believe that the primary yardstick against which proposals and institutional innovations need to be measured is whether they actually enhance Alliance defensive capabilities and make Europe more secure ... We can speak with the frankness engendered by forty years of our Alliance relationship. In our view, efforts to construct a European pillar by redefining and limiting NATO's role, by weakening its structure, or by creating a monolithic bloc of certain members would be misguided. We would hope such efforts would be resisted firmly.

While some in the Bush administration saw the memorandum as a justified defence of American interests, others were embarrassed by the premature intervention into a debate that was still taking shape and by the misrepresentation of the motives of most, if not all, of the European allies. The memorandum made it clear that the US wished to maintain NATO's central role in European security and to avoid a merger between the WEU and the EC, since the latter was 'clearly not "within the Alliance"'. Moreover, the memorandum made it clear that 'subordinating the WEU to [the EC] would accentuate the separation and independence of the European pillar from the Alliance'. This, in turn, would only serve to 'weaken the integrity of our common transatlantic security and defense which has proved successful and, in our view, will remain crucial'.[42]

Additional tensions emerged at the North Atlantic Council's 7–8 November 1991 Rome Summit, where Mitterrand reminded Bush that the end of the Cold War and the disappearance of the Warsaw Pact meant that NATO was no longer a 'holy alliance'. Bush, in a departure from the script, expressed his mounting exasperation with the European allies, when he commented, 'If, my friends, your ultimate aim is to provide individually for your own defense, the time to tell us is today'.[43] The US reaction to the prospect of the IGC is, in retrospect, somewhat surprising given that *Operation Desert Storm* was an objective lesson in the dependence of the European allies on US military and logistical capabilities. Furthermore, none of the positions of the European governments at the time of the Bartholomew memorandum could be construed as blatantly anti-NATO or anti-American. Mitterrand even went so far as to concede in a meeting with Bush that the idea of European security and defence was not incompatible with the continued existence of NATO.[44] Although the Dutch could not posture as pro-NATO as they may have liked, since they were preparing for the EC Presidency in the second half of 1991, they could not be construed as remotely anti-US or NATO. The Portuguese and the Danish were in favour of extending European competence only in those areas falling outside of NATO's geographic area (as expressed in Article VI of the Washington Treaty). Belgium, Luxembourg and Spain were closer to the French position and were in favour of adding a security element to the IGC as well as giving the WEU a more coherent role. Italy, although broadly supportive of a security pillar to the EC, was also wary of Franco-German influence and therefore supported the British position that any security element that arose out of the IGC should enhance the European pillar of NATO.

With the Bartholomew memorandum as the somewhat unfortunate foundation, the enunciation of a more focused (and diplomatic) US position vis-à-vis European security and defence followed. It came in the form of an announcement from James Baker III on 16 April 1991, in which the parameters of US support for a European security and defence identity were outlined:[45]

- The US would support the European allies where needed in their efforts to build a CFSP;
- NATO should be the principal venue for consultation and agreement on all policies bearing on the security and defense commitment of its members under the North Atlantic Treaty;
- NATO's integrated military structure should be retained;
- The European Security and Defence Identity should develop the capacity for involvement beyond Europe's borders; and
- New arrangements should be made to avoid marginalizing any allies, such as Turkey.

The announcement of NATO's *New Strategic Concept* at the meeting of the North Atlantic Council in Rome in November 1991 reinforced Baker's points. The endorsement of the ESDI as an initiative to be developed *within* the Alliance as a means of enhancing 'the Allies' ability to work together in 'the common defence' supported the American assertion that European security options would naturally serve to support the European pillar of the Alliance.[46] With the endorsement of ESDI began a struggle between the various European security institutions (primarily the WEU and NATO), which was not resolved until the North Atlantic Council's Brussels summit in 1994. In the lead up to the 1994 'grand compromise', transatlantic orientations became Europeanised while the ESDI became heavily Atlanticised. French suspicions of American hegemonic designs were further raised by the creation of the North Atlantic Co-operation Council (NACC), which was intended to facilitate dialogue with central and eastern Europe, at NAC's Rome Summit. The *New Strategic Concept* contained one significant concession to the French when it specifically endorsed the development of 'integrated and multinational European structures'[47] which, as they emerge in the context of the ESDI, will enhance the 'Allies' ability to work together in the common defence'.[48] Despite this concession, France viewed the creation of NACC as another means by which Washington could exert its influence on European security. Germany however enthusiastically backed NACC as a means of building security links with central and eastern Europe.

While the distinctions between Europeanists and Atlanticists remained the source of political controversy, the lines between them became increasingly blurred in terms of military force structure. The adoption of the *New Strategic Concept* resulted in the creation of a number of multi-national corps (seven in all) commanded by Belgium, the FRG (two), the Netherlands, the US, Britain and a joint German–Danish corps. Britain also secured command of the newly created Allied Command Europe Rapid Reaction Corps (ARRC).[49] The new security challenges and the need for smaller, highly mobile force structures, also justified the reduction in US troops in Europe to around 100 000 (from its Cold War level of over 326 000). Thus, in military terms, the distinction posed in the political forum, between Europeanists and Atlanticists, became increasingly difficult to uphold – what is European? What is 'Atlantic'?

By late 1991 a highly confusing picture had developed: primarily under US guidance NATO was substantially modified and portrayed as the 'essential forum for consultation among the allies'. The Franco-German corps was described by Germany as a means of bringing France closer to NATO and by France as a means of asserting an independent European security identity. Britain preferred to play the balancer by promoting the WEU, ostensibly as a 'European' option, but in the full awareness that it relied heavily upon NATO and would serve to buttress the European pillar of the Alliance. Germany was caught in the middle of the French pro-European initiatives and the staunch British pro-Atlanticism.

With this as backdrop, the European Council was set to meet in Maastricht on 9–10 December 1991 at a summit that would conclude the IGC.

Title V of the treaty on European Union – the CFSP

The Maastricht summit was marked by drama since it appeared that negotiations might collapse due to Britain's resistance to greater Community involvement in social policy. The main differences in the EPC area were apparent on the questions of qualified majority voting and the form of association that the WEU should have with the EU. On these two basic issues there had yet to be agreement. Hans-Dietrich Genscher (in an important role as President of the WEU foreign ministers) strongly backed the qualified majority voting formula that had been advanced by the Dutch Presidency. He stressed the importance of agreeing on a formula for 'joint action', of the type advanced in the Franco-German proposals. On the WEU question, he advocated that a 'common defence' be adopted with the WEU as an 'integral part' of the EU.

In a somewhat parallel stance, President Mitterrand also wanted the WEU to be subordinate to the EU while at the same time distancing the EU further from Washington. Felipe Gonzalez, the Spanish Prime Minister, supported France and Germany in his advocacy that the CFSP be a significant step forward from the EPC. John Major, the British Prime Minister, was broadly supportive of the CFSP but did not favour qualified majority voting. Major was also adamantly opposed to the WEU falling under the control and direction of the EU. Like Giulio Andreotti, Italy's Prime Minister, and the Dutch Prime Minister Ruud Luubers, the British also favoured the 'prospect' of a common defence policy, while remaining set against its immediate introduction. The Belgian Prime Minster, Wilfried Martens, suggested a common defence policy that could 'eventually lead' to a common defence. Martens' suggestion was eventually adopted. The suggestion that the CFSP, in part or whole, should gradually be transferred to the first pillar was not however accepted by the Dutch Presidency. In the face of these differing national positions, Desmond Dinan's comment that 'the success of the Maastricht Summit owed much to Prime Minister Lubber's negotiating skills' is appropriate.[50]

Since the IGC had debated the role of the WEU, it was important that the organisation should prepare itself in parallel discussions to those of the EU, since all WEU members were also members of the Community. Prior to approval of any CFSP, the WEU adopted a declaration that it hoped would be in accordance with the CFSP.[51] The WEU Declaration reflected the differences on the extent to which the organisation should be associated with the EU. According to Colette Mazzuchelli, in her comprehensive account of the Maastricht negotiations, progress on both the questions of association of the WEU with the EC and the procedures to be adopted within the proposed Union, was pushed forward by France and Germany:

> On each difficult issue Kohl and Mitterrand met to coordinate their actions. Although this exasperated some other member states at times, it was generally acknowledged that the Franco-German impulse was necessary to bring negotiations to a successful conclusion. France and Germany used their combined weight to force an accord on defense at Maastricht.[52]

The Maastricht summit was a success for the Franco-German partnership, which succeeded in including defence as one of the components of the CFSP while also associating the WEU with the EU. However, the details of the Franco-German draft treaty were watered down by the proposals forwarded by Britain and others, which accounts for the often vague language of the final treaty. Nevertheless, the CFSP marked a move away from political co-operation and a triumph for France, Germany and Spain, all of whom wanted to ensure that the Maastricht negotiations produced more than an 'EPC II'.

Still, the end result of the deliberations amongst the Twelve at Maastricht was an inevitable compromise between the national positions.[53] As is the nature of any document negotiated between numerous parties, contradictory trends found their way into the treaty. In the case of the Treaty on European Union (TEU) it was the inclusion of the *communautaire* approach as well as the *intergovernmental* approach that gave birth to the somewhat schizophrenic character of the CFSP. The European Commission voiced its concern about these conflicting elements as they applied to the CFSP:

> The very fact that two different working methods – the Community approach and the intergovernmental approach – coexist in the same treaty is a source of incoherence. Experience has confirmed the fears previously expressed on this subject. The single institutional framework which was supposed to ensure harmony between the various 'pillars' of the treaty has not functioned satisfactorily.[54]

Given the disparate approaches on defence and security issues expressed during the IGC, it is extremely hard to imagine that either could have been readily adaptable to *communautaire* approaches. The country most inclined to favour such an approach was Germany, who was concerned that if such an approach was not adopted, the alternative may be the re-nationalisation of defence or the rise of *ad hoc* and potentially destabilising coalitions or alliances.[55] The Netherlands was broadly sympathetic to the German approach. Belgium also expressed interest in pushing forward the WEU's closer association with the EU through the merging of the Secretariat with the CFSP and the establishment of a common budget. But, as Ambassador Giovanni Jannuzzi commented, 'while a broad consensus was to be found within the Community for expanding its powers in security matters, there was still much hesitancy over defence, partly stemming from the position of Ireland, which is a member of the European Community but not of NATO, and partly from the concern of the other member states not to undermine, still less to relinquish, the Alliance'.[56]

In spite of the treaty's flaws and shortcomings, its signing by the heads of State and Government of the TEU was an historic moment.

The general provisions of the treaty include some that are relevant to the CFSP and provide the context in which all subsequent articles elsewhere in the treaty must be interpreted. Article A states that, 'The Union shall be founded on the European Communities, supplemented by the policies and forms of co-operation established by this Treaty.' Elaborating upon this, Article C states that: 'The Union shall be served by a single institutional framework which shall ensure the consistency and the continuity of the activities carried out in order to attain its objectives while respecting and building upon the *acquis communautaire.*' Article M makes it apparent that, 'nothing in this Treaty shall affect the Treaties establishing the European Communities or the subsequent Treaties and Acts modifying or supplementing them'. Article P of the TEU formally repealed Title III of the SEA thus making the CFSP the successor to the EPC.[57]

The CFSP was thus established as the second of the three pillars of the European Union. The pillar structure was not without its potential problems since the competence for the EU's external activities was shared between the first pillar (external trade and commerce) and the second pillar which included not only security and defence issues, but human rights, democratisation and the promotion of international cooperation.

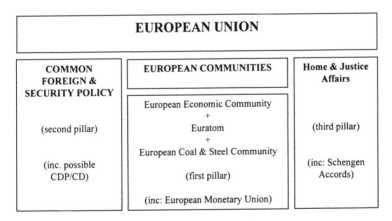

Figure 3.1   The pillar structure of the European Union.

The overall objective of the CFSP is outlined in Article B. The Union is to 'assert its identity on the international scene, in particular through the implementation of a common foreign and security policy including the eventual framing of a common defence policy, which might in time lead to a common defence'.

The TEU outlines the main features of the CFSP in Title V. (See Appendix 6.) These can be summarised as:

- CFSP is to include all questions of foreign and security policy;
- CFSP is to include the 'eventual framing' of a CDP which might 'in time' lead to a common defence;
- CFSP would make allowance for the specific character of member states' security and defence policies;
- co-operation on issues of defence are to take place *only on the basis of unanimity;*[58] and
- the WEU is to be an integral part of the European Union, which may elaborate and implement decisions and actions with defensive implications.

It is immediately apparent that the CFSP goes beyond the confines of the EPC to include *all* aspects of security policy with the addition of the European Defence Identity. The TEU also accorded the right of initiative to the Commission and attempted to integrate security and defence within a single framework. Perhaps most importantly, the TEU sought to establish a common foreign and security *policy* and not merely the promotion of co-operation, as had been the prime endeavour of the EPC. A further significant difference is that under Article 30 of the SEA it was the 'High Contracting Parties' who jointly 'formulate and implement a European foreign policy'; while under the TEU *'The Union* and its Member States shall define and implement a common foreign and security policy.'[59] The TEU subsequently refers to 'The Union' pursuing objectives,[60] and the 'Union requests'[61] – thus supporting the notion that the Union itself had become an actor in its own right.

The 'pillar' approach accepted under the Luxembourg Presidency called for the building of 'bridges' between the second and first (EC) pillars.[62] The first type of bridge is to be found in two articles of the Treaty establishing the European Community. Article 228a makes provision for the Council to adopt the necessary measures for action by the Community where an interruption or severing of economic relations with a third party is provided for by a common position or joint action emanating from the CFSP. However, a prerequisite to action under Article 228a is the adoption of a common position or joint action under the CFSP procedures. Under Article 73g, which is closely related to the aforementioned article, the Council may take 'the necessary urgent measures on the movement of capital and on payments as regards third countries concerned'. Action under this article though can only be taken if the prerequisites applying to Article 228a have been fulfilled. The second type of institutional bridge is contained in Article C which states that: 'The Union shall in particular ensure the consistency of its external activities as a whole in the context of its external relations, security, economic, and development policies.' The Council and the Commission are duly charged with responsibility to this end.

Title V, Article J 1.1, is careful to point out the intergovernmental nature of the CFSP when it states that, 'The Union *and its Member States* shall define and implement a common and foreign and security policy'.[63] The intergovernmental nature of the CFSP is further underlined by the TEU's general stipulation that the 'principle of subsidiarity'[64] shall be respected as will the 'national identities of [the Union's] Member States'.[65] The role of the Member States is reinforced by the European Council which shall 'provide the Union with the necessary impetus for its development, shall define the general political guidelines thereof'[66] and 'define the principles of and general guidelines for' the CFSP.[67] Under the TEU, provision is made for urgent action 'having regard to the general objectives of the joint action'[68] when there is no Council decision. In those circumstances where a Member State has 'difficulties in implementing a joint action' it shall be referred to the Council.[69] Article J 4.4 also ensures that the policy of the Union 'shall not prejudice the specific character of the security and defence policy of certain Member States'. Article 223 of the Treaty Establishing the European Community may also apply to the CFSP. Under the terms of this article 'No Member State shall be obliged to supply information the disclosure of which it considers contrary to the essential interests of security', and that, 'any Member State may take such measures as it considers necessary for the protection of the essential interests of it security which are connected with the production of or trade in arms, munitions, and war material'.

Not only therefore does the CFSP recognise the likelihood of clashes between the CFSP and individual Member States, but the stipulations of Title V do nothing to alter the competencies of the Member States in foreign or security policy. Although there is the expectation that 'Member States shall support the Union's external and security policy actively and unreservedly in a spirit of loyalty and mutual solidarity', there is no sanctioning procedure for states who do not. It is the job of the Council to 'ensure that these principles are complied with'

(Article J 1.4). However, in practical terms there is little that can be done to ensure compliance since, under Article L, the European Court of Justice has no jurisdiction in the CFSP field (nor in the third pillar on Cooperation in Justice and Home Affairs).[70] The Court of Justice's lack of jurisdiction serves to emphasise the political rather than the legal character of the CFSP.

Under the provisions of Article J.8 the main powers in the CFSP area are accorded to the Council of Ministers (the Council). The European Council, however, drawing upon a Council recommendation, defines the 'principles of and general guidelines for' the CFSP in those areas where the Member States have important common interests. Based on these, the Council (which replaced the old Council of Ministers on 1 November 1993) then takes 'the decisions necessary for defining and implementing the common foreign and security policy'. The Council itself is composed of Ministers from all member states and a Commission representative. It has a rotating Presidency each six months. Within the CFSP context, the Council's job is to adopt joint actions, common positions or other decisions to implement strategies. As mentioned, the TEU also charges the Council with shared responsibility (with the Commission) for ensuring consistency in the Union's external activities.[71] The Council decides, on the basis of general guidelines from the European Council, that a matter should be the subject of joint action and they shall 'define those matters on which decisions are to be taken by a ... qualified majority'.[72] Issues with defence implications however are *not* subject to qualified voting procedures and are therefore always decided on the basis of unanimity.

The Commission is to be 'fully associated with the work carried out in the [CFSP] field'. As Fraser Cameron observed, it is this seemingly modest task that has actually given the Commission a powerful role since: 'Increasingly, foreign policy is inextricably linked to economic, trade, development and interior policy.'[73] The emergence of the CFSP also allowed the Commission to undertake an internal restructure and establish a new Directorate-General (DG) for External Political Relations, to be placed under the Commissioner with special responsibility for the CFSP (DG 1A). The Commission also shares, along with the Member States, the right to refer to the Council any question relevant to the CFSP.

Given the considerable burden placed on the shoulders of the Council, it was obvious that provision for assistance must be made. This was provided by the Political Committee, consisting of the Political Directors of the Ministries of Foreign Affairs who 'shall monitor the international situation' in the areas covered by the CFSP and 'shall contribute to the definition of policies by delivering opinions to the Council'.[74] The committee also observes the implementation of agreed policies, without prejudice to the role of the Presidency or Commission. In addition, the Committee of Permanent Representatives (COREPER), consisting of Ambassadors from the Member States, examines the dossiers coming from the Political Committee to guarantee consistency between external activities of the European Communities and the CFSP. COREPER also prepares the work of the Council and carries out tasks assigned to it by the Council. Generally it divides its responsibilities amongst two parallel Committees, COREPER 1 (Permanent Representatives) and COREPER II (the Deputy Permanent Representatives). Each COREPER meeting may consist of 50+ members, including civil servants and experts. COREPER may create specialist committees, *ad hoc* committees, or working parties staffed by national experts. If there is unanimous agreement, the outcome of COREPER deliberations is put onto the Council's 'A Agenda', which the Council normally adopts. When there is no agreement, the matter is put onto the 'B Agenda' for further discussion.

As an extra-treaty activity, the EPC Secretariat was also merged into the Council Secretariat. This merger gave rise to a heated debate about whether the funding of the CFSP section of the Council Secretariat would fall under the Community budget, and thus the scrutiny of the European Parliament. The European Parliament is given a relatively marginal role, but has the right to submit questions and recommendations to the Commission. However, the views of the European Parliament, at Germany's insistence, would be 'taken into consideration' and the Parliament has the 'right to be consulted and informed'. The Community aspects of the CFSP may appear reasonably straightforward but there is a general problem with the 'departmentalization of security policy making', as Mathias Jopp has described it. In other words, security policy making is divided between the WEU, CFSP (COREPER and the Political Directors), the Commission (DG 1A and Department for Security Aspects) and the EC (external economic relations).[75]

Relations with other international organisations are addressed in Article J 2.3, in which the signatories agree to uphold a 'common position' in international organisations and conferences. This stipulation applies to NATO, the OSCE, the UN and the WEU. An important qualifier to this however is that Britain and France must 'ensure the defence of the positions and the interests of the Union' (Article J 5.4) in the context of the Security Council, in which both countries have permanent seats. The importance of this clause was emphasised by the growing number of UN mandated operations throughout the 1990s. Almost all of the UN peacekeeping operations have had a number of EU states commit forces. This raises the importance of not only making sure that the votes of the two permanent members express the general will of the Union (assuming that it is discernible) but that the use of a veto by either Britain or France should also express the concerns of the EU. The Yugoslav crisis illustrated some of the difficulties of living up to this stipulation in those circumstances in which, of the EU countries, Britain and France had most at stake and where there was division within the EU members on policy.

It should also be noted that due largely to Irish sensitivities, the TEU stated that the CFSP 'shall not prejudice the specific character of the security and defence policy of certain Member States'.[76] Along the same lines, the subsequent article declared that 'the development of closer co-operation between two or more Members States on a bilateral level' should not be prevented. These two articles significantly dilute the apparently ambitious aims of Article J.4 and point to the clear intergovernmental nature of the CFSP. This weakness is compounded by the unanimity principle, which simply encourages Member States to work outside the CFSP framework on those matters where unanimity will be difficult to gain. The work of the Contact Group on the former-Yugoslavia stands as the most obvious case in point.

The most innovative clause in Title V states that the CFSP 'shall include *all questions* related to security of the Union, including the *eventual* framing of a common defence policy (CDP), which *might* in time lead to a common defence(CD)'.[77] The treaty thus makes reference to two distinct concepts: the CDP and the CD, the latter being an important sub-component of the former. Before examining these however, the apparently limitless scope of the CFSP needs to be considered within the context of Article J 1.2, which outlines its objectives:

- To safeguard the common values, fundamental interests and independence of the Union;
- To strengthen the security of the Union and its Member States in all ways;
- To preserve peace and strengthen international security, in accordance with the principles of the United Nations as well as the principles of the Helsinki Final Act and the objectives of the Paris Charter;
- To promote international co-operation; and
- To develop and consolidate democracy and the rule of law and respect for human rights and fundamental freedoms.

These guidelines indicate that the scope of the CFSP is expansive. Although the overall effect of the treaty purportedly enables the EU to '... assert its identity on the international scene, in particular through the implementation of the CFSP...' (Article B), it is not clear how it does this. The objectives are also laden with imprecise terms – for example, what are the 'common values' of the Union and what might its 'fundamental interests' be? The CFSP further tries to provide a broad framework for the CDP and the CD. The Maastricht Treaty however was vague on exactly what a CDP and CD might actually look like. Would it, for instance, have the attributes of a classical alliance or a collective security system? In the context of post-Cold War Europe, the absence of an overt military threat obviously suggests that the eventual common defence would be more extensive than a classical military (defensive) alliance. Thus contrary to implying a somewhat restricted form of defensive co-operation the wording of the treaty, especially Articles J.4.1 and J.1.2, may actually imply that 'defence' integration is an extremely wide process and not one restricted to traditional notions of defensive alliances. There is nothing in the treaty to suggest that the CFSP is a precursor to the CDP/CD yet they are portrayed as simultaneous processes.

The role of the Western European Union

Under the TEU the WEU 'which is an integral part of the development of the Union', is *'requested* to elaborate and implement decisions and actions of the Union which have defence implications' (Article J 4.2). Willem van Eekelen commented that: 'Close reading of the word "requests" could give the impression that the Union had given a permanent mandate to WEU, but this was not the interpretation followed subsequently.'[78] In fact, only one such request has been made, in support of EU activities in Mostar, and as van Eekelen notes, the action did not even have defence implications.

When the Treaty on European Union was signed, the nine WEU members also agreed to a *Declaration of the Member States of the Western European Union on the role of the WEU and its relations with the European Union and with the Atlantic Alliance,* as a prior condition to the adoption of the CFSP.[79] Under the terms of this document it was agreed between the member states that there was a 'need to develop a genuine European security and defence identity and a greater European responsibility on defence matters'. The WEU was to be developed as 'the *defence component* of the European Union and as a means to strengthen the European pillar of the Atlantic Alliance'. To this end it 'will formulate a common European defence policy and carry forward its concrete implementation'. The WEU would therefore appear to have assumed a wider role in the formulation of a common defence policy than that implied by the TEU. But, at the same time, it was agreed that the WEU should be developed 'as a means to strengthen the European pillar of the Atlantic Alliance'. The potential tension in the WEU's charge to buttress the EU and NATO reflects the clear disagreement amongst states, especially France and Britain, about whether the CDP should be distinct from NATO or a strengthening of the European pillar of NATO. Much of the ensuing confusion about the nature of the ESDI, and its relations to the WEU, originates from the contradictory wording of Title V as well as from the WEU's Declaration.

The difficulties posed by the WEU's dual loyalties to the EU and NATO soon came to light. At the institutional level, NATO's position *vis-à-vis* the CFSP and the prospect of a revitalised WEU, appeared to be strengthened by the creation of ARRC in May, and by the decisions made at the NATO Council meeting in Copenhagen in June 1991. The Copenhagen summit reiterated that: 'NATO is the essential forum for consultation among the Allies and the forum for agreement on policies bearing on the security and defence commitments of its members under the Washington Treaty.' The communiqué also stated that 'A transformed Alliance constitutes an essential element in the new architecture of an undivided Europe' and that 'an important basis for this transformation is the agreement of the Allies to enhance the role and responsibility of the European members'.[80] The Copenhagen meeting's importance lay in the call, for the first time, for a partnership with the countries of central and eastern Europe as well as for an enhanced effort by all countries to work through the CSCE.

At its meeting in Oslo on 4 June 1992 NAC offered its support for CSCE peacekeeping activities. The offer of NATO support though was made only 'on a case-by-case basis in accordance with NAC's own procedures, peacekeeping activities under the responsibility of the CSCE, including by making available Alliance resources and expertise'.[81] Soon after, on 19 June, the WEU Council, in its Petersberg meeting, made the same offer to the CSCE and the UN. In remarkably similar wording, the WEU offered to support, 'on a case-by-case basis and in accordance with our procedures, the effective implementation of conflict prevention and crisis management measures, including peacekeeping activities of the CSCE or the United Nations Security Council'. The British Defence Secretary, Malcolm Rifkind, in advance of the June 1992 meeting of the WEU foreign and defence ministers, made a persuasive case that ARRC, the UK-Netherlands Amphibious Force and the Franco-German Eurocorps should be viewed as part of a number of complementary options open to both NATO and the WEU. This suggestion was codified in the WEU's June 1992 Petersberg Declaration, in which the Foreign and Defence Ministers attempted to strengthen the operational capacity of the WEU (see Chapter 6 for more details). Under the WEU's authority, the declaration stated that the military units of member countries could be used for crisis management ranging from low-intensity missions to tasks of combat forces in crisis management, including peacekeeping.

Enjoying its new-found sense of purpose, the WEU also reached out to the central and east European states in 1992 when it founded the Forum for Consultation. The forum consisted of WEU members, those about to join the EU and those who had signed or were about to sign Europe Agreements. It was designed to develop the capacity to conduct joint peacekeeping activities of the type outlined in the Petersberg Declaration.[82] In December NATO matched the WEU by extending an offer to the UN to assist in the implementation of UN Security Council resolutions. In response to NATO's Partnership for Peace (PfP), launched in May 1994, the WEU offered its forum members 'associate partner' status, which allowed them to participate in Council deliberations, in the Planning Cell and in 'Petersberg tasks'. Like the PfP, associate partner status carried no security guarantees or any tangible power within the organisation.

The attempt to add military structure, at least on paper, to the CFSP took shape with reasonable swiftness with the WEU's 1992 Petersberg Declaration. The declaration also eliminated some of the most glaring NATO–European rivalries and put to an end some of the blatantly duplicative WEU and NATO structures. Franco-German ambiguity concerning the Eurocorps and its relations with NATO and the WEU was also clarified in a 21 January 1993 agreement with the chief of the French General Staff, the German Inspector General and SACEUR. Under the agreement, the Eurocorps would be available to NATO for Article 5 contingencies as well as non-Article 5 tasks, such as peacekeeping or humanitarian missions. The agreement also detailed SACEUR's responsibilities for operational planning and command and control arrangements, as well as relations between SACEUR and the Eurocorps in peacetime.

The WEU's Council of Ministers was relatively quick to consider the defence aspects of the TEU. In their *Preliminary Conclusions on the*

Formulation of a Common European Defence Policy, which was formulated at the Council's meeting at Noordwijk on 14 November 1994, it was agreed that the WEU was developing both as the defence component of the EU and as the means to strengthen the European pillar of NATO.[83] The *Preliminary Conclusions* still represent one of the clearest attempts to think through the vagaries of the TEU with its somewhat artificial divide between security and defence:

> Being an element of security policy in a wider sense, the common European defence policy is directed towards the reduction of risks and uncertainties that might threaten the common values, fundamental interests and independence of the Union and its member States and towards contributing to the preservation of peace and the strengthening of international security, in accordance with the principles of the United Nations Charter as well as the principles of the Helsinki Final Act and the objectives of the Paris Charter.
>
> A common European defence policy should enhance security and stability by ensuring a commensurate European participation in collective defence, and by an active engagement in conflict prevention and crisis management in Europe and elsewhere, in accordance with Europe's importance. Institutionally and substantively, the development of a common European defence policy in WEU must be seen in the context of broader European and transatlantic relationships, which are closely intertwined.

The Noordwijk deliberations made it clear that a common defence policy must be based upon a thorough analysis of European security interests, both in Europe as well as those shared beyond. The need for a common assessment and definition of the requirements and substance of a European defence policy required, in the first place, a clear definition of security challenges facing the EU and then a determination of the appropriate responses. The *Preliminary Conclusions* had some innovative aspects as well, such as the emphasis on the need for an intelligence gathering capability and the need for a European Armaments policy. But, it did not address what precisely the challenges to Europe's security interests were.

The response to this question was provided, somewhat vaguely, in the document *European Security: a Common Concept of the 27 WEU Countries,* submitted by the Permanent Council to the WEU Council of Minister's meeting in Madrid, 14 November 1995 (including by this time Austria, Finland and Sweden). The new risks to Europe's security were listed as:

- Potential armed conflicts;
- Proliferation of weapons of mass destruction and their delivery means;
- International terrorism, organised crime, drug trafficking and uncontrolled and illegal immigration; and
- Environmental risks.

Beyond providing general assistance in helping to address the above problems, the function of the WEU was portrayed primarily as 'Petersberg tasks'. (See Appendix 5) Based on the WEU's role in enforcing embargoes in the former Yugoslavia, the Common Concept added that the WEU should attain the capability of 'mounting military operations in support of crisis management tasks' and that it may, 'on a case by case basis, also coordinate non-military resources as it has done in Mostar and on the Danube'.[84] The practicalities of addressing security risks saw the incorporation of the French concept of a 'lead nation' which would be responsible for the command arrangements for the operation, as well as other aspects such as logistics.[85] Due note was made of the WEU's generally improved ability since the TEU to respond to crises through such measures as the establishment of the Planning Cell in 1992, the identification of FAWEU, the creation of a Politico-Military Group in May 1995 and the establishment of a Situation Centre and an Intelligence Section in the Planning Cell. The Permanent Council also acknowledged the deficiencies in European capabilities. In particular, the following were identified as pressing:[86]

- Crisis management mechanisms (including procedures for force generation and assembly, and command and control procedures);
- Reconnaissance and intelligence;
- Strategic and in-theatre transport facilities;
- Standardisation and interoperability; and
- The European defence industrial base.

The WEU Council of Ministers approved the *Common Concept* at the Madrid meeting with the somewhat extravagant proclamation that it 'represents an important contribution by WEU to the process of developing the new European security architecture'.[87] Still, it is an important document since it is one of the few documents which not only attempts to assess the security challenges facing post-Cold War Europe but one that is also frank about the difficulties involved in doing so. A third document (in addition to the Madrid Declaration and the Common Concept), entitled the *WEU Contribution to the European Union Intergovernmental Conference of 1996,* was also adopted. It is addressed in the following chapter, in the lead up to the 1996 IGC.

Common interests and joint action

The European Council defined 'joint action' in its 'Declaration on Areas which could be subject to Joint Action' (otherwise known as the Asolo Declaration)[88] on 12 December 1991. The Council identified four areas in which members could have security interests in common and therefore might lend themselves to joint action. The spheres were the CSCE process (now OSCE); disarmament and arms control in Europe; nuclear non-proliferation and; economic aspects of security.

At the Maastricht summit, the Council had agreed to 'prepare a report to the European Council in Lisbon on the likely development of a CFSP with a view to identifying areas open to joint action...'.[89] In the ensuing June 1992 report, which came to be known as the Lisbon Report, the CFSP was declared to be the successor to the EPC. The report argued that the eventual formation of a common defence policy (CDP) marked a significant advance (a *'saut qualitatif '*) since it integrated the *'acquis'* of the EPC and gave it greater potential through joint actions – although the promise of extensive collaboration was not to be borne out in practice.[90] The CFSP was also regarded as a means of ensuring that the Union's external actions were more active in contrast to the reactive nature of the EPC's activities.[91] The Lisbon Report gave further shape to the concepts of 'joint action' and 'common interest' (although the idea of joint action was far from new since it was mentioned specifically in Article 30 of the SEA). Joint action was considered as a 'means for the definition and the implementation by the Union of a policy in the framework of the CFSP in a specific issue'.[92] Joint action was further intended to satisfy the objectives of the Union (as defined in Article J 1.2 of the Treaty on European Union) taking into account the Union's *acquis*, while remaining consistent with other actions adopted by the Union. Areas that were suggested as being suitable for joint action included:[93]

- Strengthening democratic principles and institutions;
- Promoting regional political stability and regional co-operation;

- Contributing to the settlement of international conflicts;
- Providing more effective assistance to international efforts to deal with emergency situations;
- Strengthening existing co-operation against arms proliferation, terrorism and illicit drugs; and
- Promoting and supporting good government.

The TEU is clear that in 'matters of *general interest*' member states shall 'endeavour to define common positions through systematic cooperation', but they shall 'implement the CFSP by joint action where they have *important interests* in common'. The existence of common interests therefore constituted the basic criterion for adopting courses of joint action (Articles J 1.3 and J.3). The factors that constitute common interest, as defined by the Council, may include the following criteria:[94]

- Geographical proximity of a given country or region;
- Interest in the political and economic stability of a region or country; and
- The existence of threats to the security interests of the Union.

A limited number of geographical areas were identified as being suitable for joint action and where it was felt that common interests were present. These areas include central and eastern Europe (in particular the Commonwealth of Independent States and the Balkans), the Mediterranean (especially the Maghreb) and the Middle East. All areas, it should be noted, where it is hard to imagine the WEU operating in without sizeable international (viz. American) backing. The European Council's Lisbon Report on the CFSP also defined 'domains within the security dimension'. Those spheres within the security dimension that may be the object of joint action were identified as:[95]

- The CSCE process;
- Disarmament and arms control in Europe (including confidence building measures);
- Nuclear non-proliferation issues; and
- Economic aspects of security (especially technology transfer).

'Joint actions' have been initiated on issues such as monitoring elections in South Africa and Russia; administrating humanitarian aid in Bosnia; EU administration of Mostar with WEU support; operating blockades on the Adriatic Sea and on the Danube river; supporting a wide variety of security issues (such as the Convention on Anti-Personnel Mines, the Non-Proliferation Treaty and the Stability Pact); and regulating the export of dual-purpose goods. 'Common positions' (positions agreed upon but not necessarily with joint action or commitment of resources as specified in Article J.2) have been adopted for diverse issues such as those pertaining to Angola, Burundi, Haiti, Iran, Libya, Nigeria, Rwanda, Sudan, Ukraine and Russia. Nearly all of the common actions have concerned economic sanctions. Most common positions have been adopted with reference to ex-Yugoslavia. The extensive use of sanctions incidentally underlines the importance of ensuring that the external activities of the Union are consistent, since the imposition of sanctions is a first pillar activity. Sanctions have been widely used both in the EPC context and the CFSP, but their effectiveness tends to depend heavily upon whether they are regulations or directives. The former is binding in all aspects while the latter specify only the goals but not the means to reach them. Sanctions in general have tended to take the form of directives and this has tended to compromise their effectiveness, as in the case of South Africa.[96] Avoidance of regulations suggests that the required consensus would be difficult to achieve. A further problem with sanctions, raised by Jacques Santer, President of the European Commission, is that they engender confusion between Community matters and those within the province of the CFSP since, for example, 'a sanction, which is a manifestly political decision, really affects trade, finance, cooperation schemes and all activities covered by Community procedures'.[97] Sanctions though comprise just one of the tools available to the Union; others include demarchés, assistance (humanitarian and other), preferential trade arrangements and the severance of diplomatic relations.

In reference to the different competencies for security and defence components, according to the European Council's Lisbon Report, 'defence implications', as opposed to 'security dimensions', are those that involve military action. A further distinction is that those issues with 'security dimensions' are subject to joint action while those issues having defence implications (covered by the procedures outlined in Article J.3) are *not* subject to the procedure of joint action. The Lisbon Report left many basic issues unanswered and in an attempt to find answers, it invited the Ministers of Foreign Affairs to begin 'preparatory work with a view to defining the necessary basic elements for a policy of the Union', which should in particular concentrate on 'the elements which will be necessary to the Union in the framework of the CFSP'.[98] In order to assist the ministers in this task, an *Ad Hoc Working Group on Security* was created under the Political Committee.

Progress towards the CFSP?

During the Maastricht negotiations the crisis in Yugoslavia erupted. This is addressed in detail in a separate chapter. Suffice it to note at this stage that the European Council's meeting in Edinburgh on 11–12 December 1992 featured a 'Declaration of Yugoslavia' in which, with surprisingly little fanfare, the EU quietly renounced exclusive responsibility for the continued unravelling of Yugoslavia.[99] A report appeared in the same month on joint action and the development of the CFSP in the field of security by the Ad Hoc Working Group on Security. The committee reiterated the joint action and interest criteria and suggested a number of outstanding issues (which were also to serve as one mandate of the working groups).[100] The wider issues included:[101]

- An analysis of European security interests in the new strategic context, 'in order to develop some common security principles on which the future Common Foreign and Security Policy will be based';
- The division of labour between the WEU and the Union in the security field;
- The question on how to ensure that the CFSP shall not prejudice the 'specific character of the security and defence policy of certain member states and shall respect the obligations of certain member States under the North Atlantic Treaty';
- The relationship between the CFSP and those of other international organisations;
- The definition of issues having defence implications, to which joint action procedures will not apply; and
- The implications of the eventual framing of a common defence policy, which might in time lead to a common defence.

At the request of Hans van den Broek a high-level Group of Experts on the CFSP were commissioned to produce a report covering the above issues in preparation for the 1996 IGC. The Group of Experts in fact comprised a number of different groups, each dedicated to a particular aspect of the CFSP.[102] The expert subcommittees, normally with four to five persons, were to produce an overall report, which was to be a guide to discussions on the CFSP in the IGC. The 19 December 1994 report provided some sombre but frank reading. In one candid section the report commented:

> The problem is that there is frankly nothing to show for all of this activity, all the fresh starts and 'progress', on the contrary, there is

an increasing sense of unease at the impotence and drift highlighted week after week by current issues and their reflection in the media. This is true even of the 'joint actions' initiated in the European Council, notably at the special session marking the entry into force of the Maastricht Treaty held in Brussels on 29 October 1993. With the possible exception of the Stability Pact these have quickly turned out to be poorly planned, hard to implement and disappointing both in terms of scope and in terms of their meagre results.[103]

The report also highlighted the weak state of the EU's relations with the WEU whereby the latter could, in conformity with Article J.4 of the Treaty on European Union, become an 'integral part of the development of the Union'. It further commented that the WEU 'is still nowhere near ready to think about setting up an actual force projection capability endowed with the necessary intelligence, command and logistical resources'.[104] It also focused attention on the 'fraught issue' of the linkage between Article V of the Brussels Treaty and the commitments entered into under the Washington Treaty whereby the same articles in the respective treaties implied vastly different levels of commitment.[105] Dual membership of the WEU and NATO could therefore imply more binding commitments than those desired or understood under the Washington Treaty. The report concluded, 'the inertia and incompetence of the CFSP and WEU are the inward and outward reflection of a lack of capacity or will to act, particularly as regards the threat and/or use of force by the Union'.[106]

The High-level group of experts, faced with the evidence of 'dysfunction, deficiencies and a lack of either any political will or the necessary sense of urgency', went on to consider what steps should be taken to give the CFSP and the WEU 'a modicum of the substance and consistency which has so far been desperately lacking'.[107] Their report recommended:

- The immediate establishment of a 'genuinely independent permanent central analysis and evaluation capability in Brussels' which should cover all areas of the CFSP but with special responsibility for the evaluation of ongoing risks and threats to Community interests;
- The preparation of strategies, to be discussed by the European Council, which should reflect the range of options actually available to the Union and to report annually to the European Council and Parliament; and
- The establishment of a Standing Committee of Chiefs of Staff for the WEU modelled on NATO's Military Committee and backed up

by the existing Planning Cell and the creation of other 'medium and long-range operational requirements units or agencies to draft equipment specifications for the three forces'.[108]

The report also devoted considerable attention to the promotion of synergy and the investigation of horizontal issues between the Union's three pillars. One suggested synergy was to 'reconcile [the Union's] emergent defence and security identity with the maintenance of an efficient and competitive scientific, technological and industrial base for weapons production'. The issue of energy supplies, and more specifically the prospect of growing dependence on oil supplies from the Persian Gulf, was also raised with the recommendation that the linkage between oil revenue, foreign policy and weapons programmes be studied in joint Commission/WEU/Presidency studies. Progress toward common defence, within the meaning of Article V of the Brussels Treaty, was supported but only in consultation with the other major partners, including the United States. Finally, and controversially, the report of the High-level Group of Experts urged that the European intervention force (based on the Eurocorps and other multinational units) must 'from the outset receive political and financial backing from those Member States who do not wish to participate, either because they lack the capability or for their own political reasons'.[109]

Maastricht, the WEU and the new world order

The contradictions and vagaries found in the agreements establishing the CFSP reflect the differing national interests of the Member States. Perhaps unsurprisingly, given the sensitive nature of foreign and security policy, the move from co-operation to common policy is more of an incremental process than a leap. The reluctance to consider CFSP questions in the early 1990s only changed as a number of successive developments in Europe altered the context of European security.

The first and most obvious change was the disintegration of the Soviet Union in December 1991. This development dramatically altered the perception of threats to western security. Second, the difficult task of putting 'military flesh' onto diplomatic bones was embarked upon at the very same moment that western Europe appeared increasingly impotent in the face of the dissolution of Yugoslavia and the eruption of brutal ethnic warfare. Third, the unification of Germany changed the geopolitics of Europe and opened up the possibility of Germany assuming a major role in European security. Even if reluctant, Germany itself realised that its status and economic leverage demanded a commensurate security role. The European Council welcomed the 'positive and fruitful contribution that all Germans can make following the forthcoming integration of the territory of the German Democratic Republic into the Community'.[110] Fourth, at the end of the Cold War the US placed greater emphasis on its domestic agenda as the full social and economic costs of the Cold War became more evident to Americans, especially the minorities and poor. Fifth, the presence of a number of volatile scenarios or actual conflicts on west Europe's doorstep, which could not be answered by nuclear or conventional deterrence provided through NATO, exerted pressure to formulate a working CFSP.

Yet despite the various developments and the TEU, very little was *common*. The much trumpeted, but somewhat vacuous, promotion of 'western values' was to appeal to the central and east Europeans in particular, but it had a hollow ring amongst the EU members. Nowhere was this more clear than in the case of the former Yugoslavia where, as Vlad Sobell observed:

> Western divisions, or the specific interests of each country, for so long stood in the way of a credible posture: former Yugoslavia has had a unique way of bringing back to life all the ghosts of the continent's troubled past. A common EU foreign policy – defined as a degree of consensus sufficient to enable the EU to act with one voice on such vital issues – is, therefore, still a long way off.[111]

Fundamental differences still remained concerning the very purpose and end-goal of the integration process. The Danes and British were already known to be less than enthusiastic about the deepening process, but doubts were by no means confined to these two countries. The result of the Danish referendum, the first of which was held on 2 June 1992, yielded a tantalisingly close result. A narrow majority (50.7 percent) of Danes voted against approving the TEU. The French referendum, held on 20 September 1992, also showed close results with a slight majority (51 percent) in favour. Although French concerns were similar to European ones, the strong lobby against the TEU was composed largely of farmers, who used the referendum as a chance to demonstrate their extreme discontent with Mitterrand's perceived failure to adequately defend their interests in the Community. The French debate was also coloured by perennial anxieties about joining a German-led and dominated Europe.

The British discussion on the TEU was influenced by the referendum votes from both Denmark and France, both of which had the effect of strengthening Conservative opposition to the TEU. The traumatic events of September 1992, which led to the withdrawal of the British pound and Italian lira from the Exchange Rate Mechanism (ERM) also created a highly negative climate in the debate. Arguably, the TEU would never have passed through the House of Commons had it not been made a matter of a vote of confidence in July 1993. Prior to this however was the second Danish vote, held on 18 May 1993, conducted under a new Social-Democratic government, which resulted in a more convincing majority in support of the TEU (56.8 percent). This majority had only been secured by allowing the Danish government certain 'opt-out' clauses in some critical areas of each of the three pillars. Denmark's *à la carte* approach to European union provided a model for the British debate and made some of the Euro-sceptics more willing to vote in favour of the bill. As a result, the British bill squeezed through the Parliament on 2 August 1993, but only after a tense vote that threatened to bring the government down. Ironically, it was Germany, commonly regarded as the champion of the deepening process, who ratified the bill last, in October 1993. Not only was ratification slow, it was overly complicated by a prolonged legal struggle in the Federal Constitutional Court in Karlsruhe over the issue of whether the TEU limited the constitutional rights of German citizens. The government insisted upon safeguards being added while the *Bundestag* secured the right to make the third stage of EMU a matter for parliamentary consent, to protect the Deutschmark.

The obvious public concerns over TEU and the fundamental differences between the Member States on basic issues cast doubt on the continuity of the 'permissive consensus' on security and defence issues that had existed for much of the Cold War period. In general, it could be argued that consensus, such as it was, was based on the assumption that the élites knew what was best for the their publics.[112] The French and Danish referenda not only illustrated the extent to which élites were out of touch with their publics, but posed the logical corollary that, having ignored public opinion for so long, élites had little idea of how much policy legitimacy was needed to make further integration publicly acceptable. This observation applies with more force to foreign and security policy since, more than other aspects of integration, it has historically been 'a private club, operated by diplomats for diplomats, and some of that same ambiance has persisted to this day'.[113]

The second significant outcome of the ratification process was that it considerably watered-down the TEU. The introduction of opt-out clauses allowed certain vital interests to be upheld, without forcing the Member(s) involved with the choice of leaving the Union. The future vitality of the Union will obviously depend upon the prudence and frequency with which the opt-out options are exercised. The clauses are also disruptive in the sense that some states are viewed as more 'deeply' integrated than others and this, in turn, has reinforced the idea of a multi-speed and multi-level approach to integration.

Third, the ratification debates illustrated the evident tension between intergovernmentalism and the *communautaire* impulses emanating from Brussels. In spite of the tensions caused by the common agricultural policy (CAP), pre-Maastricht integration was not an issue that threatened national identity (except possibly that of the French) or went to the core of issues of sovereignty. By contrast, the Maastricht process (which could be portrayed as an attempt to fibrillate a middle-aged heart attack victim), attempted to reinvigorate the entire integration process. Unsurprisingly, the attempt to push the integration process so far, so fast, was bound to encounter resistance from nation–states with profound concerns about the possible effects of union upon their sovereignty.

The significant changes in Europe that occurred between the 1990–1 and 1996 IGCs also posed the question of what type of membership criteria the EU (and other organisations) should insist upon in response to the inevitable requests for membership from the east. The proposals for a *Pact on Stability in Europe* forwarded by the French Prime Minister, Edouard Balladur, at the European Council's 20–1 June 1993 Copenhagen meeting, marked a significant attempt at more formally including the central and east European countries.[114] The Pact consisted of a series of agreements or 'codes of good conduct' ambitiously designed to 'resolve the problem of minorities and to strengthen the inviolability of frontiers'. The European Council Heads of State and Government called upon the Council to 'implement the initiative as a joint action within the framework of the CFSP'. The Pact carried an unmistakable French *imprimatur* and also that of Balladur himself and, for these reasons, it was regarded with some suspicion in the *Assemblée* as well as outside France.

The basic principles established by the Stability Pact nevertheless found resonance in the EU and thus were adopted in a slightly modified form (chiefly by dropping the idea of territorial revision) as the second Joint Action under the CFSP. A high-level working group was established to start discussions with the target states – the six central and east Europe Agreement countries, Slovenia and the three Baltic states.

The Europe Agreements, starting in December 1991 when agreements were signed with the Visegrad 'Three' (which soon became four with the division of Czechoslovakia into two separate countries) sought to strengthen political and economic reform and prepare them for potential membership of the Community. Ironically, those states with some of the most severe minority and or frontier problems did not appear on the list of countries 'principally concerned' but rather were 'Other countries invited'.[115] Instead, the emphasis was on targeting those countries that 'have the prospect' of becoming EU members. Negotiations began in earnest in December 1993, followed by a series of round tables taking place in 1994 focusing on the Baltic states and the Central European countries respectively, and culminated in the signing of the Pact of Stability in Paris in March 1995. The negotiations involved not only the EU plus the ten central and east European countries, they also kept Russia, the US and Canada informed and included a number of organisations such as the WEU, the UN, the OSCE and the Council of Europe. The focus on borders, on minority problems and on the principle of 'good neighbourliness' meant that the process fell increasingly under the purview of the OSCE and the Council of Europe. Attempts by the Council of Ministers, meeting in Lisbon in May 1995, to draw up a *Common Reflection on the new European Security Conditions* made little real progress beyond some operational developments. It is also worth noting that the Pact excluded the post-Yugoslavia states and thus perhaps failed to address the main security problem of the region.

At its meeting of 29 October 1993, the European Council adopted some theoretical and conceptual aspects of the CFSP suggested by various working groups. Although the theoretical aspects of the CFSP were elaborated both for the EU and the surrounding regions (central and eastern Europe, the Mediterranean,[116] the Maghreb and the Middle East), a matching common defence (CD) component was still lacking. The outcome of successive WEU meetings left the substance of any CD vague. This vagueness remains a major limitation upon the WEU's ability to define, let alone assume, its defence duties.

The task of defining a common European defence policy (CDP) fell to the Permanent Council of the WEU. On 10 November 1994, the Permanent Council produced a preliminary report on the definition and scope of the CDP.[117] The preliminary report directed CDP towards the 'reduction of risks and uncertainties that might threaten the common values, fundamental interests and independence of the Union and its member States', as well as to the more general objective of the 'strengthening of international security'.[118] Moreover, CDP should enhance security and stability by ensuring a 'commensurate European participation in collective defence, and by an active engagement in conflict prevention and crisis management in Europe and elsewhere, in accordance with Europe's importance'. The idea of 'European participation' implies either the existence of 'European' forces or some type of multi-national framework into which national forces are slotted. Either way, the assumption that there is the ability and will to express a European voice in defence affairs clearly existed. Fundamental to the projected CDP is the 'collective defence approach to defence', as established under the Modified Brussels Treaty and the Washington treaties. The report then outlines four levels of responsibilities and interests in the defence field:[119]

- The security and defence of WEU peoples and territories;
- The ability to project security and stability throughout Europe;
- The ability to foster stability in the southern Mediterranean countries; and
- The promotion of security, stability and democratic values in the wider world, including through the execution of peacekeeping and other crisis management measures under the authority of the UN Security Council or the CSCE (now OSCE), acting either independently or through the WEU or NATO.

The levels of responsibility are rather unsurprising and mirror NATO statements, however they do beg the question of what is 'European' security? If defence is a sub-component of wider 'security' issues, it is then up to the EU to determine those security challenges facing the Union and then to determine what might merit a military or 'defensive' response, or what might call for other forms of non-military response. In short, the question of differences or overlap between security and defence becomes important and not just a question of semantics. The continuing elaboration of a CFSP will obviously help the WEU in its task of defining the 'defence component' of European security.

The Permanent Council's Preliminary Conclusions also displayed some disagreement over the role of nuclear weapons. The *1987 Platform on European Security* viewed the British and French nuclear deterrents as important contributions to European and international peace and stability. In concurrence with this the Council's report originally proposed that: 'Under the present circumstances of European defence, there is no alternative, for the foreseeable future, to a strategy of deterrence and defence based on conventional and nuclear weapons. Only the nuclear component of these forces is able to confront a potential aggressor with an unacceptable risk.'[120] Norway was unhappy with this passage however and proposed deletion of it. In this recommendation, seven other countries supported Norway, including the United Kingdom.

The Council's report also stressed the complementary nature of the WEU's development of a European CDP as reinforcing the European pillar of NATO. The Combined Joint Task Force (CJTF) concept (see Chapter 5) was viewed as an 'innovative model to combine European security and defence co-operation with political solidarity within the Alliance, while making economic use of resources and offering the possibility for non-NATO members to participate'.[121] The Kirchberg Declaration as well as the Council's report welcomed the endorsement of the principle that NATO would make available its collective assets and capabilities for WEU operations, 'preserving WEU's own planning procedures and capabilities'.[122] The Council's report did not however comment upon whether the WEU's planning procedures, which were (and are) still at a very tentative stage of development, could possibly cope with such a contingency. The degree to which NATO capabilities, not just military forces, continue to be 'separable but not separate' remains to be seen. The development of the CJTF concept and the now widespread joint NATO–PfP military and command exercises (which occasionally present some unusual images such as American and Russian troops training together on Polish soil) is nevertheless important and a challenge. It is significant because the CJTF offers the WEU an obvious lifeline but it is also a challenge because the CJTF fits uneasily with the more European defence and security oriented advocates, such as France. In short, the CJTF concept may have presented interested observers with a somewhat counterintuitive example of military collaboration preceding the formulation of any overarching political integration to provide the policy framework in which collaboration takes place.

The Council further briefly considered the construction of a European CDP and how the WEU might assist in the deliberations of the 1996 IGC. The importance of solidarity was stressed but, even so, potential transatlantic rifts were evident. For instance, the Council wrote that: 'WEU should examine developments in the transatlantic partnership which represent an important common interest with the aim of introducing joint positions *agreed in WEU into the process of consultation* in the Alliance.'[123]

While there is a certain logic to negotiating agreed 'European' positions, there is nevertheless the danger of open rifts developing between the US and its European partners since the impression may be given that the US is negotiating with a bloc which presents pre-agreed positions and demands to the North American members of NATO. It is by no means clear that Washington would regard a European debating chamber as entirely neutral or collaborative. The dramatic changes in the French position *vis-à-vis* NATO make it somewhat less likely that the consultation process within the WEU will be adversarial to the transatlantic relationship, but it does not discount the possibility.

An interim assessment of the CFSP

From the moment the EPC became the CFSP a general weakness in the Union as a whole was apparent. What had been created was not a union as such, but a series of pillars distinguishing between the economic, political and security aspects of the EU's external behaviour. The different intergovernmental and supranational applications of policy-making to the CFSP and to external economic relations respectively, also created a general impression of incoherence on the part of the Union. The lack of any real intent to subsume national foreign and security identities into a collective European framework both during and after the 1990–1 IGC suggests that the results of the CFSP from 1993 to the 1996 IGC could be portrayed as the balance of national interests and no more.

The exact nature of what is 'common' or 'European' in the CFSP is perhaps unclear, yet the fact that realist prognostications failed to materialise suggests that there was a net benefit to collaboration. In the absence of a mutual threat the larger European powers would have reverted to the pursuit of national interests. However, the timing of the pre-Maastricht IGC indicates the opposite; namely, that the lifting of the common threat made the pursuit of common security a possibility. In support of this a liberal institutionalist perspective suggests that the willingness of the Member States to express common coincidences of national preferences (joint actions or common positions) should not be underestimated since it represents the formalization of co-operation and willingness to follow agreed procedures.[124] On balance, the general willingness of EU members to work through CFSP mechanisms may be precisely due to the vagaries of the TEU. The TEU though served to perpetuate the same paradox which lay at the centre of the EPC. The preservation of national rights to decide on involvement or non-involvement in common positions or joint actions was at odds with the institutional mechanisms enabling them to operate jointly. The increase of such mechanisms under the TEU also increased the expectations from outside parties that European states would collaborate.

For an insider's assessment, Commissioner Hans van den Broek identified several weaknesses to the CFSP.[125] First, he identified the *lack of political will* to act as a Union. Second, the *lack of any essential definition of common interests* not only hampered the potential for action but, where there was agreement on basic principles, it hindered the course of action to be followed. Third, *the decision-making procedure based on unanimity* implied that action may depend not on those who are most likely to fund and equip, but depends equally upon the most reluctant and maybe the weakest. Finally, the *provisions for financing joint actions* have proven to be inadequate.

The Commission's own report on the workings of the TEU was also highly critical of the CFSP.[126] Amongst the shortcomings, the Commission noted the confusion between Joint Actions and Common Positions – the two being used apparently interchangeably. The lack of any mechanisms to ensure consistency in the external activities of the EU or to resolve differences between the pillars was also noted. The role of the Presidency was also commented upon since it appeared to be used primarily as a device to promote national positions.

Finally, the institutional setting for the emergent CFSP was one of overlapping and competing competencies. The series of moves and countermoves by the WEU and NATO in the lead up to the IGC, and the ratification debates, detracted from the idea that a deliberative European security architecture was indeed emerging. What actually emerged was far more chaotic. Four general observations may be made in this regard. First, NATO was undeniably the central institution in European defence if only because it had the necessary military muscle and assets provided by its Member States. Second, from 1991 on, the variety of outreach initiatives to Central Europe began to redefine 'security Europe'. Third, although the 1992 Petersberg Declaration did not confine the WEU's role to peacekeeping and related tasks, the perception nevertheless existed that these were the WEU's defined tasks, thus underlining the collective defence duties of NATO. Finally, the enhanced visibility of the WEU as the EU's defence arm highlighted the lack of the organisation's physical ability to actually play that role. These military shortcomings of the WEU were to be addressed by two historic NAC meetings in Brussels and Berlin in 1994 and 1996, while the numerous shortfalls of the CFSP provided the agenda for the EU's 1996 IGC.

4
Expanding Europe, Decreasing Security

Less than common – the 1996 IGC

The Treaty on European Union made provision for an Intergovernmental Conference in 1996.[1] The European Council meeting in Corfu, on 24–5 June 1994, established a Reflection Group, chaired by Carlos Westendorp, and mandated that it focus on those areas of the TEU that were subject to revision, including the CFSP. Two questions had risen to the top of the agenda as the IGC approached. First, the development of a CDP/CD and second the nature of the EU–WEU relationship. Prior to the unveiling of the Reflection Group's findings, a number of other proposals surfaced. In relation to the first issue, the 1994 *Reflections on European Policy* paper prepared by German Christian Democratic Union/Christian Social Union (CDU/CSU) Parliamentary leader Wolfgang Schäuble and party foreign policy spokesman Karl Lammers, is worthy of note.[2] With regard to the second issue, the WEU's 1995 *Contribution to the European Intergovernmental Conference of 1996* is important.[3]

The CDU/CSU *Reflections on European Policy* (henceforth 'Reflections') aroused considerable controversy, not least from the French government.[4] The significance of the document lay in the fact that it shaped the debates of the IGC. This was in part because the CDU/CSU's tactic of forwarding the proposals in such a public and forceful manner meant that the *Reflections'* issues could not easily be avoided. The *Reflections* had the additional attraction of not tying Germany's hands since they emanated only from the party, not national, level.[5]

In the report's first section, in remarkably blunt language, the document warned that the Union risked becoming a 'group of loosely knit grouping of states restricted to certain economic aspects and composed of various sub-groupings'. Amongst the causes of instability in the Union mentioned were: the over-extension of the EU's institutions dealing with the demands of the Twelve members; the differentiation of interests due to different levels of socio-economic development; the differentiation of perceptions of internal and, 'above all, external priorities in a European Union stretching from the North Cape to Gibraltar'; the evolution of profound structural economic change; the growth of 'regressive nationalism'; the development of debilitating demands placed on national governments; and the emergence of questions of when and how the Central and East Europeans would be involved in the Union. The second section of the report outlined Germany's interests, as perceived by the CDU/CSU. These interests were based on the underlying fact that, 'Owing to its geographical location, its size and its history Germany has a special interest in preventing Europe from drifting apart'. If Europe were to drift apart, the document argued, 'Germany would once again find itself caught in the middle between East and West, a position which through its history has made it difficult for Germany to give a clear orientation to its internal order and to establish a stable and lasting balance in its external relations'. A reference to the 'military political and moral catastrophe of 1945' can also be viewed as a clear plea to EU colleagues to maintain the fundamentals of post-World War II European security.

The CDU/CSU unequivocally regarded its relations with France as comprising the 'hard core' of the Alliance. In accordance, *Reflections* suggested that 'no significant action in the foreign or EU policy fields should be taken without prior consultation between France and Germany'. In a stunningly direct message to Paris the report stated:

> If Germany puts forward clear and unequivocal proposals, then France must make equally clear and unequivocal decisions. It must rectify the impression that, although it allows no doubt as to its basic will to pursue European integration, it often hesitates taking concrete steps towards this objective – the notion of the unsurrenderable sovereignty of the 'Etat nation' still carries weight, although this sovereignty has long since become an empty shell.

The *Reflections'* use of the term 'hard core' of 'five or six countries' also left Britain in an ambiguous position. The document held open the hope that 'Great Britain will assume its role "in the heart of Europe" and thus in its core'.

On the CFSP, the report observed that, 'Action by the European Union in the field of [CFSP] must be based on a strategic concept which clearly defines common interests and objectives and stipulates the conditions and procedures as well as the political, economic and financial means'. The *Reflections* recommend giving priority to:

- The stabilisation of central and eastern Europe;
- The development of a wide-ranging partnership with Russia;
- The development of a common policy in the Mediterranean;
- The advancement of a strategic partnership with Turkey; and
- The reorientation of transatlantic relations.

In reference to the difficulties over Yugoslavia within the EU and with the US, the *Reflections* suggested that the 'creation of a common defence is a matter of much greater urgency than envisaged in the Maastricht Treaty'. Movement towards a common defence would, it was argued, mean reorganising relations between the EU and the WEU in accordance with Article J.4 (6) – in other words, the merging of the WEU and EU to the greatest extent possible. The recommendations also included realigning relations with NATO to allow the Europeans to 'take independent action using NATO resources and parts of the NATO staffs'.

The CDU/CSU *Reflections'* key problem was how to reconcile federalist versus national sovereignty issues in the particularly sensitive area of common defence. In grappling with this conundrum, the *Reflections* recognised that a 'nation's awareness of its sovereignty determined not only its self-perception but also its relations with other nations'. At the same time the *Reflections* realised that the 'common defence capability of this European community of states constitutes an indispensable factor in endowing the EU with an identity of its own, an identity which, however, at the same time leaves room for the sense of identity of each individual state'. Finally, with regard to enlargement of the EU towards the East, it urged that, 'Poland, the Czech and Slovak Republics, Hungary (and Slovenia) should become Members of the European Union around the year 2000'.

The second document, the WEU's *Contribution to the European Union Intergovernmental Conference of 1996*, was designed to encourage a structured debate on the question to what degree the WEU should be tied to the EU. The WEU Council of Ministers adopted the WEU's *Contribution* at its Madrid meeting on 14 November 1995. The conclusions to the document noted:

> Irrespective of the outcome of the institutional debate on European defence at the IGC, there is a broad consensus on the need to make

available the operational capabilities necessary for European military action, particularly in the field of the new tasks defined at Petersberg. The mostly organizational measures agreed to this end at Maastricht have still to be fully implemented and additional efforts are needed to deliver appropriate military assets and capabilities that are both effective and credible.

The document also noted the need to continue to strengthen ESDI and the Atlantic Alliance but more importantly, in view of the upcoming IGC, two options were foreseen regarding WEU–EU relations. The first choice favoured the preservation of the WEU as an autonomous organisation based on the belief that 'the principle of national sovereignty must continue to govern relations between European countries on defence matters, and that the intergovernmental nature of decision-making on defence matters must be preserved and this decision-making will be conducted on the basis of consensus'.[6] This option did not envisage extensive changes in the institutional or legal framework of the organisation. The maintenance of the current relationship between the EU and the WEU could provide the 'right framework'. The second option, encapsulating the 'majority view', also wanted to maximise the provisions bolstering the ESDI and to foster further collaboration between the WEU, EU and NATO. Unlike the first option, however, the second advocated the 'gradual integration' of the WEU into the EU with 'the purpose of achieving greater coherence than at present of European action in the security and defence field'.

Overall, the *WEU Contribution* made it clear that all were in favour of 'achieving greater coherence than at present of European action in the security and defence field'. Indeed, the principle of 'reinforced partnership' was designed to achieve this, but the question of how 'reinforced' or integrated the WEU should be with the EU was subject to differing opinions. The language employed in the TEU suggested that the positions of the WEU members became polarised between the options but that there was a common understanding that more needed to be done for Europe's security and defence.

Prior to the European Council's meeting in Amsterdam, the Heads of State and Government met in Dublin on 13–14 December 1996. The Irish Presidency prepared a revision of the TEU entitled *The European Union Today and Tomorrow*. Although an interesting document, the most controversial issues, such as voting rights and the role of the European Parliament, were avoided. On the issue of defence, the Presidency encouraged the inclusion of the Petersberg tasks, while on the role of the WEU the Presidency suggested that the EU's ability to 'request' the WEU for assistance should be replaced by the word 'avail'. Meanwhile, fractious Franco-German relations, prompted by a unilateral French defence review, were smoothed over by Kohl and the newly elected French President, Jacques Chirac, at the Franco-German Nuremberg summit of 9 December 1996, where their *Common Concept on Security and Defence* was unveiled. Volker Rühe's decision, in his capacity as Germany's Defence Minister, to publicly make clear that he was not informed of the details of Chirac's defence restructuring plans prior to its announcement was extraordinary given the 'overriding importance attached to the Franco-German relationship by Chancellor Kohl'.[7] If the restructuring of the French forces cast into doubt the intimacy of Franco-German defence relations, the French decision of the previous year to resume nuclear testing emphasised the differences between France and its other European allies.

Kohl's and Chirac's relations grew less cordial with both leaders' weakening of power. In France, Chirac's disastrously mis-timed call for early parliamentary elections witnessed the defeat of Alain Juppé's right-wing government and the election of Lionel Jospin's left-wing coalition. Jospin's election significantly impaired Chirac's ability to take any further initiatives. Within Germany, Kohl's position was weakened by the Bavarain Premier of the CSU, Edmund Stoiber – a well-known Eurosceptic who had been calling for the 'controlled delay' of EMU. Kohl's governing coalition depended upon the support of the Bavarian CSU. In order to keep the coalition together Kohl was forced to depart significantly from the *Reflections* document and the *Common Concept* and to adopt a strict line on EMU, which provoked the ire of Jospin.

In retrospect, the differences between France and Germany on the eve of the IGC had a twofold effect. First, it encouraged Germany to look to Britain and the US for support and, by so doing, induced Britain and others to play a more active role in shaping the second pillar of the Union. Second, although the weakening of the strong Franco-German engine inspired others to become more active, their increased activity came at the expense of formulating a CFSP that was likely to be innovative.

The 1996 IGC and the Consolidated Treaty on European Union (CTEU)

The second IGC commenced on 29 March 1996 with a European Council meeting in Turin and culminated in the 16–17 June 1997

Amsterdam summit. In the agenda prepared for the IGC by Westendorp's Reflection Group, the necessity of giving the EU 'greater capacity for external action' was one of three areas highlighted.[8] As if to stress the real-world importance of the Reflection Group's observation, Albania's rapid slide into chaos demanded a response from the EU. However, neither NATO nor the WEU responded immediately to the crisis. Instead, the OSCE proved to be the most helpful. It was Italy who eventually organised a Multinational Protection Force (a 'coalition of the willing') based on a 28 March 1997 UN Resolution advocating the 'safe and prompt delivery of humanitarian assistance' and the creation of a secure environment for those supplying such assistance.[9] It was not until 24 June that the WEU acted, providing a Multinational Advising Police Element (MAPE) confined initially to Tirana but then extended elsewhere. The lacklustre response by the EU to the Albanian crisis and the absence of any WEU role for almost three months, smacked of a missed opportunity. A decisive, concerted response could have instilled the IGC with the belief that it was actually creating a working European security mechanism, rather than finding new ways of being as unspecific as the previous IGC had been while Yugoslavia unravelled.

Aside from real-world considerations, Westerndorp's Reflection Group deliberations were muted by Britain's unequivocal position outlined during a press conference on 2 June by the Foreign Secretary, Robin Cook. He stated: 'We are anxious to make sure that Britain retains its veto over matters relating to foreign and security policy and it looks as if, on the basis of the current text, we have a real possibility that we will be able to achieve that negotiating goal at Amsterdam.' In a remark obviously aimed towards Washington, Cook added:

> We want to make it plain that the defence of Europe will remain through the North Atlantic Treaty Organisation, not through the European Union. For that reason we will be resisting a complete merger of the Western European Union with the European Union, and again I am hopeful that that is a negotiating objective we can secure at Amsterdam.[10]

Despite British intransigence it was generally recognised that to leave the treaty in its existing shape would be unsatisfactory.

The stormy passage of the CFSP through the IGC terminated with the Amsterdam Summit, the end of the Dutch Presidency and the signing of the *Treaty of Amsterdam amending the Treaty on European Union,*

the Treaties establishing the European Communities and certain related acts,
on 2 October 1997.[11] In the Consolidated Version of the Treaty on
European Union Title V, *which incorporates the Treaty of Amsterdam,*
the Provisions on the CFSP eventually appeared in Articles 11–29.[12]
Title V's title, *Provisions on a Common Foreign and Security Policy,* was
retained. For the sake of brevity, the Consolidated Version of the TEU
will be referred to as CTEU. (See Appendix 7.)

As in the TEU, the CTEU attempted to ensure that the external activities of the European Union, which are split between the first and second pillars (and to an extent the third) are consistent. Title I of the
CTEU, on 'Common Provisions', lays out the broad goals and objectives of the Union. The provisions include the stipulation that, 'The
Union shall be served by a single institutional framework which shall
ensure the consistency and the continuity of the activities carried out
in order to attain its objectives while respecting and building upon the
acquis communautaire.' Article 3 continues:

> The Union shall in particular ensure the consistency of its external
> activities as a whole in the context of its external relations, security,
> economic and development policies. The Council and the Com-
> mission shall be responsible for ensuring such consistency and shall
> cooperate to this end. They shall ensure the implementation of
> these policies, each in accordance with its respective powers.[13]

The idea of ensuring consistency or *'cohérence'* is one that logically
arose out of the incorporation of the EPC into the second pillar of the
Union.[14] Consistency in external activities is one that inevitably highlights the differences between the *communautaire* structures and procedures of the first pillar and the intergovernmental nature of the second
pillar. Article 3 of the CTEU also neglects to mention either foreign policy or defence specifically – contenting itself instead with the more
vague notions of 'external relations' and 'security'.

Overall, the most 'substantive amendments', to the CTEU's terminology were to the second and third pillars. The main changes or modifications to the TEU regarding CFSP are to be found in the following
areas:

- Redefinition of security and defence responsibilities;
- Institutional modifications;
- Voting procedures regarding unanimity and qualified majority vot-
  ing (QMV); and
- Relations with the WEU and other international organisations.

In order to assist the reader, new or modified text will be indicated in italics and, where appropriate, the original wording from the TEU will be included for comparative purposes (see also Appendix 6 and 7). The main aspects of the CTEU will be analysed according to the sub-headings suggested above.

Redefinition of security and defence responsibilities

The main objectives of the CFSP remained unchanged and were reproduced *verbatim* from the TEU. The broad aims of the CFSP, which the institutions aimed to achieve, also survived although they remained vague. The only addition, which is perhaps more a reflection on the slow progress of the CFSP than anything else, is that, *'Member States shall work together to enhance and develop their mutual political solidarity'*.

As has been noted here and in many other places, the wording of Article J 4.1 of the TEU was notoriously vague, stating that: 'The Common Foreign and Security Policy shall include all questions relating to the security of the Union, including the eventual framing of a common defence policy, which might in time lead to a common defence'.

The CTEU's attempt to specify how the CFSP should progress towards a CDP/CD encountered many of the same fundamental disagreements and reflected little specificity.[15] Article 17 of the CTEU reads:

> The Common Foreign and Security Policy shall include all questions relating to the security of the Union, including the *progressive* framing of a common defence policy, in accordance with the second subparagraph, which might lead to a common defence, *should the European Council so decide. It shall in that case recommend the adoption of such a decision in accordance with their respective constitutional requirements.*

Unlike the TEU, the CTEU was more specific about what 'questions' may be appropriate for the CFSP; these shall *'include humanitarian and rescue tasks, peace-keeping tasks and tasks of combat forces in crisis management, including peace-making'*.[16] The scope of the CFSP therefore reflected those undertakings outlined in the WEU's 1992 Petersberg Declaration (see Appendix 5). The CTEU though did not restrict the CFSP to these tasks; it merely *included* them – a qualification that is easy to miss. Aside from this, placing the onus on the European Council for progress towards a common defence, little practical difference was accomplished while the wording regarding 'constitutional require-ments' was the result of the sensitivities of not only Ireland but also those of Austria, Finland and Sweden, the latter three becoming mem-bers of the EU in 1995. As a further safeguard to possible constitutional clashes over agreements adopted through CFSP procedures, the CTEU clearly stated that: *'No agreement shall be binding on a Member State whose representative in the Council states that it has to comply with the requirements of its own constitutional procedure.'*[17]

Although the CTEU did not explicitly confine the CD to Petersberg tasks, the implication was that NATO would assume primary responsi-bility for collective defence. However, the reference to the Petersberg tasks and in particular 'peace-keeping' and 'peace-making', introduced an element of confusion. In June 1992 the UN Secretary General, Boutros Boutros-Ghali, outlined his *Agenda for Peace*. In it he foresaw many different variants of peace-keeping including peace-enforcement which was presented as a more muscular form of peace-keeping involv-ing, if need be, the use of force of the type employed in Somalia.[18] Since the CTEU did not explicitly mention 'peace-enforcement', the impli-cation was that the CD should mainly concentrate on non-military aspects of defence. This observation became all the more significant in light of the UN Security Council's post-Cold War willingness to sanc-tion intervention with broad mandates for those involved in peace-keeping operations.

Institutional modifications

One of the objections raised to the TEU and the CFSP was that it lacked a strong identity or persona. A suggested French solution to this was to appoint the equivalent of a Secretary-General or a *'Monsieur PESC'* (the French version of CFSP). The holder of this office would be a senior figure who would ensure the 'continuity, visibility and efficacy' of the Union's external actions and represent the Union in its negotia-tions with third countries. Those hoping for such an appointment were frustrated by the objection that such an office would detract from the intergovernmental nature of the CFSP process and the role of the Presidency. The later undignified spat between the Netherlands and France over who should head the Union's new central bank provides a cautionary tale with regard to appointing a *Monsieur/Madame PESC*. A compromise however was reached whereby the Presidency 'shall represent the Union in matters coming within the [CFSP]'[19] and shall be assisted by a 'high representative', who is the Secretary-General of the Council of Ministers.[20] The High Representative's duties are laid out in Article 26 of the CTEU. The announcement in June 1999 that Javier Solana, NATO's Secretary-General, had been nominated as the CFSP's first High Representative was greeted with general enthusiasm. Solana's appointment is all the more appropriate given the need to knit together CFSP and ESDI in a coherent manner.[21]

The operational and secretarial support for the new position is in the process of being developed. This development will assume increased importance as the High Representative assists in the implementation of *'common strategies'*, an idea which first appeared in the CTEU and which is designed to enable specific foreign policy actions to be taken by a majority vote, based on a unanimously agreed general strategy. The conclusions of the Cardiff Summit, ending the British Presidency in June 1998, saw fresh resolve to take the necessary decisions with regard to the appointment of the High Representative in the December Summit in Vienna, marking the end of the Austrian Presidency. The identity of the appointment and its political level can only be decided upon by the Member States themselves. Unfortunately, the question of defining the role of those services directly attributed to it, namely the Policy Planning and Early Warning Unit (PPEWU) have yet to be answered.[22] Ideally the PPEWU and the CFSP Unit of the Council Secretariat would work in close harmony. Most members would prefer that the PPEWU be a separate unit within the Directorate-General of the Council Secretariat responsible for external relations (thus separate but integrated within the Directorate-General). A minority though, alongside the Commission, would prefer the PPEWU to be autonomous within the General Secretariat, under the direct line and management of the High Representative.[23] Although the respective powers of the High Representative, the PPEWU, the Council and the Presidency are all defined in the CTEU, the relations between the constituents are ill-defined.

The Council's role remained largely unchanged in the CTEU (with the significant exception of alterations in voting rules addressed separately below). Three slight modifications were however made on the new position of High Representative and the Council. The TEU's Article 151.2 was replaced with the following: *'The Council shall be assisted by a General Secretariat, under the responsibility of a Secretary-General seconded by a Deputy Secretary-General who shall be responsible for the running of the General Secretariat. The Secretary-General and the Deputy Secretary-General shall be appointed by the Council acting unanimously.'*

A further retooling of the Council's role stated that it may *'request the Commission to submit to it any appropriate proposals'* relating to the CFSP to *'ensure the implementation of a joint action'.*[24] The Council also may, *'whenever it deems it necessary, appoint a special representative with a mandate in relation to particular policy issues'.*[25]

The role of the European Parliament remained unchanged with the verbatim reproduction of the TEU's Article J.7 as the CTEU's Article 21. The fact that there was absolutely no change in the role of the European Parliament vis-à-vis the CFSP indicated a willingness on the part of the Member States to retain as much executive control as possible. It is though worth noting that the CTEU's provisions on the financing of CFSP activities may give the European Parliament increased oversight since CFSP activities charged to the budget of the Communities are subject to the scrutiny and oversight of the parliament. Generally, 'administrative' expenditure and some forms of 'operational' expenditure (the terms are not defined and thus remain vague) may be charged to the budget of the Communities with the notable exception of operations having military or defence implications (see below).

A number of declarations were also adopted by the IGC in June 1997. These statements were designed to enhance the efficiency of the CFSP and to meet some of the criticisms voiced in the Committee of Experts' report. A WEU declaration on its role and relations with the EU and NATO included a reference to the establishment of PPEWU in the General-Secretariat of the Council under the responsibility of the Secretary-General. The unit is to be comprised of personnel drawn from the General Secretariat, the Member States, the Commission and the WEU. The responsibilities of the new unit should include:

- Monitoring and analysing developments in areas relevant to the CFSP;
- Providing assessment of the Union's foreign and security policy interests and identifying areas where the CFSP should focus in future;
- Providing timely assessments and early warning of events or situations which may have significant repercussions for the Union's CFSP, including potential political crises; and
- Producing, at the request of either the Council or the Presidency or on its own initiative, argued policy papers to be presented under the responsibility of the Presidency as a contribution to policy formulation in the Council, and which may contain analyses, recommendations and strategies for the CFSP.

The precise composition of the unit remains unclear following the rejection of proposals forwarded by Jürgen Trumpf, Secretary General of the Council of Ministers. According to one report: 'Paris wanted the unit to go considerably further than Trumpf's paper indicated, while other countries claimed it went too far.'[26] The issues to be decided, as mentioned above, include its composition, its rules of operation, its relations with the Council Secretariat and to whom it reports. The procedure for the adoption of answers to these issues is also unclear – should majority or consensus take them?

Schematically the CFSP's decision-making structure, as outlined in the CTEU, could be represented as follows:

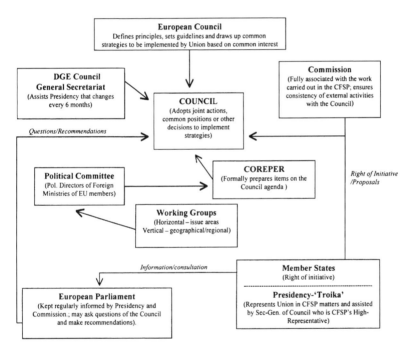

Figure 4.1   Decision-making in the EU's Second Pillar (CFSP).

Voting procedures regarding unanimity versus Qualified Majority Voting (QMV)

The question of QMV was one of the most politically sensitive since it went right to the fundamental query of the extent of the CFSP's supranational or intergovernmental nature. The concerns with the existing stipulations on QMV, laid out in Article J.13 of the TEU, centered on the vagaries of how the Council, 'when adopting a joint action and at any stage in its development', shall define 'those matters on which decisions are to be taken by a qualified majority'. The TEU was also unclear about the scope of QMV while the accession of new members and German unification called for a revision of the weighted voting procedures.

Underlying the IGC's debates on QMV was the tension between protecting vital national interests, by observing the unanimity principle, and avoiding the paralysis of the CFSP, by constant use of the veto. The CTEU upheld the unanimity principle as the general rule but in a new article it also specified that the Council shall act by qualified majority only when:[27]

- Adopting joint actions, common positions or taking any other decisions on the basis of a common strategy; and
- Adopting any decision implementing a joint action or a common position.

Qualified majority votes shall *not* however apply to decisions having military or defence implications. When the European Council establishes the principles and guidelines of the EU's external policies, it is then up to the Council of Ministers to decide *unanimously* upon the measures needed to implement the guidelines, with the exception of those mentioned above, which may be adopted by a qualified majority. Further safeguards were designed. First, the votes within the Council are to be weighted, which means in practical terms a decision must have an affirmative of 62 votes, cast by at least ten members, except when the vote is on a proposal from the Commission, in which case there must be simply 62 votes in favour.[28] However, if a member of the Council declares that, *'for important and stated reasons of national policy, it intends to oppose the adoption of a decision to be taken by qualified majority, a vote shall not be taken. The Council may, acting by a qualified majority, request that the matter be referred to the European Council for decision by unanimity'*. Second, in order to avoid the CFSP being paralysed by the need for unanimity, increased flexibility was built into the CTEU whereby an abstaining Member State *'shall not be obliged to apply the decision, but shall accept that the decision commits the Union'*, and *'the Member State concerned shall refrain from any action likely to conflict with or impede the Union based on that decision and the other Member States shall respect its position'*. If however the amount of abstentions numbers more than a third of the weighted votes, the decision shall not be adopted. These provisions give considerable political leverage to the five neutral or non-aligned states who, with the backing of a major power, may well be able to not only disassociate themselves from CFSP decisions but overturn them as well.

The CTEU would appear, at least on paper, to have found a means to combine the unanimity principle with what soon became known as 'constructive abstention'. This flexible approach seems sensible given that the need for unanimity in all cases is unlikely to be obtained. By clarifying the QMV procedures however the treaty introduced a system of (potential) multiple votes, which in some cases might override the benefits of QMV. For instance, if a member opposes the adoption of a decision to be taken by QMV, the possibility then exists for the Council, operating by QMV, to request referral of the matter to the European Council for decision by unanimity! The procedure may open up the possibility of multiple vetoes at three or four stages of the pro-ceedings and a positive outcome is still likely at some stage to rest upon unanimity.

Relations with the WEU and other international organisations

The question of the extent to which the WEU should be integrated within the Union was the subject of fierce debate. Britain and the four neutrals or non-aligned members (Austria, Finland, Ireland and Sweden) were adamantly opposed to full integration of the WEU with the EU. Britain wished to protect NATO's position as Europe's central defence organisation while the others objected to the possibility that the move would militarise the EU. For their part, Belgium, France, Germany, Italy, Luxembourg and Spain proposed a protocol that set out a timetable for the full integration of the WEU within the EU. In spite of clear differences regarding the extent of association between the WEU and the EU, the wording pertaining to the WEU in the CTEU changed significantly and reflected a stronger association between the WEU and EU. The European Council was also given new competency with regard to the possible integration of the WEU into the EU:

The Western European Union (WEU) is an integral part of the devel-opment of the Union *providing the Union with access to an operational capability notably in the context of [Petersberg Tasks]. It supports the Union in framing the defence aspects of the common foreign and security policy as set out in this article. The Union shall accordingly foster closer institutional relations with the WEU with a view to the possibility of inte-gration of the WEU into the Union, should the European Council so decide. It shall in that case recommend to the Member States the adoption of such a decision in accordance with their respective constitutional requirements.*[29]

The reservations of the neutral and non-aligned Member States as well as those of the Atlanticists were addressed in the same article with the following statement:

> The policy of the Union in accordance with this Article shall not prejudice the specific character of the security and defence policy of certain Member States and shall respect the obligations of certain Member States, *which see their common defence realised in NATO*, under the North Atlantic Treaty and be compatible with the common security and defence policy established within that framework.[30]

The onus therefore appears to once again be placed on the European Council to set the pace, or the brake, on integration of the WEU into the EU. In a potentially interesting development, it also appears to be up to the Member States themselves, based on their constitutional stipulations, to decide on whether to adopt a recommendation from the European Council in favour of integration. This presumably allows certain states, such as the neutral or non-aligned ones, to opt out. But it also exacerbates the problems of differing membership in institutions and overlapping tasks of the pillars of the Union.

In a further highly significant clause modifying Article 223 of the TEU, Article 17.1 of the CTEU states that: '*The progressive framing of a common defence policy will be supported, as Member States consider appropriate, by cooperation between them in the field of armaments.*'

Although the extent to which co-operation occurs is very much up to the individual Member States, there is nevertheless the implicit recognition that the construction of a CDP/CD will not only be difficult but divisive unless some thought is given to collaborative armaments development and procurement. A slightly cynical interpretation of this clause is that it was inserted not so much as an underpinning for a CDP but as a reaction to a series of mergers in the American defence industry.

Turning to EU–WEU relations, in somewhat elliptical wording, the CTEU states that the EU will '*avail itself of the WEU* to elaborate and implement decisions and actions of the Union which have defence implications'.[31] The difference between the somewhat awkward word 'avail' and the words, 'may request', which appear in the TEU, implies a subtle shift in the relations between the two organisations. If the EU does avail itself of the WEU, the European Council shall '*establish guidelines'* and thereafter *'all Member States of the Union shall be entitled to participate fully in the tasks in question. The Council, in agreement with the institutions of the WEU, shall adopt the necessary practical arrange-ments to allow all Member States contributing to the tasks in question to participate fully and on an equal footing in planning and decision-taking in the WEU.'*[32]

The above text apparently allows the five non-WEU states in the EU to associate fully with the WEU (see p. 273, Figure 7.2). Since they are for the most part neutral or non-aligned states and the tasks they are likely to be involved in are Petersberg-type ones, 'association' allows them to participate without the political costs of full membership of the WEU. However, such a status might create problems in terms of whether a non WEU member could 'participate fully' and on an 'equal footing' without representation or even voting rights in an organisation of which it is not a member. Further objections to those 'contributing to the tasks in ques-tion' being guaranteed an equal footing may be voiced by the major powers who are likely in most cases to be contributing (and risking) more. Although it is not touched upon in the Treaty, it is also worth conjecturing about what would happen in the event that a WEU–CJTF operation was launched. Presumably the guarantees advanced to Member States would be a disincentive for non-members to participate.

More generally, it was agreed that the WEU and EU should, within a year of the IGC, draw up arrangements for enhanced co-operation. The provisions of Article 17.3 of the CTEU were noted by the WEU as was the need to develop a role for observer members, so that they may participate 'fully and on an equal footing' in planning and decision-making in the WEU. In its relations with the EU, the WEU adopted (not for the first time) a number of measures designed to lead to enhanced collaboration, such as improving consultation and decision-making processes, holding joint meetings, harmonising the sequence of Presidencies of the WEU and EU, and emphasising close co-ordination between the staff of the Secretariat-General of the WEU and the General Secretariat of the Council of the EU.

The IGC also noted the existence of a declaration adopted by the Council of Ministers of the WEU on 22 July 1997.[33] The declaration reaffirmed the importance of strengthening efforts towards the cre-ation of a genuine ESDI and reminded the EU that the WEU was 'an integral part of the development of the EU providing the Union with access to an operational capability' (a phrase which appeared verbatim in the CTEU) and that it also was an 'essential element of the develop-ment of the ESDI within the Atlantic Alliance'. In the context of the

WEU's role in developing an ESDI within the Alliance, it was acknowledged that the Alliance 'continues to be *the basis of collective defence under the North Atlantic Treaty*' and that, 'It remains the essential forum for consultation among Allies and the framework in which they agree on policies bearing on their security and defence commitments under the Washington Treaty'.[34] For its part, the WEU was portrayed as 'an essential element of the development of the European Security and Defence Identity within the Atlantic Alliance'. Enhanced co-operation between the WEU and NATO would, according to the declaration, be augmented by:

- Crisis consultation mechanisms;
- The WEU's active involvement in the NATO defence planning process;
- Operational links between the WEU and NATO for the planning, preparation and conduct of operations using NATO assets and capabilities under the political control and strategic direction of the WEU;
- Military planning and exercises conducted by NATO in co-ordination with the WEU;
- Agreement on the transfer, monitoring and return of NATO assets and capabilities; and
- Liaison between the WEU and NATO in the context of European command arrangements.

In its ESDI guise, the WEU would 'develop its role as the European politico-military body for crisis management'. But amongst the many facets which require further attention are the 'definition of principles on the use of armed forces of the WEU States for WEU Petersberg operations'; the 'organisation of operational means for Petersberg tasks'; 'strategic mobility' and 'defence intelligence'.[35]

In the CFSP's relations with the UN, special responsibility (and trust) was accorded to France and Britain who, as UN Security Council members, should ensure that 'in the execution of their functions [they] will ensure the defence of the positions and interests of the Union, without prejudice to their responsibilities under the provisions of the United Nations Charter'.[36] This point, originally made in Article J 2.3 of the TEU with somewhat looser wording, has become increasingly important given the considerable number of UN-mandated operations involving contributions by EU Member States. The obligation to ensure the defence of the interests of the Union extends implicitly to the possible exercise of the veto. Although there are few recent instances of Anglo-French differences on the use of the veto in the Security Council, there is nevertheless the possibility that differences will arise between the two countries. For example, differences might arise over the question of lending support to US operations. This is especially the case in the Middle East where significant differences of opinion exist between the EU and Britain.

Budgetary questions

Progress was also made towards addressing the budgetary arrangements for the CFSP and those activities with defence implications. Under an Institutional Agreement signed, on 16 July 1997, between the Commission and the Council on the financing of the CFSP, it was agreed that operational expenditure should be charged to the budget of the European Communities but that the costs of military action should be borne by the Member States themselves. Under the agreement, which appeared in the *Draft* Treaty of Amsterdam, the total amount of CFSP expenditure 'shall be entirely entered in one (CFSP) budget chapter'.

The European Parliament and the Council annually secure agreement on the amount of the operational CFSP expenditure to be charged to the Communities' budget as well as the allocation of the total amount to the CFSP budget. In the absence of agreement, the amount designated for the previous fiscal year shall be allocated, unless the Commission lowers it. The amount allocated to the CFSP budget shall 'cover the real predictable needs and a reasonable margin for unforeseen actions'.[37] It was suggested that within the budget the estimated expenses could be entered under the following headings:

- Observation and organisation of elections/participation in democratic transition processes;
- EU envoys;
- Prevention of conflicts/peace and security processes;
- Financial assistance to the disarmament process;
- Contributions to international conferences; and
- Urgent actions.

The European Parliament, the Council and the Commission agreed that the amounts for the actions entered under the 'urgent actions' sub-heading cannot exceed 20 per cent of the global amount of the CFSP budget. Broadly speaking, the general terms of reference suggested in the Interinstitutional Agreement were applied in the CTEU.

The agreement is of interest not only because of the budgetary aspects of the CFSP, but also because it is an indication of the Commission's and the Council's perception of the parameters of the CFSP.

As with the TEU (Article J.11), administrative expenditure would be charged to the budget of the European Communities as would 'operational expenditure...except for such expenditure arising from operations having military or defence implications, and cases where the Council acting unanimously decides otherwise'.[38] Again, subject to the Council's unanimous decision, in those cases where expenditure is not charged to the European Communities, it shall be charged to the Member States on a weighted GNP scale. Expenditure arising from activities having military or defence implications will not be assessed for those states who make a formal declaration of non-participation and thus are not obliged to contribute.[39]

In general, the budgetary question remained contentious since a certain amount of ambiguity still exists about what constitutes 'administrative' or 'operational' expenses. Indeed, the budgetary procedures in the CTEU did not remove David Allen's 'horns of a dilemma':

> Anxious to preserve their independence and to give both the European Parliament and the Commission as little control of their CFSP activities as possible, the member states have a principled interest in paying for the CFSP themselves. However most diplomatic services have a natural resistance to multilateral calls on their often tightly restricted budgets and so have a pragmatic interest in 'losing' such expenditure in the overall Community budget.[40]

Implications of the Amsterdam treaty

The implications fall under three headings: those for the EU as an actor on the international scene; those for the WEU and NATO; and those for aspirant members of the EU.

As an actor on the international stage

The introduction of the role of 'High Representative' could both provide a more coherent voice for Europe and could introduce the idea of a spokesperson for the EU on CFSP issues, especially in crisis management, which it hitherto lacked. The EU's response to the successive crises in the Balkans has been *ad hoc* and piecemeal. The formation of the American-led 'Contact Group' on former Yugoslavia in 1994 signalled the EU's failure to act coherently and pointed to the need for a more cohesive European identity. It also highlighted the need for a response to Kissinger's famous question, 'Who do you call when you want to call Europe?' The move towards monetary union, pushed forward at Amsterdam, may also have significant knock-on effects for CFSP. The appointment of the High Representative might however pose some awkward questions for the international representation of the EU. For instance, would it be tenable for Britain and France to continue to retain their permanent seats on the UN Security Council, once a High Representative assumed his or her role? Or, would the demands for a permanent 'European' seat, as opposed to the British and French seats, on the Security Council, and maybe elsewhere, increase?

The potential for the Amsterdam mechanisms to develop into a European voice is present, but whether the Member States are willing to give the High Representative, the PPEWU and the complementary WEU mechanisms the resources and backing that may be required to make Europe an effective security and defence actor, remains an open question. The potential for a more co-ordinated response to global issues will also require an adjustment on the part of other major international actors, particularly the US, who may actually have a preference for dealing with particular EU member on a given issue. In security terms, the largest challenge to a coherent international voice is the continued preference for the EU members, especially the larger ones, to prefer *ad hoc* mechanisms, coalitions of the willing and select groups (such as the Contact Group on Bosnia).

The Effects on the WEU and NATO

The intention, at least in the Maastricht design, was to make the WEU an 'integral' part of the Union with responsibility for those aspects of the EU's work with defence implications. A good deal was done in the 1996 IGC to address the thorny problems of what are 'security implications' (and thus in the purview of the EU) and what are 'defence' related matters (in the competence of the WEU). But, without formal incorporation, the role of the WEU *vis-à-vis* the EU remains problematic. The possibility of the WEU using 'separable but not separate' NATO resources for CJTF-type operations may give the WEU some life, if only because it is an especially useful way for France to engage in quasi-Alliance operations without conceding full membership. The WEU will remain on the sidelines until there is the possibility of addressing the objections of those who most vehemently oppose its incorporation into the EU. The principle objections came from Britain, Austria, Finland, Ireland and Sweden – for differing but apparent reasons.

Perhaps one of the more unfortunate side effects of the CTEU will be to reinforce the division of European security into collective defence responsibilities falling to NATO, and Petersberg-type tasks falling to the WEU/EU. Although the treaty does not limit the purview of the CFSP to Petersberg tasks (it merely *includes* them) a tacit division of security responsibilities nevertheless emerged. The traditional tendency to give priority to national and collective defence commitments and to view other 'soft' or new security challenges as less compelling, may well hamper the development of the WEU. Even if the logic of the CTEU eventually directs the WEU towards full integration with the EU, there will be little practical difference. The reliance of the WEU upon NATO assets and, in particular US assets, will be a far more influential factor in the future of the WEU and EU.

Effects on the aspirant EU/WEU members

One of NATO's perennial concerns has been with the possibility of a 'back door' into the organisation being opened by EU–WEU membership. It does not require a vast stretch of the imagination to think of the potential awkwardness for EU–Russian relations if for instance, Estonia, became involved in a PfP or CJTF operation through its EU–WEU membership. Such a case would not only open up the obvious political concerns regarding Russian reactions but it may also compromise the non-aligned status of the other countries around the Baltic Sea. The loose association of the WEU and the EU therefore alleviates some of these 'backdoor' concerns. However, the loose association is not popular amongst the potential first round EU enlargement candidates, some of whom were not included in the first round of eastward NATO expansion. The security limbo, into which many of these states fall, further emphasises the lack of parallel process that now typifies European integration.

The obligation of the WEU to elaborate and implement decisions of the Union that deal with defence coupled with the joint obligation, shared with the Council, to allow Member States contributing to the tasks in question to 'participate fully' and 'on an equal footing' may also pose severe headaches. The 'equal footing' stipulations may have an unpredictable effect on applications to the WEU for observer or associate status with several possible outcomes. First, it will lead those who bear the major responsibilities and risks to operate outside the organisation's framework since the 'equal footing' applies to 'planning and decision taking' and not responsibility sharing. Second, it may lead to highly restrictive membership criteria for aspirant members. Third, the problems of asymmetrical EU/WEU membership may lead to sensitivities in particular circumstances, such as when the decision to 'avail' (or not to avail) is made by a non-WEU member.

None of these points are designed to imply that the EU will be any less attractive to aspirant members than before. Primary 'security' benefits arise not only from anticipated economic benefits or from mere association with the EU. As most of the EU's members are also NATO members, aspiring members could associate EU membership with proximate security benefits. Even if formal defence or security commitments do not accompany EU membership, it would be difficult for an EU member to stand by idly while the security of a fellow member was undermined. Membership of one organisation will inevitably lead to intense pressure to join the others, just as the assumption made in the Czech Republic, Hungary and Poland was that their alignment with the 'West' would not halt with NATO but would be part of a wider affiliation with other organisations such as the EU.

EU expansion and its security implications: agenda 2000

Ten central and east European countries expressed open interest in joining the EU. As a result, the Commission recommended on 16 July 1997 that preliminary negotiations should start with five (the Czech Republic, Estonia, Hungary, Poland and Slovenia) the following year in addition to the negotiations that were already underway with Cyprus. Following a change of government in Malta, its application for membership was retabled, bringing the number of potential accession members to seven. The remaining candidates – Bulgaria, Latvia, Lithuania, Romania, Slovakia and Turkey – must wait.[41] The criteria against which all applications will be measured were established at the EU Summit in Copenhagen in 1993. The criteria include:[42]

- Stable institutions that can guarantee democracy and the rule of law;
- Respect for human rights including respect for and protection of minorities;
- A functioning market economy and the ability to cope with competitive pressure and market forces within the Union; and
- The ability to accept the obligations of membership, including the aims of political, economic and monetary union.

Agenda 2000, released by the Commission on 15 July 1997, addressed the future of the EU in three sections. In terms of external policy, *Agenda 2000* calls for the Union to 'step up its activities in the external relations field'.[43] The enlargement of the Union, it was recognised, 'will affect not only the destiny of the Europeans, the Member States and the applicant countries. Through its international implications, enlargement will have an impact far beyond the new frontiers of an enlarged Europe because it will increase Europe's weight in the world, give Europe new neighbours and form Europe into an area of unity and stability'.[44] This is an especially important feature of a Union with common borders with the Ukraine, Belarus and Moldova and direct access to the Black Sea. Also of concern are the relations with ethnic Russians both within aspirant EU member states (such as Estonia) and those in contiguous countries, including the Kaliningrad *oblast*. At the same time, cooperation must be enhanced with the Mediterranean countries (through the Barcelona process), the Middle East, Asia, Latin America (including MERCOSUR) and the US (through the New Transatlantic Agenda).

More directly, on the CFSP, *Agenda 2000* argues that 'It is in the interests of the European Union to exercise political responsibility commensurate with its economic power'.[45] The report recommends accomplishing this through an 'integrated approach to external relations' making it possible to 'support a common political will with the instruments of the CFSP, those of commercial policy, development aid, or other common policies and the operational capacity of the Western European Union to carry out tasks recently included in the Treaty'.[46] Part of the 'operational capacity' will require the EU to

> acquire the capacity to take foreign-policy decisions involving the use of military resources. This is essential if the Union's external action is to be credible. It will therefore be necessary to strengthen the operational resources of the WEU, both in order to carry out the new tasks laid down in the Treaty of Amsterdam and with a view to the WEU becoming increasingly integrated in the development of the European Union itself.[47]

In Part II of the report, which included an analysis of the external dimensions of enlargement, it was noted that enlargement will 'modify the Union's geopolitical situation and its proximity to critical zones in Eastern and South-eastern Europe'.[48] With the accession of the new members may come a variety of new, but by no means unique, problems. Concerning these potential difficulties, *Agenda 2000* notes:

> Bilateral disputes involving acceding members, and the issues related to national and ethnic minorities, could burden the Union's cohesion and its CFSP, and would have to be effectively tackled before accession. Exacerbation of such problems could pose security threats to the Union independently of enlargement. The process of enlargement should provide an opportunity to address and find positive solutions to issues vital to pan-European security ... An enlarged EU will be substantially more heterogeneous in its foreign and security interests and perceptions. Definition of common interests and other CFSP decisions may thus prove more difficult. On the other hand, acceding countries should have no major problem in adopting the EU acquis in this field, while most of them would favour its development.[49]

As part of the stabilisation and democratisation process prior to application, the new members made concerted efforts to address problems relating to national and ethnic minorities. The 1994 Stability Pact's encouragement to the CEEC to address minority and border disputes as a precondition for membership led to agreements on minorities between Hungary and Romania, and Hungary and Slovakia, and Germany and the Czech Republic on the Sudeten question. However, the CEECs saw the security ramifications of EU membership as stemming from a mixture of economic, political and security factors. This was specifically recognised in a publication produced by the European Integration Studies Centre in Vilnius, Lithuania, but applies with equal force to any potential member:

> The West sees the expansion of the EU as the 'zone of peace and welfare' as 'a single security area,' i.e. not according to the rationale of the balance of power but according to the rationale of the expansion of the security community. That is why the European Union is displaying in one way or another its concern with the security policy of its future member states, even setting certain preconditions and making attempts to safeguard itself against the harm that the EU expansion might cause to the existing security community. A vivid example of the EU's concern with the security policy of the CEECs is the European Stability Pact.[50]

Still many problems remain unresolved. Tensions still exist between Hungary and Slovakia regarding minority and language rights while the problems associated with Estonia's sizeable Russian minority may be a potential catalyst for Russian intervention or at least pressure. It is by no means clear that membership of the EU itself might not be the indirect cause of enhanced cross-border tensions. Suppose, for instance, an appreciable widening of living standards were to develop between Hungarians and ethnic Hungarians in Slovakia, Romania or the Ukraine. Hungarian membership of the EU, which will presumably include compliance with the Schergen Agreement, may lead to the resurfacing of questions about the two million ethnic Hungarians living in Transylvania.

The question of how the 'autonomous process' of enlargement between the EU and NATO will contribute to European security is also discussed. *Agenda 2000* noted that there were significant links in the enlargement processes, especially the establishment of an ESDI within the Alliance following the NATO ministerial meeting in Berlin in June 1996. Nevertheless, the decision by the North Atlantic Council in Madrid in July 1997 (see below) to begin negotiations on the accession of three new members and the invitation by the EU to five new members (plus Cyprus and Malta) means that 'the issues of congruence in membership of the EU, Western European Union (WEU), and NATO remains an open and delicate question, the outcome of which may also affect the objective of integrating the WEU into the EU'.[51]

The distinct process – NATO expansion

A document issued by the EU Commission's Directorate General 1-A pointed out that the respective enlargements of the EU and NATO are 'distinct processes' and that there was 'no direct link between them, but both should contribute to the peace and stability in Europe and pose no threat to third countries'.[52] NATO's earlier September 1995 *Study on NATO Enlargement* stated that extension of the Alliance was designed to, 'complement the enlargement of the European Union, *a parallel process* which also, for its part, contributes significantly to extending security and stability to the new democracies in the East'.[53] The EU's *Agenda 2000*, as noted, preferred to describe enlargement as an 'autonomous process'.[54] The North Atlantic Council's Madrid Summit, of 8–9 July 1997, resulted in a declaration with the broad aim of reinforcing 'peace and stability in the Euro-Atlantic area'.[55] (See Appendix 8) As with other NATO summits convened since the adoption of the New Strategic Concept in 1991, the Madrid Summit's communiqué carried the reminder that NATO 'will remain the essential forum for consultation among its members and the venue for agreement on policies bearing on the security and defence commitments of Allies under the Washington Treaty'.[56]

Of the twelve countries aspiring to Alliance membership, three were invited to begin accession talks (the Czech Republic, Hungary and Poland) with the objective of signing the Protocol of Accession at the December 1997 Ministerial meeting and to see the ratification process completed by the 50th anniversary of the Washington Treaty in April 1999. For those states who were not invited to pursue membership, the Alliance reconfirmed that joining the Alliance remained open under Article 10 of the Washington Treaty and that the 'Alliance expects to extend further invitations in coming years to nations willing and able to assume the responsibilities and obligations of membership'.[57] In an effort towards this end, the Alliance encouraged an 'intensified dialogue' with the aspirant countries through the Euro-Atlantic Partnership Council (the successor to NACC and PfP).

NAC paid special attention to the Mediterranean region, arguing that 'security in the whole of Europe is closely linked with the security and stability in the Mediterranean'.[58] In recognition of its importance, the Madrid summit established a Mediterranean Co-operation Group (MCG) with responsibility for a Mediterranean dialogue. The MCG was charged to meet 'in principle' at the level of Political Advisers from national delegations with, if necessary, representatives from capitals.[59] As an important boost to enhancing the security of the region, Spain announced at the summit its willingness to participate fully in the Alliance's new command structure (once it was fully formulated).[60]

Frequent references were also made in the Council's Madrid Declaration to the development of ESDI within the Alliance. Although little had changed, it is worth reviewing the language used:

[The North Atlantic Council] endorses the decision taken with regard to European command arrangements within NATO to prepare, support, command and conduct WEU-led operations using NATO assets and capabilities (including provisional terms of reference for Deputy SACEUR covering ESDI-related responsibilities both permanent and during crises and operations), the arrangements for the identification of NATO assets and capabilities that could support WEU-led operations, and arrangements for NATO–WEU consultation in the context of such operations … We note with satisfaction that the building of ESDI within the Alliance has much benefited from the recent agreement in the WEU on the participation of all

European allies, if they were so to choose, in WEU-led operations using NATO assets and capabilities, as well as in planning and preparing for such operations.[61]

In general, the summit was hailed as an historical event since, as President Clinton proclaimed, it 'erased an artificial line drawn across Europe by Stalin after the Second World War'.[62] Still, were its achievements really that momentous?

President Clinton pre-empted his alliance partners by stating on 12 June 1997, prior to the NATO Council's historic summit, that the 'United States will support inviting three countries – the Czech Republic, Hungary and Poland – to begin accession talks to join NATO when we meet in Madrid next month'.[63] A group of nine, headed by France, had lobbied hard to admit Romania and Slovenia into the first wave, based on the argument that 'enlargement into the Balkans should balance that into Eastern Europe'.[64] Opposing the group of nine were Britain, Denmark, Iceland and Norway, all of whom supported Clinton's position, based on the argument that three new members would be cheaper, would pass though the national legislatures with more ease (especially the US Senate) and would leave some strong candidates for a second round of enlargement. On paper, Slovenia and Romania appear to have had a creditable claim to a position in the first round of enlargement but the debate was ended by the abrupt American *fiat*.

Clinton's endorsement of enlargement prior to the Madrid Summit was consistent with his administration's policy going back at least three years when, in 1994, Clinton announced that the issue was not whether NATO would take on new members but 'when and how'. The official position was most coherently elaborated upon in the February 1997 *Report to Congress on NATO Enlargement*, prepared primarily by the Department of Defense. Several points of relevance to the ESDI arise from the report. The first is that because the US already had 'the world's pre-eminent deployment capability, and substantial forces forward deployed in Europe, there will be no need for additional US forces'.[65] The extension of security guarantees eastward, in the physical sense, would be provided by existing US forces with 'improved capabilities to operate beyond their borders' provided by existing European NATO members and the 'Central European states, including likely new members'.[66] Although there were undoubtedly important contributions made to the expansion debate by European diplomats, bureaucrats and thinkers, the timetable and contents were determined from across the Atlantic.

Second, in an interesting assessment of the Clinton administration's drive for NATO expansion, Jonathan Dean reflected upon two mistaken underlying assumptions. The first is that of historicism, or the belief that general historical trends somehow become laws of historical inevitability, reflected in particular in the post-Cold War perspectives of Russia's and Germany's roles in the international system. Dean commented that, 'Administration analysis has made a wholly pessimistic analysis of the future of Russia (and of Germany as well) and had decided that Eastern Europe must be saved from possible aggression by Western action while there was still time. As the reference to Weimar revealed, NATO enlargement was for them a mental recreation of the struggle with Hitler – moved eastward.'[67] The second mistaken reason for the Clinton administration's drive toward expansion was, according to Dean, 'its conviction that doing so would preserve NATO's (and consequently the United State's) key role in Europe while allowing the United States to avoid intervention in Bosnia'.[68] Following this logic, expansion therefore provided a *raison d'être* for NATO while, hopefully, allowing the Clinton administration to remain aloof from intervention in the former Yugoslavia, or as Dean put it, 'enlargement was undertaken as a kind of bureaucratic surrogate for NATO involvement in Bosnia'.[69] Having committed itself to the expansion process for the above reasons, accompanied by strong partisan considerations, the European NATO allies had little choice but to follow. The only significant differences to be addressed at Madrid were how many should join and when those who could not start accession negotiations in the first round could expect to do so.

In a speech given by NATO Secretary-General, Javier Solana, at the Summit on 8 July 1997, the door was held open for a second round of enlargement with strong hints that Romania and Slovenia were strong contenders for membership in 1999.[70] The reasons for the admittance of the Czech Republic, Hungary and Poland, and not others is less than transparent. Moreover, it is not based solely on considerations about the security of the region *per se*, but appears to be a politically face-saving device allowing NATO to expand and thus prove its utility at a time when there were many internal questions about its mission. Any expansion also had to be minimally acceptable to Russia. Thus expansion of membership to the Baltic States in a second wave, or subsequent wave, would be deeply problematic in the likelihood of Moscow's fierce opposition. Despite this, US Secretary of State, Madeleine Albright, reiterated that NATO is 'open to all democratic market systems in Europe, which includes the Baltic states'.[71] For their part the

Baltic states remain hopeful. In response to the announcement of the new NATO members, Estonia's President, Lennart Meri, commented that the Baltic states were a 'litmus test for European security', and that 'it is fair to say that the Cold War will only finally be over when the Baltic countries have assumed their place behind the NATO Council table'.[72] However, the Baltic States' neighbours are not likely to endorse their membership. Although many Americans supported membership, encouraged by vocal ex-patriot groups, most non-Nordic Europeans, 'worried about how to defend them and reluctant to annoy Russia', do not.[73] On the eve of the conclusion of an Individual Partnership Programme with NATO, a representative of President Alexander Lukashenko of Belarus commented that 'from an historical perspective the decision to expand NATO eastward has no solid grounds and is a faulty one' and later in the speech added 'Belarus, as a land-locked country, is far from being indifferent to the situation in the Baltic region'.[74]

The ability of NATO itself to cope with the additional bureaucratic demands of not only the three new members, but the routine Ukrainian and Russian multi-level consultations and the enhanced NACC dialogue in the form of the new 28 member Euro Atlantic Partnership Council (EAPC), must also be questioned. The number of high-level meetings in the Alliance has doubled in the last three years. The additional demands have led to calls from Solana for 'urgent reforms to streamline deliberations so that future sessions are not paralyzed'.[75] Additional unforeseen knock-on effects, with particular regard to confidentiality and command structures are quite possible. The NATO-led operations in Bosnia, involving 25 countries, suggest that the military ramifications of enlargement may not be as problematic as the civilian adjustments.

The special role of Russia and the Ukraine

Underlying NATO's self-proclaimed process of 'historical transformation' were the agreements between Russia and the Ukraine.[76] Russia's preference to place the OSCE at the centre of any post-Cold War pan-European security design resulted in enhanced support shown by NATO for strengthening the role of the OSCE. More specifically, the Alliance supported developing its role as 'a primary instrument in preventive diplomacy, conflict prevention, crisis management, post-conflict rehabilitation and regional security cooperation, as well as in enhancing its operational capabilities to carry out these tasks'.[77]

Russian and NATO co-operation aimed to 'creat[e] in Europe a common space of security and stability, without dividing lines or spheres of influence limiting the sovereignty of any state'.[78] In order to further the activities and aims provided for in the NATO–Russia *Founding Act on Mutual Relations* the act's architects established a NATO–Russia Permanent Joint Council as the principal venue for consultation between the two parties in times of crisis or any other situation affecting peace and stability. The Council was also to implement 'significantly expanded' military activities and practical co-operation. In order to facilitate the meeting of both of its charges, the Permanent Joint Council established military liaison missions at various levels on the basis of reciprocity.

Broadly similar comments could apply to the Ukraine, which also has a Partnership and Co-operation agreement with the EU. The WEU started a dialogue with the Ukraine regarding, in particular, nuclear safety issues while NATO reached a significant agreement on a 'distinctive partnership' with the Ukraine at the July 1997 Madrid Summit.[79] However, the Charter on a Distinctive Partnership between NATO and Ukraine was far less formal than the agreement between NATO and Russia. It established no special structures and merely committed the parties to 'develop and strengthen their consultation and/or cooperation' in a number of political and security related subjects. Those identified were conflict prevention, crisis management, conflict resolution, political and defence aspects of NBC non-proliferation, arms exports and a range of 'soft security' issues.[80] Regular consultations were to take place at a variety of levels, including meetings at the level of the North Atlantic Council. A military liaison mission of the Ukraine was established as part of their mission to NATO. The Ukraine and NATO also expressed the need to develop a crisis consultative mechanism for 'whenever Ukraine perceives a direct threat to its territorial integrity, political independence, or security'. To support this end, NATO allies pledged to 'continue to support Ukrainian sovereignty and independence, territorial integrity, democratic development, economic prosperity and its status as a non-nuclear weapon state, and the principle of the inviolability of frontiers'.[81]

The two agreements with Russia and the Ukraine formed an important and necessary backdrop to the enlargement of NATO. Although the *Russia–NATO Founding Act on Mutual Relations* allowed Russia to be closely associated with NATO, the underlying problems of any second wave of NATO enlargement remained – especially if the Baltic states were to be included in future NATO expansion. Yet, the summit was notable for highlighting two contentious aspects of enlargement: who should be admitted and at what price?

Paying for enlargement

Although the US lead in deciding the 'who' and 'when' of NATO expansion probably saved prolonged negotiations and perhaps even gridlock, it left the European allies with little chance to alter the agenda except through the budgetary arrangements for expansion. NATO's September 1995 *Study on Enlargement* made it clear that membership for any aspirant would involve substantial costs. It was further anticipated that the effectiveness of the Alliance would be maintained by sharing 'roles, risks, responsibilities, costs and benefits of assuming common security goals and objectives'.[82] The study also reminded new members that they should not only contribute their share to NATO's 'commonly funded programmes', but they should also 'be aware that they face substantial obligations when joining the Alliance'.[83] The Alliance's military strength and cohesion, according to the study, depended in part on the 'fair sharing of risks, responsibilities, costs and benefits'.[84] The contribution levels would be calculated according to an (unspecified) 'ability to pay' criteria from the start of membership. The study further recognised that 'financial implications will be limited in the early years',[85] but new members should remember that

> Enlargement will lead to new activities and a need for increased resources … Operating and capital costs in the Civil Budget will grow. New members will be expected to contribute. Cost shares must be calculated and decisions taken concerning their obligations. Enlargement will also mean increases in the Military Budget, but the actual budgetary consequences will depend in large part on the new members' level of participation … It will be important to ensure the potential new members are fully aware that they face considerable financial obligations when joining the Alliance.[86]

The contribution to NATO's Common Infrastructure Fund was straightforward enough to calculate, based on existing NATO contributions and the relative sizes of the economies. The less obvious costs may though be crippling for the new members. For instance, new members must not only adapt themselves to NATO's norms and standards of behaviour, but must adapt themselves to NATO's strategy and force structure, which is heavily dependent upon standardisation of 'major weapon systems, and interchangeability of ammunition and primary combat supplies'.[87] It is easy to imagine that this may well lead to a similar 'one-way street' in arms trade between existing NATO members and the new ones – a relationship that typified the intra-NATO arms trade between the US and its European allies for much of the Cold War.

The cost of enlargement has been subject to much speculation. The available figures, in turn, cover such a wide spectrum of contingency costs that they have been subject to political manipulation by those in favour of or against enlargement.[88] The figures given in the February 1997 Report to Congress on NATO Enlargement suggest that the costs to NATO and new members combined will be around $2.1 to $2.7 billion per annum, for a total of around $27–35 billion over a thirteen year period.[89] The split for the costs is:

Table 4.1   Division of the costs of enlargement

Expenditure category	Annual cost	Total 1997–2009
New member costs for military restructuring	$800m–$1 billion	$10–13 billion
NATO regional reinforcement capabilities	$600m–$800m	$8–10 billion
Direct Enlargement costs	$700m–$900m	$9–12 billion
Total		$27–35 billion

Source: *Report to the Congress on the Enlargement of the North Atlantic Treaty Organization: Rationale, Benefits, Costs and Implications* (Washington, DC: Bureau of European and Canadian Affairs, US Department of State, 24 February 1997), p. 2.

In the three categories the bulk of expenditure would be spent on repair of the crumbling military infrastructures in the countries concerned.[90] The second category supposed that key shortfalls in deployability, logistics and sustainment must be corrected. It was further assumed that a 'reinforcement package' could include four divisions and six fighter wings operating under ARRC. Since the US meets all of the deployability standards, it is likewise assumed that the US will not be expected to bear a significant portion of these costs. The third and last category presupposed that there would be initial direct costs, to allow for basic interoperability in preparation for membership. A 'mature capability' would then develop over the next ten years. The US DoD presumed that countries would pay for most of their own 'direct enlargement enhancements' unless they qualified for common funding.

DoD estimates supposed that around 40 percent of the direct enlargement enhancements could be nationally funded while the remainder
could be commonly financed.

The direct enlargement costs could, it was envisaged, be split roughly
as follows:

Table 4.2   Direct enlargement costs 1997–2009

Countries	Annual amount	Total	% of total
New members	$1–1.35 billion	$13–17.5 billion	35
Non-US NATO	$0.96–1.19 billion	$12.5–15.5 billion	50
US	$0.12–0.15	$1.5–2.0 billion	15

Since the bulk of expenditure fell upon the aspirant members in the
first three years leading up to accession in 1999, the US and its
European NATO allies need not incur significant costs until the turn of
the century. For the US, the costs in terms of its overall defence budget
would amount to less than one-tenth of one percent of the defence
budget for the period. The comparable costs for the existing European
NATO members were expected to be higher but still less than one percent of their defence budgets.[91] The resource implications of NATO
expansion are not entirely clear and the Council in Permanent Session
was charged at the Madrid Summit with responsibility for conducting a
'concrete analysis' of the resource implications of the enlargement –
perhaps something that one would reasonably anticipate should have
been done before enlargement was proffered.

The *Report to Congress on NATO Enlargement* provides some of the
more commonly cited figures but these are by no means the only figures in circulation. Indeed three sets of figures have been in common
circulation. Those produced by the Congressional Budget Office (CBO)
and RAND in 1996, and the 1997 DoD figures referred to earlier. The
figures are summarised in Table 4.3.

The CBO and RAND studies assumed a variety of NATO defence pos-
tures for the new members ranging from minimalist to extensive
(including forward basing). Yet, it was also noted in both studies that
the lack of an imminent threat permitted NATO members to opt for
lower-cost options. The DoD-backed study received extensive publicity
and with the benefit of being more up to date than either of the others, it was widely presumed to be the most authoritative. In an analysis
of the DoD-backed figures appearing in the *Report to Congress on NATO
Enlargement*, the US General Accounting Office (GAO) commented that

Table 4.3   Cost estimates of NATO enlargement

Assumptions	DoD	CBO	RAND
Total cost	$27–35 billion in constant 1997 dollars	$61–125 billion in constant 1997 dollars†	$10–110 billion in constant 1996 dollars*
US cost share	$1.5–2.0 billion	$13.1 billion	$5–6 billion
Notional new NATO Members	Small group (classified)	Pol., Hung., Czech., Slovakia	Pol., Hung., Czech., Slovakia
Time period	1997–2009	1996–2010	Approx. 1995–2010
Threat assessment	Low threat	Resurgent Russia	Low Threat
Comparable force posture options	4 divisions/ 6 wings	11.7 divisions/ 11.5 wings	5 divisions/ 10 wings

*$109 billion for a defence strategy similar to the DoD's.
*$ 42 billion for a defence strategy similar to the DoD's.
Source: *NATO Enlargement: Costs Estimates Developed to Date are Notional*, 18 August 1997, GAO/NSIAD–97–209 (Washington, DC: General Accounting Office, 1997).

the report's key assumptions were 'generally reasonable' but that the DoD's 'lack of supporting cost documentation and its decision to include cost elements that were not directly related to enlargement call into question its overall estimate'. The GAO report concluded, 'Because of the uncertainties associated with enlargement and DoD's estimating procedures, the actual cost of NATO enlargement could be substantially higher or lower than DoD's estimated cost of about $27 billion to $35 billion'.[92] The GAO argued that it could not verify the DoD's pricing of many individual cost elements and that the cost estimates appeared to be based on expert 'guesstimates'. The DoD assessment also included two cost elements that could not be attributed directly to NATO enlargement. Specifically, the GAO observed that it 'found no direct link between the costs of remedying current shortfalls in NATO's reinforcement capabilities and enlargement of the alliance' and, second, it questioned whether 'all of the DoD's new member modernization and restructuring costs are attributable to NATO enlargement'.[93]

NATO enlargement also poses some difficult choices for the still fragile economies of those invited to pursue NATO membership. The opportunity cost of NATO membership is viewed by some, the IMF included, as detrimental to continued economic development and that by assuming the financial and economic responsibilities of membership 'severe burdens will thus be placed on the new member states already struggling to transform their weak economies. They will be forced to spend their scarce resources, urgently needed for stabilising their economies and saving their social security and educational systems, on new military equipment'.[94] The Czech Republic, Hungary and Poland may well find themselves in the awkward political bind of being urged by NATO ministers to contribute their share of the enlargement costs (and to buy US fighters and weapons systems) while being cautioned on the other hand by the IMF on the possible damage that may be incurred by such expenditure with, possibly, a consequent reduction in IMF support.

The costs of enlargement, such as they are, will incur an increase in military expenditure – that much is clear. The amount currently spent by the central European countries on military outlays falls below the NATO average and is only comparable with countries at the bottom of Alliance defence expenditure, such as Spain. For the aspirant members the *Report to Congress on NATO Enlargement* estimates that 'the countries of Central and Eastern Europe...are projected to spend around $80 billion in the decade ahead'.[95] For the new members, the costs of new membership spread over the 1997–2009 period may represent roughly 10–15 per cent of their existing defence expenditure.[96] The actual costs for each new member depends not only upon continued economic growth, but also upon the number of existing or anticipated programmes that support NATO membership.

Military expenditure measured as a percentage of GDP is though a very rough and not particularly accurate method of assessing actual and future military expenditure. A more reliable method is to attempt to compare military expenditure in constant prices, as do the Tables 4.4 and 4.5.

However the costs are measured, the US clearly anticipates that its costs will be minimal while those borne by its European allies will be higher. The European allies are expected to meet these costs while financing their own future military needs in the CFSP context. Enhancing the regional reinforcement capabilities of existing NATO members has been estimated by the DoD to be $600–800 million per year or $8–10 billion over a thirteen-year period.[97] As a result, the costs of enlargement that any NATO member may be willing to assume depends rather heavily on the anticipated benefits of enlargement for its defence industries. In this regard, the merging and streamlining of US defence contractors since the end of the Cold War, may well give the US decisive cost and competitive advantages over its less efficient and largely national European rivals. If however, to take one example, the European NATO members reinforce their capabilities by building their own large transport aircraft (the EUROFLAG) and not buy the US C-17, their willingness to support such expenditure both for enlargement as well as ESDI/CFSP may be much higher. The option of relying upon 'separable but not separate' NATO (read US) resources to support non-NATO operations could also prevail.

Table 4.4 Military expenditure as a percentage of GDP 1989–1996

Country	1989	1990	1991	1992	1993	1994	1995	1996
(EU)								
Austria	1.1	0.1	0.1	0.1	0.1	0.9	0.9	0.9
Belgium	2.5	2.4	2.3	1.9	1.8	1.7	1.7	1.6
Denmark	2.1	2.1	2.1	2.0	2.0	1.9	1.8	1.8
Finland[1]	1.4	1.4	1.9	2.0	1.9	1.8	1.5	1.6
France	3.7	3.6	3.6	3.4	3.4	3.3	3.1	3.0
Germany[2]	2.8	2.8	2.3	2.1	2.0	1.8	1.7	1.7
Greece	4.6	4.7	4.3	4.5	4.4	4.4	4.4	4.5
Ireland	1.0	1.1	1.1	1.1	1.0	1.2	1.1	1.1
Italy	2.3	2.1	2.1	2.1	2.1	2.0	1.8	1.9
Luxembourg	1.1	1.1	0.9	0.9	0.8	0.8	0.7	0.7
Netherlands	2.8	2.6	2.5	2.5	2.3	2.1	2.0	2.0
Portugal	2.8	2.8	2.8	2.8	2.6	2.5	2.6	2.4
Spain	2.1	1.8	1.7	1.6	1.7	1.5	1.6	1.5
Sweden	2.5	2.6	2.5	2.5	2.5	2.5	2.4	2.4
United Kingdom[8]	4.1	4.0	4.2	3.8	3.6	3.4	3.0	3.0
(EU applicants)								
Cyprus	3.7	5.1	5.0	6.2	2.8	2.8	2.3	3.4
Czech Republic[3]	n/a	n/a	n/a	n/a	2.5	2.3	1.9	1.8
Estonia[4]	n/a	n/a	n/a	3.7	1.3	1.5	1.4	1.2
Hungary[5]	2.8	2.5	2.2	2.1	1.9	1.6	1.6	1.6
Malta[5]	1.1	1.1	0.9	0.9	0.8	0.8	0.7	0.7
Poland	1.8	2.7	2.3	2.3	2.6	2.4	2.3	2.8
Slovenia[6]	n/a	n/a	n/a	1.7	1.5	1.4	1.8	1.6
(Non-EU NATO members)[7]								
Canada[8]	2.0	2.0	1.9	1.9	1.9	1.7	1.6	1.4
Norway	3.0	2.9	2.8	3.0	2.7	2.8	2.3	2.3
Turkey	3.3	3.5	3.7	3.8	3.8	3.9	3.8	4.3
USA[8]	5.6	5.3	4.7	4.9	4.5	4.2	3.8	3.6

[1]Excludes expenditure for internal security and includes pensions from 1991.
[2]Figures for 1989 and 1990 refer to FRG.
[3]Czech Republic formed 1 January 1993.
[4]Gained independence September 1991.
[5]Excludes expenditure on internal security and pensions.
[6]Declared independence in June 1991 and recognised by EC January 1992.
[7]Excludes Iceland.
[8]Figures refer to fiscal years.
Source: *SIPRI Yearbook 1998: Armaments, Disarmament and International Security* (Oxford: Oxford University Press, 1998), pp. 228–36.

As observed, the US indicated a willingness to assume 15 per cent of the direct costs of enlargement. However, it was not willing to bear any of the indirect costs, which means in monetary terms that the US share would amount to no more than $2 billion – a sum that could probably be recouped in anticipated arms sales to the aspirant NATO members.

Table 4.5 Military expenditure (in constant prices 1989–1997) (Figures are in US $ million, 1995 constant prices and exchange rates)

Country	1989	1990	1991	1992	1993	1994	1995	1996	1997
(EU)									
Austria	2146	2041	2051	2121	2141	2151	2133	2115	2100
Belgium	6051	5939	5855	4808	4566	4540	4449	4362	4410
Denmark	3224	3226	3283	3224	3230	3150	3118	3126	3170
Finland[1]	1854	1887	2180	2219	2155	2120	1909	2084	2160
France	52099	51851	52198	50527	49979	50233	47768	46596	47061
Germany[2]	53840	56760	52533	49951	44930	41906	41160	40343	39106
Greece	5001	5059	4797	4987	4866	4950	5056	5359	5702
Ireland	495	527	552	553	559	682	688	726	755
Italy	22846	21974	22283	21643	21758	21220	19376	21369	21582
Luxembourg	121	126	139	145	132	146	142	147	151
Netherlands	9907	9628	9362	9308	8549	8249	8011	8076	8014
Portugal	2435	2503	2569	2639	2547	2484	2670	2573	2815
Spain	10164	9517	9225	8529	9275	8347	8652	8451	8342
Sweden	5811	6031	5654	5435	5351	5404	5595	5744	5885
United Kingdom[8]	42714	41649	43022	38890	38022	36771	33896	34096	32837
(EU applicants)									
Cyprus	197	289	296	415	209	222	201	321	–

Czech Republic[3]	–	–	–	–	1031	965	900	902	880
Estonia[4]	–	–	–	21	29	36	36	34	52
Hungary[5]	1151	1284	987	910	819	694	612	554	530
Malta[5]	25.5	22.4	22.8	27.2	28.9	31	31.2	32.6	–
Poland	3442	3661	2536	2502	2773	2675	2720	2853	2935
Slovenia[6]	–	–	–	274	238	233	268	230	–
(Non-EU NATO members)[7]									
Canada[8]	10965	10976	9897	9963	9917	9686	9077	8262	7595
Norway	3745	3774	3660	3968	3697	3885	3383	3696	3591
Turkey	4552	5502	5655	5948	6578	6431	6606	7396	7461
USA[8]	373618	356994	313647	331280	313784	296188	278856	263727	258963

[1]Excludes expenditure for internal security and includes pensions from 1991.
[2]Figures for 1989 and 1990 refer to FRG.
[3]Czech Republic formed 1 January 1993.
[4]Gained independence September 1991.
[5]Excludes expenditure on internal security and pensions.
[6]Declared independence in June 1991 and recognised by EC January 1992.
[7]Excludes Iceland.
[8]Figures refer to fiscal years.
Source: SIPRI Yearbook 1998, Armaments, Disarmament and International Security (Oxford: Oxford University Press/SIPRI, 1998), pp. 222–7.

The enhanced NATO regional reinforcement capabilities constituted the indirect costs of enhancing rapid-reaction forces that could be used in defence of the new members. The inevitable clash over costs came dramatically on the first day of the Madrid summit. French President Jacques Chirac insisted to his American counterpart that the costs be 'zero' while Clinton insisted that the costs be 'modest'.[98] German Chancellor Helmut Kohl also expressed his dissatisfaction, describing the US cost estimates as 'manifestly exaggerating the interests of the military-industrial complex'. He further commented that: 'It is completely absurd to link NATO enlargement with cost factors as if the aim was to rearm large areas of Europe to the teeth.'[99] Naturally, the European NATO members wished to defray some of their costs of enlargement by defence contracts with the new members. But they were suspicious that the US would unfairly benefit from lucrative defence deals while at the same time assuming relatively low costs.

A further serious clash over the costs of expansion occurred at a meeting of the NATO defence ministers in Maastricht on 1–2 October 1997. According to one journalist: 'With [the economies of the European-NATO members] strapped by austerity measures and with no visible threat on the horizon, European governments are loathe to embrace the politically unpopular cause of larger defense budgets.'[100] The reluctance of the European-NATO members to assume the financial burdens of enlargement were compounded by doubts that the new members of NATO were capable or willing to assume their portion of the enlargement costs.

The potential effects of continued disputes over the costs of enlargement to existing NATO members include the willingness of the members of the NATO Council (especially the US) to make the collective assets of the Alliance available, on the basis of consultations with the North Atlantic Council, for WEU operations undertaken by the European allies in pursuit of their Common Foreign and Security Policy. Another obvious effect is the preclusion of any further French *rapprochement* with the Alliance. Cost disputes will, from the French perspective, only be resolved when financial burdens are matched by 'responsibility' sharing – that is, when commands, such as NATO's southern command (which France covets and the US has refused to negotiate on), are shared. Rancorous debates about the costs of expansion may also reverberate in the US Congress. Critics of enlargement will inevitably portray costs as unduly burdensome. It should be noted that the reappearance of the post-Cold War burdensharing debate could potentially be more injurious to overall Alliance cohesion than its Cold War variant, since there is no overarching threat to constrain the parameters of the debate.

The NATO-expansion cost debate will continue to be divisive, especially in light of the refusal of NATO itself to produce definitive figures based on its own cost assessments. According to *Jane's Defence Weekly* the US 'opposed the adoption and release of such estimates out of concern that it would become a benchmark beyond which the US Congress would not move'.[101] In spite of promises made by NATO Secretary-General, Javier Solana, and the US Secretary of Defense, William Cohen, that a NATO study would be made available in time for the 16 December 1997 NATO Council meeting, neither the report nor the Chairman's summary were made available.[102] However, even if NATO proved more 'transparent', the debate is likely to continue to have profound implications for the general process of Union expansion. Based on the three commonly-cited reports that are in the public domain, the belief that the new NATO members can absorb the costs of membership may be fanciful. Even if they can, the cost of so doing may set back progress towards EU membership. As Amos Perlmutter and Ted Galen Carpenter observed:

> The IMF requires former Warsaw Pact states to invest in economic infrastructure, and the Maastricht Treaty will accept members only on the basis of their conformity to its rigorous fiscal standards. Hungary and the Czech Republic are already experiencing serious budget crunches and are seeking ways to cut spending to meet IMF demands. Where, then, will the money come from to expand their military budgets?[103]

The budgetary issue remains one that could inflict enormous political damage on the Alliance since none of the current members are inclined to dig their hands into their pockets further. If the costs of enlargement are difficult to assess so too are the benefits of enlargement in the fiscal sense. Given the highly competitive American defence-manufacturing sector, the European allies may well expect the US to foot more of the bill of enlargement in return for a generous share of the contracts arising from the modification of the forces of the aspirant NATO members.

Public opinion and European security

Any surveys of public attitudes toward security-related issues in Europe should be assessed keeping in mind the appropriate methodological caveats, such as those pertaining to the way in which questions were posed, the sample, the use of terminology, the public understanding of terminology and the complexity and topicality of the issue at hand.[104] When participants in a United States Information Agency survey conducted in 1993 and 1996 were asked how confident they were in the ability of a number of institutions to address 'European problems', NATO enjoyed the greatest support, most notably in Britain.[105] The EU enjoyed strong support, after NATO, with more French expressing support for the EU in 1996 than NATO – Germany and Britain both continued to show their greatest support for NATO. The WEU and the OSCE followed the EU. Interestingly, those who expressed confidence or lack thereof in the institutions in 1993 and 1996 both increased, the difference being accounted for by a decline in the number of those in the 'don't know' category. Perhaps unsurprisingly, in 1993, respondents in Poland, the Czech Republic, Hungary, Slovakia and Bulgaria showed confidence in NATO, but the respondents in all countries except Poland and the Czech Republic, expressed greater confidence in the OSCE. However, with the NATO airstrikes in Bosnia and later the Madrid Summit, it is reasonable to expect far more support for NATO than the 1993 figures suggest.

In terms of who should assume more responsibility and control of European security (with the caveat that more money must be spent on defence and more responsibility must be assumed for the security of Europe) respondents in Britain were broadly in favour of keeping the security relationship with the US, while in France and Germany a majority were in favour of Europeans assuming more responsibility.[106] Two USIA surveys published in 1996 also provided some interesting insights into NATO enlargement. Majorities in Britain, Germany and France believed that enlargement would benefit the overall security of Europe. British respondents were however more cautious about hasty expansion as they feared that Russia might feel threatened. A majority (47 per cent) favoured 'not moving too quickly' while a slightly smaller number (43 per cent) favoured rapid expansion to 'address the security vacuum'. Majorities in Germany and France (72 per cent and 58 per cent respectively) favoured rapid expansion.[107] In the central and east European countries mentioned above, plus Romania and Bulgaria, a majority 'somewhat favoured' possible NATO membership in all cases except Romania, which 'strongly' favoured membership.[108]

In the EU context, support for the CFSP was relatively high. Surveys appearing in *Eurobarometer* asked respondents, amongst other things, to state whether the Member States of the EU should or should not have one common foreign policy towards countries outside the EU and whether it should have a common defence and military policy.[109] The data showed consistently higher support for defence policy and slightly less so for foreign policy (see Table 4.6). It is notable that virtually all other 'key Maastricht issues' enjoyed less support, including economic and monetary union, with the exception of teaching about the EU in schools, which commanded uniformly high levels of support.

Although the figures reveal high public advocacy for a common foreign policy toward countries outside of the EU, the numbers point to stronger support for a common defence, apart from a noticeable drop in early 1996. *Eurobarometer* commented on this drop in support but ventured no reasons as to why there should be a rapid decline (of 13 percent) between Autumn 1995 and Spring 1996. One conjectural but obvious reason is that the Dayton Accords may have appeared to threaten large commitments to future peace support activities in Bosnia of indefinite duration. The possibility of a fully-fledged common defence might have awoken the concern that there would be too

Table 4.6   Support for key Maastricht issues

Theme	Spring 1993 EB39*	Spring 1995 EB43	Autumn 1995 EB44	Spring 1996 EB45	Autumn 1996 EB46	Spring 1997 EB47
EMU	52	52	53	51	51	47
CFSP						
Common defence	77	75	73	60	68	68
Common foreign	66	67	69	66	64	63
Democratic Processes						
EP support for						
Commission	66	70	72	71	70	69
Subsidiarity	57	55	63	64	61	60
EP–Council eq.rhts.	46	51	52	58	47	48
Vote local EU[†]	48	54	54	53	54	52
Candidate EU[†]	38	45	45	43	46	43
Education and Culture						
Teaching about						
EU in schools	na	84	86	84	84	87
Support for EU TV						
& film production	na	64	66	59	64	62

*EB = Eurobarometer.
[†]elections.
Source: *Standard Eurobarometer* 47 (Brussels: EU Commission, 1997), p. 27.

little national control over the commitment of national forces to Bosnia and perhaps elsewhere. The generally successful (or, at least, better than anticipated) IFOR/SFOR operations in Bosnia may have led to a rise in confidence in the common defence policy. However, the figures and the questions do not show how the respondents differentiated between defence and foreign policy or, for that matter, between domestic aspects of the EU's work and foreign policy issues. A further questionnaire, based on fieldwork conducted in November 1996, asked samples in the fifteen EU countries to give a preference for whether certain issue areas should be subject to national or joint EU decision-making.

Table 4.7 suggests that a sizeable majority was willing to see the EU assume a substantial role in foreign policy toward countries outside the EU, with relatively few taking the position that this should be mainly a national preserve. The balance is more equal though between those favouring joint decision-making and those preferring national decision-making when it comes to defence. Several suggestions could be forwarded for why this might be. First, within the question there is an inherent ambiguity about how much decision-making should be assumed by either the EU or the Member State involved. Second, the idea of foreign policy may be quite remote to many people, suggesting

Table 4.7   National or joint EU decision-making

Decision-making area	EU	National
Third World co-operation	74	19
Fight against drugs	70	26
Foreign policy towards non-EU countries	69	23
Science & technology research	67	27
Protection of the environment	63	33
Regional support	61	32
Immigration policy	55	39
Political asylum rules	54	38
Defence	52	42
Currency	51	42
Fight against unemployment	51	45
Agriculture & fishing policy	50	43
Rates of VAT	46	44
Workers rights *vis-à-vis* employers	40	54
Radio, TV, Press	40	52
Cultural policy	37	55
Education	35	60
Health & social welfare	33	62

Source: *Standard Eurobarometer* 47 (Brussels: EU Commission, 1997), p. B.24.

that it is perhaps not vital to keep as a national preserve. Defence though is more intimately connected to ideas of national pride and even identity, which may evoke more support for the preservation of national defence decision-making authority.

Support for a common foreign policy toward countries outside the EU and for a common defence and military policy appears to have been influenced by a number of factors. For instance, in the case of demographics slightly more males than females supported CFSP but with equal opposition in both sexes. Age seemed to make little difference although those with a higher terminal education age, especially those still studying, were more likely to support the EU across a whole range of issue areas.[110] Nationally, support for a common defence and military policy was highest in Germany (particularly the former East Germany) and, unsurprisingly, lowest in Denmark and Ireland.[111] When the question specifically referred to support for a common foreign policy, backing was generally less enthusiastic, with the general national trends following closely that of a common defence and military policy. The patterns of support for a common foreign policy suggest that Ireland's reservations were aimed largely at defence and military policy, which could endanger its neutral status, while Denmark's reservations seemed to be aimed at the pace and depth of EU integration.[112] The general willingness to embrace the EU's CFSP was reflected (with the exception of the neutral or non-aligned EU members) in the extent to which publics perceived themselves as nationals, nationals and European, European and nationals, or solely European. Support generally for a common foreign policy toward non-EU countries was highest in Italy, the Netherlands, Luxembourg and France where (along with Spain) publics are above the EU average (40 percent) of those who see themselves as nationals and Europeans and *below* the EU 15 average (45 per cent) of those who see themselves as nationals only.[113] Those above the average EU support for a common defence and military policy included, in order, Germany, Greece and France which are, with the exception of the latter, also more likely to feel their nationality rather than their European identity.[114]

In an interesting twist, when asked how much trust they had in their EU neighbours, the neutral or non-aligned states registered a high degree of trust. This is striking because they are amongst the least enthusiastic backers of CFSP. Of the larger EU members, Germany commands the most trust (see Table 4.8).

When the same question was posed in relation to third countries, the EU 15 answered that they have the most trust in the Swiss. Some distance behind was the US. Significantly, in light of EU accession and NATO enlargement, the east European countries were consistently mistrusted.

The 'trust' analysis, when viewed demographically, indicated high levels of 'don't know' scores in certain sub-groups. For instance, women were less likely to express a firm opinion as were the unemployed. Trust tended to be higher amongst those who generally supported the EU, especially amongst the more highly educated. In general, the trust issue tended to elicit lower scores with more 'don't knows' than many other questions.[115]

Turning briefly to NATO expansion itself, the EU 15 data, which does not completely reflect opinion in NATO countries since membership does not overlap perfectly (Turkey is a member of NATO but not of the EU while Ireland is an EU member but not a NATO member), indicated significant levels of distrust amongst existing EU and NATO members and aspirant NATO members. Significantly, distrust of the central European nationalities was highest amongst Germans while the EU 15 mean showed not very much trust or no trust in reference to Greeks, Hungarians, Poles, Czechs, Slovaks, Russians and Turks.[116] As already mentioned, within the aspirant NATO-member countries, public support for possible NATO membership was only 'somewhat in favour', except in Romania.

Table 4.8   Trust in other EU members (EU 15)

Trust in	Lot of trust + some trust	Not very much + No trust at all*
Swedes	67	17
Dutch	65	21
Danes	64	19
Germans	64	29
Luxembourgers	63	18
Austrians	61	23
Belgians	61	25
Finns	59	20
French	59	33
Spanish	59	31
British	53	39
Portuguese	51	33
Irish	50	35
Italians	50	41
Greeks	43	41

Source: *Standard Eurobarometer*, 46 Figure 4.3 (Brussels: EU Commission, 1996), p. 43.
*Percentage 'don't know' not shown.

Examining the attitudes of the aspirant NATO members in more detail, respondents were asked if they 'support', 'somewhat support', 'somewhat oppose' or 'strongly oppose' a number of tasks which they might be asked to do if they were NATO members. The result was a majority in Poland, Albania and Romania supported sending troops to defend another country (with a fairly even balance between support and opposition in the Czech Republic). Majorities in the remaining countries were opposed. Poland and Albania also supported having NATO troops stationed in their respective countries while Romania did not. A similar outcome was obtained with regard to hosting regular NATO exercises in these countries. Poland strongly supported hosting NATO exercises (figures for Albania are not available). Regular overflights by NATO aircraft

Table 4.9   Trust in third countries (EU 15)

Nationality	Lot of trust + some trust	Not very much + No trust at all*
Swiss	69	18
Norwegians	64	18
Americans	59	32
Japanese	50	38
Hungarians	37	44
Poles	36	47
Czechs	34	47
Slovaks	30	50
Russians	24	62
Turks	21	64

Source: *Standard Eurobarometer*, 46, Figure 4.4 (Brussels: EU Commission, 1996), p. 44.
*percentage 'don't know' not shown.

Table 4.10   Attitude to possible NATO membership, central and eastern Europe countries, 1996

	Poland	Cz.Rep	Hung.	Slov.	Bulg.	Rom.	Sloven.
Strongly favour	28	17	19	18	25	56	32
Somewhat favour	44	34	38	28	27	23	39
Somewhat opposed	9	21	15	19	13	4	13
Strongly oppose	3	12	12	13	14	3	11
Don't know	16	16	16	22	21	14	5

Source: Richard Sinnott, 'European Public Opinion and Security Policy', *Chaillot Papers* 28, July 1997 (Pairs: WEU Institute for Security Studies, 1997), p. 53.

Table 4.11 Attitude to possible requirements of NATO membership, 1996

Country	Things NATO might ask a member to do…				
	Send our troops to defend another country	Have NATO troops stationed in our country	Regular exercise of NATO forces in our country	Regular overflights of our country by NATO planes	Increased proportion of national budget for military, not social, need
Poland					
Support	68	52	67	53	16
Oppose	24	38	25	37	74
Don't know	8	10	8	10	10
Czech Republic					
Support	45	31	34	30	11
Oppose	48	63	61	63	84
Don't know	7	6	5	7	5
Hungary					
Support	32	44	26	36	9
Oppose	60	49	67	57	87
Don't know	8	7	7	7	4
Slovakia					
Support	37	27	25	21	8
Oppose	54	65	69	72	85
Don't know	9	8	6	7	7

Bulgaria					
Support	34	–	27	29	21
Oppose	55	–	58	58	68
Don't know	11	–	15	13	11
Albania					
Support	58	70	–	–	39
Oppose	35	22	–	–	53
Don't know	7	8	–	–	8
Romania					
Support	51	34	41	41	17
Oppose	40	56	49	48	73
Don't know	9	10	10	11	10
Slovenia					
Support	38	32	49	37	9
Oppose	58	63	48	59	63
Don't know	4	5	3	4	28

Source: Richard Sinnott, 'European Public Opinion and Security Policy,' *Chaillot Papers* 28, July 1997 (Pairs: WEU Institute for Security Studies, 1997), p. 54.

also elicited strong support in Poland (figures for Albania again unavailable). The last category, which called on respondents to determine if they support an increased proportion of the national budget for military not social needs, was unanimously opposed by Poland.

The above figures might suggest that Poland is the only central-east European country that is wholeheartedly committed to the possible requirements of membership. Yet none of the public are in favour of increasing their national budget. Albania, for apparent reasons, is the most willing to increase the proportion of national budget spent on defence but, here as with other countries, those opposed are overwhelming. It is clearly difficult to have the benefits of NATO membership, which seem generally desirable to all countries, without increased expenditure on defence. The point borne out by Table 4.11 is not trivial since, even if a large number of the above countries begin negotiations for NATO entry, the likelihood of 'sticker shock' and public disenchantment is high and may ultimately weaken support for NATO accession or continued membership.

5
Transatlantic Relations and European Security

Leadership and post-Cold War European security

A series of attempts have been made since the end of the Cold War to make sense of the much changed international system. Francis Fukuyama's 'The End of History',[1] Samuel Huntington's 'Clash of Civilisations',[2] Aron Wildavsky's zones of conflict and zones of peace and Michael Doyle's observations on liberal states'[3] propensity not to engage in conflict with each other, are prime examples. Many of the ideas were driven by key articles, greeted as seminal, but like a young child with a new toy, they were soon discarded. Not unnaturally, theorising about the shape of the international system focused on the US role in the post-Cold War world. Two works in particular fuelled much of what became known as the declinist debate. First, Paul Kennedy's book 'The Rise and The Fall of The Great Powers', speculated about whether the US would fall prey to modern variants of imperial overstretch, whereby 'Great Powers in relative decline instinctively respond by spending more on "security" and thereby divert potential resources from "investment" and compound their long-term dilemma'.[4] In the same year that Kennedy's book appeared, David Calleo's equally provocative *Beyond American Hegemony: The Future of the Western Alliance*[5] was published. Calleo argued that post-Cold War NATO was 'essentially an American protectorate for Europe. As such, it is increasingly unviable'. Calleo further contended that it was global shifts that introduced fundamentally changed distributions of resources and power and that 'even if the fundamental common interests of the United States and Western Europe dictate a continuation of the Atlantic Alliance... the old hegemonic arrangements cannot continue without becoming self-destructive'.[6]

Unsurprisingly, mainly American academics rejected declinist arguments, continuing to believe that stability still rested largely upon America's enduring and unique ability to lead.[7] This view found its main proponent in Joseph Nye's *Bound to Lead*, in which Nye argued that in the absence of firm hegemonic leadership, instability or even chaos could ensue. Nye contended that the 'Twin dangers that Americans face are complacency about the domestic agenda and the unwillingness to invest in order to maintain confidence in their capacity for international leadership. Neither is warranted. The United States remains the largest and richest world power with the greatest capacity to shape the future'.[8] The changes in resources and power, to which Calleo refers to and which Nye disputes, depend very much upon which benchmark is used to measure relative decline or stability.

The Cold War in western Europe was marked not only by the provision of US leadership and resources, but by the assumption that the defence of the US began in Europe.[9] The end of the Cold War brought out significant contrasts in America's position, especially in its relative economic power, as it could no longer claim 45 percent of the world's economy as in did in 1945. As the contemporary international system posed no compelling or overt military threat to the US, or its European allies, inevitably the willingness of the US to lead and the receptiveness of its allies to leadership from across the Atlantic, was questioned. Although it would be inaccurate to portray the Cold War years as bereft of differences between the allies (Suez comes to mind), the gravity of the consequences of disagreements were circumscribed by the over-arching Soviet military threat. The end of the Cold War removed this constraint, most notably with reference to relations with third parties and trade.[10]

Moreover, disputes between the European allies and the US on a wide range of issues were compounded by post-Cold War diversification of national agendas in the absence of the unifying Soviet threat. For instance, the tensions between leadership in foreign policy and the domestic agenda, fuelled by unrealistic expectations of a sizeable 'peace dividend', became evident in American politics. The familiar question of orientation across the Channel or the Atlantic engaged politics in Britain. The 'new German question' was a prominent debate in France. The social and literal costs of reunification preoccupied Germany while coping with traumatic adjustments to the realities of market economies and post-communist regimes engaged Central and Eastern Europe. Russia was absorbed in coming to terms with the realities of its loss of superpower status and the tension between reformers and nationalists. These revolutions, adaptations and adjustments had a dramatic effect on virtually every aspect of international relations, the full extent of which is not yet evident.

Primus inter pares

For those who did not adhere to declinist rhetoric, it was almost a matter of faith that the United States is the 'world's strongest force for peace and freedom, and for security and prosperity'.[11] President Clinton proclaimed that: 'The burden of American leadership and the importance of it, indeed, the *essential character of American leadership* is one of the great lessons of the 20th century. It will be an even more powerful reality in the 21st century... Wherever I go, whomever I talk with, the message to me is the same: We believe in America. We trust America. We want America to lead. And America must lead.'[12] Just as modestly, Warren Christopher, the US Secretary of State, declared: 'American leadership is our first principle and a central lesson of this century. The simple fact is that if we do not lead, no one else will.'[13] In line with Clinton's enlargement and engagement strategies, US Deputy Secretary of State Strobe Talbott, argued that 'the world continues to look to the United States for leadership not just because of our economic and military might, but also because we are at our best when promoting and defending the same political principles abroad that we live by at home'.[14] In the academic community, the need for America's leadership role was just as evident. For instance, the Henry L. Stimson Center and the Overseas Development Council produced a report in 1997 entitled *The Partnership Imperative: Maintaining American Leadership in a New Era* which recognised that: 'Acting alone, the United States can neither cope with the many challenges posed by the new era, nor seize the opportunities it presents, but acting in concert with other nations it can shape the evolving international order in ways that will support US interests and values well into the next century.'[15]

Declaring leadership without a strategy though proved foolhardy. In the search for the latter-day complement to George Kennan's containment strategy, different and telling slogans were bandied, such as Dick Cheney's 'World Dominance', George Bush's 'New World Order', Al Gore's 'Global Civilization', and eventually, the winner, 'enlargement' of the community of democracies and market economies.[16] However, enlarging democracy carried with it the promise of seemingly endless queues of democratising countries waiting for handouts. Furthermore, it was far from clear what was considered to be 'foreign policy' since the 'Christopher Group' examined human rights and foreign aid in isolation from foreign policy. Christopher himself 'refused to explain to the group the basis for his decisions'.[17] As an important adjunct to enlargement, 'engagement' was also stressed as a means for the US to remain involved in peacetime activities beyond its borders (and, no doubt, to soothe external concerns of neo-isolationism).[18] Although it is easy, from a non-American perspective, to dismiss such statements as hyperbole, they were nevertheless important declarations of American conviction. They also acted as a powerful brake on neo-isolationism.

Fears of neo-isolationism were grounded in statements like that made by Under Secretary of State, Peter Tarnoff, who on 25 May 1993 put forward the controversial idea that US economic interests are 'paramount' and that, faced with finite resources, the US must define the 'extent of its commitments' and that this may 'on occasion fall short of what some Americans would like and others would hope for'.[19] Although the State Department rapidly disavowed his statement, it was in effect the *leitmotif* for post-Cold War US security policy (enshrined in the Clinton administration by PDD–25).[20] The Congressional elections of November 1994, which ushered in a Republican majority, and the appointment of Senator Jessie Helms as Chair of the Senate Foreign Relations Committee, underlined the importance of the domestic agenda in American politics and reinforced neo-isolationist tendencies. Above all, the absence of an 'enemy' or relative power against which to measure one's own superpower status had the inevitable result of introspection. As Arthur Schlesinger Jr commented: 'Dying for world order when there is no concrete threat to one's own nation is a hard argument to make.'[21]

The tension between those who advocated a primarily domestic agenda versus the more internationalist 'global leadership' role,[22] was evident in the unspoken assumption that the European allies shoulddo more to provide for their own security. At the same time, the assumptions about American willingness and ability to assume a leadership role remain largely unchanged. As irksome as the constant rhetoric about US global leadership may have been to European ears, it was nevertheless a message that, jingoism aside, had its basis in *realpolitik*.

The declinist debate notwithstanding, the US continued to be *primus inter pares*. Again, to quote President Clinton:

> Nowhere are our interests more engaged than in Europe. When Europe is at peace, our security is strengthened. When Europe prospers, so does America. We have a special bond because our nation was formed from the hopes and dreams of those who came to our shores from across the Atlantic seeking religious freedom, fleeing

persecution, looking for a better life. From the Pilgrims of 1620 to the Hungarian freedom fighters of 1956...they gave America the strength of diversity and the passion for freedom. Remarkable generations of Americans invested in Europe's peace and freedom with their own sacrifice. They fought two world wars. They had the vision to create NATO and the Marshall Plan. The vigour of those institutions, the force of democracy, the determination of people to be free – all these helped to produce victory in the Cold War. But now that freedom has been won, it is this generation's responsibility to ensure that it will not be lost again, not ever.[23]

The main instrument keeping the US engaged in Europe is NATO, which according to President Clinton is the 'bedrock of our common security'. In its *Security Strategy for Europe and NATO*, the US DoD argued that 'preserving and enhancing the effectiveness of European security organizations, especially NATO' is viewed as the 'principal vehicle for continued United States leadership and influence on European security issues'.[24] Within the Alliance, the *New Strategic Concept* and successive NATO Council communiqués, made it apparent that not only was the alliance to provide 'one of the indispensable foundations for a stable security environment in Europe', but that it was also to 'serve as a transatlantic forum for Allied consultations on any issues that affect their vital interests, including possible developments posing risks for their members' security, and for appropriate co-ordination of their efforts in fields of common concern'.[25] These essentially political tasks not only underlined the primacy of NATO in European security but also the prominent role of the US. The communiqué quoted above could just as well have read that NATO would be 'the' transatlantic forum instead of 'a' forum.

The prospect of an enhanced European security role that left America's hegemonic position essentially intact had obvious attractions for the US. Fortunately for the US (but perhaps less fortunately for security), the European allies have an interest in reaching the same end but for different reasons. The confluence of interests was defined at the two historic NATO Council meetings in Brussels in 1994 and Berlin in 1996. Together they created the illusion of the Europeanisation of NATO. As Philip Gordon observed, this resulted from the fact that 'all the main players in the Berlin agreement have an interest in claiming that the Europeanisation of NATO is happening':

France needs to claim a greater role for Europe as political cover to come back into the Alliance; Germany needs to show progress toward European political unification to reassure its elites and to convince its public to accept monetary union; Britain wants to show a strong role for the WEU to forestall calls to give the EU a defense role; and the US administration needs to be able to claim to Congress and the public that the Europeans are now prepared to shoulder more of the defence burden of transatlantic defense.[26]

At the centre of what Gordon dubbed the 'convenient myth' is the idea that WEU members can address the problem of resource constraints through the use of NATO and US assets. NATO *per se* though has very few assets of its own, with the exception of some air defence systems, petroleum–oil–lubricant (POL) pipelines, some fixed communication assets and around thirty AWACS aircraft. Beyond these Alliance assets, any military operation (whether it is WEU, NATO or an *ad hoc* coalition does not matter) is reliant upon national assets and particularly those of the US. The 'convenient myth' that the Europeans on their own could address regional problems, utilising NATO assets, was also built upon the presumption of a continued US military presence in Europe. Italy's willingness to allow unlimited use of its military facilities during the Gulf War, Spain's logistical support, Portugal's decision to allow broad access to facilities in the Azores and Turkey's support for Operation Provide Comfort II, also served as a reminder that American security commitments to Europe are essential to military projection into adjoining areas such as the Middle East Littoral or North Africa. Indeed, if developments since the end of the Gulf War are an indication, the level of activity of the US European Command (USECOM) has grown faster than any other US command area (six 'out-of-area' operations were either launched or sustained in 1994 alone).[27] The continued use of Europe-based US forces for operations in the surrounding areas is however one that is more likely than not to generate disagreement between the US and its European allies since in many areas of foreign policy, such as the Middle East, respective positions differ.

The initial reluctance of the US to become directly involved in Yugoslavia and its insistence that it was primarily a European problem, injected a note of urgency into the post-Maastricht discussions of the EU's progress towards a CFSP. Specifically, a way was needed to 'tap' American resources and assets in those cases where the US may not wish to be involved, so that US resources could be utilised in a 'European' guise. Although the US has traditionally been wary of efforts to buttress European defence collaboration, the change from the

Bush administration to that of Bill Clinton created a wider sympathy for the goals of European integration, including a more active security and defence role. The TEU in many ways complemented US interests since NATO remained the main forum for all discussions on defence while the new role of the WEU stood to enhance the 'European pillar' concept. The improvement in Washington's relations with Paris, following Chirac's accession to power along with Britain's closer association with European defence initiatives, also paved the way for a more predictable and supportive role from Washington *vis-à-vis* European security collaboration.

Westward ho?

Raymond Seitz, America's Ambassador to Britain from 1991–4, identified a number of 'false dichotomies' in transatlantic relations: first, that domestic and foreign policy are separate; second, that international economic policy can be disconnected from security policy; third, that US interests can be divided between Europe and Asia and; finally, that debates over foreign (and security) policy can be divided between unilateralists and multilateralists with little or no middle ground.[28] Speculation about a reorientation of US interest toward the Pacific Rim was fuelled by concern that with the end of the Cold War the US would lose its preoccupation with Europe, due to the rapid economic growth of east Asia but also because of the growing involvement in Latin America. European sensitivities were compounded by comments such as that by Vin Weber, a former Congressman and co-chair of Bob Dole's 1996 Presidential campaign, who commented that: 'There's almost no discussion of Europe in American politics anymore…and, quite frankly, when it does come up, it's usually in a negative context.'[29] Apprehension about a move away from Europe manifested itself in various and sometimes exaggerated ways. For instance, the German Embassy in Washington began to keep track of the movements of US Congressmen and Senators. What it found was that just over 25 per cent of the members of Congress had been to China while scarcely 10 per cent visited Europe.[30] Other evidence, such as the growth in the number of Americans of Asian and Hispanic origins, also prompted speculation that the US was somehow less interested in Europe. While demographic trends indicate that those of non-European origin are growing, those with Hispanic roots are growing faster than those with Asian ones. Moreover, the majority of Americans still claim European ancestry or ethnic origin (in the 1990 US Census, of the 249 million counted, 87 per cent indicated specific foreign ancestry and 57 per cent indicated European ancestry).[31] Some significant shifts may eventually lead to a reorientation of US policy in certain areas. For instance, nearly one in ten people in the US is foreign born (around 24.5 million) and the current leading source for first-generation US births is Mexico (with 27.2 per cent of the 1996 foreign born population), followed by the Philippines, China, Cuba, India and Vietnam. Before 1970, the countries immediately behind Mexico included Germany, Italy, Canada and Britain.[32] But it is also important, when considering such data, to consider not just numbers but the representation of the various groups in elite positions – on these grounds, Europe has little to worry about.[33]

The interest in the Pacific Rim and in the immediate post-Deng China may simply indicate that US relations with Europe are not a political issue in Washington (even the NATO enlargement issue is not especially contentious). European fears have been partially allayed by the fact that the question of how to pursue closer trade relations with China while advocating a firm stand on human rights has proven highly contentious. In spite of the fact that on several occasions Warren Christopher warned of an overly 'Euro-centric' attitude in the US and spoke of the 'primacy of Asia', the key trade interests of the US still lie in Europe.[34] Finally, the importance attached to the 'rising east' by the US Congress and policymakers alike was due not so much to a reorientation away from Europe but to the long-overdue recognition that: 'Since the days of Commodore Perry, the United States has been inconsistent in its Asia policy.'[35] More recently, the collapse of several Asian economics in 1998 has tempered optimism about Asia's long-term growth and underlined the mutual importance of the North American and European markets to each other.

The process of preserving close ties is obviously a two-way effort, but Samuel Huntington argued that preserving and promoting 'western' unity depends more on the US than on Europe. He observed that the US is pulled simultaneously in three directions: south by immigration from Latin America and its NAFTA ties with Mexico; westward by the wealth of East Asia and the efforts to develop APEC as well as migration to the US; and east towards Europe. The latter, Huntington contends, is the most important since: 'Shared values, institutions, history, and culture dictate the continuing close association of the United States and Europe.' He continues: 'Both necessary and desirable is the further development of institutional ties across the Atlantic, including negotiation of a European–American free trade agreement and creation of a North Atlantic Economic organization as a counterpart to NATO.'[36]

Trade also constitutes a strong case for, if not unity, then at least mutual-interest. The Department of State's Office of European Union and Regional Affairs confirms that, 'The EU is the United States' largest trading partner'. US–EU trade totaled some $256 billion in 1995 (up from $227 in 1994).[37] The US and the EU are also one another's most significant source of direct investment. By the end of 1994, the US had invested more than $251 billion in the EU while the EU had invested more than $274 billion in the US.[38] In addition, Europe has more of the world's GDP than any other region (35 per cent in 1992 at market exchange rates or 27 per cent at PPP exchange rates) and, in an aspect of trade often missed, Europe provides the US with relatively *balanced trade*, with only a $7 billion US merchandise trade deficit in 1993, compared to $115 billion for Asia.[39] Politically, the US and the EU moved closer with the *New Transatlantic Agenda* (discussed in more detail below), which was outlined in a speech given by US Secretary of State Christopher in Madrid on 2 June and formally adopted on 3 December 1995.

Turning to security, the vitality and enduring nature of the transatlantic link continue to be expressed through NATO. The strong (even if declining) cultural ties between Europe and the US still overshadow the cultural and institutional ties across the Pacific. According to Christoph Bertram, Europe's significance to the US lies in its ability to keep America internationally engaged. Bertram writes:

> Europe is the main, if not the only, anchor tying the United States to extra-hemispheric international order. The anchor may not hold. American may become tired of a Europe absorbed with its own identity but continuing to need the involvement and perhaps the deterrent of the United States to prosper in peace. But if that happens, the United States will be saying farewell not only to Europe but to international commitments as well…the only multilateral institution that holds US foreign policy to a procedure of day-to-day consultation and coordination with other sovereign states is the North Atlantic Treaty Organisation that links Europe and North America. If this link were to break…it would amount to the abdication of any sustained, predictable, and reliable US commitment to international order.[40]

The compelling US interests in European security are really twofold. First, Europe is not only of tremendous economic significance to the US; political and cultural factors are probably just as important. This is especially the case for the élites and none more so than Secretary of State Madeleine Albright whose refugee background serves to underscore the importance of the region to US policy. Indeed, her first meeting as secretary was with representatives of the EU.[41] Second, in America's self-appointed role as global leader, Europe is not only important in and of itself, but is notable because of its proximity to other areas of geopolitical significance, such as the Mediterranean and the Gulf. The *United States Security Strategy for Europe and NATO* recognised this fact when it observed that bilateral ties between Europe and the US are viewed as 'essential to the pursuit of shared goals outside Europe'.[42] Above all, the US security role in Europe is not only about defending US and allied interests in Europe, it is also about strengthening 'the US leadership role in European affairs'.[43] It is perfectly possible, as James Steinberg, Director of the Policy Planning Staff at the Department of State, has argued, that enhanced European capabilities will not necessarily weaken America's engagement with Europe nor undermine the effectiveness of the Alliance.[44]

In general, official US pronouncements continue to stress the cultural ties between the US and Europe. One report notes that President Clinton's four trips to Europe in 1996 reflected a historical fact: 'America has been a European power, it remains a European power, and it will continue to be a European power.'[45] The same report also mentions that 'The continent is also one of the world's greatest centers of economic power and represents a massive export market for US products ... Thus, our continued political, cultural, and economic well being is inextricably tied to Europe.'[46] Europe in this case not only implies the existing NATO members or the EU countries. Indeed, the report speaks of expanding the 'zone of stability', stating that 'prudent security investments in Central and Eastern Europe is likely to parallel the economic benefits we derived from our 40-year security relationship with our NATO allies: increasing employment opportunities, expanded selection of products, and profitable investments and exports'.[47] Perhaps, to historians, this will be one of the legacies of the Clinton era – the explicit link between free trade, expanding markets and democracy, with the US as a catalyst and guarantor which, especially in Central Europe, may give birth to stable market democracies.

Several ways of protecting and solidifying the US role in European affairs against neo-isolationists have been suggested. One of the most persistent ideas is that of an Atlantic Union, involving some form of linkage between trade and security issues, as well as closer ties between the US, Russia, NATO and the EU. Charles Kupchan and Simon Sefarty recently resuscitated the idea of an Atlantic Union, which would incorporate the EU, the WEU and NATO.[48] Kupchan's argument is framed around the observation that security is becoming increasingly divisible and is no longer a sufficient base on which to build a union, as well as upon the belief that the EU will not succeed. He advocates a 'looser but more comprehensive transatlantic union' which would ensure that 'the bridge between North America and an enlarged Europe rests on solid economic and political trestles, not just increasingly weak strategic ones'.[49] Proposals for an Atlantic Union presume that there are indeed sufficient commonalties between the US and its allies to build upon. This, as has been observed, is contestable. The open disputes between the US and Europe during the protracted GATT Uruguay round negotiations illustrate the divisions rather than the commonalties. The incorporation of the EU into an Atlantic Union would also completely undermine the CAP, since it is well known that, without the heavy subsidies, European farmers could not possibly compete with their American counterparts. Any such proposal would immediately attract the resistance of French and other farmers while, an adjustment of agricultural prices in the US, would encounter similar defiance. While it is unclear what course advancement toward European Union will take, steps towards an Atlantic Union would be even more vague. It could be that without a common external threat, there is in fact very little to tie the powers together and differences may be more difficult to resolve.

Margaret Bell, writing almost forty years before Kupchan, saw the idea of an Atlantic Union as problematic; the examples may have changed, but the general import is the same:

> However desirable in principle the Atlantic Federation might be, the Atlantic union movement has encountered difficulties on several points. The lack of identity of interests and policy of NATO nations – as witnessed by controversies over Cyprus, Suez, and the sending of arms to Tunisia – is one of these. Another is the unreadiness of members (or some of them) to subordinate their total foreign policies to NATO.[50]

In general, such schemes run the danger of overstating the commonalities between the different sides of the Atlantic while at the same time underestimating the general problems with economic union (whether the EU or NAFTA). They may also understate those areas of difference between the US and Europe, such as agricultural subsidies, the use of economic sanctions, Cuba (especially over the legitimacy and legality of the D'Amato and Helms-Burton legislation under international trade law) and disagreement in policy towards Moscow – to name but a few. The Helms-Burton legislation in particular, which exposed the EU countries to the threat of secondary sanctions, was considered by the Union to be an 'extreme case of extra-territorial law-making'.[51] It is nevertheless vital to have structures in which to discuss and manage differences. This could be done within the general framework of the *New Transatlantic Agenda*. Sir Leon Brittan promoted this role for the Agenda when he stated: 'Of course as befits the relationship between friends, and a close one, we will also have to talk about some of the difficulties, the difficulties caused for US by the legislation with regard to Cuba and the potential difficulties caused for US by the prospect of legislation relating to Iran and Libya.'[52] In variation on the theme, President Clinton called for the creation of a 'transatlantic community' built on 'closer economic and political ties' between the US and Europe. While the meaning of a 'community' versus a 'union' is not specific (and the EU may prove a misleading example in this regard), the general purport that efforts must be made to build upon mutual interests across the Atlantic is clear. One such attempt to do this, as already alluded to, is the *New Transatlantic Agenda*.

New wine in old bottles?

The *New Transatlantic Agenda* poses the immediate question of what the old one was and why there is a need for a new one? The old Transatlantic Agenda was comprised of the Atlantic Charter, the Marshall Plan, pre-1991 NATO and, more generally, the bipolar international system. The need for a new Transatlantic Agenda became apparent with the end of the Cold War, the redrawing of maps in Europe and the downscaling of the nuclear threat posed by the two armed camps. The immense cost of the Cold War, the emergence of America's European allies as trade competitors as well as partners, and the change in the nature of security further necessitated a dramatic re-thinking of trans-Atlantic relations and their security aspects.

The *New Transatlantic Agenda*, unveiled by President Clinton, Prime Minister Felipe Gonzalez of Spain and European Commission President Jacques Santer, on 3 December 1995, was intended to set transatlantic relations on a more appropriate footing for the post-Cold War era. The agenda itself is supported by a Joint *US/EU Action Plan*, consisting of a number of generally worded principles which the partners agreed should guide their trade, economic, foreign and security policies.[53] Amongst its innovations is the creation of a New Transatlantic Marketplace and the Transatlantic Business Dialogue, both launched by a conference of US and EU business leaders in Seville in November 1995. The latter has been described as a 'unique US–European business partnership in confronting additional barriers to trade'.[54]

A whole host of 'soft security' issues are also touched upon, ranging from democratisation, human rights, fighting organised crime, terrorism and drug trafficking, but by and large their mention merely codified existing collaborative efforts. The *New Transatlantic Agenda* went to considerable lengths to underline the US commitment to the 'construction of a new European security architecture in which the North Atlantic Treaty Organisation, the European Union, the Western European Union, the Organisation for Security and Co-operation in Europe and the Council of Europe have complementary and mutually reinforcing roles to play'. However it was noted that NATO remains 'the centrepiece of transatlantic security, providing the indispensable link between North America and Europe'.

Although it is assumed the US will continue to play a leadership role, the manifestation of this role will be different in the post-Cold War era. This is the case because the post-Cold War era is marked by reductions in US force levels in Europe, a greater role being played by European security organisations (such as the revived WEU) and the development of the CFSP. These factors, as well as the internal changes within NATO, mark an adjustment of the security burden towards the European allies. The transition of the burdensharing issue into a burden-shedding exercise has not however, from the US perspective, involved a fundamental reassessment of the leadership role of the US within NATO and, more generally, European security.[55] Indeed, Washington's encouragement of a greater allied role through the buttressing of the European pillar of the Atlantic Alliance did not anticipate a new transatlantic security bargain.

Despite the lofty goals of the *New Transatlantic Agenda*, a number of European security developments, such as the revived WEU, the Eurocorps, the Franco-German understanding, and the creation of national rapid reaction forces answerable to the WEU (such as FAWEU), seem to have posed an 'either-or' question for European security – *either* there is to be an adjustment in the transatlantic security framework, which reflects a larger European role, *or* European security capabilities will be developed as an alternative, not an adjunct, to the Atlantic Alliance. There is though an element of bluff to both positions: US encouragement of the European allies to assume a greater share of responsibility for their own defence has been made in the knowledge that there is little chance in the foreseeable future of the Europeans actually being able to challenge or work independently from the transatlantic framework. For the European allies, especially the French, the illusion of independent European alternatives is essential for reasons of national sovereignty, pride and to give credence to the second pillar of the EU (the CFSP). Beyond the 'either-or' predicament and in spite of the fact that few contest the need for a more effective European security role, Europe's leaders have responded 'with a mixture of apprehension and schizophrenia'.[56] This schizophrenia and inaction in general on the part of the Europeans led many in Washington to speak disparagingly of the European's attempts at building European security structures. For instance, Richard Holbrooke, better known for his role in negotiating the Dayton Accords, accused the Europeans of 'literally sleeping through the night' while Clinton was forced to negotiate a settlement in the stand-off between Turkey and Greece in the Aegean Sea in February 1996.[57] Stuart Eizenstat, the former US Ambassador to the EU, observed that: 'An effective foreign policy, even in the post-Cold War era, still requires the ability to project a credible threat of military power.'[58] In a similar vein his successor, James Dobbins, noted that: 'Until the major European nations, including Germany, are prepared to send their young men abroad to fight, and to die if necessary, in a European cause, under a European flag, and within a European command, no amount of planning for a European security identity will field a single battalion.'[59] There was also a certain amount of American *ennui* with its European allies for not assuming their full role in affairs that were closer to them. Roy Denman posed the rhetorical question of why the US should continue to assume the major role in the Middle East peace process when it is 3 500 miles to the west of its allies. His answer was simple: 'The European Union is about as capable of pursuing a common foreign policy as a rocking horse is of winning a steeplechase.'[60]

In spite of the criticism of European procrastination or ineffectiveness, there is also some historical ambivalence within the US about how 'European' (and thus independent) as opposed to transatlantic, the US would like its allies to become. In this regard, the development of the CFSP and ESDI were not harmonious with US interests since the former was portrayed at times, especially by France, not as an adjunct to the transatlantic pillar, but as a conspicuous alternative. The latter, ESDI, was viewed by some in Congress as an invitation to continue to lean somewhat heavily on US initiative, leadership and resources. The problem was thus twofold: how would the European allies square their demands for increased responsibility in European security with an apparent lack of resources and will? Second, how would the US continue to enjoy its influential role within European security with a reduced force commitment to the region and with a policy of being more selective and effective in its multilateral engagements? The answer to both questions was formulated at two historic meetings in Brussels and Berlin, in 1994 and 1996 respectively.

The beginning of the compromise ... Brussels

The US had in fact been defining its relations with ESDI through NATO at least since 1990. The communiqué of the NAC meeting in Brussels on 17–19 December 1990 declared:

> A European security and defence role, reflected in the construction of a European pillar within the Alliance, will not only serve the interests of the European states but also help to strengthen Atlantic solidarity. In this context, and as this process evolves, we will consider how the political and military structure of the Alliance must be adapted accordingly.[61]

The underlying theme – that the Alliance supported ESDI as a means of strengthening the European pillar and that NATO was still the 'essential forum' for consultation among the allies – was reiterated over the course of the next four years at various summits. The most explicit statement on the issue appeared at the North Atlantic Council's Brussels meeting on 11 January 1994:

> [NATO members] confirm the enduring validity and indispensability of our Alliance. It is based on a strong transatlantic link, the expression of shared destiny. It reflects a European Security and Defence Identity gradually emerging as the expression of a mature Europe. It is reaching out to establish new patterns of cooperation throughout Europe.[62]

The question of the WEU's role and identity was also addressed at the Brussels summit. It was agreed that NATO 'support[s] the strengthening of the European pillar of the Alliance through the Western European Union, which is being developed as the defence component of the European Union'.[63] By far the most important outcome of the summit was the move to provide the WEU with an operational capability in light of its role as the 'defence component' of the EU. The summit declaration stated that the 'Alliance's organisation and resources will be adjusted so as to facilitate this' along with a commitment to consult, 'including as necessary through joint Council meetings'. Based upon these generalities the declaration then contains the following historic paragraph:

> We therefore stand ready to make the collective assets of the Alliance available, on the basis of consultations in the North Atlantic Council, for WEU operations undertaken by the European allies in pursuit of their Common Foreign and Security Policy. We support the development of separable but not separate capabilities which could respond to European requirements and contribute to Alliance security. Better European coordination and planning will also strengthen the European pillar and the Alliance itself.[64]

The NAC, at the behest of the NATO Military Authorities, was instructed to examine 'how the Alliance's political and military structures and procedures might be developed and adapted to conduct more efficiently and flexibly the Alliance's missions, including peacekeeping, as well as to improve cooperation with the WEU and to reflect the emerging European Security and Defence Identity'. The CJTF concept was endorsed 'as a means to facilitate contingency operations'. The NAC, with appropriate advice, was further instructed to develop the concept and to establish the necessary capabilities in co-ordination with the WEU, in a manner that *'provides separable but not separate military capabilities that could be employed either by NATO or the WEU'*.[65] The 'separable but not separate' capability was a reference to the CJTF concept which was intended to comprise a network of multi-service, multi-national units that could be assembled quickly into *ad hoc* formations suitable for missions outside NATO territory (i.e. non Article 5 missions).

The Declaration marked the first time that a coherent plan emerged to harmonise the relationship and burdens between the WEU and NATO, as well as to make more amicable the competing Atlanticist and European tendencies within the two organisations. The move to multilateral and highly mobile force packages, based around regional NATO commands, was designed not only to draw from national assets but also multinational ones with varying numbers of participants.

The CJTF did not mark an end to the burdensharing debate but it did mark a significant change by shifting some of the burdens to the European allies. However, this was not matched by the assumption of greater responsibility for command and control arrangements.

The immediate effect of the Brussels summit was to solve many of the Euro-Atlanticist tensions (at least at the institutional level). For the US, the summit served national interests by, in the words of President Clinton, promoting 'greater European *responsibility and burdensharing*'.[66] The summit also confirmed NATO's primacy and thus the leadership role of the US in European security. American interests in ESDI centred on American insistence that 'NATO must remain at the center of European security'. Specifically, in a frank recognition of the realities of European security, it was recognised that 'For any major threat – including nuclear threats – the Europeans will continue to look to the United States and to NATO as the principal guarantors of their security'.[67] After the Brussels summit, ESDI was not portrayed as a threat to US interests or leadership since it was realised that 'some European states will push hard to develop a European Security and Defense Identity, but few will increase their capabilities for independent military action'.[68]

Clinton's use of the term 'burdensharing', which has traditionally been associated with host-nation support issues, was soon rejected by Washington in favour of the more expansive idea of 'responsibility sharing', which according to the US meant an 'increased allied share of roles, risks, responsibilities, costs, and benefits of meeting common security goals and objectives'.[69] Responsibility sharing started with efforts by the Clinton administration to adjust the costs of multilateral peacekeeping expenditure by decreasing US payments to the UN peacekeeping budget from almost 31 per cent to 25 per cent by the end of 1995. The difference was to be made up by 'other newly rich countries who should pay their fair share'.[70] While US support for a European defence identity within NATO was motivated by the 'inability of the EU to speak with one clear voice on foreign policy' it also served as notice to the Europeans that there may be occasions when they will have security interests that are not of direct concern to the US.[71] The Brussels communiqué not only made clear NATO's intention to 'develop' the emerging ESDI but it also, at the same time, made apparent NATO's resolve to 'endorse' the CJTF concept.

The idea of 'separable but not separate forces', which re-emerged at subsequent NAC meetings, provided an ingenuous political solution to the need for a compelling *raison d'être* for both NATO (by providing more than merely collective defence) and for the WEU (by addressing its need for an operational capability). There were however a number of practical issues which could stymie the summit declaration's mandate over the course of the next two years. Four problems in particular surfaced. First, the CJTF proposal and the 'separable but not separate forces' posed a dilemma for France since participation in a WEU-led operation using NATO assets could be misinterpreted as French back-door association with the Alliance. Second, the *modus operandi* for the precise mechanisms by which forces were released to the WEU were unclear, especially since the assets that the European allies were most likely to require were not so much NATO assets as US owned ones. Third, the close association between NATO and the ESDI, and the WEU/EU and the CFSP, emphasised the lack of symmetry in membership – Turkey being an awkward case in point. Last, the 'collective assets' of the Alliance are in fact somewhat limited and constitute some communication facilities, commands and AWACS. In personnel terms this accounts for around 13 000. The vast majority of 'NATO assets' are therefore national and, as has been observed, some of these are unique to the US. The release of 'collective assets' does little therefore to reduce the reliance upon national assets and, above all, willingness to release them.

The Brussels meeting also marked the launching of the American Partnership for Peace (PfP) initiative. The unveiling of PfP, which coincided with Clinton's first visit to Europe as President, was portrayed as an attempt to 'build a new comprehensive Euro-Atlantic architecture of security with, and not without or against Russia'.[72] It was Germany in particular who embraced the PfP concept and within twenty-four hours of the end of the NATO summit, Germany announced plans for military manoeuvres with the Poles, Czechs and Hungarians.[73]

However, the Brussels NATO Council declaration lends itself to varying interpretations. It could be construed as a move by the North American allies to scale back both their commitment ('substantial' was never defined) as well as a move to participate in European security on a more selective basis.[74] In this case, any automatic commitment to Europe would be limited to the immediate defence of the Alliance while all other security commitments would be subject to whether vital national interests of the US or its allies were involved. The emphasis on improving the European contribution to collective defence might thus have been designed to allow for shifts within US policy by an administration increasingly preoccupied with a domestic agenda, especially a comprehensive overhaul of the federal bureaucracy and the health care system.

The practical problems with the CJTF concept and the idea of 'separable but not separate' force packages were duly noted by the WEU and were the subject of much debate in the Planning Cell and amongst the Chiefs of Defence Staffs. One of the unresolved issues was whether a CJTF operation conducted by the European allies would be required to work through NATO command, even if the US chose not to be involved. The WEU's Kirchberg Declaration of 9 May 1994 accordingly welcomed the 'principle' that the 'collective assets and capabilities' of the Alliance can be made available for WEU operations. The WEU Council of Ministers nevertheless stressed that 'the modalities for making these assets available should preserve WEU's own planning procedures and capabilities'.[75] The Declaration 'underlined the importance of coordination with the Alliance on the implementation of the CJTF concept and the definition of separable but not separate military capabilities so as to ensure their effective use where appropriate by WEU, *and in that case under its command*'.[76]

The North Atlantic Council's 9 June 1994 meeting in Istanbul noted that collaboration between the WEU and NATO would be developed in accordance with the principles of 'complementarity and transparency'.[77] The Istanbul meeting also reiterated that NATO would be willing to make its collective assets available to the WEU on the basis of consultations in the North Atlantic Council. Intensive work also took place within the WEU over the next couple of years on the CJTF concept. The WEU forwarded a paper on *Criteria and Modalities for the effective use by WEU of CJTF's* to NATO in June 1994. At their Noordwijk summit in November 1994, the WEU Council of Ministers looked forward to 'intensified co-operation' between the WEU and NATO in formulating 'criteria and modalities' for the effective use of CJTFs by the WEU.[78] In May 1995, the WEU forwarded a second paper, *Mechanisms and procedures for WEU use of Alliance assets and capabilities* in which the WEU Council admitted to the Assembly that the 'strengthening of the WEU's operational role depends ... on NATO's elaboration of the combined joint task forces (CJTF) concept'.[79] The 1995 report argued that the concept was not only essential to updating NATO's military mission but an essential support component of the ESDI.

The CJTF concept received an important and vital push forward throughout 1994–5 by the prospect that the French position *vis-à-vis* NATO was changing. The linkage between NATO's and the WEU's assets and the possibility of a fundamental restructuring of the Alliance's command structure made the ongoing French *rapprochement* a matter of prudence. On 5 December 1995, on the fringes of the North Atlantic

Council's meeting in Berlin, the French Foreign Minister, Hervé de Charette, announced that France was ready to return to the 'non-integrated military bodies of the Alliance' and that henceforth the French Defence Minister would 'take part regularly in the work of the Alliance, alongside his colleagues' except for meetings of the Nuclear Planning Group.[80] The French *rapprochement* with NATO was widely welcomed and while it could have been interpreted as a change of direction in French policy towards the Alliance it was actually consistent with a core assumption in French thinking. This, as Wyn Rees points out, was that 'European and Atlantic interests would inevitably diverge over time...Thus, the longer term ambitions of the French government were consistent with those of the past, only the means had changed.'[81]

The compromise complete... Berlin

The June 1996 Berlin ministerial meeting reinforced and expanded upon the earlier Brussels decisions. The Berlin conclusions, amongst other things, restated the Alliance's determination to 'develop the ESDI within the Alliance' and to 'develop further our ability to carry out new roles and missions relating to conflict prevention and crisis management'.[82] However, the significance of the Berlin meeting lies in the fact that it marked the most specific endorsement of ESDI yet, stating that it will 'permit creation of coherent military forces capable of cooperating under *the political control and strategic direction* of the exclusively European security organisation, the Western European Union'.[83] Building upon earlier decisions made in Brussels, the NAC welcomed 'the completion of the CJTF concept'. The Berlin communiqué agreed that the CJTF concept would provide the 'Alliance with more flexible and mobile forces and headquarters elements to be used, for example, in WEU-led operations or in missions including non-NATO countries'.[84] It was assumed that the CJTF was likely to be the main tool through which the ESDI would act (though there are others, such as ARRC) and, for the foreseeable future, CJTF would also be key to the CFSP.

The communiqué further underlined the importance of the ability to mount non-Article 5 operations, guided by the concept of 'one system capable of performing multiple functions'. It was reiterated that the Alliance should remain the 'essential forum for consultation among its members' and it was agreed that 'full transparency between NATO and the WEU' was essential in 'crisis management'.[85] In order to strengthen ESDI, the NAC stressed the 'involvement of NATO and the WEU, for WEU-led operations (including planning and exercising of command elements and forces) as an 'essential part of this identity'. In spite of this note of optimism, most of the practicalities for WEU-led operations remained unfinished – for example, the 'detailed terms through which NATO assets, such as logistics or headquarter units, could be made available to the WEU on a *case-by-case basis*, as well as the appropriate command arrangements to support and conduct operations under WEU leadership, was left undecided'.[86] To remedy these problems, the Council in Permanent Session was charged with responsibility for developing appropriate arrangements. The Berlin communiqué declared:

> Among the arrangements which require detailed elaboration will be provisions for the identification and release for use by WEU of NATO capabilities, assets and HQs and HQ elements for missions to be performed by the WEU; any necessary supplement to exisiting information-sharing arrangements for the conduct of WEU operations; and how consultations will be conducted within the NAC on the use of NATO assets and capabilities, including the NATO monitoring of the use of these assets.[87]

Finally, the Berlin meeting provided some progress on the development of ESDI and, in particular, the provision of an operational capability for the WEU. The meeting could though be criticised for its general failure to move much beyond what had already been agreed to in the previous two years. The completion of the CJTF concept, as proclaimed in the communiqué, at least had the effect of forcing the difficult practical aspects of NATO–WEU cooperation to the fore. Still, the inherent tension that had emerged in Brussels was also evident in the Berlin communiqué; namely, that the American emphasis on ESDI stressed the primacy of the Alliance while arrangements for possible European-options inevitably strengthened the European caucus within the Alliance. From an American interpretation, the decisions in Berlin allowed 'our European allies to strengthen their capabilities within the Alliance. [The ministers] agreed on a process by which we can make NATO assets available for military operations led by the Western European Union, and to develop European command arrangements within the Alliance that preserve NATO's unity and the Transatlantic foundation'.[88]

The CJTF concept – ensuring US hegemony?

The WEU, even when operating in its Petersberg-task guise, has been operationally inefficient not only because 'the organisation lacks a permanent command structure and other standing military capabilities' but also because the organisation also remains divided on the role it should play in crisis situations and on 'substantive issues of policy'.[89] Even in the only existing *de facto* CJTF missions (SUPPORT HOPE and TURQUOISE, to deliver humanitarian and medical supplies in Rwanda) France and Britain relied heavily upon the US. Despite these facts, the CJTF concept provided a new and practical lease on life for the WEU while also assuring continued US leadership in European security. Furthermore, the CJTF concept also confirmed NATO's role as *primus inter pares* since the NAC effectively has veto power over *any* missions employing NATO assets. This means that the US, as a non-European and non-WEU power, has a great deal of influence in establishing initial missions but, thereafter, any mission is supposed to be under the political and military control of the Europeans with only NAC monitoring.

The continuing heavy American bias in senior command positions within NATO is a further indication of US hegemony, although there is considerable pressure from the European allies to reallocate commands, including a call for a European SACEUR.[90] Indeed, France demanded, as part of its realignment with NATO, a regional command. They expected that AFSOUTH would go to France in a forthcoming command reshuffle. Yves Boyer commented that: 'It appears that the intention is that France should acquire the same political weight in NATO as the UK and Germany. If it began to appear that no such result could be attained, officials have been reported as threatening to "go back to the starting point before the rapprochement with NATO".'[91] The extent to which the US is willing to share command and control positions with its allies is a delicate issue: the perception in Congress that the US has sacrificed too much power and influence may lead to a deterioration in US – European relations and a diminution of support for NATO. However, efforts by the European allies to assume increased responsibilities should be reflected in a readjustment of command responsibilities and, in particular, any closer French association with NATO will require adjustment on this issue.

American dominance of NATO is also reflected in the all-important command, control and release procedures for the predominantly American nuclear weapons in NATO. The reduction of nuclear weapons as a result of various agreements, such as START I, the INF Agreement and the CFE (due to its effect on dual-use weapons), removes one layer of objections to a greater European command and control role. Internal command structures are also necessary since the logic of the CJTF concept obviously calls for forces that may operate with ease under a dual-hat WEU or NATO aegis – the former clearly requires a greater European representation. Command and control structures have however proven highly resistant to change since once created they become a matter of jealous national patronage. Still, the implementation of a new force structure, introduced in the 1991 *New Strategic Concept,* necessitated a new command structure. The new structure, which became effective in July 1994, started with the reduction in the number of major NATO commands from three to two – Allied Command Europe (ACE) located near Mons, Belgium, and Allied Command Atlantic in Norfolk, Virginia. Allied Command Channel, a British command, was disbanded and absorbed by ACE. A further major change was the creation of three subordinate commands under ACE, responsible for the southern, central and northwestern regions. The subordinate commands are, respectively, AFSOUTH run by an American four-star admiral, AFCENT a German four-star general and, AFNORTHWEST a senior British four-star RAF officer. They are located respectively in Naples, Brunssum (the Netherlands) and High Wycombe (Britain). The new command structure is however not yet complete since a 'substantial further rationalisation is in prospect which, when agreed, is likely to entail the removal of an entire layer of command and a major restructuring of the remaining headquarters'.[92] The shape of the final command structure will also be determined by a major strategic assessment by NATO in 1999.

The new command structure, thus far, leaves the US with three of the top five commands (in Norfolk, Mons and Naples). As the European-sub command has gone, the French government has been pushing for the US to relinquish its command in Naples. The US has adamantly refused this demand however, arguing that they have conceded enough already to the 'Europeanisation' of the command structure by delineating extra powers to the European deputy-SACEUR whilst also observing that the Naples command covers the Mediterranean Sixth Fleet as well as the Middle East, Bosnia and North Africa.[93] In the face of an American diplomatic offensive, the support for enhanced European commands was watered down in Bonn and Madrid. Nevertheless, the Naples dispute resulted in a deadlock, with the Clinton administration clearly unwilling to compromise and the Chirac government staking its willingness to integrate into the NATO military command structure upon the Naples command. Robert Hunter, the US Ambassador to NATO, commented, '[The US] support[s] the French government's goal of greater Europeanization of the alliance, even if we don't always agree with its means'.[94] Volker Rühe, Germany's Defence Minister, backed the French demand while his British counterpart, Michael Portillo, described the position as 'unrealistic'. Italy and Spain also backed the French position, but with a discernible lack of enthusiasm. A meeting of the NATO defence chiefs in mid-November 1996 produced no agreement on this question in spite of a French compromise suggestion for a rotating US–European commander at Naples which, unsurprisingly, was rejected by the US.

The importance and potentially debilitating effects of command disputes surfaced during the Dayton negotiations. The choice of an American military commander for the Implementation Force seemed logical yet the EU Council of Ministers insisted that the civilian counterpart should be a European. Although the High Representative who was eventually agreed upon was a European, he was not selected until after a number of acrimonious disputes and also not without the US significantly paring down the power of the civilian position. As Pauline Neville-Jones observed, 'the time spent on unprofitable power plays could have been used to bring the military and civilian agendas together and to ensure greater overall coherence'.[95]

Within the CJTF framework, the command, control and intelligence (C^2I) questions have been partially addressed, but it remains to be seen how the agreed upon structures will fare in practice. Three headquarters (Striking Fleet Atlantic Command in Norfolk, Virginia, AFCENT in Brunssum and AFSOUTH in Naples) have been designated 'parent' headquarters for the CJTF nuclei. In any given CJTF headquarters there would be a mixture of permanent staff elements and non-permanent staff elements as in Figure 5.1.

An obvious problem arises if the European members of NATO wish to act independently through the NATO C^2 structures (for instance,

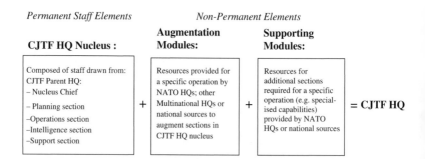

Figure 5.1   General structure of a CJTF HQ.
Source: NATO Review, Vol. 45 (4), July–August 1997, p. 35.

through ARRC): how do non-US personnel assume US command positions at short notice? Under an agreement for the US to leave its senior command posts intact (although they may not be directly associated with the CJTF operations) this immediate problem has been resolved but perhaps only to open up another. The impression, even if mistaken, may well be communicated that the US wishes to exert influence or maybe even control over European-directed CJTF operations by maintaining senior command posts. Other scenarios may arise that could lead to some highly awkward and possibly destabilising results. For instance, would the French participate in a CJTF operation when they are not proportionately represented in the command structures?

Two further issues arise in relation to command and control issues in CJTFs. First, control of operations may, as has been argued, involve the WEU taking command of operations that will include NATO assets and the tacit co-operation of the US. But, what happens if the US decides to withdraw even its tacit co-operation for internal political reasons? This happened in *Operation Sharp Guard* when fundamental differences occurred between the US and its allies about the continued need to interdict vessels carrying arms to the Bosnian Muslims (instructions were also issued to halt the exchange of military information to the US allies). Second, related to the complicated C^2 structures that are likely to prevail, the question of accountability needs to be raised. Suppose that the CJTF has been operationalised in support of a UN mandate carried out by the WEU, using NATO assets, with the co-operation of the US – who then is accountable for the outcome of a given action? One possible response may be found in the mutual finger pointing that took place in pre-Dayton Bosnia when one institution after another failed to address the deteriorating situation. Arguably, as a result, all institutions were damaged.

The question of internal command and control reorganisation is also complicated by the resistance in the US Congress to the idea of US troops serving under foreign commanders. Although there are cases of non-combat US troops serving under foreign command, there is an extreme reluctance to do so in a combat role.[96] This anxiety has been expressed in a number of official documents, most notably Clinton's May 1994 Presidential Decision Directive 25 (PDD–25) which, as has been observed, laid down the terms and conditions for US participation in multinational peacekeeping operations. Since NATO's adoption of the *New Strategic Concept* in 1991, the US has shown some flexibility on command arrangements for the new multinational corps. Within NATO the US contribution consists of substantial elements of two divisions

(3rd Infantry Division and 1st Armoured Division). The former participates in a multinational corps under the (US) V Corps commander while the latter is assigned to a German-led multinational corps as well as to ARRC. However, the multinational corps under German command places US forces under *'temporary operational control* of trusted, competent allied commanders in order to strengthen the bonds of coalition warfare'.[97] Although this may appear to signal a significant modification on the command and control issue, it is worth noting that the German-led multinational corps, as with all NATO integrated forces, comes under the command of an American SACEUR, who is of course also US CINCEUR.[98]

The CJTF concept has made the issue of reaching new command arrangements a matter of priority. Even a further reduction in key US commands would leave the US with a *de facto* operational veto over all major operations since in most foreseeable circumstances the assistance and facilities of the US would be required for logistics, communications, intelligence, heavy air-lift and sea-lift. The future development of the CJTF concept depends upon a number of conditions being met. Stanley Sloan of the Congressional Research Service summarised these conditions as:[99]

- Continuing US leadership and commitment to Europe;
- Stemming the European allies' decline in defence expenditure while developing a domestic consensus in favour of taking on military missions beyond national borders;
- Sustaining and developing Franco-American cooperation; and
- Promoting standardisation, or at least interoperability, of military equipment, supplies and operating procedures (including the extension of NATO's integrated command structure to France and any participating PfP countries).

While these are logical provisions, once they are met, there is the question of the type of leadership that the European allies may expect from the US in Europe and elsewhere. Post-Cold War American foreign policy has been characterised by prevarication rather than decisiveness, an unsure set of guiding principles, uncertainty about when and how to use force (with the exception of *Operation Desert Storm*) and uncertainty about outcomes.[100] The same comment may however be applied to the major European allies (perhaps more so) since, when military force has been used, as it was in the Gulf and Bosnia, it was implemented as the result of an American initiative. Nowhere was this more evident than in Bosnia.

6
Transatlantic and 'Euro' Options – Case Study Yugoslavia

Yugoslavia enjoyed extensive links with the EC, dating back to a trade agreement with it in 1970. As a non-aligned state, Yugoslavia was in a relatively privileged position vis-à-vis its east European neighbours. Yet it was not until 1989 that Yugoslavia indicated that it wanted to build formal links with the EC by which time others, such as Hungary, were also making similar gestures. Although the Commission did respond in 1990 with a package of arrangements, including PHARE eligibility, further progress was blocked by Belgrade's difficulties in meeting the EC's standards and strictures, such as the need for open, multi-party federal elections organised in a democratic manner. Already by 1991, secessionist strains made the organisation of federal elections well nigh impossible. Under the Yugoslav constitution, the rotating Federal Presidency was due to be assumed by a Croat, Stipe Mesić. Jacques Delors offered, on behalf of the Community, substantial economic assistance in return for a peaceable dialogue on a solution to the brewing constitutional crisis. This was not only blocked by Slobodan Milošević and other Serb nationalists, but opposed by a majority of Croats who made transparent their wish to secede from the federation in a referendum held on 19 May 1991. This followed an earlier resolution, of 20 February 1991, by which Slovenia disassociated itself from Yugoslavia. The EC, almost against all odds and defying the referendum, continued to support the idea of a federation with a rotating presidency with a variety of infrastructure programmes and by expanding PHARE. Informally, the implicit message was that potential EC membership would be endangered by Croatian independence. However, the secessionist strains gradually became more pronounced. Croatia and Slovenia gave notice of their intention to declare themselves independent states, which they formally did on 25 June 1991.

In response to Croatia and Slovenia's declarations, Yugoslav Federal forces entered Ljubljana on 27 June. Federal army units also moved into Croatia and eventually into Bosnia-Herzegovina. The EC's first reaction was to underline the importance of keeping Yugoslavia's borders unchanged and to insist upon the significance of maintaining the Federal President's office. Initial EC reactions also stressed diplomatic efforts to find a settlement, commencing with a fact-finding visit of Foreign Ministers of the EC 'Troika' (the past, current and future EC Presidents from, in order, Luxembourg, Italy and the Netherlands as well as a Commission representative). The Troika threatened suspension of EC aid unless the Yugoslav People's Army (JNA) was disengaged. It also proposed a three month suspension of any independence movements plus the election of Stipe Mesić to the rotating Presidency. The CSCE emergency consultation procedures were also activated. The result of these diplomatic endeavours was the first of numerous cease-fires that were promptly ignored. Realising the futility of their diplomatic efforts, on 5 July 1991, the Foreign Ministers of the Twelve agreed to impose an embargo upon all armaments and military equipment on Yugoslavia as a whole. It was also agreed that the Troika should continue negotiating on behalf of the Community. Indeed, the Troika's Brioni Agreement of 7 July raised hopes that some form of compromise between the republics and the federal authorities could be reached. The agreement concerned Slovenia primarily but also stipulated that a Monitoring Mission should be dispatched. At this juncture there was little else the EC could do since it had no formal military or security structures (only the EPC) and the Maastricht Summit, where such structures would be discussed, was not due until December. Moreover, the unravelling was taking place in a (nominally) sovereign state; any other form of intervention would be considered meddling in domestic jurisdiction.[1] Even when heavy fighting broke out in Slovenia in the spring, EC mediation efforts were very much geared toward keeping Yugoslavia together. The outcome of the Brioni meeting however left some room for optimism and this no doubt inspired Jacques Poos, then holding the EC Presidency, to proclaim it was 'The hour of Europe'.[2]

Poos' comments were perhaps made more wishfully than factually since, even when they were uttered, the first of many cease-fires was in the process of dissolving. The collapse of the July Brioni Accords, which were designed to act as the foundation for subsequent negotiations, saw renewed attempts to support EC monitoring missions and to negotiate cease-fires. It should be noted that the Brioni Accords extended to Slovenia and not Croatia (although an offer was made to extend cease-fire monitoring services) and certainly did not anticipate growing pressure for autonomy from Bosnia and Macedonia. The thought of armed intervention to discourage further feuding between Serbs and Croats was first broached by France at a WEU meeting in London on 7 August 1991. The idea enjoyed some support from the Belgians and Italians, but the Danes and Portuguese were less than enthusiastic. Britain also expressed reservations based on concerns about the potential size of the required forces. Unfavourable analogies were also drawn with Northern Ireland in terms of the potentiality for being bogged down in an interminable conflict. Germany meanwhile expressed reluctance based on the prevailing restrictive interpretations of its *Grundgesetz* (Basic Law) and the ability of German armed forces to intervene out of the NATO area.

More generally, the EC was fundamentally split over the question of an appropriate reaction to the ongoing fighting. Attempts to reach a settlement were launched on 12 September 1991 in The Hague under the chairmanship of Lord Carrington, who resigned as Britain's Foreign Secretary during the Falklands war, but who was selected due, in part, to his skilful handling of the 1979 London Conference on Rhodesia. Soon after the International Conference on Yugoslavia opened in The Hague, Macedonia voted for autonomy with loose ties to the Federation and, in response to attacks by the JNA on Croatia, the UN passed a resolution for a full arms embargo on Yugoslavia. The deteriorating situation did not bode well for Carrington's negotiations since one of the negotiating preconditions was that there should be no change of borders except by peaceful means. Carrington's plan aimed to secure agreement on a confederal arrangement for Yugoslavia based on existing borders with national rights guaranteed. Successive meetings in The Hague, chaired by Lord Carrington, failed however to provide a suitable solution. Serbia was given until 5 November to accept the peace plan and, if it did not, the EC threatened to proceed only with the co-operative republics. In the aftermath of attacks by the Federal Army on Dubrovnik and Vukovar, the EC voted on 8 November to withdraw all financial aid and preferences from Yugoslavia and would only restore them to those federal entities willing to observe the conditions and terms of a Hague-sponsored ceasefire. This measure was interpreted as being aimed mainly at Serbia who, alone amongst the six republics, rejected the peace plan. The perception that the EC was not neutral (in public) led Milošević to seek a UN-brokered arrangement under Cyrus Vance. The EC appeared, with the advent of a UN-monitoring force, to become a secondary actor.

Germany's recognition – leadership or breaking ranks?

The dissolution of no less than thirteen EC-backed cease-fires and the growing evidence that the independence of Croatia and Slovenia was becoming *de facto*, opened up the question of their *de jure* recognition. On 16 December 1991, Germany, who had threatened to recognise Slovenian and Croatian independence as a means of influencing Milošević, managed to persuade its EC colleagues to agree to the conditional recognition of their independence on 15 January 1992[3] (Britain was not represented at this meeting). Recognition was however dependent upon certain general conditions being met by Croatia and Slovenia, as laid out in a report by the Badinter Commission, which took its name from Judge Robert Badinter of France. However, not one EC member insisted upon fulfilment of these as an absolute condition. The conditions included support for the ongoing EC and UN peace efforts, constitutional protection for ethnic minorities and the observance of human rights. Prior to the agreed upon 15 January deadline, the Badinter Commission's constitutional experts were to deliver an assessment of progress towards the stipulated conditions. However, Germany recognised the independence of Croatia and Slovenia on 23 December without waiting for the Badinter Commission report or for the support of its EU colleagues. How should one interpret this extraordinary action, which would appear to fly in the face of any attempt at EC solidarity in the immediate aftermath of the Maastricht Summit where, amongst other things, the *Common* Foreign and Security Policy was discussed?

President George Bush, Cyrus Vance (the UN envoy to Yugoslavia), Lord Carrington and the UN Secretary General, Perez de Cuellar, all denounced the recognition. Lord Carrington, in particular, was justifiably upset since The Hague conferences had made it abundantly clear that there would be no recognition until a peace settlement was agreed to and implemented. Recognition was however warmly welcomed by Austria and the Vatican, both of whom had urged it. Analysts and academics have also commented negatively upon Germany's premature recognition. David Buchan, for instance, claims that: 'Germany fatally undermined the EC-sponsored peace conference by pushing its EC partners into recognizing Croatia's independence, and, by extension, Bosnia's independence.'[4] But, as Catherine McArdle Kelleher commented: 'Whatever the unanticipated consequences, the EC at least took action in the face of deafening silence from the Bush administration.'[5]

Under the Badinter Commission's terms it was far from certain that Croatia would meet criteria for independence and recognition. Germany's Foreign Minister, Hans Dietrich Genscher, had made it plain that he would not regard the Commission's findings as binding and that 'Germany intended to proceed, unilaterally, with recognition, whatever the outcome'.[6] By the time the Badinter Commission and its five-member Arbitration Committee delivered its report in the new year (which recommended that only Macedonia and Slovenia be granted recognition), the report was only of academic interest since the EC, under German pressure, ignored the findings. Macedonia, which was blocked from recognition by Greece, did not gain independence either. Laura Silber and Allan Little commented that 'the EC's first confident experiment in common foreign policy-making ended in shambles, the Community's own carefully formulated legal and diplomatic mechanisms shot down by old-fashioned political expediency'.[7]

It is tempting to interpret Kohl's actions and Genscher's announcement of recognition right after the Maastricht Summit of the EC in terms of geopolitics. For instance, David Schoenbaum and Elizabeth Pond comment:

> The British Foreign Office in particular understood German pressure for EC recognition of Slovenia and Croatia at the end of 1991 as an attempt to reconstitute a special German sphere of geopolitical influence in the Balkans in collusion with Croatian heirs of the old Ustashi (and the half million Croats in Germany), with the Bavarian, Austrian, and German Roman Catholic hierarchies, and with the suspect German nationalists at the *Frankfurter Allgemeine Zeitung*. In this view, recognition legitimated mistreatment by Croatia of its Serb minority and made inevitable the spread of fighting to Bosnia – and Germany was deliberately condoning these iniquities in forcing its EC partners to recognize the new states.[8]

This is not however an entirely convincing argument, as Peter Jakobsen and others have argued. Jakobsen's main critique is that the 'power politics' interpretation is wanting since, if this were the true motive, recognition should have been granted in October (as a threat against the Serbs) and not after the Maastricht summit. Jakobsen views the recognition as an *Ersatzhandlung* or 'a symbolic policy aimed at defusing the public pressure for action rather than helping the Croats and Slovenes'.[9] All of the German political parties, except the communists, supported recognition, while the Catholic Church in Germany was highly vocal in speaking out in defence of the Catholics in Croatia and Slovenia. Croat pressure groups were also highly involved. Internal considerations and a response to organised public pressure by the Kohl government as well as entreaties from Austria and the Vatican, offer more compelling explanations for the premature recognition. Other explanations include the fact that Genscher and Kohl were more concerned with demonstrating German strength and the vitality of Kohl's leadership. Wolfgang Krieger makes this point when he argues:

> Bonn's decision in favour of recognition was preceded by increasingly heated discussions during which the German Foreign Office lost control of the situation. Those promoting recognition did so for the most part because they genuinely believed it would deter Serbian forces from expanding the conflict and that the international community – meaning the CSCE, the United Nations, the EC, or all of them combined – could exert effective pressure to end the hostilities. The reason why Kohl felt impelled to recognize Slovenia and Croatia before Christmas is neither easy to determine with absolute certainty nor very important to the course of the Yugoslav war ... the most likely explanation is that the chancellor, who had to face a nervous party congress in Dresden in December, wanted to demonstrate leadership. With economic and social developments going badly in eastern Germany, his only triumphant line was the 'great success for us' he termed the EC decision on diplomatic recognition.[10]

The debate over what prompted Germany's premature recognition and its subsequent effects on Europe's ability to speak with a 'single voice' will continue but as a *causus belli* explanation it is, as Kreiger argues, deeply unsatisfactory.

The premature German recognition did however indirectly open up the question of Bosnia's future. The use of the same recognition mechanism in Bosnia, namely a referendum on independence, as recommended by the Badinter Commission, had the potential to be a recipe for disaster. Unlike Croatia and Slovenia, any referendum on Bosnia's future would inevitably lead to division along ethnic lines, given the highly complex ethnic structure of the republic. This is exactly what occurred in March 1992. More generally, it appeared that remarkably little consistency was used in the application of the Badinter Commission's guidelines. Bosnia was recognised in April 1992 in the face of compelling evidence of the use of force and intimidation by Bosnian Serbs during the referendum. Meanwhile Macedonia, which appeared to meet most if not all of the criteria, was not recognised in the face of Greek intransigence until April 1993 (with Greece continuing to oppose recognition on grounds of irredentism).

In spite of the moral sentiment that may have contributed to the German recognition of Croatia and Slovenia, the underlying issue of what an appropriate role for Germany might be in any multilateral action, had yet to be addressed. Having effectively forced the hand of France and Britain, as well as posing a very awkward test case for EC solidarity in light of the newly signed Maastricht Treaty, Germany retreated into the wings for much of 1992. One positive outcome of the 'premature recognition debate' was that, having staked Germany's leadership role in European foreign policy, the stake would later bring pressure to bear upon Kohl's government to take an active security role.

The London peace process and the Vance–Owen Peace Plan

After the EC's failure to agree on dispatching a peacekeeping force to Croatia, the UN General Assembly approved the creation of such a force on 27 November 1991, with the proviso that a cease-fire was to be agreed upon first. The UN Security Council endorsed the proposal on 21 February 1992 in Resolution 743. Within the EC there was little agreement over whether to contribute forces or not and if so under what guise (unilateral, or multilateral through the WEU). The question of a similar force for Bosnia emerged in April as fighting spread. By early June the situation in Sarajevo had significantly worsened and by 8 June the UN agreed to send a small protection force to it to keep the airport open, should there be a cease-fire. The EC's response to the deteriorating situation in and around Sarajevo was once again unclear. EC endeavours were given fresh impetus by the unilateral efforts of President Mitterrand in late June. His exertions led to the securing of the airport by Canadian peacekeepers in early July, so that the humanitarian relief flights could continue. Although Mitterrand did consult with Kohl and Mario Soares (Portugal held the EC Presidency at that time), the British were excluded and as a result were highly critical. The divergent French and British positions only served to underline the apparent difficulty that the major EC powers had in co-ordinating their actions in spite of the recently signed TEU. Germany, while supporting the initiative and the more general call for peacekeeping efforts, continued to voice constitutional objections against the involvement of German troops.

By 1992 it was obvious that achieving political or military consensus within the EU (and WEU) member countries would be well nigh impossible. It was to the UN that the EU turned. At a joint EC–UN sponsored conference in London on 26–7 August 1992, involving twenty-two countries, a number of principles were adopted. These however proved untenable as fighting continued unabated. Despite set-backs, the chief negotiators for the EU and the UN, who were respectively former British politician Lord David Owen and former US Secretary of State Cyrus Vance, continued in their attempts to broker a compromise based on the idea of a single Bosnian state with highly autonomous provinces. A series of conferences arranged by the Owen–Vance team in Geneva proved to be inconclusive however. The Vance–Owen negotiating team, both men acting as co-chairmen of the steering committee of the conference, signified a more dominant role for the UN and a back seat role for the EC. While the negotiations continued, the UN Security Council passed resolution 770 on 13 August calling for Member States to use 'all measures necessary' in support of a humanitarian effort in Bosnia. France responded the following day with an offer to protect those delivering humanitarian assistance and, four days later, Britain forwarded a similar proposition (in part because Britain had assumed the Presidency of the EC and wanted to appear to be taking the initiative).

Throughout 1992 the UN's peacekeeping presence grew, especially in the Krajina region of Croatia. During this time the EC continued its attempts at diplomatic mediation, with a small group of EC monitors remaining involved in the region. In general, the EC's record during 1991–2 was mixed and largely negative. George Ross commented that, 'the Community provided some opportunities for the protagonists to negotiate rather than kill each other. But killing nevertheless overwhelmed negotiations. From the deepening point of view, this series of diplomatic failures demonstrated the difficulty of running a common foreign and defence policy'.[11] However, it should be noted that the EC was preoccupied through most of the year in salvaging the Maastricht Treaty from near disaster following the Danish and French rejections of the treaty in referenda in June and September respectively.

The lessons learned from the Yugoslav crisis for the EC were many and varied. As with other organisations, like the CSCE, the EC was caught at a particularly difficult time in its transition from primarily an economic organisation, with the weak parallel EPC process, into something far more ambitious and comprehensive. At an early and premature date, the unfolding crisis in Yugoslavia served as a rehearsal for the many problems to be faced in building a common foreign and security policy. As a result, the EC's responses were often incoherent and, in 1992, the imposition of sanctions was only achieved with difficulty, in spite of the massive public outpouring of outrage throughout the EC publics. In the end, it was the UN and NATO who finally took decisive action. In October 1992, the UN Security Council passed resolution 781 in support of its earlier August resolution. The new resolution imposed a ban on all military flights in the airspace of Bosnia-Herzegovina and provided the much-needed protection for the delivery of humanitarian assistance. The passage of the resolution marked NATO's first involvement with the provision of AWACS support for UNPROFOR.

The London peace process and the much-maligned Vance–Owen Peace Plan (VOPP) of January 1993 for a reconstituted Bosnia, were both noble efforts that did little to address the human misery and suffering occurring on the ground. The VOPP and its successor, the Owen–Stoltenberg Plan, had the positive feature of securing the support of the EU through the first half of 1993. However, the rejection of VOPP by the Bosnian Serbs in a referendum of 16–17 May made the chances for any further negotiated settlement gloomier than ever. Meanwhile, in the face of persistent violations of the military flight ban over Bosnia-Herzegovina, the UN Security Council adopted Resolution 816 in March, which permitted the use of force in cases of violation of the airspace. *Operation Deny Flight* began the following month.

The VOPP stood little chance of effective implementation without the active support of Washington. Unfortunately, the Clinton administration, which was highly critical of the VOPP, undermined it. The reluctance of the Bosnian Muslims to discuss the VOPP was, according to Andreas Kintis, due to the 'USA's assurances to the Bosnian Muslims that the Clinton administration would not subscribe to any solution which would force the Muslims to make territorial concessions'.[12] Further differences between the US and the European allies arose in April 1993 when the Clinton administration advocated lifting the September 1991 UN arms embargo so that arms supplies could reach the Bosnian Muslims. The EC foreign ministers not only opposed this move at their meeting on 5 April, but viewed it as potentially escalatory. The White House remained critical, or at best distant, from European peace initiatives viewing them as imposed settlements which, to be successful, would require action to implement them. The Clinton administration preferred to await compromises suggested by the warring parties themselves before any active US participation on the ground would be considered. The VOPP however, in spite of considerable criticism, remained the best plan on the table. Certainly it was better than the hard-to-calculate impact of America's 1994 'lift and strike' policy (lifting of the arms embargo against the Croats and Muslims with the possibility of punitive strikes against the Serbs). This was later changed to 'lift, lift' strategy (lifting economic sanctions against Serbs as well as the arms embargo against Bosnia). From a US perspective the 'lift, lift' policy negated the need for the large UN forces envisaged under the Vance–Owen proposals. The US position enjoyed no support in the European capitals, including Bonn. Two arguments were raised against the 'lift, lift' suggestion. First, although sanctions were imperfect the arms that were 'leaking' were smaller weapons and the (albeit imperfect) embargo still served to reduce casualties. Second, the arms embargo limited conflict. In its absence, conflict could spread to Kosovo, Macedonia and even beyond the former Yugoslavia's territory.

On 25–26 April 1993, the so-called Bosnian–Serb Assembly rejected decisively the proposed territorial settlements contained in the VOPP. The deteriorating situation on the ground prompted the UN Security Council to declare that Sarajevo and five other Muslim enclaves were 'safe areas'. The growing concern with the lack of progress and the apparent need for armed intervention, supported by public opinion in the EC, led to the adoption of a joint action plan by France, Russia, Spain, the United Kingdom and the US on 22 May. The joint action plan meant the abandonment of the VOPP to the consternation of Belgium, Germany, Italy and the Netherlands. An agreement to divide Bosnia-Herzegovina into Croat, Muslim and Serb areas on 15 June signalled the final end of the VOPP.

At the successor Geneva conference, chaired by David Owen and Thorvald Stoltenberg, Alija Izetbegovic, President of Bosnia- Herzegovina, accepted the division of the territory into Croat, Muslim and Serb constituent republics on 30 July 1993. In a meeting on 8 November of the foreign ministers, for the first time assembling in their CFSP guise rather than the EPC one, a Franco-German initiative was launched with the idea of lifting sanctions against Belgrade in return for territorial concessions. The initiative met staunch opposition, once again, from Washington. However, the idea of using the alleviation of sanctions in return for territorial concessions arose again at a meeting of the EU foreign ministers on 22 November. It was agreed that some sanctions against Serbia could be suspended if Bosnian Serbs would agree to surrender a further 3.3 percent of their occupied lands. Subsequent meetings of the international conference in Geneva saw little progress and growing disenchantment with EU mediation efforts. The shelling of Sarajevo's packed market place on 5 February 1994 saw active demands from the EU, especially from France, for the urgent convening of the North Atlantic Council.

The reaction to the shelling of the market once again illustrated the difficulty of reaching consensus upon a course of action amongst the Twelve. Belgium, France and the Netherlands were highly supportive of military action to alleviate the siege of Sarajevo. Greece, at the time occupying the Presidency, was implacably opposed to the use of military force. The French were in favour of military action but only after the issuance of an ultimatum demanding the withdrawal of all Bosnian Serb heavy artillery surrounding the city. Britain meanwhile expressed caution, while Germany continued to hide behind its constitutional fig leaf. Progress towards air strikes was facilitated by strong US support for the French position and by the UN Secretary General's request to implement an exclusion zone around Sarajevo for heavy artillery and, in case of non-compliance, air strikes. Greece continued to oppose the air strikes but agreed not to block the action. On 17 February 1994 the Russian special envoy, Vitaly Churkin, negotiated his own agreement to secure the Bosnian Serb withdrawal of heavy artillery. The subsequent Bosnian Serb attacks on Gorazde in April, one of the UN's declared 'safe areas', underlined to the EU foreign ministers their fundamental inability to back up diplomacy with military action, except through NATO. In the aftermath of these attacks the preference, once again, was for an intensified diplomatic effort.

A Russian call on 19 April 1994 for an international summit on Bosnia-Herzegovina resulted in the formation of the Contact Group, comprising senior representatives from Britain, France, Germany, Russia and the US. The failure of the Contact Group's first peace plan, which awarded 51 per cent of Bosnia-Herzegovina's territory to a Muslim–Croat Federation, resulted in a fresh resolve to tighten sanctions against Serbia and Montenegro. The US also added that if the Bosnian Serbs failed to accept the Contact Group's plan by 15 October it would urge the UN Security Council to lift the arms embargo on Bosnia-Herzegovina. The Bosnian Serbs did not accept the plan and on 11 November, true to its word, the US unilaterally lifted its arms embargo against former Yugoslavia, much to the consternation of the EU. 1994 concluded with the signing of a four-month cease-fire amongst the warring parties.

The NATO airstrikes against Bosnian Serb positions in May 1995 resulted in retaliation by the Bosnian Serbs in the form of a bombardment against Tuzla and Sarajevo and the taking of UNPROFOR personnel as hostages (often near or in the compounds holding their confiscated heavy weapons). The European response to the taking of UN peacekeepers by Bosnian Serbs and their use as 'human shields' at sensitive military installations likely to be targeted by UN forces, led to a French initiative to create a Rapid Reaction Force (RRF) whose task would essentially be that of peace-enforcement. The 10 000 strong RRF was also mandated to assist in humanitarian supply efforts, to protect the UN weapons-free zones, to resupply UNPROFOR forces as needed, and to protect and defend UN forces. The approval of the RRF proposal by Britain and the Netherlands on 3 June 1995 and the formal endorsement of the RRF into UN operations made obvious what had long been apparent – traditional interpositionary peacekeeping was of limited utility in Bosnian or Somalia-type situations. The RRF was to provide protection for UNPROFOR, a role that served to keep alive the awkward notion that 'traditional' peacekeeping could co-exist with more muscular forms of peacekeeping. More importantly, the RRF provided the necessary protection for the repositioning of UNPROFOR troops for the August air strikes against Bosnian Serb positions. The RRF also provided critical intelligence for the strikes. The need for a more vigorous military profile, beyond that of UNPROFOR, was underlined when in July the Bosnian Serb forces attacked Srebrenica and Žepa (both UN designated safe areas) and, in the case of the former, occupied it.

Carl Bilt, a former Swedish Prime Minister, replaced Lord Owen as the EU's mediator on 12 June 1995. On 21 July the defence and foreign ministers of the Contact Group, along with representatives of the prime contributors to the peacekeeping operations, met at Lancaster House in London for a one-day summit. As a result of the deliberations, Boutros Boutros Ghali agreed to surrender his right of veto over NATO air strikes to General Bernard Janvier, UNPROFOR's French commander. This had the important result of increasing NATO's credibility and the threat of air strikes. The main framework for a settlement was ironed out by a US initiative on 8 September 1995 by which Bosnia-Herzegovina would continue to exist with its pre-war borders but henceforth would be comprised of the Republika Srpska and a Federation of Bosnia Herzegovina. The subsequent agreement to a 60-day cease-fire in October paved the way to the Dayton negotiations that commenced on 1 November. The Dayton Accords, signed in Paris on 14 December, provided for the creation of up to a 60 000 strong

NATO stabilisation force (SFOR), the abolition of the international conference on former Yugoslavia and support for the OSCE to prepare and
monitor elections across Bosnia-Herzegovina.

Following the expiry of the SFOR I mandate in Bosnia on 20 June
1998, the new SFOR mission immediately took effect. SFOR II was
maintained at around the same force level as its predecessor (around
30 000) until the Bosnian legislative elections in September 1998. The
SFOR II Staff Headquarters included, for the first time, 150 officers of
the Eurocorps Staff Headquarters, comprising approximately one third
of its staff. SFOR II also included a special unit of some 600
Argentinean and Italian military police.

In the ongoing Yugoslav crisis there were a few areas in which the EU
proved itself to be effective or at least where it displayed some potential. For instance, the EU helped expose the methodical abuse of
Bosnian women by Serb forces. The EU's February 1993 report, which
detailed the grisly evidence of rape being used as part of a systematic
process of ethnic cleansing, led to demands from the EU members for
the establishment of a Committee of Experts to examine the allegations of 'ethnic cleansing', mass rape and concentration camps. This,
in turn, led the UN to establish an international war crimes tribunal in
The Hague in November 1993. In a second development, in a 'civil
intervention', the EU assumed responsibility for administrative functions of the city of Mostar in October 1993. Additionally, in a joint
EU/WEU activity (the first of its kind) the WEU assumed responsibility
for training a joint Bosnian–Croat police force. Again, in another first,
the role of the EU Ombudsman was expanded into the CFSP area with
responsibility for addressing complaints arising from the EU or joint
activities with the WEU in Mostar. More generally, the Community co-
operated with UNPROFOR in establishing EC monitoring missions
(ECMM) in Dubrovnik, in supervising the withdrawal of Serb forces
and in monitoring the exchange of prisoners. In spite of these more
positive aspects of the EU's performance, the EC/EU fundamentally
failed to alter anything without US assistance.

The WEU and Bosnia

Within a few months of the July 1991 arms embargo it was obvious to
all observers that the embargo was having little effect. The breakdown
of the initial peace negotiations in November 1991 led to calls for more
extensive sanctions against Yugoslavia. New sanctions were imposed a
month later on Serbia while at the end of May 1992 comprehensive

sanctions were introduced. However, the efficacy of sanctions was soon called into question since it was unclear how much influence the Serbs enjoyed over the Bosnian Serbs.

With the failure of economic sanctions, the EC members began to formulate other means to end the fighting. In July 1992, WEU naval forces joined those of NATO to monitor the Adriatic Sea in two separate, but co-ordinated operations, in compliance with UN Security Council resolutions. This NATO–WEU Operation is often forwarded as an example of successful collaboration between security organisations and proof that the European security architecture can and does work. For instance, the WEU Minister's Ostend Declaration of 19 November 1996 declared that the operation (the first combined operation between the WEU and NATO) 'has served as a positive demonstration of the strengthening ties and intensifying cooperation between the two Oganizations'.[13] Perhaps as a matter of chance rather than foresight the WEU operation *Sharp Vigilance* and the NATO counterpart *Maritime Monitor* were co-ordinated through Italian commands – CINCNAV and COMNAVSOUTH respectively.[14]

The circumstances surrounding the NATO and WEU operations called for collaboration not only as a matter of common sense but, in light of UN Security Council Resolution 820 of 17 April 1993, imposing a full economic blockade on Serbia and Montenegro, as a necessity. The WEU, anxious to implement its new-found Petersberg tasks, responded before NATO, who was engaged in the broader question of what its role should be in multilateral operations in support of the UN. On 8 June 1993, the Councils of NATO and the WEU met in joint session and concluded that the monitoring operations involved considerable wasteful duplication of effort on the part of the two organisations. According to Willem van Eekelen, the WEU Secretary-General, this duplication was due to 'the speed of events and the fact that both organisations were defining their new roles'.[15] The June meeting led to the establishment of a single command and control operation for *Operation Sharp Guard*, the successor to the separate monitoring operations, under the political oversight of the NATO and WEU Councils and the operational command of NATO's COMNAVSOUTH. This arrangement met predictable resistance from France. A compromise was reached with the establishment of an Adriatic Military Committee over which both the WEU and NATO Councils exerted joint control. The formation of the single command structure symbolised the end of the largely French manufactured competition between the WEU and NATO. The diminution of French resistance to NATO-led operations effectively clarified the status of the WEU vis-à-vis the Alliance: it would become the European pillar of the Alliance that would act in concert with NATO except when the US did not wish to participate and, in those circumstances, the WEU would be used in an independent European operation.

Operation Sharp Guard commenced on 15 June 1993, but proved relatively short-lived. Aside from disagreements on how effective the operation was, fundamental differences existed between the US and its European partners over the need to continue to interdict vessels that might be carrying arms to the Bosnian Muslims. In November 1994, the US ceased to participate in the operation and instructions were issued to halt the exchange of military information with the former partners. As Maynard Glitman commented, this was 'hardly the role one would have expected for the "leader of the Alliance" '.[16] The problem rested not so much on institutional turf battles but in transatlantic differences. Ironically, it was these differences that bound together the WEU members and led to their common and unusually public criticism of the US in the press and in the WEU Council's 14 November 1994 Noordwijk Declaration.[17] The US decision to halt its co-operation with the embargo must also be viewed in the light of the NATO Council's January Brussels meeting in which the basic concept behind the CJTF was presented (see Chapter 5). At the centre of the CJTF concept, and indeed ESDI, was the assumption that a consensus between the European and North American allies would be reached and even if the latter chose not to participate in any given action, they would not inhibit their European partners. The abrupt unilateral US decision to cease implementation of the embargo sent out worrying signals about the reliability of the CJTF concept.

In fairness, the intractable nature of the Bosnian problem proved a severe challenge to all European security organisations. Ultimately, the failures and shortcomings are not the responsibility of the organisations themselves, but that of the Member States and their willingness to act through the organisations. Former Italian President, Oscar Luigi Scalfaro stressed the 'great responsibility' of WEU members in their dual status as EC and NATO members to 'set an example of unity through consensus, a unity that will be the keystone of a future pan-European security architecture'.[18] In this goal, the members failed except for in their common resistance to US threats to lift the arms embargo. The crisis in Bosnia also came at a time when all of the European security-related institutions, not to mention those with a more international outlook, were in transition. The EU had no processes or institutional structures for addressing foreign and security policy problems. The WEU was ill-equipped to undertake any decisive intervention and the UN headquarters included NATO personnel, without Americans or Germans, but with French. Washington, for its part, preferred to see the crisis initially as a local European one and was disinclined to become involved and thus stymied a major role for NATO until mid 1995. The situation was also exacerbated by the fact that every security institution was designed to deal with inter-state conflict. No organisation had any appreciable experience of dealing with the complexities of ethnically inspired intra-state conflict. Aside from *Operation Sharp Guard*, the Bosnian crisis illustrated that Europe, in security terms, was quite unable to take the initiative and mount a major military operation. The earlier stages of the break-up of Yugoslavia, prior to US involvement, also provided a salutary example of what Europe without a US military presence could be like. Even Mitterrand, towards the end of his second administration, admitted that *rapprochement* with NATO was compelling.

The enthusiasm with which the Community set about to make this 'Europe's hour' turned out to be a conceit. Arguably, the point of realisation came after a joint initiative launched by Mitterrand and Bush in December 1992. The initiative made it transparently clear that any ethnic cleansing in Kosovo would provoke a military response. The stationing of a multinational but primarily US 'trip wire' force in Macedonia in 1993 gave substance to the threat and served to contain the conflict for a few years. The advent of a new administration in Washington, which lead to NATO involvement in the crisis and a resolve to use force, further underlined to the Europeans their dependence upon the US.

In an interesting aside on the role of the WEU, both in the context of the Bosnian crisis but also more generally, Willem van Eekelen recounts an incident which appears to question whether the political will exists amongst the EU Members to work through or with the WEU. The meeting of which van Eeklen writes was the 22 November 1993 meeting of the Twelve in Luxembourg:

> To my surprise, it appeared that the Twelve had invited the generals in charge of the UN operations, Cot and Briquemont, and had asked them to plan alternative routes for the humanitarian convoys. Nobody from WEU had been invited, not even from our Planning

Cell which had been dealing with the Yugoslav crisis for some time. I was particularly disappointed as this happened during the Belgian Presidency of the EU, a country which had always supported closer links between the European Union and WEU... In practice, this episode marked the end of WEU involvement in the general management of the Yugoslav crisis.[19]

The dissolution of Yugoslavia prompted not only soul-searching in European capitals but also some profound debates with policy ramifications. For instance, within Germany the possibility of military involvement in the former Yugoslavia sparked a protracted discussion on the constitutionality of such action. The constitutional debate was only resolved on 12 July 1994, when the Federal Constitutional Court decided that intervention outside the delineated NATO area was not a violation of the Basic Law. Although nominally about conflicting interpretations of the *Grundgesetz*, this very public discussion was also about the deep-seated historical reservations concerning any involvement of the *Bundeswehr* in the former Yugoslavia. It should also be noted that Germany's participation in the Contact Group in 1994, along with Britain, France, Russia and the US, had the implicit effect of strengthening Germany's case for a Permanent Seat on the Security Council.[20] In retrospect it is surprising that the composition of the Contact Group, created in April 1994, involved Germany, which had no military stake in Bosnia but excluded Italy, which was the main support for the naval embargo as well as air strikes.

It is not clear if the WEU could have assumed a more active role, as France urged it should in June 1991. In all likelihood its role was bound to be circumscribed since the constitutional debate in Germany imposed a highly restrictive interpretation on the willingness of Germany to contribute to out of (NATO) area operations. Furthermore, Britain's reluctance to engage in military action in 1991, based on analogies with Northern Ireland, would also have stifled a more active WEU role. Although the WEU and NATO subsequently assumed roles in implementing UN resolutions, it is nevertheless significant that consensus on a course of action was not reached in any of the European security structures. More importantly, there were evident tensions between the WEU and the UN that foreshadowed future problems. For example, since the WEU is not formally a 'regional arrangement' (in the sense specified in Article 52 of the UN Charter) it remains unclear whether the WEU requires a formal legal mandate, such as a

Security Council resolution, as the basis for any action. Or, as the French maintained, it is able to undertake peacekeeping or other operations with the legal authority of the EU? Obviously, any formal link between the WEU and the UN would imply UN authorisation for military actions beyond the purely self-defensive. This, in turn, would bring into question the 'independent' nature of the European security identity.

In addition to its role in enforcing the embargo in the Adriatic, the WEU was also involved in two small but nonetheless important operations. Both met with some success. The first was the blockade on the Danube. As with the Adriatic embargo, the Danubian blockade owed its genesis to the Italian Presidency. It was also co-ordinated by an Italian commander with operations headquarters in Calafat, Romania, while a German deputy was located in Mohacs, Hungary. The need for WEU involvement stemmed from the inability of the riparian states (Bulgaria, Hungary and Romania) to monitor the Danube effectively without assistance. Moreover, during the course of 1992 it became obvious to observers that the main sources of arms into Serbia were through Macedonia and via the Danube. On 5 April 1993, the WEU Council consented to assist the three riparian states. Although the blockade undoubtedly helped to stem the flow of arms into Serbia, other supply routes circumvented the embargo and blockade. As an unfortunate footnote to the Danubian operations the three riparian states complained about the negative consequences of the blockade upon their economies and, in spite of their rights under international law, none received recompense.

The second operation in which the WEU was involved in was the EU administration of Mostar. The WEU assisted in the training of a police force. The WEU's inclusion stemmed from a 5 October 1993 request from the General Affairs Council of the EU and was facilitated by a co-operative attitude between the German Presidency of the EU and the Luxembourg Presidency of the WEU. This collaborative spirit was only marred by persistent British reluctance to fully support an operation without NATO involvement. Despite initial British reticence, the joint EU/WEU operation was established by April 1994 under Hans Koschnick with a contingent of roughly 190 personnel from the WEU. Overall the operation fell under the EU's aegis, as did the financing of the operation. However, the arrangements for financing it were to prove contentious since, by financing it through the EU, the European Parliament had a role to play under the Treaty on European Union. The British objections were mainly aimed at the more general implications for Community overview of (intergovernmental) second pillar activities through the control of the budget.

NATO and Bosnia

The progression of events up to and in 1995 was not encouraging for any of the international institutions involved in Bosnia. The Bosnian Serbs appeared to operate with impunity; attempts to circumscribe their operations only resulted in the kidnapping of UN peacekeepers. Within the UN, differences were evident on virtually every conceivable subject ranging from when and if UNPROFOR should withdraw and whether peacekeepers should be used for peace enforcement. In general, UNPROFOR seemed to be suffering from a crisis of morale and leadership after the fall of the so-called 'safe area' of Srebrenica to Bosnian Serb forces on 11 July, followed by attacks against Žepa, also a safe area. American willingness to use air strikes was also resisted by some of the European allies. There were a number of reasons for this, the most compelling of which was that the Europeans had sizeable numbers of troops on the ground who were likely to be the object of reprisals against air strikes.

The path to NATO's involvement in the Balkan conflict can be traced back to December 1992 when NATO extended its support for peacekeeping activities to the UN. By mid 1993, NATO was given prime responsibility for the protection of the six UN 'safe areas' in Bosnia Herzegovina. It was only in August 1995 when, after forty months of sporadic engagement (and the loss of 10 000 civilian lives in Sarajevo alone) that NATO became a major actor in the conflict. At this time, NATO unleashed five waves of airstrikes against Serbian positions throughout Bosnia Hezegovina. The catalyst was another mortar attack against a crowded market place in Sarajevo and repeat violations by Serb aircraft of the 'No Fly Zone'. NATO had shot down Serb aircraft in January 1995, which were violating the zone in *Operation Deny Flight*. The fighting also looked set to escalate following a successful Croatian offensive in the Krajina. Significantly, the Lancaster House conference of 21 July saw the UN Secretary General surrender his right of veto over air strikes to UNPROFOR's commander, General Bernard Janvier, thus clearing a major potential objection to the strikes. The initiative for *Operation Deliberate Force* was from the US and, given the massive scale of what followed, it could only really have emanated from there. The airstrikes of 30 August, which marked the first use of NATO forces in conflict, involved over 200 sorties of NATO planes (including 48 US planes). Ultimately, the airstrikes were to have a profound effect on the conflict in Bosnia and paved the way to the negotiating tables at Dayton. Beyond this, as Bhaskar Menon commented:

> The breadth and intensity of the airstrikes stood in stark contrast to the cumulative record of sporadic and ineffectual military action orchestrated under the aegis of U.N. forces and the notorious 'dual key' arrangement, which provided the U.N. civilian leadership a veto over NATO military action... It took the shelling of the civilians in Sarajevo – now coupled with the very real spectre of a costly, militarily dangerous, and politically humiliating withdrawal of UNPROFOR – to mobilize a response from the Western powers. That response would seek to circumvent the United Nations; the robust application of NATO military power, supported by active American diplomacy, would define a new phase in the Balkan War.[21]

The December 1995 Dayton Peace Accords, backed by a 60 000 strong NATO implementation force (IFOR) and 20 000 US troops, resulted in NATO assuming prime responsibility for securing the peace and enforcing the cease-fire arrangements. However, statements by President Clinton and Secretary of Defense William Perry in early 1996 that the US contingent would remain no longer than a year complicated NATO's role. Their statements reflected worries held by the US public and Congress about Somalia-type 'mission creep' and protracted involvement. The US eventually prolonged its commitment of troops through 1998 as part of a smaller SFOR. On 20 February 1996 NATO signalled its willingness to organise and lead a multinational force in Bosnia and Herzegovina following the end of SFOR's mandate in June 1998, with the objective of assisting the parties in further progress towards 'self-sustaining stability'. The force, which retains the SFOR nomenclature, has the mission 'to deter renewed hostilities and to contribute to a secure environment for the ongoing civil implementation efforts in order to stabilize and consolidate the peace in Bosnia and Herzegovina'.[22] SFOR continues to provide broad support for the implementation of the civil aspects of the Peace Agreement, including the promotion of democratic institutions, and bolsters the authority of other international organisations working in the region, such as the Office of the High Representative (Carlos Westendorp), the UN's High Commissioner for Refugees, the International Criminal Tribunal for Former Yugoslavia, the UN International Police Task Force, as well as the authorities of Bosnia Herzegovina.[23]

Lessons from Bosnia for European security

The lessons stemming from the dissolution of Yugoslavia and the ensuing crises are still being drawn. What follows therefore are a few brief, but necessarily tentative, conclusions. The first four conclusions pertain to the EU itself and the second group is a reflection of the more general problems facing European security.

First, the disintegration of Yugoslavia occurred at a point when the Community was making the transition from EPC to CFSP. This had several obvious results. The crisis was addressed primarily through EPC mechanisms, such as they were. The strong backing for diplomatic solutions is thus not surprising given the absence of any other realistic alternatives. The Bosnian crisis was not so much a test of the Union's capabilities (or those of the CFSP) but, rather, a reflection upon the well-known weaknesses of the EPC mechanisms. The mechanisms to enable the EU to address such a crisis, quite aside from questions of political will, were still in their infancy and most only surfaced with the Amsterdam Treaty.

Second, the EC/EU lacked structures to field the human or financial resources necessary to address a crisis of this magnitude. In retrospect, it is worth considering whether the vehement disagreements between the EU and the US over the question of lifting sanctions were not prompted, at least in part, by the paucity of the options available to the EU through the CFSP.

Third, the EC/EU failed to speak with a 'single voice' at virtually any stage of the unfolding crisis. Its ability to do so was further compromised by the formation of the Contact Group that recognised *de facto* differences of influence amongst the EU members. The recognition that some are more equal than others would seem contrary to the aspirations of the Union to present a united face to the international community. Indeed, one of the more worrying aspects of the crisis was the preference for the main EU actors to act outside the newly established CFSP framework in, for example, the Contact Group or the RRF.

Fourth, the EU's post-crisis assistance mechanisms would also appear to leave considerable room for improvement. An *ad hoc* EP delegation visiting Bosnia-Herzegovina in February 1998 criticised the 'bureaucratic, inappropriate and inefficient approach the EU has adopted in its reconstruction aid actions in Bosnia'.[24] The Union's assistance was co-ordinated through the PHARE programme, which the EU criticised as 'totally ineffective and inappropriate in an emergency situation such as Bosnia'.[25] The EU representative in Sarajevo was also found to be chronically short-staffed and under funded, resulting in 40 million ECUs tagged for reconstruction in Bosnia (in 1997) not being spent due to lack of human and other resources on location. The visiting EP delegation concluded: 'In reality the European Union is paying the most, much more than the United States, but it has no real presence on the ground and its action is not really visible on location. *There is very simply no European face in Bosnia.*'[26] The prime culprits for this predicament were identified by the EP delegation as the Commission and the Council with Commissioner Hans van den Broek bearing a 'large part of the responsibility'.

The more general observations stemming from the dissolution of Yugoslavia are also fourfold. First, the willingness of the US to be involved, or not, is clearly critical to almost any conceivable military operation. America's NATO allies appear to have neither the ability nor the will to mount their own peacekeeping operations. Indeed, the catalyst for the airstrikes against Bosnian Serb targets was assertive US leadership. Moreover, it was clear that in the face of conjectured US non-participation in SFOR, prior to the renewal of its mandate in June 1998, the other major contributors (mainly Britain and France) were reluctant to guarantee the fragile peace. In 1997 the British Foreign Secretary, Malcolm Rifkind, went so far as to state, 'let no-one expect our forces to stay in Bosnia when US forces leave...we went in together...we will leave together'.[27]

Second, the second-generation peacekeeping employed in Bosnia following the NATO air strikes fell outside the realms of traditional or first generation peacekeeping and, indeed, outside the purview of the UN itself. Russian President Boris Yeltsin attempted on 12 September 1995 to halt the airstrikes (backed only by China) in a resolution presented to the Security Council. He also complained to Washington and the European capitals that Russia was being ignored. Yeltsin's claim was true, but was not limited to Russia. Vigorous US leadership dissolved nearly all aspects of the 'dual key' arrangements with the UN and usurped the Security Council's participation as well. The bombing campaigns were controlled by NATO but directed largely by the US. The use of airstrikes in a peace enforcement role raises the more general problem of the limits of peacekeeping and, in particular, whether some of the central tenets of traditional peacekeeping, such as impartiality, are feasible or appropriate.

Third, all of the security-related European institutions failed to prevent war. Moreover, the process of apprehending and prosecuting the perpetrators of crimes against humanity has been slow. The work of the

International Criminal Tribunal for former Yugoslavia (ICTY) has proven slow and inconclusive and this must call into doubt the extent that it may provide a legal deterrent to future ethnic cleansing as in, for instance, Kosovo. NATO's role in assisting the ICTY has also proven problematic with two suspects being wrongly apprehended on separate occasions because of mistaken identity and the apparent inability (or unwillingness) to bring some of the prime offenders before the Court. The Dayton peace accords also failed to endorse the undesirability of ethnically homogenous states (with unknown but potentially serious knock-on effects for dealing with future ethnically driven conflicts), while the crisis produced wholly unhelpful mutual finger pointing amongst the organisations involved.

Fourth, Europeans have been forced to re-evaluate their self-image. Europeans had become accustomed to thinking of themselves as living in a humane and civilised region. The response to the crisis in Bosnia gave reason to pause for thought about the nature of that civilisation. Bosnia also served as a warning that pragmatism, political expediency, or even opportunism should not be the only guide for Europe's security arrangements. Europe must have morality and vision as well. A good, but complicated, starting point is the realisation that self-determination does not necessarily equal independence and statehood or licence to deny the fundamental freedoms of others.

Postscript Albania and Kosovo ... typical crises of the post-Cold War?

The observation that the Yugoslav crisis was primarily a test of the old EPC mechanisms and not those of the CFSP or ESDI has some credibility. The same argument cannot however be applied to the situation in March 1997 in Albania, following the collapse of 'pyramid' investment schemes and the resultant violence and anarchy in the country. The situation in Albania should have presented a chance for the EU to demonstrate categorically that CFSP can and does work. It would also have bolstered the WEU as well. Instead, Albania became a missed opportunity. The Albanian crisis was, as the Italian Minister of Foreign Affairs, Lamberto Dini, commented, 'A very typical crisis of the post-Cold War, too far from the US to be of interest for it, and too near Europe to be ignored by it'.[28]

The EU Council, meeting in Apeldoorn and Rome, was unable to agree on the need for a concerted EU peacekeeping operation. José Cutileiro, the WEU's Secretary-General, 'voiced doubts about the ability of his organisation, which had been asked for military assistance by the Albanian government, to conduct a successful mission in the country'.[29] The task of co-ordinating a response was therefore passed to the OSCE who, after several weeks and more suffering in Albania, concluded that UN authorisation for the use of armed force in Albania was necessary. It was only on 11 April that an Italian advance force went ashore at Vlora followed later by 6000 troops from other EU members (Austria, Denmark, France, Greece and Spain) as well as non-members (Romania and Turkey). Critics soon dubbed 'Operation Alba' as 'Operation Alibi'.[30] It was also only on 13 May 1998 that Secretary General Cutileiro indicated that the 'WEU is ready to assume the responsibilities of political monitoring and strategic leadership of a Petersberg mission', while President of the WEU Assembly, Luis Maria de Puig, called for 'preparation for action'.[31] Perhaps, as indicated by Cutiliero's remarks at the WEU's Ministerial Council meeting in Rhodes on 11–12 May, the WEU's lacklustre performance can be accounted for by the fact that it was still in the 'consolidation phase' of its relations with the EU and NATO and moreover the WEU Military Committee had yet to be activated.[32]

As a matter of good luck rather than anything else, the situation in Albania stabilised and there was no need for external intervention. Unlike the crisis in Bosnia, the emergency in Albania was of ideal size and nature to have served as a show-case example of the WEU mounting a Petersberg mission while at the same time demonstrating to all the EU's coming of age as a security actor. Instead, the EU contented itself with passing the buck to the OSCE. Both Bosnia and Albania are somewhat discouraging examples of how ESDI and CFSP remain more of an aspiration than a reality.

Kosovo: on the brink?

'The European Union should prove it has learnt the lessons of Bosnia by acting decisively to bring about peace in the southern Balkans' wrote Carl Bildt with reference to Kosovo.[33] The tense situation in Kosovo cannot though be separated from the general failure to find a settlement for the southern Balkans in general. The deterioration in Kosovo was evident to many observers for a number of years and certainly since the turn of 1997–8 when the Kosovo Liberation Army (KLA) made their first appearance. Is it, as Carl Bildt has suggested, a case of *déjà vu*?

Unlike many other post-Cold War intra-state conflicts, Kosovo is a good deal more grey and ambiguous. First, Kosovo is not a sovereign entity. Since the early 1970s Kosovo (and Vojvodina to the north) has achieved a high degree of autonomy akin in some ways to the six constituent republics of the Yugoslav federation.[34] However, it was only the republics, not the provinces like Kosovo, which were accorded the right of secession. Moreover, the efforts of the KLA are specifically aimed to replace autonomy with independence for *all* Albanians in the Balkans, not just those in Kosovo. The ethnic composition of Kosovo's two million inhabitants, which is 90 percent Albanian[35] and the remainder Serb, makes any open vote for continued autonomy or independence highly unlikely from Belgrade's perspective (moreso now given the widespread evidence of attempts at ethnic cleansing by the Serb security forces in Kosovo).[36] Second, Albanians outside Albania are not a nation and thus it is not clear that the principle of self-determination applies. Albanians are also a minority within Serbia and Montenegro.

The historical and cultural importance accorded to Kosovo by the Serbs makes the idea of a peaceable secession unthinkable. Kosovo is intimately connected in the Serb mind with the cradle of Serbian culture, with tales spun around the defeat of Tsar Lazar, a legendary Serb figure, by the Turks at The Field of Blackbirds (Kosovo Polje) in 1389 and the subsequent rule by Turks for the next five hundred years. Kosovo, according to Serb history, was then liberated from Turkish rule in the First Balkan War of 1912. The Serb army (with its Montenegrin ally) then attempted to consolidate its hold on Kosovo by expelling Turks, Muslims and Albanians. Following Austria's insistence, Serbia and Montenegro surrendered part of their territory to the new state of Albania. From the Serb perspective, interwar rivalries were not the cause of the deep enmity between Serbs and Albanians. Rather, as Aleksa Djilas points out, enmity is rooted in 'centuries of discrimination against the Serbian Orthodox Church and oppression of Serb peasants by Muslim Albanian lords and their followers'.[37]

With the driving out from Yugoslavia of German forces at the end of World War II, fighting immediately erupted between Albanian and Yugoslav forces for the control of Kosovo, the former being outnumbered by around four to one. Mass protests followed in 1968 with the first hint of some form of self-rule but it was not until 1974 that the new Yugoslav constitution granted Kosovo autonomy. The 1980s saw further protests over alleged harassment of Kosovo Albanians and in 1989 Slobodan Milošević removed Kosovo's autonomy. Predictably, thereafter both the protests and the casualties mounted. In 1990, Albanian students started what was to be a six-year boycott of state schools and colleges which was to spread into other areas of state activity resulting in a bureaucratic divorce of the Albanians in Kosovo from the Serb-dominated apparatus. In 1991, the Albanian parliament recognised Kosovo as an independent republic and in the following year the intellectual Ibrahim Rugova was elected president of the self-proclaimed republic. In October 1992, Serb and Kosovo Albanian leaders held the first of what was to be a number of talks aimed at an elusive mutually agreeable arrangement. As an unpopular spin-off from the Bosnian conflict, Serb authorities settled several hundred Croatian Serb refugees in Kosovo which, once again, provoked protest from the Kosovo Albanian leaders. The number of guerrilla attacks increased in 1997 while the state prosecutor made the first charges against members of the illegal National Movement for the Liberation of Kosovo and the suspected leader of the KLA was killed in a battle with police.

By the beginning of 1998 heavily armed Serb police and army groups surrounded Prekaz, which was believed to be a KLA stronghold. In response to growing tensions, the US and four European powers agreed to an arms embargo, with Russia in opposition. Massive protests were staged in Pristina against the violence and the US Special Envoy, Richard Gelbard, publicly accused the Serb authorities of using brutal and overwhelming force. The foreign ministers of the Contact Group (Britian, France, Germany, Italy, Russia and the US) meeting in London on 9 March 1998 and in Bonn on 25 March, agreed that 'the situation in Kosovo is not simply an internal matter, but also has a direct impact on the stability of neighbouring countries and jeapordizes peace in the Balkans'.[38] The imposition of UN Security Council resolution 1160, imposing an arms embargo against the Federal Republic of Yugoslavia (FRY) on 31 March by a vote of 14 to 1 (China arguing that it is an internal matter and thus opposing the resolution), sent a clear message to all parties to the conflict that the situation in Kosovo was of legitimate concern to the international community.[39] Resolution 1160 called for, amongst other things, the 'withdrawal of the special police units and ceased action by security forces affecting the civilian population', a peaceful resolution to the conflict, an enhanced status for Kosovo and greater autonomy for it as well as meaningful self-administration. As a further reminder of the international concern, the resolution urged the Office of the Prosecutor of the International Tribunal to begin gathering information pertaining to the violence in Kosovo.[40]

Following the UN Security Council vote in favour of an arms embargo and with Gelbard's urging, Belgrade attempted a diplomatic solution to the crisis by announcing an April referendum on international intervention in Kosovo. Ibrahim Rugova rejected the referendum while 95 percent of Serbs rejected any such intervention. Although limited progress was made in some areas, such as the return to schools and colleges of Kosovo Albanian students, militants stymied any substantial progress. Richard Holbrooke's 'shuttle diplomacy' commenced in May with joint talks between Milošević and Rugova. In response to the growing concern voiced by NATO and other security organisations at the situation in Kosovo, UN Secretary General, Kofi Anan, warned the Alliance that it must secure a Security Council mandate prior to any intervention.

In response to the deteriorating situation in Kosovo the six-nation Contact Group met but showed little coherence. In mid June 1998 NATO mounted a short-notice air exercise, *Determined Falcon*,[41] in order to remind Milošević of the potential consequences of continued repression. William Cohen, US Secretary of Defense, asserted that the exercise proved that NATO was 'united in its commitment to seek a ceasefire ... and demonstrated its capacity to rapidly mobilise some very significant lethal capacity'.[42] Immediately following the air exercise on 16 June, Russian President Boris Yeltsin persuaded Milošević to open negotiations with Kosovo Albanians (excluding independence parties or members of the KLA). Milošević however refused to remove the 'special police forces' that allegedly protected the Serbian minority in Kosovo. He also linked the withdrawal of Yugoslav troops to the cessation of 'terrorist activities' by the KLA based on the sure knowledge that the KLA would capitalise on any withdrawal to secure key points and perhaps, in retaliation, endanger the Serb minority. The prospect of a negotiated settlement was greeted pessimistically by NATO members. For its part, the EU Council adopted a common position (based on Article J.2) to freeze the funds held abroad by the FRY and Serbia, grounded upon evidence of continuing repression in Kosovo. With ironical timing, the WEU Secretary-General speaking on the occasion of the 50th anniversary of the WEU, ruled out intervention in Kosovo 'in the foreseeable future'.[43] Commissioner Hans van den Broek, at the same venue, said that consideration could be given to sending a 'European contingent' to UNPREDEP.[44]

In August, following a massive Serb offensive against Junik (which was believed to be a KLA stronghold), the UN called for a cease-fire. In the following month, on 23 September, the UN Security Council adopted resolution 1199. The Security Council argued that resolution 1199 and the earlier resolution (1160) provided the legal backing for any use of military force in Yugoslavia.[45] Acting under Chapter VII of the UN Charter, the Security Council demanded the following in resolution 1199:

i) That all parties, groups and individuals immediately cease hostilities and maintain a cease-fire in Kosovo, FRY, which would enhance the prospects for a meaningful dialogue between the authorities of the FRY and the Kosovo Albanian leadership and reduce the risks of humanitarian catastrophe;

ii) That the authorities of the FRY and the Kosovo Albanian leadership take immediate steps to improve the humanitarian situation and to avert the impending humanitarian catastrophe; and

iii) That the FRY, in addition to the measures called for under resolution 1160, implement immediately the following concrete measures towards achieving a political solution to the issue of Kosovo:

–Cease all action by the security forces affecting the civilian population and order the withdrawal of security units used for civilian repression;

–Enable effective and continuous international monitoring in Kosovo by the European Community Monitoring Mission and diplomatic missions accredited to the FRY, including access and complete freedom of movement to such monitors;

–Facilitate in agreement with the UNHCR and ICRC the safe return of refugees and displaced persons to their homes and allow free and unimpeded access for humanitarian organisations and supplies to Kosovo; and

–Make rapid progress towards a clear timetable, in the dialogue... with the Kosovo Albanian community called for in resolution 1160, with the aim of agreeing confidence-building measures and finding a political solution to the problems of Kosovo.

Neither of the UN resolutions were specific on how many of the Serb security forces should be withdrawn. It is a safe assumption that those security units used 'for civilian repression' is a reference to the euphemistically named 'special police' units. These were, according to Serb claims, all withdrawn. The Yugoslav Deputy Information Secretary, Miodrag Popovic, rejected the complete withdrawal of Yugoslav troops with the following argument: 'Who in their right mind would do so? Is there a country in the world that would do so, especially with an armed rebellion on their hands?'[46] Contrary to Serb claims, western press sources estimated some 1000 of the 10 000 special police remained while 60 per cent of the total force sent to put down the independence movement in Kosovo remained.[47] The withdrawal of all Serb forces would logically have implied the introduction of an intervention force to impose stability that would have also involved disarming the KLA. Relatively little was known about the KLA but it was estimated to be around 35 000 strong. Still less was known about its command structure and organisation except that it was organised around local 'units'. Such units presumably can vanish or reconstitute at will, which may pose a long-term challenge to stability in Kosovo.

The day after resolution 1199 was adopted, NATO issued an ACTWARN for a limited air option and a phased air campaign in Kosovo. The ACTWARN took NATO to a heightened level of readiness and allowed NATO commanders to identify the required assets.[48] In a press conference on 24 September 1998 at the Defence Ministers meeting at Vilamoura, Portugal, US Secretary of Defense Cohen observed that 'NATO has used air power in the past to help force an end to the fighting in Bosnia', while US Chairman of the Joint Chiefs of Staff, General Henry S. Shelton, assured the press that 'NATO has military plans to deal with the situation in Kosovo, should our diplomatic efforts fail to produce a solution'.[49]

Russia, as a permanent member of the Security Council, challenged the adequacy of the Security Council resolutions as the basis for military action. NATO's Secretary General, Javier Solana, argued on behalf of the NATO members that the Security Council's 23 September resolution in particular provided sufficient grounds for action. The case however for a further 'enabling' resolution could be construed from the final passage of resolution 1199 which read, 'should the concrete measures demanded in this resolution and resolution 1160 not be taken, [the Security Council shall] *consider further action and additional measures to maintain or restore peace and stability in the region'*. (Emphasis added) The implication therefore was that if Milošević failed to comply, his obstruction would trigger further *consideration* of measures to be taken, including the use of force, and this was not a matter for the unilateral decision of any one Security Council member. In the face however of an impending humanitarian disaster and the certainty of a Russian veto, the US, and perhaps Britain, was not inclined to wait to 'consider further action'.[50]

Although it may have been preferable to have a further resolution, it did not appear to be a necessity since the collective defence stipulations of Article 51 of the UN Charter had already been invoked. Nor, it appears, was the threat of a Russian veto in the Security Council a serious impediment. Cohen argued that not only was no authority necessary from the Security Council, since any action would fall under Article 51 of the UN Charter by which NATO could legitimately defend its collective interests, but also that 'we ought not to subordinate NATO's ability to act' to a Security Council veto.[51] Cohen echoed the views of Bob Dole who was sent by President Clinton on a fact-finding mission to Kosovo. Dole's conclusion was that 'it's time to do something...I don't believe any political pressure, economic, any kind of pressure will work'.[52] The view of the US was accorded special weight because, in spite of the nominal NATO nature of the proposed air strikes, up to 80 percent of the forces would be American. Of the other potential contributors, Britain was broadly in agreement with the US position while France expressed a preference for an additional resolution prior to any action taking place.

The combined effects of resolutions 1160 and 1199 certainly established the political case for intervention but the resolutions did not prescribe what type of use of force may be appropriate as had been the case in resolutions on, for example, Somalia. Legal issues aside, by invoking Article 51 of the UN Charter and the right to collective self-defence, NATO ran a risk. Unilateral action by NATO could undermine the validity of future UN–NATO co-operation and could also invite similar responses by other security organisations, or even individual states, regarding military intervention. In particular, it may have negative effects on Russia's relations with NATO members.[53] The Russian Ambassador to the UN, Sergei Lavrov, called for a settlement 'exclusively through peaceful political methods on the basis of granting broad autonomy for Kosovo'. The wider effects on Russian–NATO relations could however be detrimental, most notably to the future of the Partnership Council and Russia's future willingness to remain involved.

On 29 September 1998 the Serb Prime Minister, Mirko Marjanović, announced the defeat of the separatists and the withdrawal of forces from Kosovo. In spite of this, Serb forces continued attacks on villages in the Drenica region. There was also evidence that the 'Serbian forces were digging in for the winter', especially along the roads to Pristina.[54] This was in spite of the announcement by Marajanović to the Yugoslav parliament on 29 September that the special police forces would be withdrawn from Kosovo. The 29th was also the day on which the defeat of the KLA was proudly announced. At its height, in July, the KLA controlled approximately half of Kosovo and in response to

Marajanovic's claim that it had been defeated, it pronounced that on the contrary, it was 'just the beginning' of the fighting. Then, in a tactical move, aimed to enhance Milošević's image as a warmonger, the KLA announced a unilateral cease-fire, effective 8 October.

The sticking point in the Holbrooke–Milošević negotiations was over the need for an 'expanded international monitoring force' to ensure that resolutions 1160 and 1199 were being fully complied with. At the eleventh hour, under the threat of imminent air attacks, an agreement was reached on 13 October. Under the deal, Milošević agreed to allow unarmed foreign observers to monitor the withdrawal of Serb troops from Kosovo and participate in negotiations that would restore greater self-rule to the province.[55] At the time of the arrangement all NATO members agreed to sanction air strikes. The agreement allowed for 2000 OSCE observers as well as NATO overflights as part of the monitoring efforts. It was hoped that the presence of foreign observers, albeit unarmed, would encourage the return of the 50 000 or so refugees hiding in the woods and hills. At the time of writing, following the first inconclusive round of talks at Rambouillet between Serb representatives, Albanian Kosovars and the Contact Group, a number of issues remain open.

First, the return of refugees to their homes assumes that there is something to return to. Since many homes were destroyed or sufficiently damaged return is unrealistic, no matter what agreement may be reached. Many villages were torched by Serb forces because they were allegedly KLA strongholds. *The Economist* in late October 1998 noted that some 200 villages were destroyed and 'few of the 250 000 displaced people are going home. Large areas of central and western Kosovo are empty'.[56] Moreover, foreign aid and assistance was sporadic in the face of a bitter winter. Although the worst of a humanitarian disaster may have been averted, dangers remain apparent for the young and old in particular.

Second, the Holbrooke–Milošević deal averted air strikes but did not secure a settlement of the longer-term problems. The unenviable task of securing a longer-term agreement fell to Holbrooke's right hand man, US mediator and Ambassador to Macedonia Chris Hill, who developed a plan that went some of the way to meeting ethnic Albanian demands for autonomy.[57] Under the plan, Kosovo would be reserved 30 seats in the Yugoslav parliament and given places in the federal government and judiciary. Kosovo would also have its own parliament, while the federal army would remain within ten kilometres of Kosovo's international borders with Albania and Macedonia, and

Serbia would relinquish all control over Kosovo's police force. A new police force would be constituted in proportion to Kosovo's ethnic composition under an ethnic Albanian Interior Minister and a Serb deputy. Under the plan the Yugoslav Federation would retain control over foreign affairs, customs, foreign trade and monetary policy.

Third, a definitive settlement rests upon the exact status of Kosovo and whether autonomy could, at some point, lead to independence. Chris Hill and Secretary of State Madeleine Albright have pointedly refused to discuss independence for Kosovo. Hill's plan calls only for a 'reassessment' of the status of Kosovo after three years. However, there are a number of problems on the horizon including complaints by Fehmi Agani, adviser to Ibrahim Rugova, that the plan leaves the status of Kosovo unclear, creating the possibility that the more radical elements in the KLA might reject the plan.[58] The plan also makes provision for the holding of regional and local elections within nine months, under OSCE supervision. The elections may lead to further instability since ethnic Albanians have largely boycotted elections since 1989 when Kosovo was stripped of its autonomy which, in effect, bolstered Milosevic's ruling Serbian Socialist Party (SSP). The loss of an absolute majority in 1997 forced the SSP to form a coalition with the nationalist Radical Party under Vojislav Šešelj who is, at the time of writing, deputy Prime Minister. Šešelj's threat to pull out of the coalition if 'foreign peacekeepers' were allowed into Kosovo may usher in more political instability. Alternatively, Šešelj may decide to leave the coalition in pursuit of his own political ambitions.

The settlement remained shaky and sniping and retaliatory attacks continue.[59] Although the Holbrooke–Milošević agreement allowed for the continued presence of 25 000 Serb police in all of Kosovo's main towns, this police force was increasingly surrounded by better armed KLA members who apparently had little difficulty receiving weapons and supplies through Albania and elsewhere. The OSCE verification mission, which was unarmed, was also very slow in starting its duties (William Walker, the head of the mission, only arrived in Kosovo on 11 November). As a general example of the parlous state of the settlement, the North Atlantic Council released a press statement on 19 November 1998 expressing 'its deep concern about the deteriorating security situation in Kosovo' provoked by a number of incidents carried out by both Serb and Albanian Kosovo elements. These incidents 'risk creating a dangerous cycle of provocation and response which, if continued, could destabilize the ceasefire, reverse the recent improvement in the humanitarian situation, and jeopardize the arrangements being put into place by NATO and OSCE verification of compliance with the relevant UN Security Council resolutions'.[60]

The tenuous ceasefire secured by the Holbrooke–Milošević agreement was supposed to be the precursor to peace talks early in 1999. The first round of talks, held near Paris at Rambouillet in February 1999, between representatives of the Belgrade administration, KLA representatives and the six-nation Contact Group, sought to secure agreement for a permanent end to hostilities. A settlement would have meant the KLA agree to disarm and postpone, for at least three years, independence in return for limited autonomy. The Serbs were expected to agree to up to 30 000 troops on its soil to monitor the agreement, under threat of air strikes if they persisted in a military build up.

After the inconclusive end of the first round of talks a second round convened in mid March. By this time the violence had worsened, with both sides vying for position prior to the commencement of negotiations. Although, at the time of writing, the prospects for a settlement looked mixed, a number of outcomes to the conflict, which has so far left 2000 dead and some 300 000 displaced, can be foreseen. The first possible outcome is that an agreement is signed under the renewed threat of NATO air strikes and the emplacement of a sizeable NATO force into Kosovo. There are however signs that, aside from Britain and the US, reactions to this scenario are mixed amongst the NATO members. Even if a NATO intervention force is put into position the underlying political questions remain unresolved unless the NATO members are willing to assume responsibility for an indefinite presence. The threat of air strikes may also prove problematic in practice since it makes little sense to target Serb forces in Kosovo when the infrastructure and bulk of the forces are in Serbia proper. The military logic of the situation would seem to suggest comprehensive strikes against both Serb *and* KLA positions wherever they may be with the goal of neutering their military power. But, given the unpopularity and politically debatable effects of the US and British air strikes against Saddam Hussein's regime, the goals and objectives of any air strikes need to be realistic and should have the backing of at least the major NATO powers.

Second, if there is no agreement and Milošević guesses (with some justification) that NATO or the European allies will not intervene for a variety of reasons, including potential casualties, the Serb forces will be free to systematically eradicate the KLA and presumably set into flight many more Albanian Kosovars. In March 1999, NATO began to position an extraction force in Macedonia with the task of evacuating the unarmed OSCE observers if need be. One can only hope that NATO can extract all if indeed they become targets, or even hostages, in the hostilities. In this scenario not only NATO but all European security organisations or mechanisms, including CFSP, would lose all credibility. The credibility issue is especially relevant since, with much fanfare, NATO celebrates its 50th anniversary in April. In short, NATO cannot fail in Kosovo and, if it does, celebrations might well turn into a requiem.

Third, an agreement is reached and in due time (perhaps 2002) Kosovo moves towards complete independence. Such an outcome would rely firstly upon the willingness of the more radical factions in the KLA to accept limited autonomy in the uncertain interim. It would also rely upon other political figures in Belgrade exercising considerable sway over Milošević. This seems a remote possibility. The Serb parties who solely intend to buy 'breathing room' may well agree to the acceptance of such an agreement under duress. The question of whether such a settlement might not prompt others within existing entities or states, such as Macedonia or Montenegro, to push for secession also needs to be weighed.

Bosnia, as has been observed, posed a severe challenge to European security but the excuse that the crisis occurred in a very difficult transition period – where there were no European security 'structures' in place, at a time when NATO was adjusting to post-Cold War security and when the US was unsure about its foreign policy obligations and responsibilities – had some justification. No such justification applies with Kosovo and that is precisely why the crisis will make or break all of the organisations, structures and plans so carefully made or adapted since the end of the Cold War.

Lessons from the testing ground

Carl Bildt observed that: 'Kosovo is a testing ground. Here we will see if the lessons of the wars in Croatia and Bosnia have been learnt. So far, there are only faint signs that this has been the case. The EU is as hesitant, NATO as unwilling, Russia as unreluctant and the US as much a solo player as ever.'[61] The difficulties encountered in addressing the problems of Kosovo are part of a wider change in the nature of post-Cold War conflict from inter-state to intra-state warfare. Nearly all of the major armed conflicts in the international system at present, with the sole exception of the dispute over Kashmir between India and Pakistan (and more recently Eritrea and Ethiopia), are intra-state conflicts. While intra-state strife is obviously not a new phenomenon, it remains true that those security organisations that survived the Cold War, of which there are very few, remain geared to the problems of addressing inter-state conflict. NATO is one of the few organisations with effective military potential to have survived the Cold War. In spite of its efforts to emphasise the collective security aspects of its work, it remains primarily a collective defence organisation, as laid down in its founding treaty. The WEU is also geared towards collective defence under the terms of the 1954 Modified Brussels Treaty. Both organisations were founded with the heavily armed nuclear camps of the Cold War in mind and, accordingly, relatively little thought was given to the possibility of grappling with intra-state conflict. The complexity of addressing intra-state warfare, such as that in Kosovo, goes well beyond just the immediate conflict since it raises fundamental questions about order in the international system, the role of the state itself and those circumstances in which a state should be deemed less than sovereign.

In general, the Cold War taboo against intervention in the domestic affairs of a sovereign state has been undermined for two reasons. First, rarely is an intra-state conflict confined to the state in question. Normally, there will be regional or international ramifications to the fighting, such as refugee movements across borders, arms transactions and the disruption of economic and political activity. Any one of these, or a combination thereof, could legitimately be claimed to represent a threat to international peace and stability and trigger a response. Second, the proven violation of a specific group (or groups) within a state by another group could instigate an international response based on proof of the systematic violation of human rights. All of these expressions of public international law have been used in UN Security Council resolutions and have led to interventions of various types. The enthusiasm for exploiting these arguments has though waned perceptibly as the complexity and cost of intra-state conflict have become apparent (Somalia in particular) while the lack of 'quick fix' solutions has also been equally clear (nowhere moreso than Bosnia).

Kosovo is yet another depressing example of the hideous complexity of intra-state clashes and, for different reasons, it follows the litany of other less than satisfactory attempts to address intra-state conflict in Somalia, Rwanda, Burundi and Yugoslavia. Other confrontations, such as the bloody struggle in Chechnya or those in the Caucasus, remained essentially off limits to regional or international security organisations. Part of the problem lies in the very structure of the international system, which is founded on the twin pillars of statehood and

sovereignty. In turn, statehood and sovereignty have become intimately connected to the ideas of the territorial inviolability of borders,
the right of individual or collective self-defence and nationalism. These
notions shaped not only collective defence but also much of the Cold
War's history, especially the *raison d'être* of the two principal antago-
nists – both dedicated to collective defence. The post-Cold War emergence of intra-state conflict is not a new phenomenon but merely an
indication that the tensions contributing to it were subsumed in the
wider struggles of the Cold War.

A further important shaping force has to be added to those of statehood and sovereignty, that of self-determination. This has proven a notoriously slippery term to grapple with (both legally and politically) ever
since it was enunciated as one of US President Woodrow Wilson's famous
post World War I points. It is not always clear who self-determination
applies to and whether the exercise of self-determination should *ipso
facto* lead to secession from an existing state. All of these elements
come together (again) in Kosovo. What was (and perhaps still is) at
stake in Kosovo is truly of historic importance since past attempts to
stem inter-state conflict have been largely unsuccessful. Success in
Kosovo would not only have immediate benefits for the Balkans, and
more generally Europe, but would fuel the wider debate about security,
the nation-state and how to address intra-state conflict.

The lessons arising from Kosovo seem to be fourfold. First, the CFSP
has some utility as a means for shaping and voicing EU opinion and as
a forum for the pursuit of diplomatic solutions to crises. Beyond these
two functions, CFSP appears to have had relatively little effect, for
example, the threat or implementation of sanctions was ineffectual.
Moreover, in Bosnia and Kosovo arms continued to find their way to
the protagonists. Even where sanctions did have some effect, it is far
from clear that they were adequate to deter nationalist forces from conflict. More generally, sanctions have the habit of hitting their intended
targets last of all and the most vulnerable first.

Second, the ability to mount peacekeeping operations for a sustained
period of time relies heavily on US support and goodwill. Although
Britain and France have greater numbers involved in SFOR, both
expressed their reluctance to continue military involvement without
an American presence. The implications for European security and
defence would therefore tend to support the British assertion, made in
the October 1998 at the 'informal' Pörtschach summit, that the
defence of Europe should be built around ESDI and thus active US
involvement. The possibility of 'Europe only' options, made possible

by the development of the CJTF concept, is a useful development but it remains unclear whether there would be the political will (absent the US) to agree upon the need for military action or to mount and sustain an operation. Certainly, NATO's ACTWARN relied heavily upon US air power, intelligence and communications. The threat of air strikes would also, presumably, have involved the launch of sea borne cruise missiles which, based on the Sudan, Afghan and Iraqi cases, would seem to be the preferred weapon for low-risk strikes.

Third, the complex ethnic dimension to the conflict in Kosovo (and elsewhere) may demand a long-term peacekeeping presence. The reliance upon the tactical use of air power to achieve immediate goals often fails to address the underlying problems (this is as true in Iraq as in Bosnia or Kosovo). The attraction of tactical air strikes is obvious: it affords a relatively cheap and almost risk-free option compared to involvement on the ground. Air strikes in Bosnia and, more particularly in the US anti-terrorist strikes in Sudan and Afghanistan in 1998, have illustrated a tendency to exaggerate the accuracy of the systems involved and have often had negative political consequences (by allegedly or really hitting civilian targets). Air strikes must be backed by follow-up plans and the willingness to deal with the consequences of airstrikes (or the threat thereof) *on the ground*. The difficulty encountered by Holbrooke in securing a climb down by Milošević was due, in part, to the latter's (correct) suspicion that there was disagreement on the strikes themselves and a lack of any concrete follow-up plans. Even after the climb down the 2000 OSCE monitors were deployed painfully slowly while questions remained about how to secure their safety (this is especially important bearing in mind the hostage taking of UN officials by Serb forces in Bosnia). The search for 'quick fixes' to the types of problems encountered in the Balkans is likely to prove elusive. Perhaps it would be more constructive to think of Cyprus as a model for stability in the Balkans.

Lastly, conflicts in the Balkans have a habit of shaping Europe's destiny. Kosovo had all of the ingredients to set the Balkan powder keg off. The application of long-term solutions will not be easy and it is not only a question of resources but primarily one of political will. The ability to frame consensual positions amongst the EU members in the CFSP context has proven problematic. Beyond this, the earlier reluctance of the US to place its troops in harm's way has underlined the incorrect assumption that peacekeeping, including post-conflict settlement, is a low cost activity. The preference for reliance on 'remote' solutions (economic sanctions, communiqués, threat of force and air strikes) has generally led to an under-appreciation of the profound complexities behind the conflicts. Even smaller crises, apparently tailor made for the CFSP, such as that in Albania, portrayed the Europeans as indecisive and divided. The piecemeal and often disparate approaches to the crises in Bosnia, Croatia and Kosovo failed to account for the *common* consequences that the spread of fighting into a general Balkan war could have.

The Cold War legacy that Europe has inherited continues to be based upon defensive organisations and structures, albeit in transition. This heritage had led to an understandable concentration on conflict management. In future the long-term stability of the Balkans, and elsewhere, will depend upon the ability to develop effective conflict *prevention* mechanisms.[62]

7
Progress towards Defining a Common European Security and Defence Policy: Illusion or Practice?

Many hurdles have yet to be crossed on the road defining the CFSP and a European defence policy. The problems outlined here are by no means exhaustive; rather the goal of this chapter is to discuss those that appear to pose notable challenges. Although the development of CFSP has begun the process of moving the Union away from mere statements that involve little real practical commitment, numerous obstacles must be overcome if CFSP is to be a potent tool for stability in the region and beyond.

Seven obstacles are highlighted and discussed in this chapter. First, relations between the European security bodies and, second, the military effectiveness of these same entities. Third, the more specific question of command, control, communication and intelligence will be considered. Fourth, the perennial issue of finance is discussed. Fifth, and very much connected to the previous issue, is that of the future of European defence industries. Sixth, the question of who should be 'in' which organisation is still one that complicates Europe's security map and due consideration is given to whether the asymmetrical membership of the various organisations will prove a significant impediment to the formation of a genuine ESDI. Within this section three special cases are highlighted, those of the neutral and non-aligned countries, the Central and East European countries (CEEC) and Turkey. Seventh, the question whether a European security identity can emerge in light of the tendency of the larger states, in particular, to consider defence planning a national preserve is examined.

Relations between the European security bodies

European security, as has been shown, will rely upon a number of complex linkages between institutions, including the EU, WEU, NATO, the

OSCE and the UN. The CFSP will though depend particularly upon good relations being established between the first three. In particular those between the EU and the WEU are of special importance given the latter's role as an 'integral part of the development of the Union'. It is therefore somewhat sobering to reflect upon how much has to be done in this regard as observed by the President of the WEU Assembly, Lluis Maria de Puig, 'in general relations between WEU and NATO were better than those between the WEU and the European Union'.[1]

The WEU Declaration attached to the Treaty on European Union stated that the objective is to 'build up the WEU in stages as the defence component of the European Union', and to 'develop the WEU as a means to strengthen the European pillar of the Atlantic Alliance'. Also worthy of note is that the WEU agreed to 'act in conformity with the positions adopted in the Atlantic Alliance'.[2] The Petersberg Declaration also stressed the interdependent nature of the European security architecture and emphasised that the WEU, 'together with the European Union, was ready to play a full part in building Europe's security architecture'.[3] Thus far, this has involved the synchronisation of dates and venues of meetings, the harmonisation of work methods, co-operation between the secretariats and various efforts to harmonise the terms of respective presidencies.[4] The Commission is also regularly informed of WEU activities and, where appropriate, consulted. Closer co-operation has also been encouraged between the Parliamentary Assembly of the WEU and the European Parliament. The Parliamentary Assembly of the WEU meets twice a year in Paris in plenary session and, as such, plays a unique role as the only European parliamentary organ with a defence mandate and the only democratic body able to address defence issues.

The close involvement of the Commission and the European Parliament in the future of the WEU and the revising of Article J.4 of the Treaty on European Union in the lead up to the 1996 IGC, seem to have ignored the specification in the treaty that revisions will be undertaken on the basis of a report submitted by the Council (of the EU) to the European Council. (Article J.4.6) Rather oddly, the WEU Council is not accorded a role in the revision process. These omissions, in turn, open up the broader issue of which body (or bodies) has ultimate authority in security and defence matters. It would seem logical to suggest that, at least in the revision process, it should be the WEU Assembly. On many occasions, ministers acknowledged that the WEU will be one of the 'essential elements' of the future European security architecture in accordance with the decisions taken by the European

Council in the Maastricht Declaration. Ministers furthermore stated that they were prepared to support 'on a case-by-case basis and in accordance with our own procedures, the effective implementation of conflict prevention and crisis management measures, including peace-keeping activities of the CSCE or the United Nations Security Council'.[5]

The above statement gives rise to many questions, such as the exact nature of 'the procedures' that are referred to, the issue of how the WEU can 'effectively implement' such a wide variety of tasks and the mechanisms and procedures by which the WEU would support the OSCE or the UN? A provisional answer was supplied by the Petersberg Declaration that proved to be of enormous political significance for several reasons. First, by embracing such a range of tasks the WEU *temporarily* distanced itself from the more purely defence-oriented NATO missions and thus helped to ease tensions between the organisations. Second, the link established with CSCE (now OSCE) and UN missions in effect obviated the constraints of having to work within NATO's geographically delineated area. Finally, the declaration paved the way for the January 1994 NATO Council decision to make the 'collective' assets of the Alliance available to the WEU for operations undertaken by the European allies.

The Petersberg Declaration appeared, for a short time, as a re-birth of the WEU since it gave the WEU a mission, it was not hampered with NATO's out-of-area issues and it had the foundations of military force and support to enable the WEU to carry out its new mandate. The WEU's new-found mission and prominence was however short-lived for two reasons. First, the difficulties that the EC had in formulating a coherent policy towards the Yugoslav crisis hindered it and, even when it did become militarily involved, it could not do so without consider-able NATO assistance. Second, NATO assumed Petersberg-type tasks after the Oslo and Brussels NATO Council meetings on 19 June and 17 December 1992, respectively. Thus, within a matter of months the WEU's *raison d'être* was challenged. Post-Cold War European security has, if anything, been characterised by a competition for roles rather than a harmonious vision of how the organisations might collaborate.

The assumption by NATO of some Petersberg-type tasks opened up a still unresolved debate about the role of the WEU. More specifically, it pointed to the changing nature of peacekeeping itself which has increasingly strayed from its traditional, interpositionary practice into more muscular forms such as peace enforcement. The incorporation of the Petersberg tasks into the TEU and CTEU constitutes only part of the WEU's broad responsibilities, but since they are the only mandate with coherence at the moment, the impression that they are the WEU's *raison d'être* can be forgiven. In practical terms this has been borne out by the WEU's assumption of responsibility of policing or customs operations, such as that on the Danube, that other organisations may be unwilling or unable to take on. NATO, meanwhile, would engage in *peace-enforcement*. While NATO has not strayed from its collective defence origins until Kosovo, it is clear that the more muscular forms of peacekeeping offer the Alliance an effective use of its defensively oriented arsenal.

The evolution of the division of responsibilities between the organisations reflects the adjustments that NATO and the WEU have undergone since the end of the Cold War. There is though little chance of the WEU moving beyond the quasi-policing functions that it has undertaken until the WEU's association with the EU is further clarified. NATO's assumption of tasks more closely associated with peace-enforcement, alongside its traditional collective defence duties, relies heavily upon continued US military support. In the event of the WEU being formally incorporated into the EU or, with the launching of a CJTF or multilateral European operation, the issue of military effectiveness would have to be addressed. Also given the fact that the 1992 Lisbon European Council statement on the CFSP envisaged the 'defence' component as being confined quite narrowly to military action, the question of Europe's military reliability is important.

Military effectiveness

The prolongued discussions regarding the eastward expansion of NATO and, to a lesser extent the EU and the WEU, distracted attention from the state of NATO and WEU militaries. As Michael O'Hanlon pointed out, 'only the US is in a position to deploy large numbers of forces well beyond its national borders and operate them there for an extended period of time'.[6] This was only too apparent to the European allies during the 1990–1 Gulf operations. O'Hanlon commented that 'there is so much military competence in Europe that to have so little of it reliably available for warfighting in the Persian Gulf, emergency peace-enforcement in Africa, or perhaps a crisis in Asia, is deeply troublesome'.[7]

The European Alliance members have made remarkably little attempt to address their continued dependence on their American allies. Even the CJTF concept has, if anything, reinforced the European assumption that key US assets will be available even when Washington may not wish to be involved in an operation and that 'European' defence and security may be had on the cheap. The European allies' dependency in key areas has led some American commentators to wonder if the forces of its allies are not becoming 'hollow'. Again, O'Hanlon put the case bluntly:

> European governments and militaries have to realise that the Cold War is over, and that defending national territory should no longer be the driving impetus behind their military planning... Having the capacity to transport less than 50,000 relatively lightly armoured soldiers quickly to a trouble spot, and needing many months to send significant amounts of armour, is inadequate. Despite spending two-thirds of what the US does on defence, Europeans have less than 10% of the transportable defence capability for long-range action... This situation is unsustainable.[8]

Progress has been made in some areas but the overall picture continues to reflect the gist of O'Hanlon's arguments.

While the obvious current shortcomings of the WEU are recognised internally, the Petersberg Declaration stated somewhat fancifully, that the WEU members 'intend to develop and exercise the appropriate capabilities to enable the deployment of WEU military units by land, sea or air to accomplish these tasks'.[9] The WEU's ability though was more basic than the Petersberg Declaration suggested since the organisation was by-passed for much of the Cold War. The amount of institution building required to make the WEU anything like an effective military organisation was therefore far greater than that of its NATO counterpart. There has been progress but it is barely an outline. In October 1992, a Planning Cell of forty military personnel was established in the Secretariat-General's office in Brussels. It was charged with responsibility for preparing contingency plans for the employment of forces under WEU auspices; to make recommendations on C^3I arrangements; and to maintain a list of units which 'might be allocated to the WEU' for specific operations.[10] The most important aspect of the cell's undertaking was to establish and plan contingencies for WEU multinational forces that could be used either in a UN context or in co-operation with NATO. The 15 May 1995 Council of Ministers meeting in Lisbon provided the WEU with new decision-making and planning structures, such as a Politico-Military Group to advise the council on crises and crisis management, as well a Situation Centre and an intelligence section within the Planning Cell. It was also agreed that the WEU's rules of engagement should be drawn up for implementing 'Petersberg tasks'. However, the structures subsequently proposed begged the question of how the WEU would attain the raw intelligence needed to make decisions and, indeed, how it would communicate decisions.

In spite of the efforts outlined in the Petersberg Declaration and elsewhere, the WEU remains of questionable military utility. Unlike NATO, it does not have a Supreme Commander or peacetime headquarters. Moreover, the assumption that the Eurocorps would, in effect, form the brunt of the WEU's military capability is questionable given the continuing vagaries of the French *rapprochement* with the Alliance.[11] The Council's Luxembourg meeting of 22 November 1993 advocated that the Eurocorps would be deployed as a unified corps in the framework of the WEU to serve the goals of the European Union if NATO fails to act, or if the Europeans choose to act outside of the Alliance. However, the relatively heavy reliance upon US intelligence and logistical support raised the question of the extent to which the US would want to see its resources used in a purely European context. It might also give rise to inevitable command and control headaches that posit the possibility of not just WEU–NATO dual-hat commands, but a triple-hat, if the Franco-German Defence Council is added to those operations involving the Eurocorps.

The 10–11 January 1994 NATO Brussels Summit marked a useful attempt, at least on paper, to answer some of the institutional problems relating to the creation of workable European and Transatlantic security networks (see Chapter 5). At Brussels, the NATO heads of state and government resolved to adapt the Alliance's political structure to 'reflect both the full spectrum of its roles and the development of the emerging European Security and Defence Identity'. In this goal they endorsed the 'concept of the Combined Joint Task Forces'. NATO also expressed support for the 'strengthening of the European pillar of the Alliance through the Western European Union, which is being developed as the defence component of the European Union'.[12] The role of the US has proved to be critical in these highly flexible arrangements. In theory, the CJTF concept allows for either, or both, organisations to draw upon military assets, depending upon the countries involved and the task at hand. Since NATO, like the WEU, has no forces exclusively at its disposal, it is up to the contributing states to contribute adequate forces to multinational operations.

The CJTF concept may in practice raise three problems. The first is obviously that a disproportionate amount of the assets are not only

American but in certain areas, such as aerial electronic jamming capacities, exclusively American. The use of either organisation is therefore critically dependent upon US goodwill and support. Second, without prior planning and at least some agreements on what is needed for an assignment, the CJTF runs the same risks as UN peacekeeping operations. Namely, that it will not know who will turn up, when they will turn up, what they will be armed with, how they will be trained and for how long they intend to participate. Clearly, these are problems that are less apparent in the specifically European context compared to the international one, but there are still significant disparities in training and equipment (not to mention income) levels to make this a valid concern.

Relations between the WEU and NATO have become even more murky with the development of forces answerable to the WEU (FAWEU). According to the WEU Council of Ministers, 'the fulfilment of [FAWEU] missions will not prejudice the participation of their units in the common defence missions provided for by Article V of the Modified Brussels Treaty, and Article 5 of the Washington Treaty'.[13] In the WEU Council's May 1995 Lisbon Declaration certain forces were designated as FAWEU and were open to all WEU member states. FAWEU forces were identified as:

- The EUROCORPS (European Corps), in which France, Germany, Belgium, Spain and Luxembourg participate;
- The Multinational Division (Central), consisting of units from Belgium, Germany, the Netherlands and the United Kingdom;
- The UK/Netherlands amphibious force;
- The EUROFOR (Rapid Deployment Force), in which France, Italy, Portugal and Spain participate;
- The EUROMARFOR (European Maritime Force) in which France, Italy, Portugal and Spain participate;
- Offers of national units by 24 of the 28 WEU members; and
- The British–French air group based at High Wycombe (FBEAG) (not as a standing operational unit but a structure to exploit and develop complementarities).

There are however serious uncertainties about which force 'packages' may be counted upon and provided for, in terms of pre-planning and training, in any particular eventuality in the CD or European pillar context. For instance, EUROMARFOR consists of pre-structured packages while EUROFOR has no pre-assigned forces. The Franco-British air group is not a standing operational unit while the Multinational

Division Central is a standing force. Moreover, of these packages, what can be counted on for planning and training purposes is also unclear.

As with all of the forces that may be answerable to one or the other organisation, a preliminary and important clarification needs to be made about the legal basis of any proposed deployment. Article 5 of the North Atlantic Treaty involves the full power (including nuclear) of the US but generally members are only committed to take such action as deemed necessary. The same article of the modified Brussels Treaty is more binding upon members, however, as José Cutileiro observed, 'Petersberg-type missions' are difficult to foresee, 'the WEU must have the military tools ready and then it is up to the nations to decide whether and when to use them'.[14] This interesting position arises from the respective treaties and the nature of the WEU's possible military involvement, which appears to offer more formal guarantees. But Petersberg-type missions are likely to afford more selectivity. While the Washington Treaty is somewhat more flexible, its collective defence mission is unlikely to allow as much choice in the event of an appeal being made to Article 5. In either scenario, if the WEU or some European 'coalition of the willing' is to be militarily effective, action must be based on reliable intelligence.

The problems of forming and operating with multinational forces are profound, whether in the WEU, NATO or any other context. Operations *Desert Shield* and *Storm* leave room for some optimism about the ability of 'coalitions of the willing' to collaborate successfully in the air and maritime environments. As Roger Palin observed, the greatest differences between European forces and thus difficulties are to be found on the land environment. Palin also reminds us that, prior to 1989, apart from the Allied Command Europe (ACE) Mobile Force–Land and the Jutland Corps HQ, *no multinational integration existed below principal subordinate commander or operational level.*[15]

To assist the FAWEU a Planning Cell was created at the WEU Council's meeting in Bonn on 19 June 1992. A four-star admiral was appointed to head the cell with approximately fifty personnel from twelve countries, divided into six main 'departments', which included:

- Communication and information systems;
- Co-ordination (internal and external);
- Intelligence;
- Logistics/movements and finance;
- Operations and exercises; and
- Plans.

The Planning Cell exists, according to Cutileiro, to 'carry out generic planning for possible operations, to provide rules of engagement and standing operational procedures for headquarters, to update details of forces that might be available for WEU operations and to prepare exercise plans'.[16] The number of staff, as indicated, is small and there is a 'tendency to focus on those tasks that are among its own priorities'.[17] In practice, FAWEU is little more than a database of forces and assets kept by the Planning Cell. It is ultimately up to the individual members whether they contribute or not to any actions outside of the territorial confines of the Member States. The FAWEU may be called upon when the Council gives the political directive. The Planning Cell will then call upon a 'lead nation' (who and how this emerges is vague) to head the operation with the cell acting as liaison with the council. David Greenwood noted that, 'while there are good practical reasons for nominating a lead nation for new bi-national or multi-national formations, the corollary – that some countries must accept junior partner status – may not be appealing to those member states so designated'.[18] The lead nation will also have to be a NATO member since the WEU Ministerial Council meeting, held in Ostend on 19 November 1996, encouraged the formation of 'militarily coherent and effective forces' within the ESDI framework. Such forces though were only under 'the *political control and strategic direction* of the WEU' – thus implying that issues of military command and control rest squarely in NATO's hands.[19]

Generally, the WEU's crisis management mechanisms are incomplete, although it is worth noting in passing that the WEU Assembly adopted a motion at the end of 1997 approving the creation of the WEU's own rapid reaction force (RRF). The WEU's RRF would comprise, at a minimum, a light infantry division (10–12 000 troops), with air and sea support, for operations in which it does *not* make use of NATO assets. The WEU Military Committee recognised that such a force would also imply a more common approach to arms procurement in Europe. However, the more modest improvements to the WEU's capabilities suggested in the Amsterdam Treaty, those of the High Representative of the CFSP and the PPEWU, have yet to materialise. Until they do, there will be obvious deficiencies in the ability to mount Europe-only peacekeeping or crisis management missions. The lack of agreement on who should occupy the High Representative's position has also hindered development of the PPEWU, which falls under the High Representative's control. In an interim report in April 1998, the British Presidency noted the Council's agreement to provide credits for

1999 in view of the recruitment of twenty high level personnel for the unit (spread over three permanent agents and seventeen temporary agents, including in the latter a Commission representative, a WEU representative and one from each Member State).[20] This assumed that an appointment of a High Representative would be made in December 1998, under the Austrian Presidency. The interim report also suggested a division of responsibilities between the PPEWU and the CFSP Unit:

i) The CFSP Unit would be more specifically responsible for assisting the Secretariat of the Presidency, the High Representatives, working groups, the Political Committee, COREPER and the General Affairs Council and for political dialogue including follow-up activities; and

ii) The PPEWU would be more specifically responsible for systematic follow-up and analysis, for planning for future areas of CFSP activity, for early warning and crisis prevention, for options concerning policies to be followed on current and future CFSP issues, for assisting the High Representative and Presidency draw up common CFSP measures (especially new common strategies) and for networking with key figures and organisations (including the WEU).

Of the FAWEU, the Eurocorps has generated the most optimism regarding the ability of the Europeans to actually mount 'Europe-only' military action. The FAWEU are, by and large, earmarked or tagged forces and their availability at short notice must therefore by questioned. The Eurocorps may, in time, mark an exception and be a standing force that can be used either to support CJTF operations or those of the WEU. Although named a 'Eurocorps' it only includes five EU members with a peacetime strength of around 50 000 troops, 700 tanks and 2700 tracked or wheeled vehicles which, according to General Forterre, commander of the Eurocorps, 'probably [makes] the European Corps by far the most powerful armed landforce in Western Europe'.[21] Because of its potential, the Eurocorps deserves further examination.

The Eurocorps

The Franco-German summit held at La Rochelle, on 22 October 1992, launched the 'Eurocorps', which was to become operative in October 1995. The Eurocorps' birth was met with unease in London, primarily because of Kohl's description of the corps as being 'complementary to

NATO' as well as 'part of the way to a European defence identity'.[22] Expansion of the brigade was effectively blocked until the issue of its identity and affiliation was answered. It was not until December that a solution was engineered between France and the US – in any 'warlike situation' control of the Eurocorps would go to NATO while, in peacetime, the corps would be freestanding.[23]

The French extension of invitations to other interested parties to contribute forces to the corps was unsettling to Washington. Brent Scowcroft, President Bush's National Security Advisor, communicated to his opposite number in the Federal Chancellery in Bonn that this development was not entirely welcome.[24] Despite reservations, the corps began to take shape. The 40 000–50 000 strong force was charged with four main functions: first, common defence in accordance with Article 5 of the Washington Treaty and Article V of the Modified Brussels Treaty; second, humanitarian and rescue tasks; third, peacekeeping tasks; and fourth; tasks of combat forces in crisis management. The Eurocorps was formally made 'answerable to WEU' (FAWEU), alongside the Multinational Division Central (Belgium, the Netherlands and the United Kingdom) and the British–Dutch Amphibious Force, at the WEU Ministerial Council meeting in Rome in May 1993.

The Chiefs of Defence Staff of the five Eurocorps countries (France and Germany plus, Belgium, Luxembourg and Spain) further defined the tasks for the corps as well as its relations to the Alliance.[25] The corps had already established its headquarters in Strasbourg in 1992 and its staff grew to the current level of around 1000 including 200 officers (from all three services). The forces at the disposal of the Eurocorps now stand at three armoured or mechanised divisions (Belgian, French and German), the Franco-German brigade and a Spanish mechanised division. The forces are retained under national command in peacetime since the corps' responsibilities only extend to planning and training. In time of crisis or need, operational command would be transferred from national command to the corps with agreement by the Member States. Forterre argues that the 'Forces thus made available would be easily sufficient for the Corps to undertake operations under Article 5 of the Washington Treaty'.[26]

By late 1998 the Eurocorps reached corps-size strength. The Eurocorps' composition is expressed in Figure 7.1. Although the Eurocorps was portrayed in some quarters as a German–French challenge to ARRC, it appeared to offer several distinct advantages over the ARRC. It offered, in the first place, greater French collaboration in European defence, including the possibility of stationing French forces on German soil.

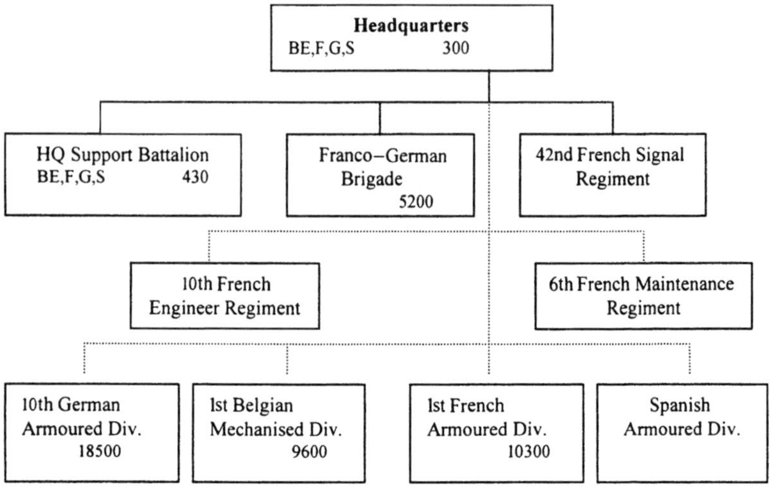

Figure 7.1   The components of the Eurocorps.
Key: BE = Belgium, F = France, G = Germany, S = Spain. Numbers denote personnel size.
Source: Dieter Mahncke, 'Towards A Common European Defence: The European Corps', *CFSP Forum*, 1/95, p. 4.

Second, the Eurocorps allowed a greater role for the *Bundesweher* in a European context and also encouraged a more active role for Germany in its own defence as well as that of its neighbours. However, since neither France nor Germany was willing to assign troops to the Eurocorps on a permanent basis, the commitment, as such, was largely political.

Detractors of the Eurocorps were though quick to point out that the corps would still be largely dependent upon non-Eurocorps assets for certain critical areas such as airlift, and certain types of intelligence. In theory the corps could offer a skeleton, in-theatre, land or joint forces command post. General Pierre Forterre suggested that: 'In the event of a live engagement, the headquarters could be used as the army command post for Article 5 missions in central Europe.'[27] At the CRISEX 96 exercise the Eurocorps successfully mounted a forces HQ of around 400. In spite of the rapid progress made in just over five years, there are however difficulties to be overcome. These are, according to Forterre, interoperability, equipment, language and relations with other organisations or structures. The operational procedures are those employed by NATO, which does not pose a problem in itself, but the procedures fail to balance manoeuvres between NATO and the WEU so that forces and operational elements are equally adept at operating in either capacity on a regular basis. Equipment used is characterised by diversity and not uniformity with, for example, three different tanks and four infantry vehicles (this is not though a problem unique to the Eurocorps). Language is a 'critical issue' since with four official languages (Dutch, French, German and Spanish) and two working languages (French and German – to which should be added English in a quasi-official capacity since it is used for communications with the WEU or NATO) and the possible addition of more if membership grows, the challenges to effective communication in peace and war scenarios need addressing.

Relations with the WEU have been strengthened through a directive between the Eurocorps' commander and the Planning Cell Director establishing, amongst other things, what mutual assistance is to be provided and what information is to be exchanged. Relations have not though extended to strategic level information that might translate political directives into military action for in-theatre commanders. Relations with NATO are less well developed and are mostly in the initiatory stage between the Eurocorps and NATO Planning headquarters. The Eurocorps' role in the WEU/CFSP or ESDI context will depend upon the extent to which other 'Euro' forces are employed or not.

Talk of the creation of various Euro options or Euro forces often ignores some of the key elements behind any effective force, namely logistics and C^3I, or command, control, communication and intelligence (to which a fourth 'C', computers, is often now added making C^4I). In many of these areas the Europeans remain reliant upon their American counterparts. The degree to which the European allies are reliant and the possible negative effects of this became evident following the unilateral decision by the US in November 1994 to cease enforcement of the arms embargo against the former Yugoslavia. This prompted the observation by Sir Dudley Smith, President of the WEU, that Europe needed 'to be autonomous where intelligence gathering, satellite reconnaissance and logistics support' were concerned.[28]

Logistics and intelligence – getting there and knowing what's there

The discussion above provides an overview of some of the many new European post-Cold War force structures that have emerged. Although many exist on paper or as 'tagged' elements within national forces, O'Hanlon points out that it is of little use to have well-trained forces if there is not way of getting them in a timely fashion from A to B. He asks (rhetorically): 'What power can Europe project today?'

> Over a period of days or weeks, it can move several thousand troops, principally British and French and dozens of fighters. But its real weakness would manifest itself in the period from two weeks to two months after a crisis began. During that time, the US could deploy large amounts of equipment, with prepositioned ships, large transport aircraft and fast sealift followed by dedicated cargo and tanker ships. Europeans might deploy nothing in that time, unless aided by US strategic transport and would probably get armoured forces to a distant theatre like the Persian Gulf only after several months. Even then, beyond a couple of divisions, they would rely on the US for in-theatre logistics support.[29]

Some recent agreements between the WEU and the Ukraine and Russia may develop into a potentially valuable way of supplementing 'European' assets. In a *Document on Co-operation between the WEU and Ukraine in the Field of Long-Haul Transport,* signed in June 1997, it was agreed that certain air transport assets could be made available to the WEU for which use the Ukraine would be reimbursed. A similar arrangement was reached with Russia on the delivery of satellite imagery to the Torrejon satellite centre shortly before the European Council's Birmingham meeting in May 1996. However, both arrangements have more political than practical significance. Still, they nevertheless mark an imaginative way of using the enormous military assets of the former Soviet Union to the benefit of European security in those areas where the west Europeans are wanting. However, as long-term strategies for building a European defence entity with minimal reliance on the US, they are unlikely to work. As the military infrastructure of the former Soviet Union declines, it is unlikely that finances will be available to replace or update those assets loaned to the WEU. It is furthermore unlikely that the west Europeans would loan money to replace such assets, preferring to invest in the ailing west European defence industries.

The issue of sharing intelligence assets is controversial. Unlike command and control arrangements, which belong to a specific organisation, intelligence for the various European security operations is based on national resources. NATO relies heavily upon American assets and in some areas, such as airborne electronic jamming, is wholly dependent. The WEU is aware of this as a potential source of weakness in the organisation's ability to act independently in the CJTF or other contexts. The Defence Committee of the WEU recommended that links between NATO and the WEU should be strengthened 'with a view to sharing the intelligence required for operational planning and activities of European armed forces in the framework of the Petersberg tasks'.[30] While not in disagreement with this position, François de Rose argued, 'In order to ensure a sufficient capability of coherent action, the Europeans should at least provide themselves with space-based surveillance and intelligence gathering systems, as well as the means for the deployment of forces accustomed to working together and equipped with materiel which is compatible, if not standard-ized'.[31] Although de Rose and others view the development of an inde-pendent European intelligence capability as essential, the obstacles to such an advance are formidable. Three impediments in particular are noteworthy.

First, the nature of intelligence itself has changed from its Cold War variant, which focused primarily on military intelligence. Post-Cold War requirements emphasise what General Jean Heinrich described as 'military interest intelligence' or rather the 'combination of knowledge and information of all kinds that the political or military decision-maker needs in order to take his decision'.[32] This includes understanding more than mere size or disposition of military forces but also such factors as historical, ethnic and social dimensions applying primarily to intra-state conflict. The extent of the intelligence network that is required to gather such extensive data is difficult to estimate. One good indicator of effort that may be involved is to consider the extent of the US intel-ligence assets used by IFOR in north-east Bosnia.[33] These assets included over 1000 army intelligence troops, a national intelligence support team in Tuzla including CIA representatives, members of the Defense Intelligence Agency and representatives from the National Security Agency. Intelligence-gathering assets also included numerous satellites, Quickfix (EH–60 helicopter collecting electronic signals), Guardrail (army intelligence targeting system), JSTARS (US Air Force intelligence gathering), numerous listening devices, seismic monitors, infrared monitors, magnetic sensors and point-blank (human) surveil-lance. Assets held by the European allies simply cannot match those and thus their ability to build up a clear and comprehensive picture from multiple sources is significantly hindered.

Second, the increase in the number of potential sources of instability has not been matched by a cumulative national effort to answer the new intelligence requirements. As the WEU Defence Committee argued:

> The present geostrategic situation has become far too complicated for individual European nations to keep up with all the relevant developments taking place in different parts of the world and analyse them in detail. Limited and often still further diminishing intelligence budgets go hand in hand with an increasing number of hotbeds of tension and potential or real crises which may, some day, threaten Europe's economic or security interests.[34]

European-led efforts to create a common European intelligence system have, so far, largely been limited to the establishment of the WEU Satellite Centre at Torrejon, Spain. The centre operated in an 'experimental phase' from 1992–5, using mostly commercially available satellite imagery, including Helios 1,[35] SPOT, LANDSAT and even Russian military sources. Torrejon's ability to deliver high-resolution space imagery has been patchy. Its shortage of personnel to interpret the data has resulted in long delays while actual image resolution has proven inadequate. The WEU Defence Committee noted that: 'Moreover, one still has the impression that the WEU Council's support for the Satellite Centre is not wholehearted owing to differences of opinion between member states, which are resulting in the lowest common denominator for the Centre's objectives and terms of reference.'[36] This situation is all the more disturbing when one considers that, aside from the WEU's Secretariat-General, the Satellite Centre accounts for the largest number of personnel and it is also the organisation's single largest budget item, dwarfing the Secretary General which includes the Situation Centre.[37]

Third, the costs of providing for a genuinely independent intelligence capability may prove prohibitive (political objections aside). 'Independence' may in fact mean providing intelligence support for a bewildering variety of scenarios. For instance, a WEU document stated that it would 'need the appropriate mechanisms for political decision-making and military command and control. WEU's operational role should be developed in a flexible way, ensuring the capacity to, on the one hand, operate autonomously (where appropriate in close consultation with NATO) and, on the other hand, to operate together with non-WEU countries'.[38] François Heisbourg illustrated some of the potential costs of independent capabilities in the reconnaissance and intelligence field when he noted that in 1995, with the Gulf War coalition's dependence on the US in mind, Pierre Joxe (then the French

Defence Minister) launched a five million franc project for that year alone for a military-space system *'sans rival en Europe'*.[39] Aside from possible duplication of effort and expense, the real issue in this regard is the provision of *relevant* intelligence. Much of the predominantly US-backed NATO intelligence (and communication) networks were built with the anticipation of a specific threat and aggression. Since many of the contemporary threats to European security stem from intra-state tensions and activities, it may legitimately be asked whether the existing intelligence apparatus is suitable for this type of challenge. The question of whether the US is willing to invest heavily in changed or improved intelligence and surveillance when such intra-state challenges do not directly effect their national security, should also be considered.

Of the problems facing the development of an autonomous intelligence capability, the cost of providing for expensive satellite systems would seem to be the most visible challenge. The French-led efforts to develop a FF 11 000 million satellite system (Helios 2) and joint endeavours with Germany to build the FF 13 000 million Horus radar observation satellite, proved ill-fated. Franco-German co-operation in this area stemmed from a joint summit in Baden-Baden in December 1995 where Chirac and Kohl agreed to develop a joint satellite programme. Germany cited pressure on the defence budget as a reason for first delaying payments to the Helios 2 project, and then withdrawing altogether. Volker Rühe, Germany's Defence Minister, illustrated the difficulty of choice when confronted by a shrinking defence budget. In reference to the possibility of developing both the Eurofighter and a Franco-German satellite system, he rejected the latter arguing that the former is 'far more important for me as defence minister than satellites... there is no money in the budget for that'.[40] France announced plans on April 1998 to abandon the Horus project, which was to have been financed with 40 percent funding from France and the remainder from Germany. The French Defence Minister, Alain Richard, justified the decision as part of measures to save some FF 20 billion over the next four years.[41] Meanwhile, the Helios 2 project, is now going ahead with Italian and Spanish support. Britain withdrew from a $1.65 billion military satellite programme, along with France and Germany, (based on an agreement signed in December 1997) because the satellite would not be ready by 2005, when Britain's three Skynet satellites are due for replacement. The German Defence Ministry commented on how 'it was quite unusual to leave a project when a memorandum of understanding was signed only eight months ago', and added incorrectly that Britain's actions were, 'without precedent'.[42]

Even if a European consortium does produce a military satellite, there is little to indicate that there is a marked public preference for 'European' manufactured defence goods over those of, for instance, the North Americans. The decision by the Dutch in 1995 to purchase American helicopters over a Franco-German competitor illustrated the point. Choices will, it appears, be made on the basis of purchase price and longer-term reliability rather than on the basis of promoting region-wide competency.

Nevertheless, in spite of the practical and financial objections, the formation of an increasing number of security structures at the European level points to the need for intelligence structures to support their work. This, in turn, depends 'on the degree of convergence of national interests of the states concerned'.[43] This also includes the degree of convergence that will exist between the US intelligence requirements and those of the European allies and, indeed, upon American willingness to make available certain resources or information. Considering this, the WEU Defence Committee comments that

> Europeans may have to recognise, however, that for the implementation of their common foreign security and defence policy they may not be able to rely forever on the provision of US assets. The development of purely European operational capabilities should therefore be one of WEU's priorities and it should go hand in hand with the provision of Alliance assets through CJTF in the field of intelligence. A fully-fledged intelligence system, ranging from different military satellites to intelligence processing and gathering centres and including direct links with C^4I systems, would take years to develop and commission, even though the European defence industry has all the basic technologies available to build the components.[44]

One useful step to build convergence was suggested by the WEU's Defence Committee to the Assembly. The committee proposed sending a representative from each member's national intelligence service to the Planning Cell, which could not only improve the latter's ability to make assessments but develop collaborative intelligence habits. Following the establishment of the Planning Cell in October 1992 and the Council's concerns regarding intelligence support voiced two years later, agreement was reached in Lisbon in May 1995 that an Intelligence Section should be established in order to facilitate the execution of tasks mandated in the Petersberg Declaration. However, the resulting Intelligence

Section, with a mere staff of five, primarily provides analysis of intelligence data in its files at the request of the WEU Council. At present, there is no WEU intelligence policy as such. The means to even make 'an autonomous WEU analysis, has not yet been defined because of a lack of political will in the member states'.[45] This lack of will led the WEU Defence Committee to observe that the WEU should 'be able to provide the political authorities with an assessment of the strategic situation in areas where they might have to act in order to prevent conflicts. Decisions are needed now to enable the WEU to provide its own security analysis as a building block for the European common foreign and security policy by the year 2000.'[46]

The recognition of common intelligence interests may allow specialisation as well as collaboration in the acquisition, interpretation and dissemination of intelligence material. The word 'specialisation' is uppermost here since there is clearly no need for competing or duplicative intelligence systems, but at the same time there must be enough mutual reliance upon other members' intelligence specialisation to ensure that a European system develops and that national withholding of information is resisted. Since the signing of an agreement between NATO and the WEU in June 1996, intelligence documents have been exchanged, subject to guarantees referring to the distribution of documents amongst the WEU members, associate members and the observers and associate partners. It has also been suggested that ten NATO-trained intelligence analysts could work in the WEU Planning Cell's Intelligence Section, providing analyses based on messages sent by either NATO or WEU sources. The quarterly meetings between the Permanent Councils of the Atlantic Alliance and the WEU have now become a regular feature and work has begun on planning the first WEU/NATO crisis management exercises, to take place in the year 2000.[47] This too would suggest the need for NATO to strengthen WEU intelligence input.

The WEU established a variety of methods of exchanging views and information with NATO, including the joint sessions of the NATO and WEU Councils at least four times per year as well as various daily procedures. The latter are described by José Cutileiro as 'the exchange of classified information, WEU use of NATO integrated telecommunications system and regular consultations between the secretariats and military staffs'.[48] It is especially important that close communication and understanding exist between NATO and the WEU since, in many cases, they draw upon the same assets. For instance, the twelve-member ARRC, comprising up to 400000 soldiers, is a complicated mix of multinational, national and framework (in this case British) forces assigned to ten divisions under an international headquarters.

The development of a European intelligence policy is an uphill struggle given the general lack of political will as well as the complications of institutional co-operation. For the WEU, as the host of such a potential intelligence agency, the task will be to avoid duplication of NATO-assets while at the same time allowing for an independent capability should the US, in particular, not wish to be involved in a given mission. The 'non-duplication' argument, as the WEU Defence Committee noted, 'is often conveniently used as an excuse for preventing any operational structuring of WEU independently of NATO'.[49] Ideally, the Planning Cell should not only be guaranteed use of NATO protected telecommunication networks, as they currently are, but further access by the Cell to NATO intelligence databases should be secured. This though may not be sufficient since although the organisations overlap substantially, NATO's continuing main emphasis is on collective defence while the WEU's primary emphasis is on Petersberg-type tasks, and different types of tasks may well call for different types of intelligence. The WEU is more likely to require far more general analysis of political risk, from more open sources on such topics as religious movements, refugee movements and so forth. The intelligence interests of the WEU have been loosely defined as including *documentary intelligence* (permanent geographical, political, economic and military data and instability factors); *operational situational intelligence* (intelligence collection and processing to assist those in charge of carrying out an operation); and, finally, *space observation* (satellite imagery). An independent European intelligence capability with these three interests need not be duplicative. If NATO and the WEU collaborate, recognising that each may need slightly different intelligence, and if there is a greater input from national intelligence agencies directly into the Planning Cell's Intelligence Section, duplication could be minimised. As a potential support for CJTF missions, it is essential that there should be a sufficient independent capability 'to free Europeans from their dependency on the United States for intelligence which may be given or withheld but which in any event is selective and sifted by NATO'.[50]

Failure to develop a European intelligence capability, which could eventually underpin the WEU and 'Euro-options', would mean the continuation of CJTF-type arrangements, relying heavily upon the US and its good will. The importance accorded to the development of a genuinely European intelligence capability is low largely because of cost considerations. Generally, progress has been made on cost allocation within organisations, however there remain considerable problems with cost-sharing arrangements between organisations or even *ad hoc* coalitions of the willing. These problems have been exacerbated by the (unrealistic) expectation from many publics of a post-Cold War peace dividend and the extreme difficulty most politicians would face in lobbying for additional defence expenditure.

Finance

There are no formal agreements for cost sharing between the European security organisations. The absence of detailed arrangements between NATO and the WEU makes a renewed burden-sharing dispute likely. Within the WEU itself, the question of contributions from associate members still has to be addressed, both in terms of day-to-day arrangements that may be adopted and in terms of possible cost-sharing measures in relation to WEU military activities. Moreover, if cost-sharing terms were extended to associate members there would be legitimate demands for voting representation. Currently, 96.1 percent of the total budget is paid by the 'core group' (the ten full members) and the remaining amount is assumed by the associate members.[51]

In general, the pattern of financing EC/EU co-ordinated operations has been varied and somewhat *ad hoc* as in, for example, the US-led UN operations in Somalia, where the EC was unable to spend its development funds due to the ongoing conflict. Nevertheless, it was argued that the provision of funds to a Belgian battalion from the European Development Fund's budget was a legitimate use of EC funds. Although commendably flexible, the action scarcely provided a blueprint for future funding in similar circumstances. The financial dimensions of the CFSP have been notoriously stormy, involving not only economic questions but sensitive political ones too. Broadly speaking, the Community was faced with the difficult dilemma of wishing to charge as much as it conceivably could to the Community budget as administrative expenditure, while at the same time attempting to curb the EP's enhanced overview of CFSP activities through its important budgetary role within the EC. The determination of whether a CFSP joint action should be charged as administrative expenditure or operational not only caused considerable disagreement, but under-funding. The TEU introduced distinctions between 'administrative' and 'operational' expenditure under Article J.11. The former is automatically charged to the budget of the Communities while, with regard to the latter, the Council can decide unanimously to charge it to the Community budget or that it shall be assumed by the Member States. However, the problem is not merely that of deciding who should pay but of securing the payment itself. For instance, in October 1994, when the financial aspects of the joint action of November 1993 on the support for the convoying of humanitarian aid to Bosnia-Herzegovina and the administration of Mostar should have been completed, only three Member States had paid their contributions (Denmark, Greece and Ireland). As a result of this, the total expenditure for the administration of Mostar was, under a Council decision of 6 February 1995, charged entirely to the Community budget. The Commission, which had been requested to start implementing the joint action, had to resort to 'borrowing' funds from other programmes such as tobacco, fishing and PHARE.[52] Successive attempts were made since December 1993 by the EP to secure an inter-institutional settlement on CFSP financing with the medium term strategy of using 'its budgetary powers as a tool in order to get a say on the political substance of the CFSP'.[53]

The main issues pertaining to the financing of CFSP joint actions and other activities were solved as a result of the 1996 IGC. There are though two outstanding issues. First, there is ambiguity about who is responsible for the implementation of those aspects of 'common measures' involving Community expenditure under the budget. Is it the Council (as Article J 8.2 might suggest) or the Commission (Article J 18.4)? Second, any common defence policy will have to offer guidelines for procurement, financing and production in the military–industrial sector as part of the more general EU harmonisation. The main responsibility for formulating general outlines in this area will fall to WEAG, which forms the skeleton of a projected European Armaments Agency (EAA). However, merely grouping European armaments activities under a WEAG flag fails to address the still problematic link between the economies of the Member States and their general defence and other policies.

Within NATO the burden-sharing debate can be expected to continue with a greater emphasis upon burden-shedding and upon non-financial costs (especially risk-sharing).[54] The burdensharing debate will become heated not only with reference to the enlargement issue, which will serve to emphasise issues of cost-sharing and who benefits, but other issues as well, such as: What division of costs and responsibilities is appropriate for the European allies and the US? And how will NATO (and indeed the EU) balance the costs of expansion eastward with commitments to the Mediterranean? The adoption by Germany of a more active military role, as has been happening in a tentative manner since 1994, may alleviate some of the transatlantic burden-sharing pressures. What should be avoided however, are operations that appear to place undue burdens on some members (IFOR serves as an example) or engaging in a divisive east versus south rivalry for resources.

Traditionally, NATO members have paid for the troops and units they contribute to any given Alliance-related activity. Common costs are assumed through the infrastructure fund that is calculated upon the basis of a member's GDP. There is however no operational budget for multilateral operations in support of the UN or any other organisation. If, as was the case in Bosnia with IFOR and now with SFOR, NATO members are expected to contribute out of their own pockets for troops, units, logistics and so forth, two problems arise. First, the contributions from the larger powers quite naturally result in demands for commensurate command positions and political control (responsibility-sharing). Second, the assumption is that the larger member countries will assume a bulk of the burden which, inevitably, will result in donor fatigue. The possibility of establishing a fund within NATO for peace-support operations is also fraught with difficulties, such as whether this would align with UN contributions and under what conditions these funds might be used. Such a fund may put the larger full-NATO members and France at odds with each other since the latter would presumably fall outside this arrangement. Perhaps, though, there is room for some optimism if the UN is able to function as intended, with regard to compensating Member States who contribute to peacekeeping operations. Although this obviously relies upon the continued willingness of all UN members to pay their assessed dues in a timely manner.

Closely related to the finance issue is the question of what anticipated benefits and costs may arise from membership of more countries into the various organisations, both for the existing members and for the aspirants. This may be especially evident when, in the absence of an over-arching Cold War-type threat, the issue of costs of operations may be closer to the surface as well as the extent to which these costs may be offset by defence contracts.

Manufacturing security – a two way street?

One of the more persistent themes of the Cold War Alliance burden-sharing debate was the idea that greater US contributions were offset by the 'one-way' street in defence sales from across the Atlantic.

Although there were persistent demands for *juste retour*, or a 'two-way' street, implementing the necessary reforms to allow an effective European share was never considered. In the post-Cold War setting it is also clear that Europe faces stiff competition from US defence industries which benefit from the policy priority of maintaining a technological lead in defence. One American report even described the maintenance of technological superiority as the *'sine qua non* of [US] military strategy'.[55] Some, like Ethan Kapstein, went further, arguing that America's current technological edge means that there currently exists a de facto US monopoly on arms technology and trade.[56]

One way of redressing some of the American advantage in defence manufacturing is through European defence industry collaboration. The idea is not however new. The co-ordination of European armaments began with FINABEL (after the initials of the member states: France, Italy, the Netherlands, Belgium and Luxembourg), established as part of the EDC structures in October 1953. Germany joined in 1956 and Britain joined in 1972. Three years later, in February 1958, the governments of France, Germany and Italy informed NATO and the WEU of their intention to form a steering committee to select those types of weapons for which they were prepared to undertake joint study.[57] The Eurogroup, established in 1968 following an initiative from Denis Healey, Britain's Minister of Defence, promoted European collaboration on defence production within NATO in the same manner as FINABEL, in other words 'as an organisation independent of the Alliance, but within its framework'.[58] The European Council, meeting in Rome on 14–15 December 1990, advocated that the IGC should pay attention to ways of enhancing co-operation in the armaments field. One institutionalised opportunity to pursue this aim occurred when the IEPG was transferred from NATO to the WEU in December 1992. These initiatives, when considered alongside the number of CFSP joint actions or common decisions devoted to 'dual-use' goods, suggest an awareness of the need to restructure Europe's defence industries in order to underpin EPC or CFSP.

While data from SIPRI and other sources supports the contention that the percentage of world-wide arms contracts being awarded to the US has increased since the end of the Cold War, partly through the aggressive use of trade–security linkages but also due to the collapse of the old Soviet arms industry, it is an overstatement to maintain that the US enjoys a monopoly.[59] If the implication of the claimed monopoly is that European arms manufacturers should leave production to the US and not attempt to resuscitate their own defence industries, three objections may be raised. First, the US technological edge is largely the result of research and development (R&D) expenditure made during the Cold War at a time when the public was more tolerant of high defence expenditure. Given the post-Cold War reductions in the US defence budget, and those of many of its allies, it is questionable whether the US will be able to sustain its competitive edge without joint ventures of its own with companies in allied countries. Second, the existence of competitive and technologically sophisticated European companies may well be attractive to the US because they may open up the potential for European–American consortia. Third, the blurring of defence and civilian technologies could make the EU a strong actor in the defence market. The success of 'Airbus' and the European Space Administration's 'Ariane' rocket demonstrated that not only is there a market for non-US goods in the civilian and dual-use area but that some consumers may be wary of the political ramifications of sole reliance upon a single supplier.

However, for Europeans to be competitive with US defence industries significant national impediments must be addressed. As Peter van Ham observed:

> Europe is characterized by protected national defence markets, with much duplication on the research and development level. Only a few West European governments have decided to open their markets for competition and there are no signs that this will change rapidly in the coming years... For most West European governments, defence procurement is still less a matter of purchasing security at the lowest feasible cost, than a matter for domestic economic concern (i.e. maintaining technological and production capabilities and employment).[60]

Van Ham pointed out the absurdity of Western Europe attempting to produce three main battle tanks, as opposed to one in the US, or the west European production of three jet fighters with, again, only one in the US.[61] In 1985, the US had eight military aircraft manufacturers but as a result of downsizing and the merger of Boeing and McDonnell Douglas, it now has three. There were twelve missile manufacturers in 1985 and now, with Raytheon's purchase of Hughes Electronics, there are four.[62] Raytheon, Hughes and Texas Instruments combined could produce sales of $5 billion annually, compared to sales of $1.5 billion generated by Europe's largest general weapons manufacturer, Matra BAe Dynamics. If they were combined with Thomson–CSF, Aérospatiale, Dasa, Alenia and Saab, a $4 billion company could be created.[63]

Table 7.1   Downsizing defence industries: an overview

Product	United States	Europe (EU)
Helicopters	3 (being reduced to 2)	3
Missiles	4	10
Military aircraft	3 (being reduced to 2)	6
Satellites	4 (being reduced to 2)	5
Defence electronics	4 (being reduced to 3)	8
Civil aircraft	1	1

Lockheed and Martin Marietta, Boeing and McDonnell Douglas, Raytheon and Hughes Electronics, all combined to form a small number of mega defence companies (with a turnover of over $35 billion a year) that enjoy the support of the US administration. Any brief comparison of the number of European and US major defence manufacturers suggests that, when combined with declining defence budgets, the Europeans are sustaining too many production facilities (see Table 7.1).

One of the few areas in which Europe can compare with its American counterparts is in the civil aircraft manufacturing sector. The lessons learned from the process of gradually integrating Airbus[64] into one company (Airbus SCE) may apply to the integration of defence companies. Over the course of twenty-five years Airbus has managed to capture around 30 percent of the global market (the remainder belonging to Boeing) and may, according to industry predictions, capture up to half of the market. The continuing process of downsizing defence industries in the US, in the search for efficiency and new markets with, it should be remembered, a larger defence budget than that of any European ally, makes the reluctance of its allies to do the same all the more notable. Still, the combined defence budgets of the European NATO-allies could serve as the foundation of a powerful European defence industry.[65] Successful competition in the defence sector may also involve expansion into the civil sector or vice versa – indeed having dual military/civil interests may be one of the keys to long-term survival. The Deputy Director-General of Aerospatiale, Jean-Louis Fache, suggested that military activities could assist civil activities when he observed that: 'The cyclical nature of the civil aeronautics industry, its major funding and research requirements and the huge investment it demands make it necessary to carry out military activities in parallel.'[66] Some European companies like British Aerospace, Britain's largest exporter, have flourished by dividing sales between the defence and civil sector (70:30). It is however not only a difference in the number and nature (private or public) of the companies, but also a question of the amount of money spent and the focus of that expenditure.

The impediments to the restructuring of the European arms industries are primarily national, as van Ham, Jens van Scherpenberg[67] and others have pointed out. Indeed, obstructions at the European level are now non-existent. However, one often-mentioned obstacle to potential European armaments collaboration is the existence of skeletons of horrifically expensive collaborative ventures. As one official observed, 'There is supposedly a rule of thumb under which the costs of a collaborative programme are calculated by multiplying the initial base cost by the square root of the number of participants and I must say that I find very little evidence to suggest that this rule is very far from the truth'.[68] However, it is not necessarily fair to ascribe cost overrun problems to collaboration as such. The principal reasons for cost overruns can be found in the structure of the consortium, the nature of the customer (a committee) and the type of client (an industrial consortium). A system of joint international tender, as suggested by Lord Levene, former Head of Defence Procurement in the UK Ministry of Defence, under which any company from the countries involved would be allowed to bid and then, if successful, it would be obliged to sub-contract work to the value of each nation's share, seems a more efficient system.

Whatever the means of restructuring, whether through a system of joint international tender or not, the process of restructuring European defence industries, so that they compete with the US and other manufacturers, must be pursued vigorously for four reasons. First, the shrinkage in the post-Cold War global arms market calls for more competitive companies. Second, the changed circumstances of post-Cold War Europe, including less direct reliance on the US, points to the need for a rapid restructuring of European weapons manufacturers. Third, the accession of three new members to NATO in 1999 and perhaps more later will open up new arms markets as the new members are expected to standardise their weapons systems for inter-operability with existing NATO systems. Fourth, the US has traditionally been extremely reluctant to export its latest technology, even to its allies, without close supervision. Taking into account these four issues, but especially the matter of reliance on the US, the President of the WEU Assembly, Luís María de Puig, warned that:

… were the Europeans to become dependent upon the United States as sole supplier, they would soon be reduced to participating, under close political and military supervision from Washington, in missions conceived and controlled by their American partner, as was the case during the Gulf War. At the end of the day it is the future of political Europe which is at stake.

But we are also talking about the future of economic Europe, for there is an obvious link between, on the one hand, setting up a joint management of armaments by European bodies representing the states and, on the other hand, the action that will inevitably have to be taken by the industry.[69]

Along similar lines, Jacques Santer, former President of the European Commission, counselled that, '(the EU defence industries) are confronted with American counterparts who are quite simply giants in comparison to our defence companies and able to benefit from increasing civil and defence synergies. The Commission believes the Member States should accelerate industrial defence restructuring as a matter of urgency'.[70] The European Council, on a slightly different but related note, called for renewed and sustained effort in the framework of the CFSP to 'develop responsible and coherent arms export control policy throughout the Union'.[71]

There are though three formidable hurdles hindering the building of a European defence industry. First, there are very few pan-European weapons programmes that could be used as a platform for further integration. There are specific areas of collaboration, such as satellites (France's Lagardère and Britain's GEC) or the Eurocopter (Aérospatiale and Dasa), but these are not pan-European and, as *The Economist* noted, 'These ventures offer some technological synergies and economies of scale, but each component is run as a separate operating company. They have not concentrated production at their most efficient sites'.[72] Second, national requirements and priorities differ enormously. Such differences have led to, for example, the stalling of plans to build a Franco-German-British Multi Role Armoured Vehicle. France lobbied for a vehicle equipped with a large gun whereas Germany and Britain were primarily interested in a troop carrier.[73] Third, until recently, European defence industries remained jealously guarded national preserves operating in close collaboration with national governments.

The Treaty of Amsterdam made defence co-operation in the procurement of defence equipment a matter, as the Secretary-General of the EDIG, Graham Woodcock, observed, 'of political will amongst the governments involved to share their responsibilities in defence and security matters'. This is a prerequisite, Woodcock argued, 'if we are to make any real and lasting progress and not just engage in window dressing and comforting words'.[74] It should additionally be borne in mind that, at the end of 1997, approximately 70 percent of all armaments in Europe were not procured according to WEAG guidelines but under the aegis of Article 223.[75] The reason for this may be that, in spite of the modifications introduced by the treaty, defence industries remain largely immune to free market trade principles (they are not for, example, included in GATT or the WTO). In the absence of Article 223[76] it is difficult to see what would prevent US manufacturers from buying into the European arms firms (thus guaranteeing equality of treatment in its competition with European manufacturers within the European market). Although Article 223 was modified by the Treaty of Amsterdam, any acknowledgement of a significant dilution of the article would presumably also dilute European leverage in its efforts to find markets for European manufactured defence goods in the American market.[77] EU attempts to show that defence industrial issues are within its purview and subject to open market principles may, at this time, have deleterious effects.

The chicken and egg question for European armaments manufacturers is whether a CFSP should be in place before more ambitious European armaments integration is attempted? There seems to be little reason why manufacturers should wait, especially since the emergence of a fully-fledged CFSP might be a long time in the making. Increasingly stiff competition from the US, a growing number of European–American mergers and dwindling defence budgets may well push more European mergers, such as that between Dasa (which sold 30 percent of its missiles company) and Matra BAe, or that between Dynamics and Matra Marconi Space, whose satellite businesses will merge.[78] The response to the question of whether collaboration amongst European defence markets should be a prerequisite for the formation of an operational European CD, or a result of it, received an unambiguous response from Wolfgang Piller, of Daimler-Benz Aerospace:

As soon as the American competitors have restructured and harvested the fruits of synergy and mergers, they will concentrate on Europe and they will tear the European industrial base in aerospace and defence apart.

When and if, in such a foreseeable situation it became more and more apparent or likely that we were never going to achieve political union in Europe, there might be some companies which would be ready to sell their business to American competitors. It is likely that the first one to do so will achieve a price premium for throwing open the front door to American competitors.

In any such event, the remaining potential of the European aerospace and defence industries would be too small to serve as a minimum industrial and technological base for minimum European sovereignty, in which case we could never create political union.[79]

Is the US in a position to 'harvest the fruits of synergy'? The streamlining of the US defence industry, through a series of mergers and takeovers, reduced a number of large defence contractors to just three (Lockheed, Boeing-McDonnell Douglas and Raytheon). In the streamlining process the three have become not only highly competitive internationally but they are also large enough to spread their R&D costs, thereby avoiding dependency upon one big project (as was the case with Northrop and the B–2 Stealth Bomber). The US also spends almost five times as much as Europe on defence-related research and development and focuses this expenditure more tightly (currently on 'information warfare').

If the US is well advanced on its path to synergy, the question of whether it will 'tear the European industrial base in aerospace and defence apart' arises. While the European governments have made plain their desire to see a strong consolidated European arms manufacturing capacity, indeed a competency with sufficient clout against US contractors, the immediate problem arises of whether they should buy urgently needed equipment 'off the [US] shelf' or wait and develop new European technology. The question though of what is 'American' and 'European' can also be obscure. Consider the competition to supply missiles to the Eurofighter that is due to enter into service in 2004. The European offering is the Meteor missile, a venture led by Matra BAe Dynamics but which also includes GEC–Marconi (UK), Alenia (Italy), the missile division of Daimler-Benz Aerospace, LFK (Germany), Casa (Spain) and Saab (Sweden). The competition comes from Rayethon, whose team includes Shorts (Northern Ireland), Thomson-Thorn Missile Electronics (France), Diehl (Germany), Fokker Special Products (the Netherlands) and Atlantic Research (US).[80]

The European aerospace industry is the most acutely aware of the threats to its future well-being from slimmed down and efficient US competitors. Accordingly, the Eurofighter project is increasingly viewed as the basis for a consolidated European aerospace group. Because of this, George Robertson, the British Defence Secretary, was most anxious to bring France on board (they are not members of the Eurofighter consortium) arguing that, 'The French can see the writing on the wall as clearly as anyone else can'.[81] In a move to bring about just such a consolidated aerospace group, a letter of intent to remove barriers to defence industry rationalisation was signed between Britain, France, Germany, Italy, Spain and Sweden on 6 July 1998. The governments of the six signatory states stepped-up pressure on the defence industries involved by demanding a blueprint from them by mid-October on the structure of what was dubbed the European Aerospace and Defence Company (EADC).[82] The eventual aim of the consortium would be to win half the export market for fighters, which is estimated to be around 800 aircraft between 2005–2025, with a value of $70 billion, excluding those purchased by the four Eurofighter partners, China, Russia and the US.[83] The French government's decision of 22 July to reduce the governments' shareholdings in Aérospatiale opened the doors to a possible merger with BAe and Dasa.

The end of 1998 however saw a decision by Lord Simpson, Managing Director of Britain's General Electric Company (GEC), to announce the dismemberment of GEC. By the end of the year, Lockheed Martin, Northrop Grumman, BAe and Thomson-CSF were negotiating with GEC. In particular GEC was attractive to the American competitors since GEC itself had recently purchased Tracor, a relatively small US company. However BAe signed a merger deal with GEC-Marconi on 19 January 1999 and, in so doing, not only blocked a Marconi-Thomson merger but also scuppered the all but signed BAe–DASA merger. The latter, of course, was also to be the core of the EADC with Thomson as a potential third partner. The BAe, GEC, Marconi merger created the world's second largest defence industry, behind only Lockheed Martin.[84] Measured in terms of defence sales, Thomson-CSF ranks sixth while DASA ranks eleventh. The connection to Tracor, alongside BAe's work with Boeing, will also give BAe a good toehold in the US defence market.

What are the implications for the future of EADC? John Weston, BAe's chief executive, was one of the primary advocates of EADC, which under the original scheme would have included the Airbus consortium. DASA and Thomson's negative reaction to the merger may well have stymied, if not destroyed, the creation of a European defence industry of which aerospace is the largest sector. It should however be borne in mind that a Thomson-Marconi merger could have had equally negative effects on plans for EADC. The original EADC line up had included not only BAe and DASA but Thomson as well. However, Thomson proved to be a less than attractive partner due to concerns regarding its profitability as well as the significant government stake in the company. DASA is therefore unlikely to form a rival aerospace company with Thomson which still leaves the possibility of a BAe–DASA merger open. More generally, the implications of BAe's merger with GEC Marconi for US–EU defence industries point less to the creation of a 'fortress Europe' defence industry but towards a more complex transatlantic defence industry with mergers across the oceans and penetration of one another's markets. Although unlikely at present, the merger may also make the case more compelling to include defence industries in the Transatlantic Business Dialogue.

The fate of the EADC remains in the balance but some of the needs are more immediate, such as the general shortage of non-American airlift for WEU or CJTF eventualities. In this case, the choices for the EU members would appear to be either the US C–17 transport aircraft, with a payload of 78 tons and a price of around $200 million or, an adapted Airbus A340–300, with a payload of 53 tons and a cost of around $120–150 million (the latter though is not specifically designed for a military transport role and has no provision for landing ramps).[85] With this issue in mind, the WEU's Mobility Group was tasked by the Council to assess future transport requirements and communicate the findings to the Planning Cell. In response to questionnaires sent to various members, the following became evident: 'strategic air lift needs can be met using WEU existing member's military assets, third party assets and civilian commercial resources. However, under certain circumstances, availability of large military carrier aircraft fitted with ramps and military transport ships could prove to be essential.'[86]

Despite this assessment, the WEU did *not* favour a procurement programme that gave the WEU its own strategic assets. Members were also *not* generally in favour of centralising hire contracts, arguing that the WEU could instead play a co-ordinating role. Finally, members disagreed with the pooling of national assets on a permanent basis under WEU authority. As Colonel Bernard Vezinhet, Head of Logisitics/Movements and Finance Section of the WEU Planning Cell commented: 'These conclusions reflect both the present spending difficulties and a degree of resistance towards common procurement of strategic assets.'[87] Although it would be unrealistic to expect all European WEU/NATO members to fund a large number of programmes there is, as Rear Admiral Leira observed, a 'lack of a basic acquisition strategy covering overall Alliance priorities, and the scale of funding which we can bring collectively'. Leira sees the need for a 'collectively-agreed appreciation of how [the allies] are going to meet [procurement] challenges. Not on a project-by-project basis, but across the board.'[88]

The difficulties with creating a European Armaments Industry, as the essential underpinnings of CFSP and other European security structures, cannot be blamed on any shortage of dedicated multinational agencies. For instance, NATO's Conference on National Armaments Directors (CNAD) is to address the root of this issue, in other words why the Alliance needs a given armament, for what task and what end.[89] In addition to the CNAD there is the Western European Armaments Organisation (WEAO). The WEU Council of Ministers created WEAO at their Ostend meeting in November 1996. Its primary responsibility was in developing and enhancing European armaments policy, including such topics as augmenting the role of armaments co-operation within the ESDI, increasing harmonisation and interoperability, creating the conditions for a more integrated an internationally competitive European armaments business to flourish, managing the Euclid and THALES programme and improving both international and intra-European procurement practices.[90] The Assembly has, since then, pushed for WEAO's mandate to be extended beyond research and development to include 'the placing of orders for armaments in Europe and abroad and the development of an armaments export policy which would reconcile the industry's legitimate aims with the demands of a common foreign and security policy in the European Union'.[91] WEAO, which began work in April 1997, has been given its own legal personality but, as a subsidiary body to the Council, it includes states that are signatories of the Modified Brussels Treaty or of the 1955 Agreement on the status of the WEU and its staff.[92] WEU Ministers, at their in Ostend meeting, also singed a memorandum of understanding on Technology Arrangements for Laboratories for Defence European Science (THALES) which was designed to provide 'improved mechanisms for implementing government-funded joint research programmes and information exchanges'.[93] In general, the advent of WEAO is a potentially useful development but in order to avoid duplication of effort WEAO's endeavours will demand close collaboration with NATO's CNAD and the EDIG.[94]

The restructuring of the US defence industry poses problems for many European defence industries, but it may also present sales opportunities, such as that of the EH101 helicopter built by British, Italian and US contractors. The key to making collaboration attractive not only to European defence industries but beyond, will be the privatisation of defence industries. Competing with the American defence manufacturers will be difficult in many sectors but there are many other areas that may prove attractive to European competitors and, in terms of the innovation and inventiveness, the US does not have a monopoly on research and development. There are signs that the message has been taken aboard following a meeting of the Defence Ministers of France, Germany, Britain, Italy and Spain, in Paris on 20 April 1998, where it was agreed to move towards harmonising procurement and to avoid wasteful duplication of R&D efforts. In addition, a number of measures were adopted that were designed to ensure security of supplies since the elimination of over-capacity could leave individual countries without indigenous suppliers of key equipment, such as ammunition.[95] The BAe, GEC-Marconi merger also illustrates that solutions to the competitiveness and technology problem of European armaments industries may lie not only within Europe, but in transatlantic ties as well. The merger may well have done more to establish a 'two way' arms trade across the Atlantic than any protectionist measures in Europe could hope to accomplish.

The geography of post-Cold War security: the 'ins' and 'outs'

The issues addressed thus far are political ones but, in a sense, they are also technical. One of the most vexatious problems for post-Cold War security is going to be that of deciding upon membership of the various organisations and, related to this, assessing the effects upon it of its extended membership. Europe's evolving institutional security structure creates the impression of a complicated patchwork of institutions with, sometimes common, and sometimes differing, membership. Figure 7.2 below illustrates the organisations and the overlapping membership of most of them. All are included in the OSCE while many are in the Council of Europe and the relatively new Euro-Atlantic Partnership Council (EAPC). The use of different levels of membership, such as the WEU's associate member or associate partner status, or NATO's EAPC members, also poses interesting questions of what obligations may be incumbent upon full members for the various partial members.

Three sets of issues pertaining to membership will be considered. First, those of the neutral and non-aligned states who are members of the EU but not of the WEU or NATO. The specific concern in this regard is the extent to which they might neuter the CFSP and its ability to develop a common defence policy (CDP) and eventually a common defence (CD). The second group to be considered is the Central and East European countries (CEEC). The effects of their association or membership of any

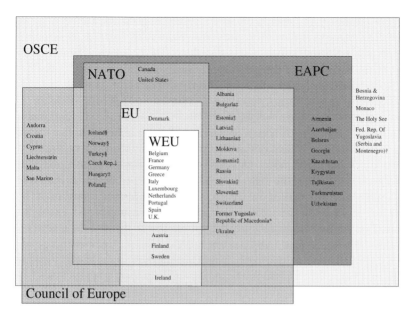

Figure 7.2   The evolving European security structure.
* Turkey recognises FYRM by its constitutional name; † Suspended; ‡ Associate
Partners of WEU; § Associate Member of WEU.

one organisation and the potential knock-on effects for Russian security are of prime concern. Third, the case of Turkey, whose claims to EU
membership have been consistently rebutted, will be considered.

The neutral and non-aligned

The post-Maastricht debates included the question of extending the
Union to the European Free Trade Area (EFTA) members.[96] The
European Commission prepared a report in July 1992 on the question
of extending membership not only to the EFTA countries, who had
applied, but also those who were likely to apply (Cyprus, Malta, Turkey
and the Central and East European countries).[97] The Commission
viewed enlargement as an issue that presented both risks and opportunities. The risks were in the dilution of the community while the
opportunities were in enhancing the stability of post-Cold War Europe.
The issue of enlargement to the EFTA countries was the least controversial of all of the projected new members – they were after all nearly
all countries who would become net payees, rather than beneficiaries,
as well as being countries that shared similar political outlooks. Official

negotiations with Austria, Finland, Norway and Sweden commenced, at the European Council's urging, in February 1993. Of the four countries, only Norway was a NATO member, and it also was the only one to reject the offer of membership.

What has been the effect of incorporating three neutral or non-aligned (NNA) countries into the EU upon Europe's security structures? The accession of the three EFTA countries on 1 January 1995 posed a number of issues with regard to NATO, but made little difference to the CFSP since Title V is, supposedly, not incompatible with neutrality.[98] Moreover, the CFSP does not raise a direct challenge to the image of neutrality, which is still held to be a defining characteristic of national identity by many within the three countries. However, the nature of the WEU's links with the CFSP has stalled a debate about the extent to which the vestiges of neutrality are compatible with the WEU's responsibility for the 'defence implications' of the Union. Membership of the EU by the three would appear to actually strengthen the security of the EU for two reasons. First, the Scandinavian members in particular have a close dialogue with the Baltic states. Specifically, their economic and cultural ties with the Baltic countries could prove critical over the question of the treatment and status of Russian minorities within the Baltics. Second, the Scandinavian countries have a long and distinguished history of involvement in UN and OSCE peacekeeping operations and observation missions. This may well add credence to future EU-backed peacekeeping operations. However, the idea of non-alignment may nevertheless translate into an extreme conservatism when faced with potential plans to create a coherent defence element to the CFSP.

Accession of the three NNAs to the EU involved not only acceptance of all of the rights and obligations of membership (the *acquis communautaire*) but also acceptance of those obligations pertaining to the CFSP. The apparent ease with which the three neutrals accepted the membership terms relating to the CFSP could be explained by the vague objectives of the CFSP (outlined in very general terms in Article J 1.2) and the reference in Article J 4.1 to the *'eventual* framing of a common defence policy, which might in time lead to a common defence' – all sufficiently indefinite to not create immediate and obvious questions regarding their status. The frequent references throughout Article J to 'general interests' or simply 'interests in common' as the basis for joint policy, suggest that the neutrals could refuse to recognise that their interests were being served by a suggested common action. If the voices of the Republic of Ireland and (perhaps) Denmark are added to those of Austria, Finland and Sweden, it becomes difficult to argue that common positions or strategies, joint decisions or joint actions, could be passed against the interests of one-third of the EU's membership. It could also be argued that the security and defence aspects of the TEU (and CTEU) serve to uphold the status of the neutrals in two ways. First, Article J 1.4 states that the CFSP 'shall not prejudice the specific character of the security and defence policy of certain Member States'. Second, any decision taken with defence implications must have unanimous backing.

In general, the concept of neutrality has had to be softened in the post-Cold War world since there are no obvious blocs from which to disassociate oneself. But the fundamental tenet of neutrality remains, as Kaj Sundberg reflected in the case of Sweden, 'non-participation in alliances in peacetime, with a view to neutrality in the event of war'.[99] There is evidently a reluctance to radically change the recipe of neutrality–non-alignment and alliance membership, which gave Scandinavia security and stability for the Cold War period.

It is quite possible that the NNAs will not join the WEU. If Ireland and Denmark adopt the same position, the chances for full convergence between the EU and WEU become remote, as does the possibility of the WEU assuming the role of NATO's European pillar. Since the WEU regards itself as the European pillar of NATO as well as an integral part of the development of the EU, any extension of membership to the WEU should *ipso facto* mean accession or at least close association with NATO as well through, for example, participation in CJTFs. Surya Subedi, an International Law professor in The Hague, argued that the accession of the neutrals prior to the defining of the CFSP 'has strengthened the position of the neutral States', and that the commitments secured by the EU from the neutral states in the CFSP context are 'no more than a hollow commitment... Under the present state of affairs, neutrals have more possibility of neutering the CFSP than Brussels has of neutering the neutrals'.[100] The currently ill-defined WEU–EU ties are the main reason that many of the potential problems outlined by Subedi have been avoided thus far. Provided the WEU remains primarily involved with Petersberg tasks, the participation of any of the neutral or non-aligned countries does not pose any fundamental inconsistencies with their NNA status. For example, forces from Austria, Finland and Sweden were involved in the WEU Police Element in Mostar and there was never a question of this being incompatible with NNA. It is however more difficult to conjecture what may happen to the formulation of a CDP with the NNAs as EU members. One possibility is a form of second-tier security membership of the various organisations, which would mirror the multi-tiered economic structure that has been suggested from time to time (giving rise perhaps to the awkward prospect of countries being in different tiers in different categories). The three countries concerned could maintain 'second tier' membership in NATO (through the Partnership for Peace and the EAPC) and in the WEU (as associate partners). This is however less than ideal and would lead to obvious voting complications and a possible weakening of the EU's *acquis communautaire*, unless an agreement could be reached that the second-tier countries would not block first-tier countries from decisions on defence and security-related matters. However, it is difficult to imagine any of the NNA countries accepting this arrangement since it would have the effect of Brussels mounting a challenge to their perceived neutrality (something that may be more unpalatable than challenges from individual capitals). Accession of aspirant CEEC to full membership may also create some odd dynamics for these three countries. Is it, for instance, imaginable that Finland and Sweden would retain some form of second-tier ranking in the event that Poland acceded to the EU, the WEU and NATO and then proceeded to make decisions with profound implications for the security of the Baltic Sea region.

An additional problem that should be mentioned in reference to the three new EU-members and associate partners of the WEU is their position on nuclear deterrence and, more specifically, the deterrent forces of Britain and France. The WEU Council of Ministers recalled in Noordwijk in 1994 that 'Europeans have a major responsibility with regard to the defence in both the conventional and nuclear field.' NATO's New Strategic Concept of 1991 also recognised that 'the independent nuclear forces of the United Kingdom and France, which have a deterrent role of their own, contribute to the overall deterrence and security of the Allies'.[101] Austria, Finland and Ireland have pointed out however that they are not party to any of these decisions and therefore disassociated themselves. Although it is difficult to envisage a scenario calling for the use of nuclear weapons, the extent to which full membership for any of these countries may be blocked by the WEU's association with the British and French nuclear deterrent forces, may be a further constraint on the WEU's growth.

Central and Eastern Europe

The explicit linkage of economic and technical assistance to broad political and economic reforms in Central and Eastern Europe was made at the European Council's Dublin Summit in June 1990. The political framework for assistance to the CEEC was firmly established in November 1990 with the CSCE's Charter of Paris, which reconfirmed the principles established in 1975 in Helsinki. The newly created dialogue with the CEEC was however rudely interrupted by dispatch of Soviet forces (including special forces) to Lithuania in early 1991. Although the situation was resolved (but not without bloodshed) with the independence of the Baltic States in the second half of 1991 and the eventual withdrawal of Russian troops in 1994, the difficult transition of the three states to independence posed a number of challenges to European security institutions. The EC was quick to recognise the independence of the states and to extend PHARE assistance to them while encouraging a resolution to their minority and border disputes through the French-inspired 1995 Stability Pact.

Moscow's extreme sensitivity to EC, WEU or NATO interference in the Baltic states resulted from concern for their sizeable Russian minorities and the need to secure access to the Kaliningrad *oblast*. Russian sensitivities *vis-à-vis* the Baltic states marked them as a special problem for the post-Cold War European security-oriented institutions. The August 1991 coup and the disintegration of the Soviet Union in December 1991 simplified matters somewhat while also clarifying the security challenges facing the region. At the top of the list was the future of the former Soviet nuclear forces in Belarus, Kazakhstan and the Ukraine. The emerging consensus of support for Yeltsin and the formation of recognition guidelines for the new states in the CEEC were the result of US-led initiatives. The articulation of the Community's responsibilities had to wait until 1992 when the Commission produced a report referring to the 'historic challenge to assume its continental responsibilities' and to contribute to the development of a 'political and economic order for the whole of Europe'.[102] In June of the following year, at its Copenhagen meeting, the European Council made it clear that its main response to the 'historic challenge' would be eastward enlargement up to the borders of the former Soviet Union. Predictably, this led to charges from Moscow that the EC was creating a 'new iron curtain' through its preferential treatment of the CEEC. The European Council's October meeting deserves passing mention since it was decided at this gathering to launch the EU's first joint action, namely, to monitor the Russian parliamentary elections of 12 December 1993. The observer mission involved participants drawn from both the Commission and the Member States. However, the need for such a mission was questionable in light of the fact that the Council of Europe, the OSCE and the UN also sent observer missions.

It was also agreed at the October meeting that a second joint action would be initiated to create a European Stability Pact along the lines laid out by French Prime Minister Edouard Balladur.

In spite of the EU's early activity in Russia, the CIS generally remained off-limits. Given the preponderant political and military influence of Russia amongst the CIS and the EU's apparent inability to mount peacekeeping activities, it was unsurprising that Yeltsin secured approval at a CIS summit in April 1994 for Russia's role as peacekeeper and border guard. In fact, Armenia and Georgia signed formal agreements for joint border policing while the election of pro-Moscow governments in Kiev and Minsk moved the Ukraine and Belarus in the same direction. The use of Russian 'peacekeeping' forces in Chechnya, Georgia, Moldova, Nagorno-Karabakh and Tajikistan, further underlined Russia's role while at the same time gave prominence to the difficulties that European institutions must surmount. As a result, the OSCE is the only European security organisation to play a modest observer role in the region. The adoption of a CIS peacekeeping role also enunciated a Russian preference for an OCSE-based European security structure in which a ten-person OCSE Steering Committee would mandate the CIS and NATO to police their respective spheres of influence. The Russian-inspired European security structure is of interest for two reasons. First, Russia clearly recognised NATO's importance but did not acknowledge the EU as being a security actor. Second, the division of Europe into spheres of security competence between the CIS and NATO gives rise to questions of how extensive Russia's 'near abroad' is – does it incorporate Central Europe or the Baltic states and what arrangements would be made with regard to the neutral or non-aligned states, such as Finland? Because of these difficulties, the EU regarded the CIS as beyond its reach and focused its attention on the CEEC.

The outreach mechanism for the EU in the CEEC was the bilateral Europe Agreements, which were signed with a number of countries. Although there is no overt security content to the agreements, the emphasis on consolidating democracy and moving towards market economies is clearly aimed at conflict prevention. The question of how to address the security element of the EU's activities was made all the more pressing with the formal applications of Hungary and Poland in April 1994 for membership. The Commission strongly recommended that there should be joint meetings of COREPER, the Political Committee and the relevant working groups, to discuss the idea of creating a European Political Area and what form of association the CEEC should have with CFSP. In spite of the ambitious proposals of the Commission and a number of bilateral initiatives, the CFSP element remained vague. However, some modest steps were undertaken in order to intensify the dialogue with the CEEC Europe Agreement countries. More specifically, on 7 March 1994, the General Affairs Council extended and deepened the dialogue with the CEEC and allowed them to associate with EU actions. The March guidelines came into force in October 1994. The first substantive action to come out of the guideline was the May 1995 joint EU–CEEC Europe Agreement statement supporting the indefinite continuation of the Non-Proliferation Treaty (NPT). In accordance with this statement, the countries involved pledged to participate in the NPT Review Conference with a pre-defined position.

The European Council made it clear at its 26 June 1994 Corfu meeting that full implementation of the Europe Agreements was a prerequisite for full membership for the ten central and east European aspirants. However, basic disagreements existed within the EU about the relative priority given to widening or deepening.[103] Indeed, the expansion of the EU eastward proved to be especially controversial in the south of Europe – a region that has been the main beneficiary of community munificence. It was at the Essen meeting of the European Council, on 9–10 December 1994, that the preparation for the accession of the associate countries of Central and Eastern Europe assumed centre stage. The question of when these countries could expect to join the EU as full members and participate in the CFSP was however couched very carefully. The Council made it plain that no firm decision on timing could be made until after the 1996 IGC and that any decisions on accession should be made with the objective of strengthening the overall process of integration. The Essen summit underlined the importance that the EU attached to intraregional co-operation and solutions to problems by offering PHARE assistance while at the same time establishing a multi-level dialogue with the CEEC. It was clear that the emphasis would remain on dialogue and not on concrete action or membership. Finally, the European Council, for its part, stressed a central role for COREPER and suggested a series of devices that would permit Europe Agreement countries to 'associate' with EU joint actions, declarations or démarches. These included:

- Meetings of the EU and CEEC Agreement countries at the same time as the European Council;

- Twice yearly meetings of the Foreign Ministers; and
- Complementary meetings of Ministers in other areas of EU activity.

Over the course of the next couple of years a rough structure for the CFSP dialogue between the EU and the CEEC emerged. The Europe Agreement countries established links through their embassies in Brussels, utilising the Correspondence Européenne (COREU) network to communicate with associate countries. Since October 1994, COREPER has held meetings with the Ambassadors of the Europe Agreement countries. In addition, a number of Working Groups were established in the second half of 1994, including with Agreement countries. The Working Groups cover a diverse selection of topics ranging from disarmament, proliferation, human rights, arms exports, OSCE and the former Yugoslavia. Although the Europe Agreement countries are permitted to 'associate' themselves with CFSP joint actions, declarations and démarches, the procedure for doing so is unclear. There are also areas of potential or actual CFSP activity that could prove awkward and possibly undermine the impact of CFSP activities. For instance, any form of activity involving the CEEC could open division lines between the Agreement countries and those who do not have such agreements. By the same token, any activity aimed at the CIS countries could generate political tension between Brussels and Moscow with, no doubt, allegations that the EU is perpetuating the division of Europe. Ultimately, designing mechanisms for effective forms of 'association' of the CEEC Agreement countries with CFSP activities is a significant problem. The real difficulty lies in the EU's lack of resolve or *acquis* to address many of the awkward questions pertaining to the region.

Another facet of the dialogue that emerged between the EC/EU and the CEEC was its geographically expansive nature. The dialogue developed from a limited discussion with the four Visegrad countries, to the Europe Agreement countries, and then to the Stability Pact signatories. At the 1996–7 IGC, the Czech Republic, Estonia, Hungary, Poland and Slovenia emerged as the front runners for membership. Although EU membership is certainly a goal for the CEEC, each also aimed to match economic stability with security through NATO membership. While each also assumed some form of association with the WEU and would, if a EU member, participate fully in the CFSP, there is little pretence that currently the real security guarantees lay anywhere other than NATO.

The dialogue with the CEEC has also expanded in the WEU context to include the associate partner countries. During the 1992 WEU

Council of Minister's Petersberg meeting, the foreign and defence ministers of the nine WEU members were joined by those of Bulgaria, the Czech Republic, Hungary, Poland, Romania, Slovakia and the Baltic States. It was agreed that: 'In view of the profound changes in Europe of the last few years, intensifying the relations between the WEU and the states of Central Europe will contribute to stability and the emergence of a new peaceful order in Europe based on partnership and co-operation, greater security and confidence, as well as disarmament.'[104] The dialogue between the WEU members and the CEEC was formalised in a WEU Forum of Consultation, consisting of the WEU Permanent Council and the CEEC Ambassadors.[105] In a document appended to the Kirchberg Declaration of 9 May 1994, the nine CEEC were granted Associate *Partners* status (see Table 7.2) which entailed the following:[106]

- The right to participate in the discussions of the Council without the ability to block decisions that are subject to consensus among the member states;
- The right to be regularly informed of the activities of the Working Groups of the Council with the possibility of being invited to participate in Working Groups on a case by case basis;
- The right to have liaison arrangements with the Planning Cell;
- The possibility to associate themselves with decisions taken by the Member States regarding Petersberg tasks; and
- The right to participate in the implementation of Petersberg tasks, including relevant training exercises, unless a majority of the Member States, or half the Member States and the Presidency, object.

After they were given Associate Partner status, arrangements were made to draw them closer to the WEU operationally, in the Petersberg context. Liaison arrangements were implemented and improved between the Associate Partners and the Planning Cell in WEU CRISEX 95–96 and, based on this, it was agreed that 'Associate Partners should be more involved in the ongoing work on the development of the operational role of WEU with regard to Petersberg missions.'[107]

Full membership of the WEU is only on offer to states who are members of the European Union. Thus Iceland, Norway and Turkey are blocked from full participation in the WEU due to their non-membership in the EU, although they are associate members. However, other European Member States of NATO were invited, at the 23 June 1992 Bonn meeting, to become Associate *Members* of the WEU 'in a way

Table 7.2 Affiliations with the Western European Union

Member States	Associate Members	Observers	Associate Partners
Modified Brussels Treaty 1954	Rome 1992	Rome 1992	Kirchberg 1994
Belgium	Iceland	Austria (1995)	Bulgaria
France	Norway	Denmark	Czech Republic
Germany	Turkey	Finland	Estonia
Greece (1995)		Ireland	Hungary
Italy		Sweden (1995)	Latvia
Luxembourg			Lithuania
Netherlands			Poland
Portugal (1990)			Romania
Spain (1990)			Slovakia
United Kingdom			Slovenia (1996)

Source: Western European Union, 1999.

which would give them a possibility of participating fully in the activities of the WEU'.[108] This offer led Iceland, Norway and Turkey to assume associate member status of the WEU on 9 May 1994 at the Council's Kirchberg meeting.[109] Associate members, as opposed to ass ciate partners or observers, are connected to the WEU communications network (WEUCOM) and also are required to make a financial contribution to the WEU, although smaller than dispensations given by full members.[110]

The communiqué resulting from the North Atlantic Council's Berlin meeting on 3 June 1996, contains the provision that plans for WEU-led operations using NATO assets should take into account the involvement of '*all* European allies if they were so to choose'.[111] The associate-member status of the three countries mentioned above, with the possibility of participating 'fully in the activities of the WEU', carries with it the possibility that 'all European members of the Alliance participate in the development of a European Security and Defence Identity within the WEU framework, according to their status'.[112] Through the associate-membership status of these countries the 'European pillar' of the Alliance acquired the requisite overlap to give the concept meaning.

The issue of whether WEU membership should be limited to EU members or NATO members was addressed in the WEU's 'Declaration II' annexed to the Treaty on European Union. According to this, invitations were extended to those states 'who are members of the European Union' to accede to the WEU 'on conditions to be agreed in accordance with Article XI of the modified Brussels Treaty'. Simultaneously, other European Member States of NATO were invited to become associate members of the WEU in a way which will give them the possibility of participating fully in the activities of the organisation'.[113] Even this formula risks creating an inner circle of full members and an outer circle of associate members and partners, the latter who have limited participation, restricted information and may not block a decision on which consensus has been agreed to by full members. The questions surrounding membership, as has been discussed, have become all the more pressing with the accession of Austria, Finland and Sweden to the EU on 1 January 1995.

Within the WEU itself, the different types of membership may be a mixed blessing as was observed at the WEU Council of Ministers in Madrid on 14 November 1995:

> The flexibility allowed by these different status of participation (together with those of the WEU associate members and associate members) enhances WEU's ability to bring together the ideas, efforts and resources of European states for the sake of stability and security in Europe. On the other hand, differences regarding status increase the asymmetry between both organizations, thereby making the full development of WEU as the defence component of the Union more complex, as two partially different groups of countries participate in the decision-making process regarding EU decisions and actions to be elaborated and implemented by WEU.[114]

The possibility of the WEU becoming a 'backdoor' into NATO has been voiced frequently but still remains an unresolved issue. For example, during a WEU visit to Washington in March 1995, the Pentagon made it clear that any full member of the WEU should also be a NATO member – which is currently the case. However, the Maastricht treaty and subsequent documents link accession to the WEU to membership of the EU – not NATO. Thus, Austria, Finland and Sweden may, if they so wish, become parties to the Brussels Treaty and not NATO. This, in turn, would create considerable difficulties for the implementation of the CJTF. If prior membership of NATO were to be made a condition of WEU membership two problems would be encountered. First, the criteria for membership of NATO are still hazy and those criteria that do exist have not been applied uniformly to the EU, the WEU or the Council of Europe. Second, if NATO membership became the criterion for WEU expansion, the Alliance would then be in the unacceptable position of exercising a veto over the eastward expansion of the WEU.

NATO launched its Partnership for Peace (PfP) initiative at its January 1994 summit. The initiative however was vague on membership details apart from the statement that 'the Alliance, as provided for in Article 10 of the Washington Treaty, remains open to the membership of other European states in a position to farther the principles of the Treaty and to contribute to the security of the Atlantic area ... we would welcome NATO expansion and would reach to democratic states to our East, as part of our evolutionary process, taking into account political and security developments in the whole of Europe'.[115] This formula was repeated in the communiqué issued after the North Atlantic Council's 1 December 1994 summit.[116] The issue of whether an aspirant state is democratic or not camouflaged the wider uncertainties about extending NATO membership east and potential Russian reactions. The concentration on Russian attitudes towards the eastward expansion of NATO has had the unfortunate effect of stifling any debate on the deepening or widening of European integration which could include the development of a CD. It has also suppressed a debate within the EU about the consequences of CFSP, CDP and CD on Russia. In general, the discussion on the expansion of NATO eastwards has become, in the words of one commentator, 'a ritual and all but futile exercise'.[117]

Turkey

Turkey's chances of securing EU membership appear distant due to persistent concerns over its human rights record, its ongoing struggle with the PKK and its potential to clash with Greece over Cyprus. Arguably though Turkey is the key to Europe's security given its location *vis-à-vis* the Caucasus, the Middle East, the Balkans and the Islamic countries bordering the Russian federation. Turkey also has the second largest armed forces in NATO. Although Turkey's record on human rights violations continues to draw international criticism, the exclusion of Turkey has left a key player in European security out in the cold. The EU's apparent reluctance to go back on its 1997 Luxembourg Summit pronouncement, which effectively put Turkey into a separate category from all other EU applicants, is the cause of serious differences between the US and the EU. Moreover, there would appear to be differences of opinion within the EU. Michael Lake, who was for eight years head of the Commission delegation to Ankara, commented (in a personal capacity) on the growing evidence of civic society in Turkey and that nearly all 'contentious issues are on the table, discussed in dozens of seminars and conferences, some financed by the Commission'.

But, Cyprus is still regarded as a 'national cause', or a matter of national honour. Lake noted, 'modern Turks are fed up with having their destiny ... and particularly their relationship with the European Union, mortgaged to Cyprus'.[118]

There is a need for a serious dialogue with Turkey but there is also a need for Turkey to address some of the more glaring objections that have made it, for right or wrong, a special case. On human rights, the evidence is that it is improving. The vendetta by the armed forces against the relatively mild Islamist party has also been a cause of concern.[119] The key issue though is undoubtedly the continuing and apparently intractable standoff over Cyprus with Greece. Following Hans-Dietrich Genscher's insistence at the Maastricht Summit, Greece acceded to full membership of the modified Brussels Treaty, making it the tenth member. This may however create severe problems for the CFSP. Disputes between Greece and the Former Yugoslav Republic of Macedonia (now abated), those with Albania and the unresolved Cyprus issue may well make agreement on a CFSP more complicated given the widely divergent views held by the ten on these issues. The purchase of S–300 missiles, ostensibly for air defence, by the Greek-Cypriots has caused severe tension between the two parts of Cyprus. This, combined with the EU's apparent willingness to move ahead with membership for the Greek-Cypriot part of the island, could pose one of the most serious challenges for European security. Indeed, as Lake points out, the missiles may bring about a paradoxical scenario, 'My personal view is that it is unacceptable to be negotiating adhesion with a government which plans to introduce Russian missiles aimed at one of our allies. Paradoxically, if the Greek Cypriots used the missiles against Turkish targets even Greece would be required to defend Turkey under the rules of NATO'.[120] The dispute over the missiles may also directly concern NATO since the radar used in conjunction with the missiles has a considerable range, including the large US base at Incirlik in Turkey, which is host to 'Northern Watch', the American – British operation to monitor air activity in northern Iraq.[121] At worst, an armed conflagration would engage Turkey and Cyprus and make it an intra-NATO dispute as well as a CFSP problem of enormous magnitude. Solicitations, forwarded by Belgium, to consider Cyprus' request to become an 'associate partner' of the WEU met with 'most strong opposition' from Britain.[122] A mishandling of the Cyprus issue has all the makings of a disaster with the capacity to render meaningless the carefully constructed post-Cold War European security structures.

With regard to membership of the European security structures three issues need clarifying as a matter of urgency. First, the issue of the expansion of NATO, the EU and the WEU needs to be addressed in the context of a *grand dessin*. The evidence seems to suggest that the expansion processes have become largely distinct and often are timed with relatively trivial considerations in mind, such as the need to expand by NATO's 50th anniversary. Second, Turkey's association with the EU and the WEU should be clarified, given its geopolitical importance for European security and the Cyprus issue. Third, a clear approach towards the Baltic states also needs to be adopted since they have the potential to be enormously sensitive for west European relations with Russia. Until these issues of membership are addressed, the idea of a European Security architecture or 'system' will remain a chimera. Some five years ago, Willem van Eekelen observed that, 'The nations making up and breathing life into the intergovernmental organisations have yet to arrive at a clear consensus response to the questions of who does what, where how and with what aims'.[123] The observation still has some truth to it.

Renationalising militaries v Euro options

The final issue standing in the way of the formation of the CFSP is the alleged tendency to renationalise defence policies. For instance, the 1994 French Defence White Paper places first priority upon defending France's 'vital and strategic interests and those with a bearing on France's international responsibilities'. The second objective is to build Europe, but this is viewed as dependent upon the willingness of Germany and the United Kingdom to pool their military assets with those of France. Furthermore, emphasis is placed upon strengthening the WEU because it is viewed as an organisation 'for asserting the European defence and security identity'.[124] In 1996, President Chirac decided to end military conscription and rely upon a professional military force. In further cuts announced on 7 July 1998 the French Defence Minister, Alain Richard, announced the government's goal to reduce the armed forces by a third, from 557000 in 1997 to 434000 in 2002. Naval cuts included the decommissioning of the aircraft carrier *Foch* and three frigates while the air force will have two squadrons of Jaguars phased out by 2001. The industrial ramifications of this included the shedding of approximately 10300 jobs (or one third) of Giat's workforce.[125]

For its part, British defence policy is designed to support its 'wider security policy, which is to maintain the freedom and territorial integrity of the United Kingdom and its dependent territories'. Reflecting Britain's international economic and political links, the 'multilateral dimension will increasingly influence [the UK's] judgement about the programmes we choose to implement'.[126] At the same time as the French 1998 defence review, the British announced their own Strategic Defence Review with the emphasis on creating a highly professional armed force while at the same time lowering expenditure. Britain's defence plans also include the commissioning of two new medium-size aircraft carriers. Both France and Britain have tried to increase military effectiveness on overall national budgets that will devote a smaller share of their GNP to the military (around 2.5 percent). Germany's 1994 'White Paper on Security and the Situation and Future of the *Bundeswehr*' stresses the importance of the Basic Law as the guide to the 'interests on which Germany bases its action in the field of security policy'.[127]

What is striking about these and other statements on defence is the lack of any clear conception of shared security interests and thus of any concept that might support a common military action. The various calls for a European Defence White Paper would certainly appear to be an initial step in the right direction but, when it comes to actually implementing common military action, reservations must be expected regarding Germany's contribution in particular. In spite of three positive judgements by Germany's Federal Constitutional Court (FCC) in Karlsruhe, which tentatively suggest that Germany will play a more active military role in regional and international security, grounds for concern remain. Under the last of the FCC's rulings in July 1994, explicit parliamentary approval, expressed by a simple majority, would be a prerequisite for an armed German military mission aside from those undertaken in self-defence or within NATO. As one of the principles of participation, Klaus Kinkel observed that it is 'desirable that a consensus be reached across the political spectrum before German troops participate in any [military missions]'.[128] It is however precisely the politicisation of security issues in a country that still has severe psychological reservations about the use of force that may well continue to circumscribe the use of the *Bundeswehr*. It will take more than a FCC ruling to motivate Germany to assume a security role that befits its economic status. This will undoubtedly be a major determinant upon whether a defence component of the CFSP becomes a reality.[129]

One of the more interesting outcomes of the Bosnian crisis was the close collaboration between American and French forces utilising

NATO assets. Additionally, Mitterrand authorised the participation of French officers in NATO planning for the protection of the UN-designated safe areas. In IFOR, French troops fell directly under NATO command for the first time since 1966. Both of these experiences led to the beginnings of a profound change of heart in France regarding NATO and paved the way for the reintegration of France into the Alliance. It was also France who took the initiative and gained US support for the NATO ultimatum that would break the Serb siege of Sarajevo. Again, in 1995, a series of Franco-US initiatives led to the December peace agreement and the announcement by the French Defence Minister, Hervé de Charette, at the 5 December NATO Council meeting, that France would resume full participation in the Military Committee and that the Defence Minister would 'regularly take part in the work of the Alliance, alongside his colleagues' – on the proviso that this would not encroach on French sovereignty.[130]

The 1994 French Defence White Paper had only mentioned participation in NATO meetings on a case-by-case basis, but it became clear that over the course of the next year that France was indeed intent on regular participation in NATO Council meetings, commencing with François Léotard's participation in the 'informal' Seville meeting and extending to the NATO Defence College and the Obergammergau SHAPE School and the Brussels Situation Centre. The only part of the Alliance that France continues to hold reservations about is the Defence Planning Committee (DPC) largely on grounds of the lack of civil accountability for SACEUR. It should also be pointed out that France's 5 December 1995 announcement was inspired, in the words of French Defence Minister, Charles Millon, by the idea of enabling its 'partners to share her convictions in favour of strengthening political control and the European identity within NATO'.[131] Unfortunately, as has been argued elsewhere, the price of the *rapprochement* seems unacceptably high since the strengthening of political control and the European identity within NATO that France has in mind is, from the US standpoint, the unnegotiable Alliance southern command.

Clearly, developments on the other side of the Atlantic will also continue to exert a strong influence on the possible re-nationalisation of European militaries. Under the Clinton administration, the failure to outline clear priorities and interests (most notably in Somalia and Bosnia), well publicised differences over senior appointments and the emergence of a Republican foreign policy agenda at variance with that of the Democratic administration, have all created a lack of faith in US leadership within the Alliance.[132] The case for an independent European security organisation may have inadvertently been made stronger by the Clinton administration.

At the centre of the problems faced in formulating a CDP for the Union is a fundamental question that has not been adequately addressed: what will the CD actually look like? Will it merely draw upon existing armed forces of the EU countries as the need arises or, will it involve deep integration of the armed forces and the dedication of a portion of the forces to a common force? The latter would certainly involve the pooling of planning, logistics, intelligence, communication, command and control and, in effect, the creation of European forces that would operate on behalf of the Union. This obviously raises difficult questions regarding control of these forces with profound implications for national sovereignty. Some countries, such as Britain, are clearly unwilling to entertain such a radical step at this stage. The issue of the apportionment of resources (both financial and human) between national, EU and international requirements could also result in considerable tensions. The alternative, 'on call' armed forces, is probably more workable politically but may actually contribute to the re-nationalisation of defence planning by demoting contributions to European structures to a visible second place.

Given that most of the contemporary challenges to Europe are of a general nature (such as drug trafficking, weapons proliferation, migratory pressures and so forth) any military response would presumably call for a concerted European response. Many of the challenges require quick reaction, non-combat uses of the military and place special demands upon intelligence collection. All of these factors point to the need for a standing force that has dedicated C^3I and logistical capabilities. The size of the force is subject to debate but the pre IGC (1996) discussions would appear to have settled on around 150 000–200 000 men and women. The goal outlined by the WEU Council of Ministers at Madrid on 14 November 1995 was for the WEU to be able to 'plan and control a Petersberg operation at up to Corps level, taking into account factors such as complexity, intensity and duration'.[133] If drawn from the fifteen EU countries or a majority thereof, the force would be sufficiently small to avoid the worst fears of loss of national control over armed forces. A standing-force, which may evolve from the Eurocorps, combined with a European Defence White Paper could serve as a valuable starting point for a CDP. The transformation of the CDP into a CD will involve a significant investment to allow the standing force to operate in a stand-alone capacity (that is, free from reliance upon US military assets). This will, once again, give rise to heated debate about the relationship between the CD and the transatlantic commitments of the Union's NATO members. The issue of how the forces communicate in the WEU context, aside from issues of language, was addressed with the signature of a Memorandum of Understanding on WEU access to NATO communications systems.[134]

The advent of not only CJTFs but more especially the multinational rapid reaction forces (RRF) implies that a significant degree of autonomy may have disappeared from Member States' hands. The future effectiveness of multinational divisions or corps would indeed seem to rest heavily upon pre-delegated arrangements. Since the RRF would, logically, be deployed early on in a crisis this may well signal a concerted response for follow-on operations. It may however also imply that Member States may exercise their autonomy through greater control of follow-on contributions. Some degree of automatic response is clearly desirable from the planning perspective but may be highly undesirable in terms of the autonomy of the Member States. Greater autonomy might however result in UN-type scenarios where there is little or no control over what forces may turn up for peacekeeping operations.

Issues of autonomy of decision-making processes will become all the more important if the above argument is extended beyond the immediate NATO and WEU context to include the PfP and Associate Partners, respectively. CJTFs may be deployed in the NATO context (involving fifteen members in practical terms)[135] but may also be utilised in a crisis affecting one of the 27 PfP members, of which 16 have Individual Partnership Programmes. Moves to enhance the PfP (in part to placate concern amongst those who did not make the first wave of expanded NATO membership) have led to a Euro-Atlantic Partnership Council designed to engage Partners in the 'planning as well as the execution' of NATO missions. What this means in practice is imprecise but the prospect of using NATO as the foundation for multilateral missions or peacekeeping efforts, possibly including the PfP, offers another avenue for the US to build a 'zone of stability'.

The lessons that can be drawn from post-Cold War crisis management, whether in Bosnia, Somalia or Rwanda, offer three discouraging conclusions. First, it is the military who often claim that little can be done to quell conflicts around the world (since most are intra-state anyway), while those who had formerly argued that force provided no solutions, now demand military responses. Second, the widespread public expectation that peacekeeping and crisis management operations should not involve casualties has put an increasing emphasis on hi-tech 'virtual' responses to conflict, especially surgical air strikes. The problems more often than not demand on-the-ground involvement and an in-depth knowledge of the history, culture and traditions of the vying groups. This, as a matter of fact, will involve considerable effort, expenditure and casualties. Rarely, if ever, can solutions be found through the laser-guided weapons tossed from fighters roaring overhead. Peacekeeping is no longer, if it ever was, a risk-free enterprise. Third, as Jonathan Eyal observed, those 'who shout loudest about a European defence identity are those who have cut their defence budgets most'.[134] Although collaborative multinational structures have emerged, such as the CJTF concept, ARRC or the Eurocorps, they were largely by-passed in times of crisis, as they were in the Albanian or Bosnian crises. Europe's future stability continues to rest upon national security structures and 'coalitions of the willing'. The continued priority given to national security is understandable given the close association between armed forces and notions of sovereignty. The logic of EMU and perhaps the merging of national defence industries into European conglomerates should direct Europe towards regional, rapid response forces, equipped with dedicated logistics and C^{3}I. Before this transpires soldiers have to be persuaded to answer one question affirmatively – is Europe worth dying for?

8
Conclusion

There are some striking similarities between current attempts to breathe life into European security structures and the 1950–4 EDC debate, although the parallels should not be exaggerated. The insecurities in Europe during the 1950s also suggested that there was an evident need for a European defence organisation to address long-term defence needs. The failure of the EDC may be attributed to disagreement over Germany's role; the issue of Britain's European versus its transatlantic priorities; French concerns about Germany's intentions; and the durability and nature of US military commitments to Europe. Although the context has changed, especially with regard to Central and Eastern Europe, the themes remain surprisingly durable. Indeed, one could question, as Robin Niblett has, whether Europe is beginning to re-fragment along the same lines as 1957, when the original six states founded the EEC? Niblett's conclusion is that at the present we are witnessing the 'emergence of a new European disunion, in the sense of a return to the rough European architecture that accompanied the launch of the Treaty of Rome'. Although he stresses that the disunion has many new aspects to it, 'with a few exceptions' the 'same fault-lines remain between those at the heart of Europe and those on its periphery'.[1] Anne Deighton made a similar point when she observed that 'it is an ironic but inescapable fact that for Western Europeans the two great security conundrums of the Cold War remain much the same in the post-Cold War period'. These are first, what will keep the US in Europe and, second, whether the Europeans actually want to construct an independent, integrated defence and security policy.[2]

There are though a number of historical differences between the situation in 1954, when the EDC dissolved, and the end of the 20th century, that deserve consideration. The first and most obvious dissimilarity is that the US was a clear and willing backstop in 1954. The failure of the EDC did not have disastrous effects on west Europe's security since all parties were aware that the US already provided for allied defence, 'agonising reappraisals' notwithstanding. The contemporary America and the international environment is different. It is no longer so self-evident that the US is as willing to play backstop for Europe's security debates nor are the stakes in terms of immediate threat so compelling.

The second main difference is that Western Europe in 1954 could not provide for its own defence in an era of nuclear deterrence. The change in emphasis from nuclear to intra-state conflict and other lesser more general security challenges takes away the EU Member States' excuse for not playing an active role. Indeed, the US insisted on numerous occasions that its European allies play such a role; most famously when Richard Holbrooke asked how many times will Europe 'sleep through the night', with reference to the 1996 Aegean crisis. The Cold War's preoccupation with nuclear weapons and the overwhelming superpower arsenals also shaped the defence requirements of the European allies. The radically changed post-Cold War European environment witnessed a painfully slow, and reluctant, adjustment on the part of the EU Member States. When it comes to the military aspects of these adaptations some even questioned that there has been any adjustment at all, such as Philip Gordon, who observed that, 'There is no sign that Europeans are prepared to do very much about their military deficiencies'.[3]

Third, the west European security institutions were largely separate throughout the Cold War. The WEU was dormant for the most part, NATO had little to do with the OSCE and the EPC was reluctant to expand its modest security aspects. This is no longer true. There are now numerous links between all of the institutions, especially the EU, the WEU and NATO. The fate of the CFSP will have a marked effect on the other institutions and its future cannot be a matter of indifference to NATO. The pillars of the EU continue to be somewhat separate (there is for instance only one common committee between the third and second pillars) but the shared responsibility between the first and second pillars for the EU's external relations makes the development of the second pillar a matter of immense importance. Its collapse would do enormous damage to the Communities. The role of the third pillar, Police and Judicial cooperation in Criminal Matters, would be made far more complicated without parallel efforts by the second pillar amongst third parties.

Fourth, the Cold War function of NATO was as much about conflict prevention in Europe as about defence (the 'keeping Germany down' part of Lord Ismay's famous dictum). The EC/EU has made war between the Member States virtually unthinkable, but not completely. The focus is no longer on Germany but on the south of Europe. Put simply, it is easier to address frictions within organisations than when the members are outside them. This important role of the CFSP should not be discounted.

The historical record also illustrates that at times of profound change it is not only institutions that find ways to adapt. The Member States of the various organisations also search for ways to respond to change. Part of this process involves evaluating the utility of the organisations in the light of changed circumstances. It is therefore not surprising that echoes of the last time of immense upheaval in Europe, following the Second World War, are still made. The parallels are helpful since a close reading of the history may avoid some of the same pitfalls although the perils of historical determinism have to be noted. The fact that European security remains confused is a reflection on the still incomplete reactions to the end of the Cold War on the part of states and the institutions of which they are members. The early post-Cold War metaphor of security architecture and its association with a deliberative process of building to a blueprint was inappropriate and unhelpful. A more relevant metaphor, suggested by Sir Michael Howard amongst others, is gardening with all of the uncertainties about what might grow and thrive.

It would be premature to predict what is evolving in European security and it would be wrong to chide the major European states too swiftly for a lack of vision. The history of the EDC illustrated that there was in fact plenty of vision but much of it competing since, more often than not, it was connected to promoting a leadership role. Compared to the security debates of the 1940s and 1950s there is more urgency to find solutions to securing and defending Europe in the post-Cold War environment. The Cold War provided the *raison d'être* for NATO as well as for the nuclear deterrent forces for Western Europe's defence. The EDC debates, the Fouchet Committee's deliberations and the prolonged slumber of the WEU, were not of critical import for the region's defence or its future. The EDC debates were of great political significance but they were also somewhat academic in the sense that they failed but Western Europe's defence was provided for anyway. This highlights the largest difference of today's debates from those of the postwar. Indeed, today, the roles of the organisations, including NATO, are being challenged in some fundamental ways as are the assumptions that can be made about the type of involvement that can be assumed by the Member States. Unlike the postwar debate, today's is not academic in the sense that there will be real world consequences if appropriate answers are not provided to meet the multifarious challenges. There is no safety blanket to pick up the pieces if the various attempts to provide for Europe's security fail. A further difference lies in the challenges that are faced. The postwar threat was evident and well enunciated in containment strategy with its military arm, nuclear deterrence. The post-Cold War era poses a bewildering variety of challenges, some of which call for provision of traditional defensive alliances, but most call for flexible structures relying upon non-traditional military functions such as policing, election monitoring, counter-terrorism and non-muscular and muscular forms of peacekeeping.

Compared to the postwar attempts at providing for Western Europe's security, the post-Cold War record is in fact glowing. Much progress appears to have been made; the London, Brussels and Berlin NATO Council meetings knitted together a group of somewhat disparate organisations through a series of consultative mechanisms, formal links, co-ordination meetings and, most importantly, through the CJTF concept. The WEU articulated its Petersberg declaration and, with it, claimed for itself an important role. In spite of the rancour, the EU moved beyond EPC to formally make security a part of the progress towards union with the TEU. The post-Cold War record at almost a decade after the Cold War ended has more to show for itself on paper than the same period after the end of the Second World War. There is however an element of *déjà vu* since most of the post-Cold War innovations are at the conceptual stage or are barely tested. The attempts in both periods to design European defence or security structures have both had the effect of emphasising the reliance upon the US to make so-called 'European' schemes practicable.

There are though, as has been observed, many challenges to European security that will not necessarily require a response from the United States, or all NATO members. There is therefore a strong case to be made for having a 'European' capability for independent action. Steps to this end have been taken. For instance, the addition of a Policy Planning and Early Warning Unit, a Planning Cell, three new agencies,[4] the satellite centre, the formulation of the 'Petersberg' tasks, the creation of procedures for co-ordinating NATO and WEU Council meetings and the beginnings of intelligence liaison with NATO, have all enhanced Europe's independent security capabilities. In spite of these developments, continued progress towards a European security and defence remains heavily reliant upon the use of NATO assets and, more particularly, American assets. At the centre of most of the European security structures that are emerging, through the WEU or EU, is the CJTF concept.

The CJTF idea defined post-Cold War European security more than any other single proposal. The profound implications of the concept led John Gerard Ruggie to note that ESDI 'does not exist in any practical terms apart from the possibility of WEU-led CJTFs, presumably using Eurocorps and other Europe-designated NATO forces'.[5] Since ESDI is therefore limited to non-Article 5 operations, Ruggie commented, 'under this concept the EU will remain unable to promise benefits of collective defense to its members who are not also members of NATO – even if they have associated themselves with the WEU, which has its own Article 5 provision and which the Maastricht Treaty designated the EU's defense component'.[6] In Philip Gordon's view the CJTF created the 'convenient myth' whereby the European allies can, for political needs, feel reassured that they have developed 'European' options that the WEU could call upon. For the US, the CJTF concept allows it to feel released from the need to intervene when there is no vital national interest involved. The success of the CJTF will nevertheless rely, somewhat awkwardly, upon US willingness to make certain key assets and resources available to its allies even though it may not be (officially) involved. In this light, the concept has reinforced US hegemony in Western Europe's security and could imply a physical veto over the ability of European allies to conduct certain operations. Such dependence may merely be a pragmatic arrangement that provides a neat solution to the interminable 'Europeanist' versus 'Altanticist' arguments. It may also pose a potential challenge to both Europe and the US since their relations are not limited to security. Negative linkages could well be established in, for instance, trade relations which could have similar knock-on effects for security associations. It would indeed be a strange, perhaps unique, scenario if the US continued to underwrite critical aspects of Europe's defences while the EU became one of the main trade competitors for North America.

Aside from the important transatlantic aspects of European security, there are a considerable number of problems or contradictions that need to be addressed in the 'Europe only' context. In the EU setting, the second pillar (CFSP) remains the weakest and the most defiantly intergovernmental. As a result of the Amsterdam Treaty, few of the intergovernmental aspects of CFSP were pruned, with the possible exception of the important arrangements on financing. The main barrier to the construction of a more *communautaire* CFSP remains the implacable opposition from the Atlanticists, led by Britain, to any extension of Brussels' competence in the security field that might damage transatlantic relations. The intergovernmental nature of the second pillar also poses problems for consistency in the external activities of the Union. Aside from the exclusion of foreign policy and defence from the EU's definition of external activities, responsibility remains divided between the first pillar and the second pillar. A number of institutional bridges exist to facilitate consistency but the main problem is to be found in the differing nature of the pillars plus the Union is unable to speak with a single voice on all occasions.

The Atlanticist versus Europeanist debate is one of the common threads running through the EDC debates, to the EPC and now to CFSP. This basic dividing line led to the WEU's marginalisation in the mid-1950s and, thirty years later, to its resuscitation. The future development of the WEU may well be stymied by the fact that the *status quo* represents the optimal role for the organisation since it balances the Atlanticist and European interests. Philip Gordon suggested that the most likely scenario for the WEU's future is that

> the WEU will remain on the course it has been on for some time – pronouncing itself relevant, making symbolic deployments to prove it, doing a few missions here and there, and very slowly building up its actual capabilities, all while leaving – both by choice and necessity – the most important tasks of European security in the hands of NATO and the United States.[7]

Prior to the 1996 IGC, the WEU recognised that it would be unwise to use the IGC to 'test the functioning of the WEU as an instrument of European defence and thus risk jeopardising its political and operational effectiveness and its function as the European pillar of NATO'.[8] The significance of the 3 June 1996 NATO Ministerial meeting in Berlin, where the basic operational principles of the CJTF concept were agreed upon, appears to be that it underlined the important supporting role that the WEU plays as the European pillar of the Atlantic Alliance. The question of how closely the WEU should be associated with the EU remains controversial though and, again, the familiar transatlantic and European divisions are apparent. An interesting and perhaps useful solution to the WEU's future role was forwarded by the Blair government with its suggestion to fully integrate the WEU into the second pillar while at the same time creating a new fourth pillar dedicated solely to defence (see below).

The history of efforts to incorporate a security or defence dimension to the European integration process illustrates a profound ambivalence about the willingness, even of the Europeanists, to actually create a European security entity possessing the genuine ability to act in the interests of Europe. The CJTF concept provides a convenient means for employing NATO assets and US resources in a 'Europe-only' context but it also fudges the central issues. Two questions arise from the continued reliance upon NATO and the US. First, is it in the interests of their security that European nations should remain highly dependent upon the US? Second, for how long will the US be willing to assume the substantial burden of addressing security problems in which it may have little or no interest and that its trade competitors choose to ignore?

The reply to the first issue is negative. Unlike its European allies, the US still has global military interests but, like them, it has a declining defence budget. The difficulties that the US encountered in finding an underlying thrust to its post-Cold War foreign and security policy are mirrored in its European allies. The lack of a common threat, which provided much of the cement for NATO and made it such a successful alliance, is now replaced by vaguer talk of 'common values' and shared cultures. Exactly what these common values are is not always obvious, especially when the post-Cold War years have been punctuated by a number of serious differences between the US and its European partners in several non-security fields, such as trade. What keeps the US in Europe undoubtedly contains an element of genuine belief in common values and cultural nostalgia, but it is shaped more profoundly by self-interest on the part of both sides.

In the case of the US, several interests can be identified. First, active involvement in Europe's security and stability helps to underpin America's superpower status. Europe was, after all, the prize of the Cold War and the symbolism of the retreat of the last Russian troops from their bases in the former East Germany, Estonia and Poland, was not lost upon potential CEEC NATO members. Furthermore, NATO is one of the few organisations in which the US can play a clearly hegemonic role. It attempted to play such a role elsewhere, most notably in the UN, but the methods it chose to bring about reforms in the organisation led to at least as much condemnation of the US as support. Second, the maintenance of forward bases in Europe serves US interests in littoral areas. *Operation Desert Storm* illustrated the importance of European gateways and base facilities for power projection to the Near and Middle East and, if need be, to North Africa as well.

This observation though has to be balanced with the consideration that the US cannot count on the support of its allies, with the exception of Britain, for such out-of-area ventures. The cruise missile strikes against terrorist targets in Afghanistan and the Sudan in August 1998 were mounted by US naval vessels operating from international waters. From the military standpoint it is therefore desirable but not essential to maintain access to European bases for force-projection reasons. Third, the maintenance of US forces in Europe is a central component of the expansion of its influence in Central and Eastern Europe. Quite simply, the attraction of NATO to so many CEEC is not just the alliance, but the fact that it is backed by the only remaining superpower. For obvious practical and historical reasons, an Alliance without the US would have far less attraction for the CEEC.

The issue for the European allies is whether US interests in Europe are sufficiently similar to their own to be incorporated seamlessly into European security structures or whether mutual self-interest is a sufficient basis upon which to ensure the security of the region. The chronologies of the WEU or other multilateral attempts to address security challenges in Europe and beyond without the US, illustrate that there has yet to be a concerted 'European response'. Instead, reactions to security problems rest upon unilateral initiatives or 'coalitions of the willing' and not upon any automatic response from the ten WEU members or fifteen EU members. Furthermore, on those occasions when the WEU mobilised, it was far from clear what positive practical contribution it made. The missed opportunity in Albania poses not only questions for the WEU but, more generally, about the willingness of the members to work through the institution. There would appear to be a marked preference to work through *ad hoc* arrangements or coalitions of the willing, whether in Bosnia, Albania or further afield. For example, the crisis in Albania saw an Italian-led coalition intervene in April 1997 to restore order following the descent of the country into civil unrest. Of the eight countries who participated each had their own reasons for wishing to be involved, ranging from French support for the idea of a 'European response', Greek concerns about regional security to Romania's wish to launch a last-minute bid to impress NATO prior to the Madrid summit (apparently Hungary, feeling secure in the knowledge that an invitation would be forwarded to join NATO, did not feel the same pressure). More importantly, at least seven countries had reasons for *not* participating. An *à la carte* approach to security challenges in and around Europe may indeed recognise the fact that not all will feel threatened equally but it also renders any pretence of a 'European' response as nonsense. As long as armed forces remain predominantly under national control, selectivity will not be avoided. The formation of dedicated and standing European forces, building, for example, upon the FAWEU concept or the Eurocorps, under multinational control to provide a European response would seem the logical, if distant, answer. While the European allies ponder the design of European security options and the extent to which they wish to be involved, their reliance upon the US becomes more transparent.

The response to the first question would, therefore, actually be that there is currently sufficient self-interest on the part of the US and its European allies to continue current commitments. Mutual self-interest is not however the same as common interest. The former does not require the enunciation of principles or the formation of common values that bind together the parties. However, the establishment of common interest does. The lack of any overarching threat, which in Cold War parlance was what was meant by 'common values', leaves the problem of identifying the foundations of transatlantic security co-operation. The values though are not so common, as was illustrated over the issue of lifting the arms embargo in Bosnia or the Helms–Burton legislation, and as American cultural nostalgia for the 'old country' becomes more distant with each generation and demographic changes there might be less to build common edifices upon. Still, identifying common interests and values should not be that difficult since they lie in the carnage and wreckage of the Balkans.

The second question, considering how long the US will wish to remain engaged, has already been partially answered. In general, successive reactions to European security and defence schemes from the White House have been marked by schizophrenia. As Anne Deighton noted, US policy towards Europe was 'particularly unsettled between 1990 and 1994'.[9] Clear and consistent encouragement for the European allies to assume more of the common defence burdens only emerged post-1994, with the CJTF concept under the Clinton administration. The history of European security and defence initiatives may well have encouraged an inconsistent approach since few of the schemes came to fruition and none challenged America's hegemonic position. Normally the schizophrenia in US–European relations was the result of the tension between the economic and political aspects of European integration. The political (and security) support given to Western Europe during the Cold War facilitated the formation of the

EEC and what has now become a potential trade competitor. The short-term response, as indicated above, is that there is clearly sufficient self-interest for the US to remain involved in Europe's security. The potential however in the long-term for the non-security aspects of transatlantic relations to have negative consequences on America's willingness to underwrite its defence and security contributions to Europe also have to be considered. The role of the New Transatlantic Agenda, the Transatlantic Business Dialogue and the New Transatlantic Marketplace could play a critical role in ensuring that non-security aspects of transatlantic relations do not endanger security aspects. While an Atlantic Union is a long way off, there is certainly need for a transatlantic institution to exist, with an overview of the various aspects of the New Transatlantic Agenda and transatlantic security relations. Although there is an active exchange of information and there are visits between the EP and the national legislatures with Congress, and vice versa, something more formal is needed. Perhaps a Transatlantic Parliamentary Assembly composed of rotating members from the EP and Congress would be a logical next step in answering the question of why the US should remain interested in Europe.

In addition to the two questions posed, the context in which transatlantic relations and European security are discussed will be influenced decisively, for better or for worse, by enlargement. What started out as the parallel process of NATO and EU expansion soon became the distinct process. NATO has expanded before the EU and, by all accounts, the expansion of the latter will be far more difficult and time consuming. Meanwhile, it is quite possible that the EU will be unable to solve the contradictions and disagreements pertaining to its second pillar and the development of a CDP and CD posed by its last expansion in 1995, with Austria, Finland and Sweden.

NATO expansion to the Czech Republic, Hungary and Poland is built upon the premise that it is a suitable organisation to address the security challenges of the region. The future may reveal however that NATO is in many ways an unsuitable body to provide security not only because it is not designed to answer many of the non-military problems of the region, but also *because of what it is* – a largely American-backed collective defence organisation. The historical baggage associated with NATO as well as American hegemony may become decisive (and negative) issues in a second round of membership negotiations, which will probably include at least Estonia (strengthened by its invitation to begin negotiations for EU membership) if not the remaining Baltic states. Neither the WEU nor the EU carries the same association, especially for an unstable Russia, which might construe NATO absorption of the Baltics as an anti-Russian move. This suggests that a greater WEU role might be politically more tolerable. The process of NATO expansion may also fall foul of European politics and, in particular, Greek–Turkish animosity over Cyprus which is a candidate for EU membership. The unpredictable reaction from Russia to NATO enlargement to the Baltic states, combined with the erratic changes of the Russian government, economic instability and widespread civil unrest, may also prompt caution in the ratification process for NATO enlargement.

Scenarios for the future

The political capital within the EU is clearly heavily invested in European Monetary Union (EMU). What happens with EMU will have an effect on CFSP. A successful EMU could provide the impetus for further effort in the second pillar but it may also prompt a rethink by the US of its continued willingness to support Europe. The failure, or postponement, of EMU could prompt compensatory efforts in the other pillars. It may also have the opposite effect of diluting federalist tendencies yet further. The fate of CFSP will have far less of an impact upon the Union or transatlantic relations, but it will have some implications. It is clear that it would be immensely difficult for the EU to continue without a second pillar or for the Union to revert to an EPC-style parallel process for four reasons. First, the Maastricht Treaty and numerous subsequent documents have made it clear that the CFSP is part of the 'general process of integration within the European Union' and also that the WEU is an 'integral part' of the EU. The separation of the CFSP from the more general integration process would not only make negotiable all other aspects of the union and open up the flood gates for Member States' exceptionalism, but it would also undermine much of the *raison d'être* of the WEU. Second, the expansive post-Cold War parameters of security, which include many non-military aspects of security, will also of necessity demand close collaboration since many of the issues falling under the second pillar rubric will have profound implications for other pillars. Third, the collapse of the second pillar would weaken the EU as an international actor and might lead outside states to exploit differences rather than adjust to consensus. Fourth, the CFSP and the CDP/CD in particular may be undesirable to a number of countries but there are no clear alternatives that would knit together the interests of the Atlanticists and Europeanists in a way that links the CFSP with the WEU and NATO.

The main difficulty would appear to be not so much one of whether the CFSP will survive but whether it will ever be anything more than marginal. It will survive because the EU serves the general interests of the Member States in some way or another, varying from state to state. Even those who are less than enamoured with the EU would hesitate to be portrayed as openly damaging the institution. Part of the paradox of the EPC and CFSP is that there is a perceived utility in their existence, from both within the EU and from outside, yet there seems to be a profound reluctance to provide them with the necessary political and financial resources. Two astute observers of EU affairs summarised the paradox facing the CFSP in the 1990s thus:

> Expectations of West European governments, as a group, has risen: from the former socialist states, from a deliberately less committed American administration, from less-developed countries operating through the UN, even from active groups within their domestic publics. Capabilities had been adjusted, but – as in previous negotiations over strengthening the institutions and decision-making procedures of EPC – only modestly and reluctantly. There remained 'a dangerous tension' at the heart of CFSP: a 'capability-expectations gap' which reflected the contradiction between the ambitions of EU member governments to play a larger international role and their reluctance to move beyond an intergovernmental framework in doing so.[10]

The 'capability-expectations gap' with regard to the security and defence aspects of CFSP can be explained on several levels. It is, in part, connected to entrenched national positions, which recognise the benefits and strengths of common positions in external relations, but also include strongly held feelings of national autonomy. The latter prevail largely because what is aimed at is a CFSP – not just a CFP. The positive aspects of foreign and security policy co-ordination have been demonstrated in a number of ways ranging from increased efficiency, better mutual understanding, reinforcing other (non-military) forms of solidarity and confidence building, reducing threat perceptions, and the ability to bring consensus in numbers and, if necessary, force in numbers, to bear upon a given problem. Integration in the security arena however poses special challenges to *national* values and even identity since much of a state's history, for better or worse, is wrapped up in armed forces.

Generally, Christopher Hill's capabilities-expectations gap [CEG] may have narrowed, since as he argued, 'the punctured balloon of hopes for the CFSP should have closed the CEG by bringing expectations back into line with capabilities'.[11] In the specific CDP/CD context the activation of the Eurocorps, the identification of FAWEU and the CJTF's 'separable but not separate' forces concept, may all have led to rather high expectations. These expectations however have been downgraded by three factors. First, the formation of a CDP/CD is constrained by a lack of military capabilities. The few options that do not rely upon NATO and, more significantly, US assets ensure that the CD remains peripheral. Second, the lack of a generally agreed upon CDP and the fact that defence procurement remains for all practical purposes outside the EU treaties means that the development of common positions will be hampered by national (and business) interests. The close involvement of EU states in defence industries further suggests that reaching common positions or the adoption of joint actions will tend to be easier in the case of low-key peripheral activities, such as observer missions, training, patrols and natural disaster responses. Third, the CFSP mechanisms have developed considerably beyond the somewhat rudimentary EPC mechanisms. The development of 'joint actions', 'common positions', 'common strategies' and modified voting rules as well as those for finance, have strengthened the likelihood of consistency and coherence. Any such mechanisms are only useful if they are adhered to and, indeed, used. Quite aside from the issue of institutional improvements there is the willingness of the Member States themselves to actuallly use the mechanisms at their disposal. Even when decisions have been made in the CFSP context, CFSP has failed more often than not to act with a 'single voice'. For example, with Germany's premature recognition of Croatia and Slovenia; the failure of the Dutch Presidency in 1997 to persuade its EU partners to co-ordinate their actions regarding Albania through CFSP; and the U-turn on the EU's position regarding the Helms–Burton legislation. The modifications introduced by Maastricht and Amsterdam have done little to lessen the Member States' intergovernmental grasp over CFSP while they have arguably diminished the capabilities-expectations gap.

The shortcomings of the CFSP generally will have obvious detrimental effects for any CDP/CD. The preference thus far has been to continue to formulate national defence priorities with only cursory acknowledgement of the importance of the CDP/CD. Whatever further changes are instituted to CFSP, the right to a national veto and non-participation in any activities involving the use of military force, will be jealously guarded by the Member States. Indeed, the use of military force is a matter of such acute sensitivity that it is difficult to imagine it otherwise. It is also likely that the right of veto on the part of those who will be the main contributors and risk takers will also be upheld. In light of this, what are the alternatives for the future of the security and defence dimensions of the CFSP?

There would seem to be three main alternatives: some type of multi-speed Europe; a continuation of the *ad hoc* arrangements which have prevailed until the present; and the construction of a new forth pillar dedicated to defence.

Multispeed security

There are several variants of the first option. It could comply with the proposals forwarded by the German CDU/CSU Parliamentary group or could follow the Balladur proposals for a number of concentric circles. In practical terms, the multi-speed CFSP based on 'variable geometry' was implicitly recognised with the formation of the Contact Group on Bosnia and Kosovo. The existence of some heavyweight foreign policy actors who will have more influence and say in the CFSP, and especially in defence matters, is recognised but not a basis upon which to construct any common positions or actions when the overall objective is for the EU to speak with 'a single voice'. The variable geometry Europe was primarily designed to address the differing economic capabilities of the members and their ability to meet economic convergence criteria for monetary union. In the CFSP realm the question is not so much one of the ability to contribute to a CFSP but of the political will to do so. While it is important to recognise that the CFSP is not common in the same sense that, for instance, the Common Agricultural Policy is, a piecemeal approach would also violate the spirit, if not the word, of the Treaty of Maastricht. The treaty declares that the CFSP is designed to 'safeguard the common values, fundamental interests, independence and integrity of the Union'. It also commits Member States to 'support the Union's external and security policy actively and unreservedly in a spirit of loyalty and mutual solidarity'.[12]

While these recommendations have the attraction of recognising that some states wish to integrate, and are able to integrate, at different speeds, they are perhaps more problematic than beneficial. For instance, the assumption that the economic and political hard core would *ipso facto* constitute the central group of the CFSP and Europe's common defence is one that is debatable on several grounds. Where, for instance, would Britain fall in such a construct? Presumably, the reservations held towards EMU would place it outside the central group yet, in terms of the CFSP, as one of the two nuclear powers and one of the two permanent members of the Security Council, it can scarcely be considered a marginal actor. A two (or multi) speed Europe also appears to ignore important differences between the character of the pillars. The first pillar is primarily *communautaire* in approach while the second pillar remains resolutely intergovernmental. While a variable speed CFSP might work, it is difficult to see how such a concept would function in conjunction with a variable-speed first pillar (the group of eleven EMU countries and the remaining four). Finally, the existence of a central group of CFSP actors would presumably encourage the second or third tier members to expect the central ones to act and assume risks. In the event that weaker members did not support a position or activity, it could also widen political differences within the EU and WEU.

More of the same

The CFSP cannot continue as it has without fundamental reform because it has hit a barrier, created by the underlying intergovernmental nature of the second pillar and the tentative linkage of defence with the second pillar, beyond which it is immensely difficult to go forward. The inclusion of aspects of security in the EPC context was acceptable since the Cold War preoccupation was very much centered on collective defence. But the 'security plus' approach of the TEU was more controversial since security was more evident and collective defence less so, in light of the dissolution of the Warsaw Pact. Attempts to more formally include defence in the Amsterdam Treaty met strong resistance, not only because of concerns about diluting transatlantic ties, but also because the IGC gave rise to many of the same issues that arose in the EDC debates. A European defence would also suggest a move towards standing European armed forces, a step that is viewed with deep suspicion by Britain, in particular.

The changing nature of security and the inclusion of defence into the CFSP framework, alongside differing national perspectives, have together contributed to the impasse. The enlargement of both the EU and NATO will only exacerbate the problems of CFSP. The 'Europe only' options for military action under CFSP rely heavily upon the CJTF concept. The linkage of CFSP to defensive roles, through the ability of the EU to 'avail itself' of the WEU and its ability in turn to request the release of NATO assets, poses two challenges. First, the linkage between CFSP, a defensive role, and NATO assets is awkward for the neutral and non-aligned countries. The four countries involved, plus Denmark, will probably not object to participation in Petersberg tasks but anything beyond this would create a challenge to their constitutional and political sensitivities. Second, the inter relationship between the organisations could lead to growing involvement of new EU members in CJTF operations and perhaps WEU membership as well. Estonia's position is of particular concern in this regard since any such scenario would have highly negative effects upon relations with Russia and the relevant organisations.

The future of the CFSP therefore rests upon the ability to incorporate defence as an integral part of the EU's role whilst not alienating the US and the Atlantic Alliance in general and to preserve and expand the foreign and security elements of the CFSP, whilst respecting the individual positions of the Member States. One design to accomplish this was forwarded by the British at a meeting in October 1998.

Britain's fourth pillar

Prime Minister Tony Blair's stated goal for the British EU Presidency, lasting from 1 January to 30 June 1998, was that the United Kingdom should 'lead in Europe'. Robin Cook, the Foreign Secretary, said in the autumn of 1997 that the UK 'now has a government with a secure majority and a strong leader able to seize the opportunity to shape the direction of Europe'.[13] The agenda of the 1998 UK presidency must be placed in the context of the Prime Minister's drive to distance himself from the Conservative legacy regarding Britain's role in the 'new cooperative approach to Europe'.[14] The Presidency was very much linked to Labour's domestic agenda and to the continued disarray within the Conservative Party, where the 'Europe' question is highly divisive.[15]

It is worth noting briefly that the UK Presidency was silent on the defence aspects of the CFSP and, in particular, the issue of the closeness of the WEU's association with the EU. The reluctance to address this issue, given the EU's relative impotence in Bosnia and Kosovo, sprang not only from Britain's well-publicised pro-NATO stance but also from the potential domestic political repercussions coming from the Conservative Eurosceptics to any hint of selling out Britain's defences to Brussels. Only well after the UK Presidency was finished did Blair unveil a plan to abolish the WEU, by having its political functions taken over by a new fourth pillar of the EU and having its military side revert to NATO. Nevertheless, the proposed fourth pillar has to be seen in the light of the Blair government's desire to play a leading role in Europe, as established during the UK Presidency.

The fact that the Blair government chose to make its bid in the defence realm is unsurprising given the difficulties that would be faced by a similar bid in other areas of EU activity (such as economic, political or social affairs). The timing of the bid, after the UK Presidency, may also be explained by the relatively short period of the Presidency; whether six months affords enough time to introduce and implement major changes. The first reports of the British defence plans were in the *Financial Times*[16] shortly after the UK Presidency ended. The plans were based on a booklet by Charles Grant of the Centre for European Reform.[17] Robert Cooper of the Foreign and Commonwealth Office was, according to *The Economist*, set the task of writing a confidential paper on the future of Europe. Its central thrust was that 'Britain should champion the reform of European institutions, to increase their legitimacy and to make them more effective'.[18] Cooper also argued that a final constitutional settlement should be sought for Europe but that a bridging strategy was necessary. The idea forwarded by Cooper and Grant was that Britain should propose the strengthening of Europe's role in defence. Unfortunately, the subsequent elaboration of Britain's lead in this capacity lacked the intellectual coherence of their arguments.

Grant argued that defence is a logical area in which Britain could assume a prominent role since 'Britain and France are the only countries capable of projecting power beyond Europe'.[19] By reversing the traditional hostility to the concept of European defence and Britain's tendency to line up with the US, Grant contended that Britain could radically redefine its role and image in Europe. The post-Amsterdam European security architecture also lent itself to such an initiative. Grant described it as an 'unsatisfactory mess' based on the WEU ('an organisation in search of a role'), the French remaining 'semi-detached from NATO', while the EU's 'nascent foreign policy is weakened by its disconnection from any military organisation that could support its positions'.[20] Grant speculated that in the spring of 1998 Blair 'may have realised that, if the British could appear to be better Europeans in this area, they might win considerable credit with their partners; and that in the strange world of EU politics, it is possible to buy good will by making concessions that are more symbolic than substantial'.[21]

The essence of Grant's proposals can be summarised as follows:

- Britain should strengthen European defence without damaging NATO or upsetting the US and it should do this by deepening bilateral military relationships (especially with the French);
- Britain should try and broker a compromise between the US and France on the latter's full reintegration into the NATO command structure;
- Britain should not flag in its efforts to lead the restructuring of the European defence industry; and
- Britain should propose the abolition of the WEU. Its political functions would merge with the EU, becoming the 'fourth pillar', and its military functions would be subsumed into NATO and Article V of the Modified Brussels Treaty (obliging members to defend each other from attack) would be transferred to the fourth pillar.

The perceived benefits of this course of action would be, according to Grant:[22]

- The WEU would be 'put out of its misery' since it cannot develop further without duplicating NATO's role;
- The CFSP would be strengthened since, if the EU were able to call on military assets, its pronouncements on foreign and security policy would carry more clout;
- The reforms would settle the issue of Europe's defence identity and convince all that NATO has a future as 'Europe's only functioning military organisation' and this should help maintain the US military presence in Europe;
- Establishing a fourth pillar would make it easier for the EU to admit countries unwilling or unable to join a defence organisation; and
- Russia is less likely to take exception to EU enlargement if the military guarantee does not apply to all members (thus the Baltic Republics would not joint the fourth pillar).

The Blair government's unveiling of Britain's initiative on European defence was made at the EU Pörtschach summit on 24–5 October 1998, held under the auspices of the Austrian Presidency. The way was paved with select interviews with a number of European newspapers prior to the summit. Blair made it clear that Britain was willing to drop its long-standing objection to the EU having a defence capability but that he was not talking of a European army and that: 'Nothing must happen that in any way impinges on the effectiveness of NATO.'[23] Blair noted that the Kosovo crisis clearly indicated that Europe had responsibilities and obligations; adding that 'We should be prepared to think more boldly and more imaginatively about how we do that'.[24]

The Pörtschach summit, ostensibly called to discuss 'real problems', included the outlining of a number of defence options for the EU:[25]

- The strengthening of the European security and defence identity within NATO;
- The dissolution of the WEU and its integration into the EU; and
- The establishment of modern and flexible European forces.

While Blair's 'proposals' lacked the details of the Grant-Cooper underpinnings, their main importance lay in the significant reversal of Britain's traditional resistance to EU responsibility in security and defence affairs. Schematically, the gist of the proposals can be summarised as follows:

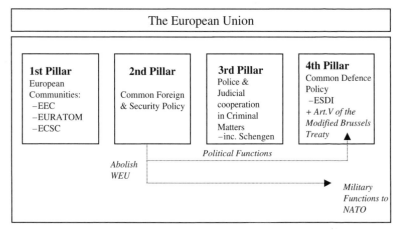

Figure 8.1   Britain's 'Fourth Pillar' Proposals (based on the Pörtschach Proposals and the St. Malo Declaration).

Soon after the Pörtschach summit Austrian Defence Minister, Werner Fasslabend, called a summit of the fifteen EU defence ministers, on 4 November 1998 in Vienna, to discuss prospects for European defence after the entry into force of the Amsterdam Treaty and to discuss crisis management. Much of the focus was upon George Robertson, the British Defence Secretary, but he did little to elaborate upon the fourth pillar. He did however stress that all Britain had done was to present 'options'. Robertson noted that Europe had reached a 'defining moment' for defence policy and that Bosnia and Kosovo had raised the question of 'when we press the button for action, is it connected to a system and a capability that can deliver?'[26] He emphasised the need for 'armed forces that are deployable and sustainable, that are modern, powerful and flexible, that are mobile, survivable and are highly capable'. The institutional options were not, 'about removing defence from the control of national governments', or about creating a 'standing European army', nor to undermine or duplicate NATO.[27] The question of the merger of the WEU into the EU raised, according to Robertson, 'a number of difficulties'. His preferred solution was to explore other options such as 'merging some elements of the WEU into the EU and associating other elements more closely with NATO, or perhaps creating a more distinct European dimension within NATO'.[28]

The opaque nature of the British proposal of the exact fate of the WEU appears to be for political reasons, especially with regard to French and Dutch sensitivities. Until the French rapprochement with NATO is complete, the WEU will continue to be an important vehicle for French input into European security and defence debates. The Dutch Defence Minister, Frank de Grave, made it clear at the informal defence ministers meeting that 'for the time being WEU will remain the organisation that provides the Union with an operational capability'.[29] Jean-Pol Poncelet, the Belgian Defence Minister, noted that the six founding members of the EU had already pronounced themselves to be in favour of the gradual incorporation of the WEU into the EU and he also called for a White Paper on European Defence which should 'provide the guidelines and European vision currently lacking in the definition of NATO's new strategic concept'.[30] Ireland's Defence Minister, Michael Smith, underlined Ireland's willingness to contribute to Petersberg tasks since peacekeeping is a 'defining element' in Irish foreign policy but that the legitimacy of such operations should be provided by the OSCE or the UN. Smith spoke in favour of enhancing the 'interaction' between the EU and the WEU as well as for a 'definition of rights' for the non-allied Observers (Austria, Finland, Ireland, Sweden and Denmark).[31]

José Cutilero, the WEU's Secretary General, argued that the WEU gives Europeans 'decisional autonomy' for the execution of Petersberg tasks. He also recalled that the WEU operates 'at 18' (the ten full members, plus the observers and the associate members and partners). Thus, according to Cutilero, 'through WEU, all European Union members and all NATO European allies work together now on politico military aspects of European security on a permanent basis', and Central and East European countries 'participate collectively in European deliberations on security matters'.[32]

The combined effect of the Pörtschach summit and the informal meeting of the EU defence ministers in Vienna was to reopen the debate on European security and defence, prior to the ratification and enforcement of the Treaty of Amsterdam. The subsequent General Affairs Council meeting saw continued reflection on the different European schemes for security and defence. Italian Foreign Minister, Lamberto Dini, who was also President in Office of the WEU Council, acknowledged that 'despite the existence of the WEU and the good will of the European Union, Europe has often been unable to act in crisis situations'. He added that the WEU's decision-making mechanisms in particular and its membership 'has demonstrated that it is an ineffective body' and that the WEU–EU link must therefore be reviewed.[33] The WEU Council, with the participation of the EU Foreign and Defence Ministers, met 'at 18' on 16 November 1998, where Cutilero summarised the outcome of the proceedings by observing that: 'If we are really interested in using our capacities in Petersberg-type operations, we basically have to do two things: pick up and combine the appropriate forces where they are and find the political will to use them within the framework of a European multinational action.'[34]

The outlining of British 'options' for Europe's defence can be interpreted in a number of ways. First, the fourth pillar idea may be an attempt to persuade the British public that Britain is playing a leading role in Europe (and a smokescreen for the more politically sensitive debate about EMU). Second, the proposed abolition of the WEU and the concentration of defence into a new fourth pillar may only serve to make obvious what is apparent anyway – that much of Europe's security and defence depends upon the good will and support of Washington. By inadvertently highlighting this, the Blair government may actually draw attention to the strength and durability of Britain's transatlantic leanings. Third, the options may provide a useful solution to the impasse in the CFSP's development by removing defence from the second pillar and creating a new fourth pillar. Even if the creation of a new pillar merely moved the problems from one pillar to another, it may afford the chance for the second pillar to develop, for new Member States to join and for the constitutional and political sensitivities of all to be catered to.

St Malo: a glimpse down the road

Britain's initiatives in the multilateral context were matched by proposals in the bilateral framework. As a result of a meeting between President Chirac and Prime Minister Blair a joint Franco-British declaration was issued on European defence.[35] The declaration called for the Treaty of Amsterdam to be made 'a reality' which, amongst other factors, would involve endowing the Union with 'the capacity for autonomous action, backed by credible military forces, the means to decide to use them and a readiness to do so'.[36] As per other declarations, the different situations of countries in relation to NATO and of individual states were observed. The declaration's main impact was to call for a far more autonomous European military capability than had hitherto been enunciated:

> In order for the European Union to take decisions and approve military action where the Alliance as a whole is not engaged, the Union must be given appropriate structures and a capacity for analysis of situations, sources of intelligence and a capability for relevant strategic planning, without unnecessary duplication, taking account of the existing assets of the WEU and the evolution of its relations with the EU. In this regard, the European Union will also need to have recourse to suitable military means (European capabilities pre-designated within NATO's European pillar or multinational European means outside the NATO framework).[37]

The declaration also noted that strengthened European armed forces would need to be supported by a 'strong and competitive European defence industry and technology'.

What significance should be attached to the St Malo declaration? In some ways the declaration marks a highly significant development, particularly with regard to Britain's willingness to associate itself more closely with European security and defence. It is also welcome in the sense that, from a military perspective, any credible European military option will have to be built around Franco-British co-operation. However, the wording continues to obfuscate on some important issues and perhaps national differences in the British and French positions. For instance, the declaration calls for the Union to develop the capacity for 'autonomous action' while acting in conformity with 'our respective obligations in NATO'. What does this mean when the British preference has traditionally been to develop ESDI while France's incomplete *rapprochement* with NATO may lead to a preference for less dependence upon NATO? Or, is the call for autonomous action on the part of the Blair administration an attempt to pressure Washington into greater support for ESDI on a concrete and predictable basis? Nevertheless, the call for an 'autonomous' capability clearly recognises that there will be circumstances in which the EU members may wish to act where the US may not.[38] The need for 'unnecessary duplication' may also point in the direction of the abolition of the WEU in favour of a direct link between the EU and NATO through, for example, a new fourth pillar devoted to defence. The WEU has virtually no assets *per se* and the evolution of its relations with the EU remains ambiguous following the 1996 IGC. By taking both of these into account, the conclusion may well be that there is no real further role for the WEU. The call for a 'strong and competitive' European defence industry also recognised what had long been apparent; a commitment to joint European defence industrial projects forms the essential underpinning to any genuinely autonomous European military capability.

Generally, the welcome impact of the St Malo declaration as a positive development for European security was undermined by open differences a few days later between France (and other EU members) and Britain over the US and British bombing of Iraq. The February 1999 announcement of a merger between BAe and the Marconi defence division of GEC, in preference to a BAe merger with Daimler-Chrysler Aerospace (Dasa), also seemed to call into question the sincerity of the British commitment to the declaration.[39] Until the deal was announced it had been assumed that the BAe-Dasa merger would be the first step in forming a unified six country European aerospace and defence company (EADC). Siegmar Mosdorf, government co-ordinator for the aerospace industry in the Federal German government, estimated that the Airbus and EADC processes had been set back by 'at least two years', during which time it is expected that Boeing's production problems may be fully solved.[40]

The combined significance of the 'fourth pillar' and St Malo proposals, in so far as they deserve such a description, is threefold. First, they marked Britain's bid for leadership in Europe based on the only credible area open to Britain to influence its neighbours. Second, Britain's willingness to voluntarily enter into discussions about European defence is a major development which, arguably, removes one of the major impediments to progress in this area. And, last, any progress in European security and defence is inconceivable without the active involvement of Britain and France. The history of efforts at integration in this field illustrates that either or both can make or break the best of schemes.

Déjà vu?

There is one interesting and rather surprising parallel between the post EDC years and the current ones. In both cases the future direction of European security and defence may well depend upon an initiative from that unlikely European partner, Britain. The idea for a fourth pillar has considerable attraction since it increases the flexibility of the EU to accommodate the security requirements of all members, including the neutral and non-aligned Member States, and provides a way forward beyond the impasse reached at Maastricht over the defence elements of the CFSP. It is also difficult to see how the WEU can develop further without duplicating the functions and resources of NATO while its full incorporation into NATO, minus the Article V commitments, would seem to make much sense. The emphasis on security can then be put where it belongs, in Europe, and that of defence where it has belonged since 1949, with the Atlantic Alliance.

No matter how the fourth pillar initiative is interpreted, the 'options' provoked a debate that will not go away, not even with the enforcement of the Amsterdam Treaty. The Blair government has not actually suggested anything radically new but it has publicly pointed out the fundamental contradictions and problems at the heart of the security and defence elements of the CFSP. If the fourth pillar options are adopted, and they are not that far away from French and German thinking on the matter, it may prove to be one of the most remarkable developments in European defence policy and the most substantial enhancement to Britain's European credentials.

No matter what happens, security and defence will remain a fundamental component of the ongoing attempts to build a European union. In post-Cold War Europe security can be provided in many different ways, ranging from economic, social to political variants, and it is not the exclusive preserve of the second pillar. At the same time, post-Cold War Europe has proven itself to be unstable with numerous challenges stemming from intra-state tensions. As the events in Bosnia, Kosovo and Albania have shown, the EU cannot remain hermetically sealed from the events surrounding it; the success of the European Communities has made sure of that. The future should include not only an enhanced second pillar, perhaps with a defence-oriented fourth pillar, but a growing emphasis upon conflict prevention. The ability to achieve that task with a credible single European voice, backed by military force, needs to be developed. That credible voice continues to be American, not European, and the EU capitals can only hope that the European allies continue to be at the centre of Washington's foreign and security interests.

The intergovernmental nature of the second pillar is unlikely to change (this would apply with equal force to any fourth pillar). The history of European security and defence collaboration would not though support a purely realist approach whereby nation states are unwilling to surrender control over 'high politics' in all circumstances. Nor would it completely support a neo-functionalist approach since security and defence has so far resisted the 'spill over' into the full application of the *acquis*. The latter though helps to explain far more than the realist approach. The economic pressures to merge European defence industries, commencing with the aerospace industry, may well prove to be the first manifestation of spillover from the economic to the defence sectors. Perhaps more important than the economic pressures pushing the EU members towards more European security and defence is the price of this autonomy. This is all too apparent in Bosnia and Kosovo. Bosnia came perilously close to discrediting the CFSP as well as NATO. Kosovo may yet do so. This alone should be sufficient to compel the EU members to provide a commitment to comprehensive European security and defence. It is worth recalling that the building blocks for such an enterprise resulted from ideas formulated behind the barbed wire of prisoner-of-war camps at a time when the threat of further inter-state conflict was uppermost in the minds of those advocating European integration. The challenge now is that of intra-state dissolution and conflict. The response to predominantly intra-state conflict will, as it did in the 1940s, require vision and commitment.

Appendix 1: The Brussels Treaty

Treaty of economic, social and cultural collaboration and collective self-defence

Signed at Brussels on 17 March 1948

between His Majesty in respect of the United Kingdom of Great Britain and Northern Ireland, His Royal Highness the Prince Regent of Belgium, the President of the French Republic, Her Royal Highness the Grand Duchess of Luxembourg, and Her Majesty the Queen of the Netherlands

Article I

Convinced of the close community of their interests and of the necessity of uniting in order to promote the economic recovery of Europe, the High Contracting Parties will so organize and co-ordinate their economic activities as to produce the best possible results, by the elimination of conflict in their economic policies, the co-ordination of production and the development of commercial exchanges.

The co-operation provided for in the preceding paragraph, which will be effected through the Consultative Council referred to in Article VII as well as through other bodies, shall not involve any duplication of, or prejudice to, the work of other economic organizations in which the High Contracting Parties are or may be represented but shall on the contrary assist the work of those organizations.

Article II

The High Contracting Parties will make every effort in common, both by direct consultation and in specialized agencies, to promote the attainment of a higher standard of living by their peoples and to develop on corresponding lines the social and other related services of their countries.

The High Contracting Parties will consult with the object of achieving the earliest possible application of recommendations of immediate practical interest, relating to social matters, adopted with their approval in the specialized agencies.

They will endeavour to conclude as soon as possible conventions with each other in the sphere of social security.

Article III

The High Contracting Parties will make every effort in common to lead their peoples towards a better understanding of the principles which form the basis of their common civilization and to promote cultural exchanges by conventions between themselves or by other means.

Article IV

If any of the High Contracting Parties should be the object of an armed attack in Europe, the other High Contracting Parties will, in accordance with the provisions of Article 51 of the Charter of the United Nations, afford the Party so attacked all the military and other aid and assistance in their power.

Article V

All measures taken as a result of the preceding Article shall be immediately reported to the Security Council. They shall be terminated as soon as the Security Council has taken the measures necessary to maintain or restore international peace and security.

The present Treaty does not prejudice in any way the obligations of the High Contracting Parties under the provisions of the Charter of the United Nations. It shall not be interpreted as affecting in any way the authority and responsibility of the Security Council under the Charter to take at any time such action as it deems necessary in order to maintain or restore international peace and security.

Article VI

The High Contracting Parties declare, each so far as he is concerned, that none of the international engagements now in force between him and any other of the High Contracting Parties or any third State is in conflict with the provisions of the present Treaty.

None of the High Contracting Parties will conclude any alliance or participate in any coalition directed against any other of the High Contracting Parties.

Article VII

For the purpose of consulting together on all the questions dealt with in the present Treaty, the High Contracting Parties will create a Consultative Council, which shall be so organized as to be able to exercise its functions continuously. The Council shall meet at such times as it shall deem fit.

At the request of any of the High Contracting Parties, the Council shall be immediately convened in order to permit the High Contracting Parties to consult with regard to any situation which may constitute a threat to peace, in whatever area this threat should arise; with regard to the attitude to be adopted and the steps to be taken in case of a renewal by Germany of an aggressive policy; or with regard to any situation constituting a danger to economic stability.

Article VIII

In pursuance of their determination to settle disputes only by peaceful means, the High Contracting Parties will apply to disputes between themselves the following provisions.

The High Contracting Parties will, while the present Treaty remains in force, settle all disputes falling within the scope of Article 36, paragraph 2, of the Statute of the International Court of Justice by referring them to the Court, subject only, in the case of each of them, to any reservation already made by that party when accepting this clause for compulsory jurisdiction to the extent that that Party may maintain the reservation.

In addition, the High Contracting Parties will submit to conciliation all disputes outside the scope of Article 36, paragraph 2, of the Statute of the International Court of Justice.

In the case of a mixed dispute involving both questions for which conciliation is appropriate and other questions for which judicial settlement is appropriate, any Party to the dispute shall have the right to insist that the judicial settlement of the legal questions shall precede conciliation.

The preceding provisions of this Article in no way affect the application of relevant provisions or agreements prescribing some other method of pacific settlement.

Article IX

The High Contracting Parties may, by agreement, invite any other State to accede to the present Treaty on conditions to be agreed between them and the State so invited.

Any State so invited may become a Party to the Treaty by depositing an instrument of accession with the Belgian Government.

The Belgian Government will inform each of the High Contracting Parties of the deposit of each instrument of accession.

Article X

The present Treaty shall be ratified and the instruments of ratification shall be deposited as soon as possible with the Belgian Government.

It shall enter into force on the date of the deposit of the last instrument of ratification and shall thereafter remain in force for fifty years.

After the expiry of the period of fifty years, each of the High Contracting Parties shall have the right to cease to be a party thereto provided that he shall have previously given one year's notice of denunciation to the Belgian Government.

Appendix 2: The North Atlantic Treaty

Washington, DC – 4 April 1949

The Parties to this Treaty reaffirm their faith in the purposes and principles of the Charter of the United Nations and their desire to live in peace with all peoples and all governments. They are determined to safeguard the freedom, common heritage and civilisation of their peoples, founded on the principles of democracy, individual liberty and the rule of law. They seek to promote stability and well-being in the North Atlantic area. They are resolved to unite their efforts for collective defence and for the preservation of peace and security. They therefore agree to this North Atlantic Treaty:

Article 1

The Parties undertake, as set forth in the Charter of the United Nations, to settle any international dispute in which they may be involved by peaceful means in such a manner that international peace and security and justice are not endangered, and to refrain in their international relations from the threat or use of force in any manner inconsistent with the purposes of the United Nations.

Article 2

The Parties will contribute toward the further development of peaceful and friendly international relations by strengthening their free institutions, by bringing about a better understanding of the principles upon which these institutions are founded, and by promoting conditions of stability and well-being. They will seek to eliminate conflict in their international economic policies and will encourage economic collaboration between any or all of them.

Article 3

In order more effectively to achieve the objectives of this Treaty, the Parties, separately and jointly, by means of continuous and effective self-help and mutual aid, will maintain and develop their individual and collective capacity to resist armed attack.

Article 4

The Parties will consult together whenever, in the opinion of any of them, the territorial integrity, political independence or security of any of the Parties is threatened.

Article 5

The Parties agree that an armed attack against one or more of them in Europe or North America shall be considered an attack against them all and consequently they agree that, if such an armed attack occurs, each of them, in exercise of the right of individual or collective self-defence recognised by Article 51 of the Charter of the United Nations, will assist the Party or Parties so attacked by taking forthwith, individually and in concert with the other Parties, such action as it deems necessary, including the use of armed force, to restore and maintain the security of the North Atlantic area.

Any such armed attack and all measures taken as a result thereof shall immediately be reported to the Security Council. Such measures shall be terminated when the Security Council has taken the measures necessary to restore and maintain international peace and security.

Article 6

For the purpose of Article 5, an armed attack on one or more of the Parties is deemed to include an armed attack:

- on the territory of any of the Parties in Europe or North America, on the Algerian Departments of France, on the territory of Turkey or on the Islands under the jurisdiction of any of the Parties in the North Atlantic area north of the Tropic of Cancer;
- on the forces, vessels, or aircraft of any of the Parties, when in or over these territories or any other area in Europe in which occupation forces of any of the Parties were stationed on the date when the Treaty entered into force or the Mediterranean Sea or the North Atlantic area north of the Tropic of Cancer.

Article 7

This Treaty does not affect, and shall not be interpreted as affecting in any way the rights and obligations under the Charter of the Parties which are members of the United Nations, or the primary responsibility of the Security Council for the maintenance of international peace and security.

Article 8

Each Party declares that none of the international engagements now in force between it and any other of the Parties or any third State is in conflict with the provisions of this Treaty, and undertakes not to enter into any international engagement in conflict with this Treaty.

Article 9

The Parties hereby establish a Council, on which each of them shall be represented, to consider matters concerning the implementation of this Treaty. The Council shall be so organised as to be able to meet promptly at any time. The Council shall set up such subsidiary bodies as may be necessary; in particular it shall establish immediately a defence committee which shall recommend measures for the implementation of Articles 3 and 5.

Article 10

The Parties may, by unanimous agreement, invite any other European State in a position to further the principles of this Treaty and to contribute to the security of the North Atlantic area to accede to this Treaty. Any State so invited may become a Party to the Treaty by depositing its instrument of accession with the Government of the United States of America. The Government of the United States of America will inform each of the Parties of the deposit of each such instrument of accession.

Article 11

This Treaty shall be ratified and its provisions carried out by the Parties in accordance with their respective constitutional processes. The instruments of ratification shall be deposited as soon as possible with the Government of the United States of America, which will notify all the other signatories of each deposit. The Treaty shall enter into force between the States which have ratified it as soon as the ratifications of the majority of the signatories, including the ratifications of Belgium, Canada, France, Luxembourg, the Netherlands, the United Kingdom and the United States, have been deposited and shall come into effect with respect to other States on the date of the deposit of their ratifications.

Article 12

After the Treaty has been in force for ten years, or at any time thereafter, the Parties shall, if any of them so requests, consult together for the purpose of reviewing the Treaty, having regard for the factors then affecting peace and security in the North Atlantic area, including the development of universal as well as regional arrangements under the Charter of the United Nations for the maintenance of international peace and security.

Article 13

After the Treaty has been in force for twenty years, any Party may cease to be a Party one year after its notice of denunciation has been given to the Government of the United States of America, which will inform the Governments of the other Parties of the deposit of each notice of denunciation.

Article 14

This Treaty, of which the English and French texts are equally authentic, shall be deposited in the archives of the Government of the United States of America. Duly certified copies will be transmitted by that Government to the Governments of other signatories.

Appendix 3: Modified Brussels Treaty

Treaty of economic, social and cultural collaboration and collective self-defence signed at Brussels on 17 March 1948, as amended by the 'protocol modifying and completing the Brussels Treaty'

Signed at Paris on 23 October 1954

[The High Contracting Parties]

Resolved:

To reaffirm their faith in fundamental human rights, in the dignity and worth of the human person and in the other ideals proclaimed in the Charter of the United Nations;

To fortify and preserve the principles of democracy, personal freedom and political liberty, the constitutional traditions and the rule of law, which are their common heritage;

To strengthen, with these aims in view, the economic, social and cultural ties by which they are already united;

To co-operate loyally and to co-ordinate their efforts to create in Western Europe a firm basis for European economic recovery;

To afford assistance to each other, in accordance with the Charter of the United Nations, in maintaining international peace and security and in resisting any policy of aggression;

To promote the unity and to encourage the progressive integration of Europe;

To associate progressively in the pursuance of these aims other States inspired by the same ideals and animated by the like determination;

Desiring for these purposes to conclude a treaty of collaboration in economic, social and cultural matters and for collective self-defence;

Have agreed as follows:

Article I

Convinced of the close community of their interests and of the necessity of uniting in order to promote the economic recovery of Europe, the High Contracting Parties will so organise and co-ordinate their economic activities as to produce the best possible results, by the elimination of conflict in their economic policies, the co-ordination of production and the development of commercial exchanges.

The co-operation provided for in the preceding paragraph, which will be effected through the Council referred to in Article VIII, as well as through other bodies, shall not involve any duplication of, or prejudice to, the work of other economic organisations in which the High Contracting Parties are or may be represented, but shall on the contrary assist the work of those organisations.

Article II

The High Contracting Parties will make every effort in common, both by direct consultation and in specialised agencies, to promote the attainment of a higher standard of living by their peoples and to develop on corresponding lines the social and other related services of their countries.

The High Contracting Parties will consult with the object of achieving the earliest possible application of recommendations of immediate practical interest, relating to social matters, adopted with their approval in the specialised agencies.

They will endeavour to conclude as soon as possible conventions with each other in the sphere of social security.

Article III

The High Contracting Parties will make every effort in common to lead their peoples towards a better understanding of the principles which form the basis of their common civilisation and to promote cultural exchanges by conventions between themselves or by other means.

Article IV

In the execution of the Treaty, the High Contracting Parties and any Organs established by Them under the Treaty shall work in close co-operation with the North Atlantic Treaty Organisation.

Recognising the undesirability of duplicating the military staffs of NATO, the Council and its Agency will rely on the appropriate military authorities of NATO for information and advice on military matters.

Article V

If any of the High Contracting Parties should be the object of an armed attack in Europe, the other High Contracting Parties will, in accordance with the provisions of Article 51 of the Charter of the United Nations, afford the Party so attacked all the military and other aid and assistance in their power.

Article VI

All measures taken as a result of the preceding Article shall be immediately reported to the Security Council. They shall be terminated as soon as the Security Council has taken the measures necessary to maintain or restore international peace and security.

The present Treaty does not prejudice in any way the obligations of the High Contracting Parties under the provisions of the Charter of the United Nations. It shall not be interpreted as affecting in any way the authority and responsibility of the Security Council under the Charter to take at any time such action as it deems necessary in order to maintain or restore international peace and security.

Article VII

The High Contracting Parties declare, each so far as he is concerned, that none of the international engagements now in force between him and any other of the High Contracting Parties or any third State is in conflict with the provisions of the present Treaty.

None of the High Contracting Parties will conclude any alliance or participate in any coalition directed against any other of the High Contracting Parties.

Article VIII

1. For the purposes of strengthening peace and security and of promoting unity and of encouraging the progressive integration of Europe and closer co-operation between Them and with other European organisations, the High Contracting Parties to the Brussels Treaty shall create a Council to consider matters concerning the execution of this Treaty and of its Protocols and their Annexes.
2. This Council shall be known as the 'Council of Western European Union'; it shall be so organised as to be able to exercise its functions continuously; it shall set up such subsidiary bodies as may be considered necessary: in particular it shall establish immediately an Agency for the Control of Armaments whose functions are defined in Protocol No. IV.
3. At the request of any of the High Contracting Parties the Council shall be immediately convened in order to permit Them to consult with regard to any situation which may constitute a threat to peace, in whatever area this threat should arise, or a danger to economic stability.
4. The Council shall decide by unanimous vote questions for which no other voting procedure has been or may be agreed. In the cases provided for in Protocols II, III and IV it will follow the various voting procedures, unanimity, two-thirds majority, simple majority, laid down therein. It will decide by simple majority questions submitted to it by the Agency for the Control of Armaments.

Article IX

The Council of Western European Union shall make an annual report on its activities and in particular concerning the control of armaments to an Assembly composed of representatives of the Brussels Treaty Powers to the Consultative Assembly of the Council of Europe.

Article X

In pursuance of their determination to settle disputes only by peaceful means, the High Contracting Parties will apply to disputes between themselves the following provisions;

The High Contracting Parties will, while the present Treaty remains in force, settle all disputes falling within the scope of Article 36, paragraph 2, of the Statute of the International Court of Justice, by referring them to the Court, subject only, in the case of each of them, to any reservation already made by that Party when accepting this clause for compulsory jurisdiction to the extent that that Party may maintain the reservation.

In addition, the High Contracting Parties will submit to conciliation all disputes outside the scope of Article 36, paragraph 2, of the Statute of the International Court of Justice.

In the case of a mixed dispute involving both questions for which concilia-tion is appropriate and other questions for which judicial settlement is appro-priate, any Party to the dispute shall have the right to insist that the judicial settlement of the legal questions shall precede conciliation.

The preceding provisions of this Article in no way affect the application of relevant provisions or agreements prescribing some other method of pacific set-tlement.

Article XI

The High Contracting Parties may, by agreement, invite any other State to accede to the present Treaty on conditions to be agreed between them and the State so invited.

Any State so invited may become a Party to the Treaty by depositing an instrument of accession with the Belgian Government.

The Belgian Government will inform each of the High Contracting Parties of the deposit of each instrument of accession.

Article XII

The present Treaty shall be ratified and the instruments of ratification shall be deposited as soon as possible with the Belgian Government.

It shall enter into force on the date of the deposit of the last instrument of ratification and shall thereafter remain in force for fifty years.

After the expiry of the period of fifty years, each of the High Contracting Parties shall have the right to cease to be a party thereto provided that he shall have previously given one year's notice of denunciation to the Belgian Government.

The Belgian Government shall inform the Governments of the other High Contracting Parties of the deposit of each instrument of ratification and of each notice of denunciation.

Appendix 4: Single European Act (extract)

18 February 1986, Done at The Hague; 1 July 1987, entered into force

TITLE III: Provisions on european cooperation in the sphere of foreign policy

Article 30

European Cooperation in the sphere of foreign policy shall be governed by the following provisions:

1. The High Contracting Parties, being members of the European Communities, shall endeavour jointly to formulate and implement a European foreign policy.
2. (a) The High Contracting Parties undertake to inform and consult each other on any foreign policy matters of general interest so as to ensure that their combined influence is exercised as effectively as possible through coordination, the convergence of their positions and the implementation of joint action.

    (b) Consultations shall take place before the High Contracting Parties decide on their final position.

    (c) In adopting its positions and in its national measures each High Contracting Party shall take full account of the positions of the other partners and shall give due consideration to the desirability of adopting and implementing common European positions.

    In order to increase their capacity for joint action in the foreign policy field, the High Contracting Parties shall ensure that common principles and objectives are gradually developed and defined.

    The determination of common positions shall constitute a point of reference for the policies of the High Contracting Parties.

    (d) The High Contracting Parties shall endeavour to avoid any action or position which impairs their effectiveness as a cohesive force in international relations or within international organisations.
3. (a) The Ministers for Foreign Affairs and a member of the Commission shall meet at least four times a year within the framework of European Political Cooperation. They may also discuss foreign policy matters within the framework of Political Cooperation on the occasion of meetings of the Council of the European Communities.

    (b) The Commission shall be fully associated with the proceedings of Political Cooperation.

    (c) In order to ensure the swift adoption of common positions and the implementation of joint action, the High Contracting Parties shall, as far as possible, refrain from impeding the formation of a consensus and the joint action which this could produce.

4. The High Contracting Parties shall ensure that the European Parliament is closely associated with European Political Cooperation. To that end the Presidency shall regularly inform the European Parliament of the foreign policy issues which are being examined within the framework of Political Cooperation and shall ensure that the views of the European Parliament are duly taken into consideration.

5. The external policies of the European Community and the policies agreed in European Political Cooperation must be consistent.

   The Presidency and the Commission, each within its own sphere of competence, shall have special responsibility for ensuring that such consistency is sought and maintained.

6. (a) The High Contracting Parties consider that closer cooperation on questions of European security would contribute in an essential way to the development of a European identity in external policy matters. They are ready to coordinate their positions more closely on the political and economic aspects of security.

   (b) The High Contracting Parties are determined to maintain the technological and industrial conditions necessary for their security. They shall work to that end both at national level and, where appropriate, within the framework of the competent institutions and bodies.

   (c) Nothing in this Title shall impede closer cooperation in the field of security between certain of the High Contracting Parties within the framework of the Western European Union or the Atlantic Alliance.

7. (a) In international institutions and at international conferences which they attend, the High Contracting Parties shall endeavour to adopt common positions on the subjects covered by this Title.

   (b) In international institutions and at international conferences in which not all the High Contracting Parties participate, those who do participate shall take full account of positions agreed in European Political Cooperation.

8. The High Contracting Parties shall organise a political dialogue with third countries and regional groupings whenever they deem it necessary.

9. The High Contracting Parties and the Commission, through mutual assistance and information, shall intensify cooperation between their representations accredited to third countries and to international organisations.

10. (a) The Presidency of European Political Cooperation shall be held by the High Contracting Party which holds the Presidency of the Council of the European Communities.

   (b) The Presidency shall be responsible for initiating action and coordinating and representing the positions of the Member States in relations with third countries in respect of European Political Cooperation activities. It shall also be responsible for the management of Political Cooperation and in particular for drawing up the timetable of meetings and for convening and organising meetings.

   (c) The Political Directors shall meet regularly in the Political Committee in order to give the necessary impetus, maintain the continuity of European Political Cooperation and prepare Ministers' discussions.

(d) The Political Committee or, if necessary, a ministerial meeting shall convene within forty-eight hours at the request of at least three Member States.

(e) The European Correspondents' Group shall be responsible, under the direction of the Political Committee, for monitoring the implementation of European Political Cooperation and for studying general organizational problems.

(j) Working groups shall meet as directed by the Political Committee.

(g) A Secretariat based in Brussels shall assist the Presidency in preparing and implementing the activities of European Political Cooperation and in administrative matters. It shall carry out its duties under the authority of the Presidency.

11. As regards privileges and immunities, the members of the European Political Cooperation Secretariat shall be treated in the same way as members of the diplomatic missions of the High Contracting Parties based in the same place as the Secretariat.

12. Five years after the entry into force of this Act the High Contracting Parties shall examine whether any revision of Title III is required.

Appendix 5: WEU Council of Ministers Petersberg Declaration

Bonn, 19 June 1992

(Part II only)

II. On strengthening WEU's operational role

1. In accordance with the decision contained in the Declaration of the Member States of WEU at Maastricht on 10 December 1991 to develop WEU as the defence component of the European Union and as the means to strengthen the European pillar of the Atlantic Alliance, WEU Member States have been examining and defining appropriate missions, structures and means covering, in particular, a WEU planning cell and military units answerable to WEU, in order to strengthen WEU's operational role.
2. WEU Member States declare that they are prepared to make available military units from the whole spectrum of their conventional armed forces for military tasks conducted under the authority of WEU.
3. Decisions to use military units answerable to WEU will be taken by the WEU Council in accordance with the provisions of the UN Charter. Participation in specific operations will remain a sovereign decision of Member States in accordance with national constitutions.
4. Apart from contributing to the common defence in accordance with Article 5 of the Washington Treaty and Article V of the modified Brussels Treaty respectively, military units of WEU member States, acting under the authority of WEU, could be employed for:

   - humanitarian and rescue tasks;
   - peacekeeping tasks;
   - tasks of combat forces in crisis management, including peacemaking.

5. The planning and execution of these tasks will be fully compatible with the military dispositions necessary to ensure the collective defence of all Allies.
6. Military units will be drawn from the forces of WEU Member States, including forces with NATO missions – in this case after consultation with NATO – and will be organized on a multinational and multi-service basis.
7. All WEU Member States will soon designate which of their military units and headquarters they would be willing to make available to WEU for its various possible tasks. Where multinational formations drawn from the forces of WEU nations already exist or are planned, these units could be made available for use under the authority of WEU, with agreement of all participating nations.
8. WEU Member States intend to develop and exercise the appropriate capabilities to enable the deployment of WEU military units by land, sea or air to accomplish these tasks.
9. A Planning Cell will be established on 1 October 1992, subject to practical considerations, under the authority of the Council. It will be located with the Secretariat-General in a suitable building in Brussels. The Council has

today appointed Maj.Gen. Caltabiano (Italian Air Force) as its first Director. The Planning Cell will be responsible for:

- preparing contingency plans for the employment for forces under WEU auspices;
- preparing recommendations for the necessary command, control and communication arrangements, including standing operating procedures for headquarters which might be selected – keeping an updated list of units and combinations of units which might be allocated to WEU for specific operations.

10. The Council of Ministers approved the terms of reference for the Planning Cell.

Appendix 6: Treaty on European Union (extract)

(Maastricht, 7 February 1992)

Title V: Provisions on a common foreign and security policy

Article J

A common foreign and security policy is hereby established which shall be governed by the following provisions.

Article J.1

1. The union and its Member States shall define and implement a common foreign and security policy, governed by the provisions of the Title and covering all areas of foreign and security policy.
2. The objectives of the common foreign and security policy shall be:

   - to safeguard the common values, fundamental interests and independence of the Union;
   - to strengthen the security of the Union and its Member States in all ways;
   - to preserve peace and strengthen international security, in accordance with the principles of the United Nations Charter as well as the principles of the Helsinki Final Act and the objectives of the Paris Charter;
   - to promote international cooperation;
   - to develop and consolidate democracy and the rule of law, and respect for human rights and fundamental freedoms.

3. The Union shall pursue these objectives:

   - by establishing systematic cooperation between Member States in the conduct of policy, in accordance with Article J.2;
   - by gradually implementing, in accordance with Article J.3, joint action in the areas in which the Member States have important interests in common.

4. The Member States shall support the Union's external and security policy actively and unreservedly in a spirit of loyalty and mutual solidarity. They shall refrain from any action which is contrary to the interests of the Union or likely to impair its effectiveness as a cohesive force in international relations. The Council shall ensure that these principles are complied with.

Article J.2

1. Member States shall inform and consult one another within the Council on any matter of foreign and security policy of general interest in order to

ensure that their combined influence is exerted as effectively as possible by means of concerted and convergent action.

2. Whenever it deems it necessary, the Council shall define a common position. Member States shall ensure that their national policies conform on the common positions.

3. Member States shall coordinate their action in international organizations and at international conferences. They shall uphold the common positions in such fora. In international organizations and at international conferences where not all the Member States participate, those which do take part shall uphold the common positions.

Article J.3

The procedure for adopting joint action in matters covered by foreign and security policy shall be the following:

1. The Council shall decide, on the basis of general guidelines from the European Council, that a matter should be the subject of joint action. Whenever the Council decides on the principle of joint action, it shall lay down the specific scope, the Union's general and specific objectives in carrying out such action, if necessary its duration, and the means, procedures and conditions for its implementation.

2. The Council shall, when adopting the joint action and at any stage during its development, define those matters on which decisions are to be taken by a qualified majority. Where the Council is required to act by a qualified majority pursuant to the preceding subparagraph, the votes of its members shall be weighted in accordance with Article 148(2) of the Treaty establishing the European Community, and for their adoption, acts of the Council shall require at least fifty-four votes in favour, cast by at least eight members.

3. If there is a change in circumstances having a substantial effect on a question subject to joint action, the Council shall review the principles and objectives of that action and take the necessary decisions. As long as the Council has not acted, the joint action shall stand.

4. Joint actions shall commit the Member States in the positions they adopt and in the conduct of their activity.

5. Whenever there is any plan to adopt a national position or take national action pursuant to a joint action, information shall be provided in time to allow, if necessary, for prior consultations within the Council. The obligation to provide prior information shall not apply to measures which are merely a national transposition of Council decisions.

6. In cases of imperative need arising from changes in the situation and failing a Council decision, Member States may take the necessary measures as a matter of urgency having regard to the general objectives of the joint action. The Member State concerned shall inform the Council immediately of any such measures.

7. Should there be any major difficulties in implementing a joint action, a Member State shall refer them to the Council which shall discuss them and seek appropriate solutions. Such solutions shall not run counter to the objectives of the joint action or impair its effectiveness.

Article J.4

1. The common foreign and security policy shall include all questions related to the security of the Union, including the eventual framing of a common defence policy, which might in time lead to a common defence.
2. The union requests the Western European Union (WEU), which is an integral part of the development of the Union, to elaborate and implement decisions and actions of the Union which have defence implications. The Council shall, in agreement with the institutions of the WEU, adopt the necessary practical arrangements.
3. Issues having defence implications dealt with under this Article shall not be subject to the procedures set out in Article J.3.
4. The policy of the Union in accordance with this Article shall not prejudice the specific character of the security and defence policy of certain Member States and shall respect the obligations of certain Member States under the North Atlantic Treaty and be compatible with the common security and defence policy established within that framework.
5. The provisions of this Article shall not prevent the development of closer cooperation between two or more Member States on a bilateral level, in the framework of the WEU and the Atlantic Alliance, provided such cooperation does not run counter to or impede that provided for in this Title.
6. With a view to furthering the objective of this Treaty, and having in view the date of 1998 in the context of Article XII of the Brussels Treaty, the provisions of this Article may be revised as provided for in Article N(2) on the basis of a report to be presented in 1996 by the Council to the European Council, which shall include an evaluation of the progress made and the experience gained until then.

Article J.5

1. The Presidency shall represent the Union in matters coming within the common foreign and security policy.
2. The Presidency shall be responsible for the implementation of common measures; in that capacity it shall in principle express the position of the Union in international organisations and international conferences.
3. In the tasks referred to in paragraphs 1 and 2, the presidency shall be assisted if needs be by the previous and next Member States to hold the Presidency. The Commission shall be fully associated in these tasks.
4. Without prejudice to Article J.2(3) and Article J.3(4), Member States represented in international organisations or international conferences where not all the Member States participate shall keep the latter informed of any matter of common interest. Member States which are also members of the United Nations Security Council will concert and keep the other Member States fully informed. Member States which are permanent members of the Security Council will, in the execution of their functions, ensure the defence of the positions and the interests of the union, without prejudice to their responsibilities under the provisions of the United Nations Charter.

Article J.6

The diplomatic and consular missions of the Member States and the Commission Delegations in third countries and international conferences, and their representations to international organisations, shall cooperate in ensuring that the common positions and common measures adopted by the Council are complied with and implemented. They shall step up cooperation by exchanging information, carrying out joint assessments and contributing to the implementation of the provisions referred to in Article 8c of the Treaty establishing the European Community.

Article J.7

The Presidency shall consult the European Parliament on the main aspects and the basic choices of the common foreign and security policy and shall ensure that the views of the European Parliament are duly taken into consideration. The European Parliament shall be kept regularly informed by the Presidency and the Commission of the development of the Union's foreign and security policy. The European Parliament may ask questions of the Councils or make recommendations to it. It shall hold an annual debate on progress in implementing the common foreign and security policy.

Article J.8

1. The European Council shall define the principles of and general guidelines for the common foreign and security policy.
2. The Council shall take the decisions necessary for defining and implementing the common foreign and security policy on the basis of the general guidelines adopted by the European Council. It shall ensure the unity, consistency and effectiveness of action by the Union. The Council shall act unanimously, except for procedural questions and in the case referred to in Article J.3(2).
3. Any Member State or the Commission may refer to the Council any question relating to the common foreign policy and may submit proposals to the Council.
4. In cases requiring a rapid decision, the Presidency, of its own motion, or at the request of the Commission or a Member State, shall convene an extraordinary Council meeting within forty-eight hours or, in an emergency, within a shorter period.
5. Without prejudice to Article 151 of the Treaty establishing the European Community, a Political Committee consisting of Political Directors shall monitor the international situation in the areas covered by common foreign and security policy and contribute to the definition of policies by delivering opinions to the Council at the request of the Council or on its own initiative. It shall also monitor the implementation of agreed policies, without prejudice to the responsibility of the Presidency and the Commission.

Article J.9

The Commission shall be fully associated with the work carried out in the common foreign and security policy field.

Article J.10

On the occasion of any review of the security provisions under Article J.4, the Conference which is convened to that effect shall also examine whether any other amendments need to be made to provisions relating to the common foreign and security policy.

Article J.11

1. The provisions referred to in Articles 137, 138, 139 to 142, 146, 147, 150 to 153, 157 to 163 and 217 of the Treaty establishing the European Community shall apply to the provisions relating to the areas referred to in this Title.
2. Administrative expenditure which the provisions relating to the areas referred to in this Title entail for the institutions shall be charged to the budget of the European Communities. The Council may also:

   - either decide unanimously that operational expenditure to which the implementation of those provisions gives rise is to be charged to the budget of the European Communities; in that event, the budgetary procedure laid down in the Treaty establishing the European Community shall be applicable;
   - or determine that such expenditure shall be charged to the Member States, where appropriate in accordance with a scale to be decided.

Appendix 7: Consolidated Version of the Treaty on European Union

(*Incorporating changes made by the Treaty of Amsterdam, signed 2 October 1997*)

Title V – Provisions on a common foreign and security policy

Article 11 (ex Article J.1)

1. The Union shall define and implement a common foreign and security policy covering all areas of foreign and security policy, the objectives of which shall be:

   - to safeguard the common values, fundamental interests, independence and integrity of the Union in conformity with the principles of the United Nations Charter;
   - to strengthen the security of the Union in all ways;
   - to preserve peace and strengthen international security, in accordance with the principles of the United Nations Charter, as well as the principles of the Helsinki Final Act and the objectives of the Paris Charter, including those on external borders;
   - to promote international cooperation;
   - to develop and consolidate democracy and the rule of law, and respect for human rights and fundamental freedoms.

2. The Member States shall support the Union's external and security policy actively and unreservedly in a spirit of loyalty and mutual solidarity.

   The Member States shall work together to enhance and develop their mutual political solidarity. They shall refrain from any action which is contrary to the interests of the Union or likely to impair its effectiveness as a cohesive force in international relations.

   The Council shall ensure that these principles are complied with.

Article 12 (ex Article J.2)

The Union shall pursue the objectives set out in Article 11 by:

- defining the principles of and general guidelines for the common foreign and security policy;
- deciding on common strategies;
- adopting joint actions;
- adopting common positions;
- strengthening systematic cooperation between Member States in the conduct of policy.

Article 13 (ex Article J.3)

1. The European Council shall define the principles of and general guidelines for the common foreign and security policy, including for matters with defence implications.
2. The European Council shall decide on common strategies to be implemented by the Union in areas where the Member States have important interests in common.

    Common strategies shall set out their objectives, duration and the means to be made available by the Union and the Member States.
3. The Council shall take the decisions necessary for defining and implementing the common foreign and security policy on the basis of the general guidelines defined by the European Council.

    The Council shall recommend common strategies to the European Council and shall implement them, in particular by adopting joint actions and common positions.

    The Council shall ensure the unity, consistency and effectiveness of action by the Union.

Article 14 (ex Article J.4)

1. The Council shall adopt joint actions. Joint actions shall address specific situations where operational action by the Union is deemed to be required. They shall lay down their objectives, scope, the means to be made available to the Union, if necessary their duration, and the conditions for their implementation.
2. If there is a change in circumstances having a substantial effect on a question subject to joint action, the Council shall review the principles and objectives of that action and take the necessary decisions. As long as the Council has not acted, the joint action shall stand.
3. Joint actions shall commit the Member States in the positions they adopt and in the conduct of their activity.
4. The Council may request the Commission to submit to it any appropriate proposals relating to the common foreign and security policy to ensure the implementation of a joint action.
5. Whenever there is any plan to adopt a national position or take national action pursuant to a joint action, information shall be provided in time to allow, if necessary, for prior consultations within the Council. The obligation to provide prior information shall not apply to measures which are merely a national transposition of Council decisions.
6. In cases of imperative need arising from changes in the situation and failing a Council decision, Member States may take the necessary measures as a matter of urgency having regard to the general objectives of the joint action. The Member State concerned shall inform the Council immediately of any such measures.
7. Should there be any major difficulties in implementing a joint action, a Member State shall refer them to the Council which shall discuss them and seek appropriate solutions. Such solutions shall not run counter to the objectives of the joint action or impair its effectiveness.

Article 15 (ex Article J.5)

The Council shall adopt common positions. Common positions shall define the approach of the Union to a particular matter of a geographical or thematic nature. Member States shall ensure that their national policies conform to the common positions.

Article 16 (ex Article J.6)

Member States shall inform and consult one another within the Council on any matter of foreign and security policy of general interest in order to ensure that the Union's influence is exerted as effectively as possible by means of concerted and convergent action.

Article 17 (ex Article J.7)

1. The common foreign and security policy shall include all questions relating to the security of the Union, including the progressive framing of a common defence policy, in accordance with the second subparagraph, which might lead to a common defence, should the European Council so decide. It shall in that case recommend to the Member States the adoption of such a decision in accordance with their respective constitutional requirements.

    The Western European Union (WEU) is an integral part of the development of the Union providing the Union with access to an operational capability notably in the context of paragraph 2. It supports the Union in framing the defence aspects of the common foreign and security policy as set out in this Article. The Union shall accordingly foster closer institutional relations with the WEU with a view to the possibility of the integration of the WEU into the Union, should the European Council so decide. It shall in that case recommend to the Member States the adoption of such a decision in accordance with their respective constitutional requirements.

    The policy of the Union in accordance with this Article shall not prejudice the specific character of the security and defence policy of certain Member States and shall respect the obligations of certain Member States, which see their common defence realised in the North Atlantic Treaty Organisation (NATO), under the North Atlantic Treaty and be compatible with the common security and defence policy established within that framework.

    The progressive framing of a common defence policy will be supported, as Member States consider appropriate, by cooperation between them in the field of armaments.

2. Questions referred to in this Article shall include humanitarian and rescue tasks, peacekeeping tasks and tasks of combat forces in crisis management, including peacemaking.

3. The Union will avail itself of the WEU to elaborate and implement decisions and actions of the Union which have defence implications.

    The competence of the European Council to establish guidelines in accordance with Article 13 shall also obtain in respect of the WEU for those matters for which the Union avails itself of the WEU.

    When the Union avails itself of the WEU to elaborate and implement decisions of the Union on the tasks referred to in paragraph 2 all Member States of the Union shall be entitled to participate fully in the tasks in question. The Council, in agreement with the institutions of the WEU, shall adopt the necessary practical arrangements to allow all Member States contributing to the tasks in question to participate fully and on an equal footing in planning and decision-taking in the WEU.

   Decisions having defence implications dealt with under this paragraph shall be taken without prejudice to the policies and obligations referred to in paragraph 1, third subparagraph.
4. The provisions of this Article shall not prevent the development of closer cooperation between two or more Member States on a bilateral level, in the framework of the WEU and the Atlantic Alliance, provided such cooperation does not run counter to or impede that provided for in this Title.
5. With a view to furthering the objectives of this Article, the provisions of this Article will be reviewed in accordance with Article 48.

Article 18 (ex Article J.8)

1. The Presidency shall represent the Union in matters coming within the common foreign and security policy.
2. The Presidency shall be responsible for the implementation of decisions taken under this Title; in that capacity it shall in principle express the position of the Union in international organisations and international conferences.
3. The Presidency shall be assisted by the Secretary-General of the Council who shall exercise the function of High Representative for the common foreign and security policy.
4. The Commission shall be fully associated in the tasks referred to in paragraphs 1 and 2. The Presidency shall be assisted in those tasks if need be by the next Member State to hold the Presidency.
5. The Council may, whenever it deems it necessary, appoint a special representative with a mandate in relation to particular policy issues.

Article 19 (ex Article J.9)

1. Member States shall coordinate their action in international organisations and at international conferences. They shall uphold the common positions in such fora.

   In international organisations and at international conferences where not all the Member States participate, those which do take part shall uphold the common positions.
2. Without prejudice to paragraph 1 and Article 14(3), Member States represented in international organisations or international conferences where not all the Member States participate shall keep the latter informed of any matter of common interest.

   Member States which are also members of the United Nations Security Council will concert and keep the other Member States fully informed. Member States which are permanent members of the Security Council will, in the execution of their functions, ensure the defence of the positions and the interests of the Union, without prejudice to their responsibilities under the provisions of the United Nations Charter.

Article 20 (ex Article J.10)

The diplomatic and consular missions of the Member States and the Commission Delegations in third countries and international conferences, and their representations to international organisations, shall cooperate in ensuring that the common positions and joint actions adopted by the Council are complied with and implemented.

They shall step up cooperation by exchanging information, carrying out joint assessments and contributing to the implementation of the provisions referred to in Article 20 of the Treaty establishing the European Community.

Article 21 (ex Article J.11)

The Presidency shall consult the European Parliament on the main aspects and the basic choices of the common foreign and security policy and shall ensure that the views of the European Parliament are duly taken into consideration. The European Parliament shall be kept regularly informed by the Presidency and the Commission of the development of the Union's foreign and security policy.

The European Parliament may ask questions of the Council or make recommendations to it. It shall hold an annual debate on progress in implementing the common foreign and security policy.

Article 22 (ex Article J.12)

1. Any Member State or the Commission may refer to the Council any question relating to the common foreign and security policy and may submit proposals to the Council.
2. In cases requiring a rapid decision, the Presidency, of its own motion, or at the request of the Commission or a Member State, shall convene an extraordinary Council meeting within forty-eight hours or, in an emergency, within a shorter period.

Article 23 (ex Article J.13)

1. Decisions under this Title shall be taken by the Council acting unanimously. Abstentions by members present in person or represented shall not prevent the adoption of such decisions.

    When abstaining in a vote, any member of the Council may qualify its abstention by making a formal declaration under the present subparagraph. In that case, it shall not be obliged to apply the decision, but shall accept that the decision commits the Union. In a spirit of mutual solidarity, the Member State concerned shall refrain from any action likely to conflict with or impede Union action based on that decision and the other Member States shall respect its position. If the members of the Council qualifying their abstention in this way represent more than one third of the votes weighted in accordance with Article 205(2) of the Treaty establishing the European Community, the decision shall not be adopted.

2. By derogation from the provisions of paragraph 1, the Council shall act by qualified majority:

- when adopting joint actions, common positions or taking any other decision on the basis of a common strategy;
- when adopting any decision implementing a joint action or a common position.

If a member of the Council declares that, for important and stated reasons of national policy, it intends to oppose the adoption of a decision to be taken by qualified majority, a vote shall not be taken. The Council may, acting by a qualified majority, request that the matter be referred to the European Council for decision by unanimity.

The votes of the members of the Council shall be weighted in accordance with Article 205(2) of the Treaty establishing the European Community. For their adoption, decisions shall require at least 62 votes in favour, cast by at least 10 members.

This paragraph shall not apply to decisions having military or defence implications.

3. For procedural questions, the Council shall act by a majority of its members.

Article 24 (ex Article J.14)

When it is necessary to conclude an agreement with one or more States or international organisations in implementation of this Title, the Council, acting unanimously, may authorise the Presidency, assisted by the Commission as appropriate, to open negotiations to that effect. Such agreements shall be concluded by the Council acting unanimously on a recommendation from the Presidency. No agreement shall be binding on a Member State whose representative in the Council states that it has to comply with the requirements of its own constitutional procedure; the other members of the Council may agree that the agreement shall apply provisionally to them.

The provisions of this Article shall also apply to matters falling under Title VI.

Article 25 (ex Article J.15)

Without prejudice to Article 207 of the Treaty establishing the European Community, a Political Committee shall monitor the international situation in the areas covered by the common foreign and security policy and contribute to the definition of policies by delivering opinions to the Council at the request of the Council or on its own initiative. It shall also monitor the implementation of agreed policies, without prejudice to the responsibility of the Presidency and the Commission.

Article 26 (ex Article J.16)

The Secretary-General of the Council, High Representative for the common foreign and security policy, shall assist the Council in matters coming within the scope of the common foreign and security policy, in particular through contributing to the formulation, preparation and implementation of policy decisions, and, when appropriate and acting on behalf of the Council at the request of the Presidency, through conducting political dialogue with third parties.

Article 27 (ex Article J.17)

The Commission shall be fully associated with the work carried out in the common foreign and security policy field.

Article 28 (ex Article J.18)

1. Articles 189, 190, 196 to 199, 203, 204, 206 to 209, 213 to 219, 255 and 290 of the Treaty establishing the European Community shall apply to the provisions relating to the areas referred to in this Title.
2. Administrative expenditure which the provisions relating to the areas referred to in this Title entail for the institutions shall be charged to the budget of the European Communities.
3. Operational expenditure to which the implementation of those provisions gives rise shall also be charged to the budget of the European Communities, except for such expenditure arising from operations having military or defence implications and cases where the Council acting unanimously decides otherwise.

   In cases where expenditure is not charged to the budget of the European Communities it shall be charged to the Member States in accordance with the gross national product scale, unless the Council acting unanimously decides otherwise. As for expenditure arising from operations having military or defence implications, Member States whose representatives in the Council have made a formal declaration under Article 23(1), second subparagraph, shall not be obliged to contribute to the financing thereof.
4. The budgetary procedure laid down in the Treaty establishing the European Community shall apply to the expenditure charged to the budget of the European Communities.

Appendix 8: Madrid Declaration on Euro-Atlantic Security and Cooperation Issued by the Heads of State and Government

Madrid, 8 July 1997

1. We, the Heads of State and Government of the member countries of the North Atlantic Alliance, have come together in Madrid to give shape to the new NATO as we move towards the 21st century. Substantial progress has been achieved in the internal adaptation of the Alliance. As a significant step in the evolutionary process of opening the Alliance, we have invited three countries to begin accession talks. We have substantially strengthened our relationship with Partners through the new Euro-Atlantic Partnership Council and enhancement of the Partnership for Peace. The signature on 27th May of the NATO–Russia Founding Act and the Charter we will sign tomorrow with Ukraine bear witness to our commitment to an undivided Europe. We are also enhancing our Mediterranean dialogue. Our aim is to reinforce peace and stability in the Euro-Atlantic area.

   A new Europe is emerging, a Europe of greater integration and coopera-tion. An inclusive European security architecture is evolving to which we are contributing, along with other European organisations. Our Alliance will continue to be a driving force in this process.

2. We are moving towards the realisation of our vision of a just and lasting order of peace for Europe as a whole, based on human rights, freedom and democracy. In looking forward to the 50th anniversary of the North Atlantic Treaty, we reaffirm our commitment to a strong, dynamic partnership between the European and North American Allies, which has been, and will continue to be, the bedrock of the Alliance and of a free and prosperous Europe. The vitality of the transatlantic link will benefit from the develop-ment of a true, balanced partnership in which Europe is taking on greater responsibility. In this spirit, we are building a European Security and Defence Identity within NATO. The Alliance and the European Union share common strategic interests. We welcome the agreements reached at the European Council in Amsterdam. NATO will remain the essential forum for consulta-tion among its members and the venue for agreement on policies bearing on the security and defence commitments of Allies under the Washington Treaty.

3. While maintaining our core function of collective defence, we have adapted our political and military structures to improve our ability to meet the new challenges of regional crisis and conflict management. NATO's continued contribution to peace in Bosnia and Herzegovina, and the unprecedented scale of cooperation with other countries and international organisations there, reflect the cooperative approach which is key to building our common

security. A new NATO is developing: a new NATO for a new and undivided Europe.

4. The security of NATO's members is inseparably linked to that of the whole of Europe. Improving the security and stability environment for nations in the Euro-Atlantic area where peace is fragile and instability currently prevails remains a major Alliance interest. The consolidation of democratic and free societies on the entire continent, in accordance with OSCE principles, is therefore of direct and material concern to the Alliance. NATO's policy is to build effective cooperation through its outreach activities, including the Euro-Atlantic Partnership Council, with free nations which share the values of the Alliance, including members of the European Union as well as candidates for EU membership.

5. At our last meeting in Brussels, we said that we would expect and would welcome the accession of new members, as part of an evolutionary process, taking into account political and security developments in the whole of Europe. Twelve European countries have so far requested to join the Alliance. We welcome the aspirations and efforts of these nations. The time has come to start a new phase of this process. The Study on NATO Enlargement – which stated, inter alia, that NATO's military effectiveness should be sustained as the Alliance enlarges – the results of the intensified dialogue with interested Partners, and the analyses of relevant factors associated with the admission of new members have provided a basis on which to assess the current state of preparations of the twelve countries aspiring to Alliance membership.

6. Today, we invite the Czech Republic, Hungary and Poland to begin accession talks with NATO. Our goal is to sign the Protocol of Accession at the time of the Ministerial meetings in December 1997 and to see the ratification process completed in time for membership to become effective by the 50th anniversary of the Washington Treaty in April 1999. During the period leading to accession, the Alliance will involve invited countries, to the greatest extent possible and where appropriate, in Alliance activities, to ensure that they are best prepared to undertake the responsibilities and obligations of membership in an enlarged Alliance. We direct the Council in Permanent Session to develop appropriate arrangements for this purpose.

7. Admitting new members will entail resource implications for the Alliance. It will involve the Alliance providing the resources which enlargement will necessarily require. We direct the Council in Permanent Session to bring to an early conclusion the concrete analysis of the resource implications of the forthcoming enlargement, drawing on the continuing work on military implications. We are confident that, in line with the security environment of the Europe of today, Alliance costs associated with the integration of new members will be manageable and that the resources necessary to meet those costs will be provided.

8. We reaffirm that NATO remains open to new members under Article 10 of the North Atlantic Treaty. The Alliance will continue to welcome new members in a position to further the principles of the Treaty and contribute to security in the Euro-Atlantic area. The Alliance expects to extend further invitations in coming years to nations willing and able to assume the responsibilities and obligations of membership, and as NATO determines that the inclusion of these nations would serve the overall political and strategic

interests of the Alliance and that the inclusion would enhance overall European security and stability. To give substance to this commitment, NATO will maintain an active relationship with those nations that have expressed an interest in NATO membership as well as those who may wish to seek membership in the future. Those nations that have previously expressed an interest in becoming NATO members but that were not invited to begin accession talks today will remain under consideration for future membership. The considerations set forth in our 1995 Study on NATO Enlargement will continue to apply with regard to future aspirants, regardless of their geographic location. No European democratic country whose admission would fulfil the objectives of the Treaty will be excluded from consideration. Furthermore, in order to enhance overall security and stability in Europe, further steps in the ongoing enlargement process of the Alliance should balance the security concerns of all Allies.

To support this process, we strongly encourage the active participation by aspiring members in the Euro-Atlantic Partnership Council and the Partnership for Peace, which will further deepen their political and military involvement in the work of the Alliance. We also intend to continue the Alliance's intensified dialogues with those nations that aspire to NATO membership or that otherwise wish to pursue a dialogue with NATO on membership questions. To this end, these intensified dialogues will cover the full range of political, military, financial and security issues relating to possible NATO membership, without prejudice to any eventual Alliance decision. They will include meeting within the EAPC as well as periodic meetings with the North Atlantic Council in Permanent Session and the NATO International Staff and with other NATO bodies as appropriate. In keeping with our pledge to maintain an open door to the admission of additional Alliance members in the future, we also direct that NATO Foreign Ministers keep that process under continual review and report to us.

We will review the process at our next meeting in 1999. With regard to the aspiring members, we recognise with great interest and take account of the positive developments towards democracy and the rule of law in a number of southeastern European countries, especially Romania and Slovenia.

The Alliance recognises the need to build greater stability, security and regional cooperation in the countries of southeast Europe, and in promoting their increasing integration into the Euro-Atlantic community. At the same time, we recognise the progress achieved towards greater stability and cooperation by the states in the Baltic region which are also aspiring members. As we look to the future of the Alliance, progress towards these objectives will be important for our overall goal of a free, prosperous and undivided Europe at peace.

9. The establishment of the Euro-Atlantic Partnership Council in Sintra constitutes a new dimension in the relations with our Partners. We look forward to tomorrow's meeting with Heads of State and Government under the aegis of the EAPC.

The EAPC will be an essential element in our common endeavour to enhance security and stability in the Euro-Atlantic region. Building on the successful experience with the North Atlantic Cooperation Council and with Partnership for Peace, it will provide the overarching framework for all aspects of our wide-ranging cooperation and raise it to a qualitatively new level. It will deepen and give more focus to our multilateral political and security-related discussions, enhance the scope and substance of our practical cooperation, and increase transparency and confidence in security matters among all EAPC member states. The expanded political dimension of consultation and cooperation which the EAPC will offer will allow Partners, if they wish, to develop a direct political relationship individually or in smaller groups with the Alliance. The EAPC will increase the scope for consultation and cooperation on regional matters and activities.

10. The Partnership for Peace has become the focal point of our efforts to build new patterns of practical cooperation in the security realm. Without PfP, we would not have been able to put together and deploy so effectively and efficiently the Implementation and Stabilisation Forces in Bosnia and Herzegovina with the participation of so many of our Partners.

We welcome and endorse the decision taken in Sintra to enhance the Partnership for Peace by strengthening the political consultation element, increasing the role Partners play in PfP decision-making and planning, and by making PfP more operational. Partners will, in future, be able to involve themselves more closely in PfP programme issues as well as PfP operations, Partner staff elements will be established at various levels of the military structure of the Alliance, and the Planning and Review Process will become more like the NATO force planning process. On the basis of the principles of inclusiveness and self-differentiation, Partner countries will thus be able to draw closer to the Alliance. We invite all Partner countries to take full advantage of the new possibilities which the enhanced PfP will offer.

With the expanded range of opportunities comes also the need for adequate political and military representation at NATO Headquarters in Brussels. We have therefore created the possibility for Partners to establish diplomatic missions to NATO under the Brussels Agreement which entered into force on 28th March 1997. We invite and encourage Partner countries to take advantage of this opportunity.

11. The Founding Act on Mutual Relations, Cooperation and Security between NATO and the Russian Federation, signed on 27th May 1997 in Paris, is a historic achievement. It opens a new era in European security relations, an era of cooperation between NATO and Russia. The Founding Act reflects our shared commitment to build together a lasting and inclusive peace in the Euro-Atlantic area on the principles of democracy and cooperative security. Its provisions contribute to NATO's underlying objective of enhancing the security of all European states, which is reinforced also through our actions here in Madrid. It provides NATO and Russia a framework through which we intend to create a strong, stable and enduring partnership. We are committed to working with Russia to make full use of the provisions of the Founding Act.

Through the new forum created under the Founding Act, the NATO–Russia Permanent Joint Council, NATO and Russia will consult, cooperate and, where appropriate, act together to address challenges to security in Europe. The activities of the Council will build upon the principles of reciprocity and transparency. The cooperation between Russian and NATO troops in Bosnia and Herzegovina and between the staffs at SHAPE demonstrate what is possible when we work together. We will build on this experience, including through PfP, to develop genuine cooperation between NATO and Russia. We look forward to consulting regularly with Russia on a broad range of topics, and to forging closer cooperation, including military-to-military, through the Permanent Joint Council, which will begin work soon.

12. We attach great importance to tomorrow's signing of the Charter on a Distinctive Partnership between NATO and Ukraine. The NATO–Ukraine Charter will move NATO–Ukraine cooperation onto a more substantive level, offer new potential for strengthening our relationship, and enhance security in the region more widely. We are convinced that Ukraine's independence, territorial integrity and sovereignty are a key factor for ensuring stability in Europe. We continue to support the reform process in Ukraine as it develops as a democratic nation with a market economy.

We want to build on steps taken to date in developing a strong and enduring relationship between NATO and Ukraine. We welcome the practical cooperation achieved with the Alliance through Ukraine's participation within IFOR and SFOR, as well as the recent opening of the NATO Information Office in Kyiv, as important contributions in this regard. We look forward to the early and active implementation of the Charter.

13. The Mediterranean region merits great attention since security in the whole of Europe is closely linked with security and stability in the Mediterranean. We are pleased with the development of the Mediterranean initiative that was launched following our last meeting in Brussels. The dialogue we have established between NATO and a number of Mediterranean countries is developing progressively and successfully, contributes to confidence-building and cooperation in the region, and complements other international efforts. We endorse the measures agreed by NATO Foreign Ministers in Sintra on the widening of the scope and the enhancement of the dialogue and, on the basis of their recommendation, have decided today to establish under the authority of the North Atlantic Council a new committee, the Mediterranean Cooperation Group, which will have the overall responsibility for the Mediterranean dialogue.

14. We welcome the progress made on the Alliance's internal adaptation. Its fundamental objectives are to maintain the Alliance's military effectiveness and its ability to react to a wide range of contingencies, to preserve the transatlantic link, and develop the European Security and Defence Identity (ESDI) within the Alliance. We recognise the substantive work which has been carried out on the development of a new command structure for the Alliance; the implementation of the Combined Joint Task Forces (CJTF) concept; and the building of ESDI within NATO. We attach great importance to an early and successful completion of this process. Building on the earlier reductions and restructuring of the Alliance's military forces, it will provide the Alliance with the full range of capabilities needed to meet the challenges of the future.

15. We welcome the substantial progress made on the development of a new command structure which will enable the Alliance to carry out the whole range of its missions more effectively and flexibly, support our enhanced relationship with Partners and the admission of new members, and provide, as part of the development of ESDI within NATO, for European command

arrangements able to prepare, support, command and conduct WEU-led operations.

We note that essential elements of the new command structure have been identified and will form the basis for further work. We must maintain the momentum of this work. We have, accordingly, directed the Council in Permanent Session, with the advice of the Military Committee, to work on the resolution of outstanding issues with the aim of reaching agreement on NATO's future command structure by the time of the Council Ministerial meetings in December.

16. Against this background, the members of the Alliance's integrated military structure warmly welcome today's announcement by Spain of its readiness to participate fully in the Alliance's new command structure, once agreement has been reached upon it. Spain's full participation will enhance its overall contribution to the security of the Alliance, help develop the European Security and Defence Identity within NATO and strengthen the transatlantic link.

17. We are pleased with the progress made in implementing the CJTF concept, including the initial designation of parent headquarters, and look forward to the forthcoming trials. This concept will enhance our ability to command and control multinational and multiservice forces, generated and deployed at short notice, which are capable of conducting a wide range of military operations. Combined Joint Task Forces will also facilitate the possible participation of non-NATO nations in operations and, by enabling the conduct of WEU-led CJTF operations, will contribute to the development of ESDI within the Alliance.

18. We reaffirm, as stated in our 1994 Brussels Declaration, our full support for the development of the European Security and Defence Identity by making available NATO assets and capabilities for WEU operations. With this in mind, the Alliance is building ESDI, grounded on solid military principles and supported by appropriate military planning and permitting the creation of militarily coherent and effective forces capable of operating under the political control and strategic direction of the WEU. We endorse the decisions taken at last year's Ministerial meeting in Berlin in this regard which serve the interests of the Alliance as well as of the WEU.

We further endorse the considerable progress made in implementing these decisions and in developing ESDI within the Alliance. In this context we endorse the decisions taken with regard to European command arrangements within NATO to prepare, support, command and conduct WEU-led operations using NATO assets and capabilities (including provisional terms of reference for Deputy SACEUR covering his ESDI-related responsibilities both permanent and during crises and operations), the arrangements for the identification of NATO assets and capabilities that could support WEU-led operations, and arrangements for NATO-WEU consultation in the context of such operations. We welcome inclusion of the support for the conduct of WEU-led operations in the context of the ongoing implementation of the revised Alliance defence planning process for all Alliance missions. We also welcome the progress made on work regarding the planning and future exercising of WEU-led operations, and in developing the necessary practical arrangements for release, monitoring and return of

NATO assets and the exchange of information between NATO and WEU within the framework of the NATO-WEU Security Agreement.

We note with satisfaction that the building of ESDI within the Alliance has much benefitted from the recent agreement in the WEU on the participation of all European Allies, if they were so to choose, in WEU-led operations using NATO assets and capabilities, as well as in planning and preparing for such operations. We also note the desire on Canada's part to participate in such operations when its interests make it desirable and under modalities to be developed. We direct the Council in Permanent Session to complete expeditiously its work on developing ESDI within NATO, in cooperation with the WEU.

19. The Alliance Strategic Concept, which we adopted at our meeting in Rome in 1991, sets out the principal aims and objectives of the Alliance. Recognising that the strategic environment has changed since then, we have decided to examine the Strategic Concept to ensure that it is fully consistent with Europe's new security situation and challenges. As recommended by our Foreign Ministers in Sintra, we have decided to direct the Council in Permanent Session to develop terms of reference for this examination, and an update as necessary, for endorsement at the Autumn Ministerial meetings. This work will confirm our commitment to the core function of Alliance collective defence and the indispensable transatlantic link.

20. We reiterate our commitment to full transparency between NATO and WEU in crisis management, including as necessary through joint consultations on how to address contingencies. In this context, we are determined to strengthen the institutional cooperation between the two organisations. We welcome the fact that the WEU has recently undertaken to improve its capacity to plan and conduct crisis management and peacekeeping operations (the Petersberg tasks), including through setting the groundwork for possible WEU-led operations with the support of NATO assets and capabilities, and accepted the Alliance's invitation to contribute to NATO's Ministerial Guidance for defence planning. We will therefore continue to develop the arrangements and procedures necessary for the planning, preparation, conduct and exercise of WEU-led operations using NATO assets and capabilities.

21. We reaffirm our commitment to further strengthening the OSCE as a regional organisation according to Chapter VIII of the Charter of the United Nations and as a primary instrument for preventing conflict, enhancing cooperative security and advancing democracy and human rights. The OSCE, as the most inclusive European-wide security organisation, plays an essential role in securing peace, stability and security in Europe. The principles and commitments adopted by the OSCE provide a foundation for the development of a comprehensive and cooperative European security architecture. Our goal is to create in Europe, through the widest possible cooperation among OSCE states, a common space of security and stability, without dividing lines or spheres of influence limiting the sovereignty of particular states.

We continue to support the OSCE's work on a Common and Comprehensive Security Model for Europe for the Twenty-First Century, in accordance with the decisions of the 1996 Lisbon Summit, including consideration of developing a Charter on European Security.

22. We welcome the successful holding of elections in Albania as a vital first step in providing the basis for greater stability, democratic government and law and order in the country. We stress, in this context, the importance of a firm commitment by all political forces to continue the process of national reconciliation. We also welcome the crucial role of the Italian-led Multinational Protection Force, with the participation of several Allies and Partners, in helping to create a secure environment for the re-establishment of peace and order. We value the efforts of the OSCE as the coordinating framework for international assistance in Albania, together with the important contributions made by the EU, WEU and the Council of Europe. We are following closely events in Albania and are considering measures through the Partnership for Peace to assist, as soon as the situation permits, in the reconstruction of the armed forces of Albania as an important element of the reform process. Continued international support will be essential in helping to restore stability in Albania.

23. We continue to attach greatest importance to further the means of non-proliferation, arms control and disarmament.

We welcome the progress made since the Brussels Summit, as an integral part of NATO's adaptation, to intensify and expand Alliance political and defence efforts aimed at preventing proliferation and safeguarding NATO's strategic unity and freedom of action despite the risks posed by nuclear, biological and chemical (NBC) weapons and their means of delivery. We attach the utmost importance to these efforts, welcome the Alliance's substantial achievements, and direct that work continue.

We call on all states which have not yet done so to sign and ratify the Chemical Weapons Convention. Recognising that enhancing confidence in compliance would reinforce the Biological and Toxin Weapons Convention, we reaffirm our determination to complete as soon as possible through negotiation a legally binding and effective verification mechanism. We urge the Russian Federation to ratify the START II Treaty without delay so that negotiation of START III may begin.

We support the vigorous pursuit of an effective, legally binding international agreement to ban world-wide the use, stockpiling, production and transfer of anti-personnel mines. We note the positive developments in the Conference on Disarmament. We further note the progress made by the Ottawa Process with its goal of achieving a ban by the end of the year.

24. We continue to attach utmost importance to the CFE Treaty and its integrity. In this context, we welcome the entry into force of the CFE Flank Agreement on 15th May 1997 and underline its importance for regional stability. We share the commitment of all thirty States Parties to continue full implementation of the CFE Treaty, its associated documents, and the Flank Agreement. We confirm our readiness to work cooperatively with other States Parties to achieve, as expeditiously as possible, an adapted CFE Treaty that takes account of the changed political and military circumstances in Europe, continues to serve as a cornerstone of stability, and provides undiminished security for all. NATO has advanced a comprehensive proposal for adaptation of the CFE Treaty on the basis of a revised Treaty structure of national and territorial ceilings. The Allies have already stated their intention to reduce significantly their future aggregate national ceilings

for Treaty-Limited Equipment. We look forward to working with other States Parties on the early completion of a Framework Agreement on CFE adaptation.

25. We reaffirm the importance of arrangements in the Alliance for consultation on threats of a wider nature, including those linked to illegal arms trade and acts of terrorism, which affect Alliance security interests. We continue to condemn all acts of international terrorism. They constitute flagrant violations of human dignity and rights and are a threat to the conduct of normal international relations. In accordance with our national legislation, we stress the need for the most effective cooperation possible to prevent and suppress this scourge.

26. The steps we have taken today, and tomorrow's meeting with our Partners under the aegis of the EAPC, bring us closer to our goal of building cooperative security in Europe. We remain committed to a free and undivided Euro-Atlantic community in which all can enjoy peace and prosperity. Renewed in structure and approach, strengthened in purpose and resolve, and with a growing membership, NATO will continue to play its part in achieving this goal and in meeting the security challenges in the times ahead.

27. We express our deep appreciation for the gracious hospitality extended to us by the Government of Spain. We are looking forward to meeting again on the occasion of the 50th anniversary of the North Atlantic Treaty in April 1999.

Appendix 9: Historical Highlights of Attempts to Create a European Common Foreign and Security Policy

1952–4	European Defence Community	The EDC aimed to establish a common defence system supported by foreign policy coordination. Six countries sign the EDC Treaty but France fails to ratify.
1962	Fouchet Plan	French diplomat Christian Fouchet establishes an intergovernmental committee on political union. The committee draws up a draft design for a European Union of States, including plans for foreign and security policy integration; the plan is rejected because it is deemed too inter-governmental by some.
1969	Hague Summit	Leaders of the Six call for a 'United Europe' which should be capable of assuming international responsibilities including, by association, those relating to security.
1970	Luxembourg Report	Foreign Ministers create intergovernmental apparatus for political cooperation (EPC), including political and economic aspects of security.
1973	Copenhagen Report	Foreign Ministers of Nine review EPC process and establish procedures for consultation prior to decisions in the foreign policy area.
1981	London Report	Foreign Ministers agree to 'associate' the Commission with the EPC process at all levels. Joint action replaces cooperation as main objective.
1986	Single European Act	EPC institutionalised and parties agree to jointly 'formulate and implement a European foreign policy.' Also agree that 'common principle and objectives' are developed and defined.
1992	Treaty on European Union	CFSP established as intergovernmental second pillar of the European Union. Security included as formal part of co-operation. WEU requested to 'elaborate and implement' decisions and actions of the EU with 'defence implications'. Limited oversight by European Parliament.
1997	Treaty of Amsterdam	CFSP to apply to all questions relating to the security of the EU, including framing of a common defence. WEU to foster closer ties and clearer procedures for voting and budgetary matters. Secretary-General of the Council becomes the High Representative for the CFSP.

Appendix 10: Franco-British Summit – Joint Declaration on European Defence

Saint-Malo, 4 December 1998

The Heads of State and Government of France and the United Kingdom are agreed that:

1. The European Union needs to be in a position to play its full role on the international stage. This means making a reality of the Treaty of Amsterdam, which will provide the essential basis for action by the Union. It will be important to achieve full and rapid implementation of the Amsterdam provisions on CFSP. This includes the responsibility of the European Council to decide on the progressive framing of a common defence policy in the framework of CFSP. The Counsil must be able to take decisions on an intergovernmental basis, covering the whole range of activity set out in Title V of the Treaty of European Union.

2. To this end, the Union must have the capacity for autonomous action, backed up by credible military forces, the means to decide to use them and a readiness to do so, in order to respond to international crises.

   In pursuing our objective, the collective defence commitments to which member states subscribe (set out in Article 5 of the Washington Treaty, Article V of the Brussels Treaty) must be maintained. In strengthening the solidarity between the member states of the European Union, in order that Europe can make its voice heard in world affairs, while acting in conformity with our respective obligations in NATO, we are contributing to the vitality of a modernised Atlantic Alliance which is the foundation of the collective defence of its members.

   Europeans will operate within the institutional framework of the European Union (European Council, General Affairs Council and meetings of Defence Ministers).

   The reinforcement of European solidarity must take into account the various positions of European states. The different situations of countries in relation to NATO must be respected.

3. In order for the European Union to take decisions and approve military action where the Alliance as a whole is not engaged, the Union must be given appropriate structures and a capacity for analysis of situations, sources of intelligence and a capability for relevant strategic planning, without unnecessary duplication, taking account of the existing assets of the WEU and the evolution of its relations with the EU. In this regard, the European Union will also need to have recourse to suitable military means (European capabilities pre-designated within NATO's European pillar or national or multinational European means outside the NATO framework).

4. Europe needs strengthened armes forces that can react rapidly to the new risks, and which are supported by a strong and competitive European defence industry and technology.

5. We are determined to unite in our efforts to enable the European Union to give concrete expression to these objectives.

Notes and References

Introduction

1. Robert Rhodes James, *Anthony Eden* (London: Weidenfeld and Nicolson, 1986), p. 347.
2. For a discussion of the expansive nature of security see, Michael T. Klare and Daniel C. Thomas (eds), *World Security: Challenges for a New Century* (New York: St Martin's Press, 1994) (Second edition).
3. *SIPRI Yearbook 1998: Armaments, Disarmament and International Security* (Oxford: Oxford University Press, SIPRI, 1998), p. 17.
4. 'Petersberg-type tasks' take their name from the WEU's Petersberg Declaration of June 1992 describing a number of new missions, mainly associated with peacekeeping, for which the organisation could bear prime responsibility.
5. Two notable recent contributions are Anne Deighton (ed.), *Western European Union 1954–1997: Defence, Security, Integration* (Oxford: St Antony's College, Oxford, 1997) and Willem van Eekelen, *Debating European Security 1948–98* (The Hague: Sdu Publishers, 1998).
6. WEU Council of Ministers, *Common Reflections on the New European Security Conditions*, 15 May 1995, Introduction, Para. 4.
7. Two notable exceptions are Simon Nuttall, *European Political Co-operation* (Oxford: Clarendon, 1992) and Panayiotis Ifestos, *European Political Co-operation: Towards a Framework of Supranational Diplomacy?* (Aldershot: Avebury, 1987).
8. The 'Dual-Track' decision was made by the NATO Council in December 1991. Under the agreement NATO agreed to deploy a number of Pershing II and ground-launched cruise missiles (GLCMs) as a deterrent to the Soviet Union's intermediate range missiles located in central Europe (primarily the SS–20). The intention was to deploy them as a deterrent in the first instance (track 1) but also to use the deployments as a means of inducing arms control negotiations on this category of missile (track 2).
9. John Mearsheimer, 'Back to the Future', *International Security*, Summer 1990 (15), p. 47.
10. See François Heisbourg, 'The Future Direction of European Security', in Manfred Wörner, Hikmet Çetin, François Heisbourg, Simon Lunn and Janusz Onyszkiewicz (eds), *What is European Security After the Cold War?*, (The Philip Morris Institute for Public Policy Research, December, 1993), pp. 36–50.
11. See, for instance, Ernst B. Hass, *Beyond the Nation State: Functionalism and International Organization* (Stanford: Stanford University Press, 1964), Robert O. Keohane and Joseph S. Nye, *Power and Interdependence* (Boston: Little, Brown, 1977) and Stephen D. Krasner (ed.), *International Regimes*, (Ithaca: Cornell University Press, 1983). It should however be noted that functionalism owes its roots to the decidedly European David Mitrany. See David Mitrany, *The Functional Theory of Politics* (London: Martin Robertson, 1975).

12. Ernst Haas, *The Uniting of Europe: Political, Economic, and Social Forces 1950–57* (Stanford: Stanford University Press, 1968), p. xix.

13. Ibid., p. xxix.

14. For instance K. Booth and Steve Smith, *International Relations Theory Today* (University Park: The Pennsylvania State University Press, 1995); M. Calingaert, *European Integration Revisited* (Boulder, Colorado: Westview, 1996); C.W. Kegley Jr., *Controversies in International Relations Theory: Realism and the Neoliberal Challenge* (New York: St Martin's Press, 1995); R.O. Keohane, *After Hegemony: Cooperation and Discord in the World Political Economy* (Princeton: Princeton University Press, 1984); R.N. Lebow and T.Risse-Kappen, *International Relations Theory and the End of the Cold War* (New York: Columbia University Press, 1995); J. Rosenau, *The Study of Global Interdependence: Essays on the Transnationalism of World Affairs* (New York: Nichols, 1980); and P.R. Viotti, and M.V. Kauppi, *International Relations Theory* (New York: Macmillan, 1996).

15. For instance: C. Angarita and P. Coffey, *Europe and the Andean Countries: A Comparison of Economic Policies and Institutions* (London: Pinter Publishers, 1988); K.K. Bhargava and R.M. Husain, *SAARC and European Union: Learning and Cooperation* (New Delhi: Har-Anand Publications, 1994); S. Brüne, J. Betz, W. Kühne, *Africa and Europe: Relations of the Two Continents in Transition* (Münster: LIT Verlag, 1994); E. Frey-Wouters, *The European Community and the Third World: The Lomé Convention and Its Impact* (New York: Praeger, 1980); R.L. Grant, *The European Union and China: A European Strategy for the Twenty-First Century* (London: RIIA/Asia Pacific Programme, 1995); M. Holland, *The European Community and South Africa: European Political Cooperation Under Strain* (London: Pinter Publishers, 1988); M. Kaiser and H. Werner, *ASEAN and the EC: Labour Costs and Structural Change in the European Community* (Singapore: ASEAN Economic Research Unit, Institute of Southeast Asian Studies, 1989); R.J. Langhammer and H.C. Rieger, *ASEAN and the EC: Trade in Tropical Agricultural Products* (Singapore: ASEAN Economic Research Unit, Institute of Southeast Asian Studies, 1988); J. Lodge, *The European Community and New Zealand* (London: Pinter Publishers, 1982); T.D. Mason and A.M.Turay (eds), *Japan, NAFTA, and Europe: Trilateral Cooperation or Confrontation?* (New York: St Martin's Press, 1994); D. McAleese (ed.), *Africa and the European Community after 1992* (Washington DC: Economic Development Institute, 1993); C. Piening, *Global Europe: The European Union in World Affairs* (Boulder, Colorado: Lynne Rienner, 1997); R.W.T. Pomfret, *Mediterranean Policy of the European Community: A Study of Discrimination in Trade* (New York: St Martin's Press, 1986); S.K Purcell and F. Simon (eds) *Europe and Latin America in the World Economy* (Boulder, Colorado: Lynne Rienner, 1995); J. Shanti, *EC and India in the 1990s: Towards Corporate Synergy* (New Delhi: Indus, 1993); R.Taylor, *China, Japan and the European Community* (London: Athlone Press, 1990); and W. Zartman (ed.), *Europe and Africa: The New Phase* (Boulder, Colorado: Lynne Rienner, 1992).

16. For instance: R. Faini and R. Portes, *European Union Trade with Eastern Europe: Adjustment and Opportunities* (London: Centre for Economic Policy Research, 1995); N.V. Gianaris, *The European Community, Eastern Europe and Russia: Economic and Political Changes* (Westport, Connecticut: Praeger,

1991); G. Merritt, *Eastern Europe and the USSR: The Challenge of Freedom* (London: Kegan Page, 1991); T. Palanki, *The EC and Central European Integration: The Hungarian Case* (Boulder, Colorado: Westview, 1991); J. Pinder, *The European Community and Eastern Europe* (New York: Council on Foreign Relations, 1991); and P. van Ham, *The EC, Eastern Europe and European Unity: Discord, Collaboration and Integration Since 1947* (London: Pinter Publishers, 1993).

17. A.J. Blinken, *Ally versus Ally: America, Europe and the Siberian Pipeline Crisis* (New York: Praeger, 1987); W.C. Cromwell, *The United States and the European Pillar* (Basingstoke: Macmillan, 1992); K. Featherstone and R.H. Ginsberg, *The United States and the European Community in the 1990s: Partners in Transition* (New York: St. Martin's, 1993); N.V. Gianaris, *The European Community and the United States: Economic Relations* (New York: Praeger, 1991); J. Joffe, *The Limited Partnership: Europe, the United States and the Burdens of Alliance* (Cambridge, Massachusetts: Ballinger, 1987); J. Lepgold, *The Declining Hegemon: The United States and European Defense, 1960–90* (New York: Greenwood, 1990); R. Perle, *Reshaping Western Security: The United States Faces a United Europe* (Lanham, Maryland: University Press of America, 1991); J. Peterson, *Europe and America in the 1990s: Prospects for Partnership* (Brookfield, Vermont: Edward Elgar, 1992); R. Schwok, *US–EC Relations in the Post-Cold War Era: Conflict or Partnership?* (Boulder, Colorado: Westview, 1991); J. Steinberg, *An Ever Closer Union: European Integration and Its Implications for the Future of U.S.–European Relations* (Santa Monica, California, RAND, 1993); L. Tsouklais, *Europe, America and the World Economy* (Oxford: Basil Blackwell, 1986); and G. Yannopoulos, *Europe and America: 1992* (New York: Manchester University Press, 1991).

18. For instance: A. Bloed and R.A. Wessel, *The Changing Functions of the Western European Union: Introduction and Basic Documents* (Dordrecht: Martinus Nijhoff, 1994); S. Bulmer and W. Wessels, *The European Council: Decision-Making in European Politics* (London: Macmillan, 1987); A. Cahan, *The WEU and NATO: Strengthening the Second Pillar of the Alliance* (Washington DC: Atlantic Council, 1990); R. Corbett, F. Jacobs, and M. Shackleton, *The European Parliament* (3rd ed.) (London: Cartermill, 1995); G. Edwards and D. Spence (eds), *The European Commission* (Harlow: Longman, 1994); C. Hill (ed.), *The Actors in Europe's Foreign Policy* (New York: Routledge, 1996); and F. Laursen and S.Vanhoonacker (eds), *The Ratification of the Maastricht Treaty: Issues, Debates, and Future Implications* (Maastricht: EIPA, 1994).

19. For instance: S. Duke, *Europe's New Security Disorder* (London: Macmillan, 1994); C. McA. Kelleher, *The Future of European Security: An Interim Assessment* (Washington DC: The Brookings Institution, 1995); J-P. Maury, *La Construction européenne, la sécurité et la défense* (Paris: Universitaires de France, 1996); S. Nuttall, *European Political Cooperation* (Oxford: Clarendon Press, 1992); E. Regelsberger, P. Schoutheete de Tervarent, and W. Wessels, *Foreign Policy of the European Union: From EPC to CFSP and Beyond* (Boulder, Colorado: Lynne Rienner, 1997); J.P. Rogers, *The Future of European Security: The Pursuit of Peace in an Era of Revolutionary Change* (New York: St Martin's Press, 1993); R. Rummel (ed.), *Toward Political Union: Planning a Common Foreign and Security Policy* (Boulder, Colorado: Westview, 1992); and P. Tsakaloyannis, *The European Union as a Security Community: Problems and*

Prospects (Baden-Baden: Nomos, 1996); Martin Holland (ed.), *Common Foreign and Security Policy: The Record and Reforms* (London: Pinter, 1997); Anne Deighton (ed.), *Western European Union 1954–1997: Defence, Security, Integration* (Oxford: St Antony's College, Oxford, 1997); B. Heuser, *NATO, Britain, France, and the FRG: Nuclear Strategies and Forces for Europe, 1949–2000* (New York: St Martin's Press, 1997); J. Peterson and H. Sjursen (eds), *A Common Foreign Policy for Europe? Competing visions of the CFSP* (London: Routledge, 1998); G. Wyn Rees, *The Western European Union at the Crossroads: Between Trans-Atlantic Solidarity and European Integration* (Boulder, Colorado: Westview Press, 1998); and Willem van Eekelen, *Debating European Security 1948–98* (The Hague: Sdu Publishers, 1998).

20. See for instance P. Bender, *East Europe in Search of Security* (London: Chatto and Windus for IISS, 1972); N. Brown, *European Security 1972–80* (London: RUSI-Institute for Defence Studies, 1972); W. Fox and W. Schilling, *European Security and the Atlantic System* (New York: Columbia University Press, 1973); P. Hassner, 'Change and Security in Europe Pt.1', *Adelphi Papers* No. 45 (and Part II, No. 49), (London: IISS, 1968), and O. Pick and J. Critchley, *Collective Security* (London: Macmillan, 1974).

1 The European Defence Community

1. For an overview of twentieth century European federalism see, Elisabeth du Réau, *L'Idée d'Europe au XXe Siècle* (Bruxelles: Editions Complexe, 1996); for a longer-term perspective see, J.B. Duroselle, *L'Idée d'Europe dans l'Histoire* (Paris: Denoël, 1965).

2. Quoted in Altiero Spinelli, 'European Union and the Resistance', in Ghita Ionescu, *The New Politics of European Integration* (London: Macmillan, 1972), p. 5.

3. Ibid., p. 6

4. Ibid., p. 7.

5. Jean Monnet, *Mémoires* (Arthème Fayard, 1976), p. 427.

6. Sir Anthony Eden, *Full Circle* (London: Cassell, 1960), pp. 29–30.

7. Ibid., p. 30.

8. François Duchêne, *Jean Monnet: The First Statesman of Independence* (New York: W.W. Norton and Company, 1994), p. 227.

9. Jean Monnet, *Mémoires*, p. 489.

10. Draft note dated 1 August, Ibid., loc. cit.

11. On 6 September 1950 Robert Schuman complained that there had been no reply from Washington but, according to one interpretation, the French statements were a 'transparent scheme' to 'spread their inflation among all the allies, collectivise the cost of the Indochina War, and make the United States underwrite the military budgets of the Europeans'. Ibid., loc. cit.

12. Quoted in Phil Williams, *The Senate and U.S. Troops in Europe* (London: Macmillan, 1985), pp. 37–8.

13. Konrad Adenauer, *Memoirs 1945–53* (Chicago, Henry Regenery Company, 1965), p. 284.

14. Dean Acheson, *Present at the Creation: My Years in the State Department* (New York: W.W. Norton and Company, 1969), p. 443.

15. *Department of State Bulletin*, Vol. XXIII, 9 October 1950, p. 588.
16. Acheson, *Present at the Creation*, p. 443.
17. Adenauer, *Memoirs*, p. 289.
18 Ibid., p. 291.
19. *Department of State Bulletin*, Vol. XXIII, 2 October 1950, p. 530.
20. Adenauer, *Memoirs*, p. 290.
21. Heinemann was Präses of the Synod of Protestant Churches in Germany.
22. Adenauer, *Memoirs*, p. 291.
23. Jean Monnet, *Mémoires*, p. 501.
24. Duchêne, *Monnet*, p. 229.
25. Jean Monnet, *Mémoires*, p. 502.
26. Eden, *Full Circle*, p. 32.
27. Elisabeth du Réau, *L'Idée d'Europe au XXe Siècle,* pp. 209–10.
28. Eden, *Full Circle*, op. cit.
29. Acheson, *Memoirs*, p. 458.
30. Ibid., loc. cit.
31. Jean Monnet, *Mémoires*, p. 500.
32. Duchêne, *Monnet*, p. 229.
33. Adenauer, *Memoirs*, p. 297.
34. Ibid., loc. cit.
35. Ibid., loc. cit.
36. Ibid., p. 298.
37. Who was described by the Secretary of State as 'less than reliable', Dean Acheson, *Present at the Creation*, p. 488.
38. See in particular, Phil Williams, pp. 43–109; Acheson, pp. 491–6; and Major-General Edward Fursdon, *The European Defence Community: A History*, pp. 105–22.
39. Acheson, *Present at the Creation*, p. 492.
40. Ibid., p. 495.
41. Ernst B. Haas, *The Uniting of Europe: Political, Social and Economic Forces 1950–7* (Stanford: Stanford University Press, 1968), p. 30.
42. Adenauer, *Memoirs*, p. 358.
43. Duchêne, *Monnet*, pp. 231–2.
44. Adenauer, *Memoirs*, pp. 358–9.
45. Duchêne, *Monnet*, p. 232.
46. Ibid., loc. cit.
47. Acheson, *Present at the Creation*, p. 570.
48. In addition to his duties as Chancellor Adenauer also assumed the duties of Federal Minister of the Exterior.
49. Adenauer, *Memoirs*, pp. 363–4.
50. Ibid., pp. 383–400.
51. Ibid., p. 404.
52. Ibid., p. 405.
53. Ibid., p. 406.
54. Ibid., loc. cit.
55. Ibid., p. 407.
56. *Department of State Bulletin*, Vol. XXVI, March 10, 1952, pp. 367–8.
57. Acheson, *Present at the Creation*, p. 645. Article 4 of the North Atlantic Treaty bound its members to consult together whenever, in the opinion of any of

them, the territorial integrity, political independence or security of any of the Parties is threatened.

58. Adenauer, *Memoirs*. p. 416.
59. Ibid., p. 425.
60. Duchêne, *Monnet*, p. 234.
61. *Draft Treaty Embodying the Statute of the European Political Community* (Luxembourg: 1953), Article 2. Cited in Hans A. Schmitt, *The Path to European Union: From the Marshall Plan to the Common Market* (Baton Rouge: Louisiana State University, 1962), p. 211.
62. Elisabeth du Réau, *L'Idée d'Europe au XXᵉ Siècle* , p. 212.
63. See especially Major-General Edward Fursdon, *The European Defence Community: A History* (London: Macmillan, 1980).
64. Eden, *Full Circle*, pp. 36–7.
65. Ibid., p. 38.
66. Ibid., p. 48.
67. Duchêne, *Monnet*, p. 237.
68. The British delegation was officially headed by Winston Churchill but illness prevented him and his French counterpart, Prime Minister Joseph Laniel, from playing major roles.
69. Eden, *Full Circle*, p. 55.
70. Leonard Mosley, *Dulles: A biography of Eleanor, Allen, and John Foster Dulles and their family network* (New York: The Dial Press/James Wade, 1978), p. 324.
71. *NATO Final Communiqués 1949–74* (Brussels: NATO Press and Information Service), p. 80.
72. Eden, *Full Circle*, p. 58.
73. For example, in response to a request from Molotov to discuss the EDC with Mendès-France, Molotov was told that he would have to wait until after the Indo-China issue was settled.
74. See Jacques Bariety, 'La décision de réarmer l'Allemagne, l'échec de la CED et les Accords de Paris, *Revue Belge de Philologie et d'Histoire*, No. 71, 1993, pp. 354–383.
75. Fursdon, p. 297.
76. Ernst Haas, *The Uniting of Europe: Political, Social, and Economic Forces 1950–7* (Stanford, California: Stanford University Press, 1968), pp. 125–6.
77. Simon Nuttall, *European Political Co-operation* (Oxford: Clarendon Press, 1992), p. 37.
78. Adenauer himself was not in a strong position after the 1953 elections that left the CDU with a majority of one seat in the *Bundestag*.
79. Eden, *Full Circle*, p.148. See also Dwight D. Eisenhower, *The White House Years: Mandate for Change 1953–56* (New York: Doubleday and Company Ltd., 1963), p. 402.
80. Eden, p. 149.
81. Eisenhower, *The White House Years*, pp. 403–4.
82. Eden, p. 151.
83. Willem van Eekelen persuasively argues that there are reasons to doubt the authenticity of Eden's idea since the same suggestion had been made prior to this by Sir Frank Roberts to the Foreign Secretary and also by Harold Macmillan, then Housing Minister. See Willem van Eekelen, *Debating European Security 1948–98* (The Hague: Sdu Publishers, 1998), p. 8.

84. Eisenhower, *The White House Years*, pp. 405–6.
85. Ibid., p. 406.
86. Eden, p. 168.
87. Ibid., loc. cit.
88. Eisenhower, p. 406.
89. Ibid., p. 407.
90. The restrictions on West Germany's arms manufacturing took the form of a letter, signed by Adenauer, appended to the Modified Brussels Treaty. The word 'manufacture' was deliberately used and accepted by all parties.
91. *European Yearbook*, Vol. 2 (The Hague: Martinus Nijhoff, 1956), pp. 313–41.
92. Alfred Cahen, 'The Emergence and Role of the Western European Union', in Michael Clarke and Rod Hague (eds), *European Defence Co-operation: America, Britain and NATO* (Manchester: Manchester University Press, 1990), p. 55.
93. Eden. p. 170 (Emphasis added).
94. G. Wyn Rees, *The Western European Union: Between Trans-Atlantic Solidarity and European Integration* (Boulder, Colorado: Westview Press, 1998), p. 9.
95. Article 13 of the 1949 Washington Treaty merely states that after a period of twenty years any party may 'cease to be a party one year after its notice of denunciation has been given to the Government of the United States of America'.
96. Alfred Cahen, *The Western European Union and NATO: Building a European Defence Identity within the Context of Alliance Solidarity* (London: Brassey's, 1989), p. 5.

2   The Rebirth of European Security

1. *Foreign Relations of the United States (FRUS)*, 1955–7, Vol. IV, 'Telegram from the U.S. Delegation at the North Atlantic Council Ministerial Meeting to the Department of State' (Washington DC: USGPO, 1986), pp. 19–20.
2. These were Antoine Pinay, Gaetano Martino, and Christopher Steel, respectively.
3. *FRUS*, 1955–7, Vol. IV, p. 20.
4. 'New Impetus for European idea', speech by Chancellor Konrad Adenauer, *The Bulletin* (Press and Information Office of the German Federal Republic, 4 Oct. 1956), quoted in M. Margaret Ball, *NATO and the European Union* (London: Stevens and Sons Ltd., 1959), p. 403.
5. M. Senghor, Rapporteur of the General Affairs Committee of the WEU, *Proceedings*, Vol. 1, p. 71, Para. 23, op. cit., pp. 404–5.
6. *Foreign Relations of the United States*, 1955–57, Western European Security and Integration, Vol. IV, 'Despatch 2661', 15 June 1955, p. 307n.
7. Ibid., 'Telegram from the Secretary of State to the Embassy in Germany', 1 July 1955, pp. 307–8.
8. Ibid., loc. cit.
9. Ibid., 'Memorandum of a conversation, Washington', 25 January 1956, pp. 390–1.
10. Ibid., 'Memorandum of a conversation, Department of State, Washington', 22 November 1955, p. 350.
11. Ibid., 'Telegram from the Ambassador in France (Dillon) to the Department of State', 7 February 1956, pp. 407–8.

12. Council of Europe, Consultative Assembly, *Official Report*, 1 May 1957, Vol. 1, pp. 73–9.
13. Other signatories to the Stockholm Convention were Austria, Denmark, Norway, Portugal, Sweden, and Switzerland. Finland and Iceland joined later.
14. See, for instance, Article 113 (addressing Common Trade policy), Article 132 (dealing with association with overseas territories), Article 228 (the power to make international treaties and agreements) and Article 238 (agreements with third countries).
15. Article 223 of the Treaty of Rome reads, in part: (a) No Member State shall be obliged to supply information the disclosure of which it considers essential to the interests of its security, (b) Any Member State my take such measures as it considers necessary for the protection of the essential interests of its security which are connected with the production of or trade in arms, munitions and war material; such measures shall not adversely affect the conditions of competition in the common market regarding products which are not intended for specifically military purposes...
16. These points are made in Douglas Johnson, 'De Gaulle and France's Role in the World', in Hugh Gough and John Horne (eds), *De Gaulle and Twentieth Century France* (London: Edward Arnold, 1994), pp. 93–4.
17. The memorandum is referred to in Sophie Vanhoonacker, 'La Belgique: responable or bouc émissaire de l'échec des négotiations Fouchet?', *Res Publica*, 1989 (4), Vol. XXXI, p. 515.
18. The lack of British enthusiasm for de Gaulle's policies was to prove a crucial hindrance to the achievement of de Gaulle's aims.
19. Simon J. Nuttall, *European Political Co-operation* (Oxford: Clarendon Press, 1992), p. 38.
20. Ibid., p. 41.
21. In an typically blunt summation of his views de Gaulle was quoted as saying, 'quelles sont les réalités de l'Europe? Quels sont les piliers sur lesquels on peut la bâtir? En vérité, ce sont les Etats, des Etats qui sont certes, très différents... (mais) ... qui sont les seules entités qui ont le droit d'ordonner et le pouvoir d'être obéis. Se figurer qu'on peut bâtir quelque chose d'efficace pour l'action, et que ce soit approuvé par les peuples en dehors ou en-dessus des Etats, c'est un chimère'. Quoted in C.W.A. Timmermans, 'The Uneasy Relationship Between the Communities and the Second Union Pillar: Back to the 'Plan Fouchet?', *Legal Issues of European Integration*, No. 1, 1996, pp. 64–5.
22. Jean Lacouture, *De Gaulle: The Ruler 1945–70* (New York: W.W. Norton and Company, 1991), p. 349.
23. For details see Vanhoonacker, *Res Publica*, pp. 520–2.
24. Alfred Pijpers, 'National Adaptation and the CFSP: The Case of the Netherlands', *Legal Issues of European Integration*, No. 1, 1996, p. 81.
25. Quoted in Catherine McArdle Kelleher, *Germany and the Politics of Nuclear Weapons* (New York: Columbia University Press, 1975), pp. 140–1.
26. 564, H.C. Deb., cols. 798–9, quoted in M. Margaret Ball, *NATO and the European Union*, p. 419n.
27. The missile system had been viewed by Prime Minister Macmillan as the 'key to Britain's "special relationship" with the U.S'. Kennedy's Ambassador

to London, David Bruce, and the British Ambassador to Washington, David Ormsby-Gore, failed to warn Washington of the potential gravity of the cancellation of the agreement while Macmillan appears to have chosen to ignore the doubts about the technical efficacy of the Skybolt system voiced by U.S. Secretary of Defense, Robert McNamara. See Theodore C. Sorensen, *Kennedy* (New York: Harper and Row, 1965), p. 565.

28. Ibid., loc. cit.
29. Ibid., p. 566.
30. Ibid., p. 569.
31. 'The Bermuda Meeting, *NATO Letter*, Vol. V (4), 1 April 1957, p. 10 (Emphasis added).
32. *Committee of Three on Non-Military Co-operation in NATO* (Paris: NATO Information Division, 14 Dec. 1954), Para. 40.
33. Simon Nuttall, op. cit. p. 46.
34. Kennedy is quoted as saying, 'That is why [the US] deplores the fact that your treaty has been made outside NATO and without taking the opinions of others into account'. Jean Lacouture, *De Gaulle*, p. 376.
35. Ibid., loc. cit.
36. Ibid., p. 382.
37. For a comprehensive overview of the changes in nuclear strategy during this period, and others, see Beatrice Heuser, *NATO, Britain, France and the FRG: Nuclear Strategies and Forces for Europe, 1949–2000* (New York: St Martin's Press, 1998), pp. 33–57.
38. US General Accounting Office, *Comptroller General's Report to the Congress, Movement of American Forces from France*, Department of Defense B–161507 (GAO: Washington D.C., 1967), p. 4.
39. For general details of the Luxembourg compromise see, Derek W. Urwin, *The Community of Europe: A History of European Integration since 1945* (New York: Longman, 1991), (2nd ed.), pp. 113–5.
40. Alfred Cahen, 'Relaunching the Western European Union: Implications for the Alliance', *NATO Review*, August 1986 (No. 4), pp. 6–9.
41. Members of the Eurogroup are Belgium, Denmark, the Federal Republic of Germany, Greece, Italy, Luxembourg, the Netherlands, Norway, Portugal, Spain, Turkey, and the United Kingdom. The IEPG's composition is identical but also includes France.
42. The technical sub-groups are: EURO/NATOTRAINING (training); EUROLOG (logistics); EUROCOM (communications); EUROMED (medicine); EURO-LONGTERM (operational concepts).
43. The debate was prompted by Senator Mike Mansfield in a series of debates between 1966–74. For full details of the debate see Simon Duke, *The Burdensharing Debate: A Reassessment* (London: Macmillan, 1993), pp. 53–86.
44. Nixon's 'one-and-a-half' war strategy required sufficient American forces with the ability to fight one major and one relatively small conflict simultaneously, based on the assumption that the major conflict would be in Europe.
45. Quoted in Duke, *The Burdensharing Debate*, p. 62.
46. The Yaoundé Convention (Yaoundé I) of Association between the Community and Seventeen African states and Madagascar was signed in 1964.
47. A parallel report was to be produced on progress towards economic and monetary union, which later became known as the Werner Report.

48. Quoted in Derek W. Urwin, *The Community of Europe: A History of European Integration since 1945* (second edition) (London: Longman, 1995), p. 148.

49. 'Report of the Ministers of Foreign Affairs of the Member States on the Problems of Political Unification' (the Davignon Report), *EC Bulletin*, 11/1970 (Luxembourg, 1970).

50. *Luxembourg Report*, 'Report by the Foreign Ministers of the Member States on the Problems of Political Unification', 27 October 1970, Part 2, Ministerial Meetings, I (a–b).

51. *Luxembourg Report*, Part II, Section IV, Matters within the scope of the consultations.

52. Simon Nuttall has perceptively commented that, 'The link between the CSCE and the Community's own policy towards the East European countries was not fortuitous ... The governments of the Six intended that the political guidelines for the Community's common commercial policy should be set by them rather than by the Commission'. Simon Nuttall, pp. 60–1.

53. *Luxembourg Report*, Part III, Para. 1.

54. The four new members signed their treaties of accession in the Palais d'Egmont on 22 January 1972.

55. Norway would later withdraw as the result of a referendum on 24–5 September which showed that 53.9 percent of those who voted were opposed to membership while 46.1 percent were in favour.

56. Bull.-EC, 9-1973, pp. 14–21, *The Copenhagen Report*, Second Report on European Political Co-operation on Foreign Policy, 23 July 1973, Part I (i).

57. See note 55.

58. *The Copenhagen Report*, Part I, (ii).

59. Ibid., Part II, 12 (b).

60. Ibid., Part II, 12.c (ii–iii) (Emphasis added).

61. Peter Brückner, 'The European Community and the United Nations', *European Journal of International Law* (1), 1990, p. 177.

62. Henry Kissinger, *Years of Upheaval* (Boston: Little, Brown and Company, 1982), pp. 716–7.

63. Henry Kissinger, *Years of Upheaval*, pp. 173–4.

64. Ibid., p. 700.

65. *Rapport d'Information déposé par la Délégation de L'Assemblée Nationale pour les Communautés Européennes, L'Europe et sa sécurité: bilan et avenir de la politique étrangère et de sécurité commune (PESC) de L'Union européenne* (France: Assemblée Nationale, 31 mai 1994), p. 12.

66. Elfriede Regelsberger, Philippe de Schoutheete de Tervarent, and Wolfgang Wessels, (eds), *Foreign Policy of the European Union* (London: Lynne Rienner Publishers, 1997).

67. Simon Nuttall, pp. 152–3.

68 Bull.-EC, S.3/81, pp.14–17, *Report on European political cooperation*, London, 13 October 1981, Preamble.

69. Greece became the tenth member of the EC on 1 January 1991.

70. The reference to Gymnich-type agreements takes its name from the location of an informal meeting of the European Foreign Ministers (then at nine) in 1974. At the meeting it was agreed that before a Community member could initiate consultations with a third party through the EPC process, there should be consultation amongst the other members. If they agreed,

the Member State holding the Presidency should be authorised to begin consultations (in the case in point, with the U.S.). More generally Gymnich-type agreements refer to informal arrangements based on a gentleman's agreement.

71. *London Report*, Para. 10.
72. *London Report*, Preamble.
73. See Genscher–Colombo Plan of 6 Nov. 1981 in *EC Bulletin*, No. 11 (1981), pp. 99–104.
74. Emilio Colombo, 'European Security at a time of radical change', *NATO Review*, Vol. 40 (3), June 1992, Web edition at ⟨www.nato.int/docu/review/articles/9203-1.htm⟩.
75. Sanctions were imposed against Argentina based on Article 113 of the Treaty of Rome. It is though worth briefly noting that the Commission suggested the imposition of sanctions.
76. Fred Kaplan, 'Postwar Order Crumbling', *The Boston Globe*, 17 November 1989, p. 3.
77. Quoted in Panos Tsakaloyannis, *The European Community as a Security Community: Problems and Prospects* (Baden-Baden: Nomos Verlagsgesellschaft, 1996), p. 62.
78. Geoffrey Howe, 'Bearing More of the Burden: In Search of a European Foreign and Security Policy', *The World Today*, Vol. 52 (1), January 1996, p. 23.
79. The differences appear in Nuttall, pp. 246–7.
80. *Statement by Mr Santer, President-in-Office of the European Council*, 11 December 1985, Strasbourg, Doc. 85/317.
81. *Treaties Revising the Treaties establishing the European Communities and Acts Relating to the Communities* (the Single European Act), 11 June 1986, Title I, 'Common Provisions', Article 1.
82. *Single European Act*, Title III, 'Provisions on European Cooperation in the Sphere of Foreign Policy', Art. 30.
83. Ibid., Article 30, Para. 2 (a) (Emphasis added).
84. Ibid., Article 30, Para. 2 (c).
85. Ibid., Article 30, Para. 2 (d).
86. Ibid., Article 20, Para. 5.
87. Ibid., Article 30, Para. 4.
88. The Secretariat consisted of the Presidency-in-Office of EPC together with a seconded official from the two preceding and two following Presidencies. For further details see *Ministerial Decision on the Application of Certain Aspects of Title III of the Single European Act*, Doc. 28/090, 28 February 1986. For further details of the role of the EPC Secretariat see, *Question No. H–341/86 by Sir Peter Vanneck concerning the Secretariat for EPC*, 10 December 1986, Doc. 86/387.
89. *Single European Act*, Title III, Article 30, Para.10 (g).
90. Ibid., Article 30, Para. 6 (a) (Emphasis added).
91. See note 31 above.
92. SEA, Article 30, Para. 6 (b).
93. Ibid., Article 30, Para. 6 (c).
94. Ibid., Article 30, Para. 5.
95. *Statement on the Term-of-Office of the British Presidency*, Strasbourg, 10 December 1986, Doc. 86/402.

96. Panayiotis Ifestos, *European Political Co-operation: Towards a Framework of Supranational Diplomacy?* (Aldershot: Gower Publishing Group, 1987), p. 358.

97. Article IV of the Modified Brussels Treaty actually stipulates that the signatory members and any other organs established by them 'shall work in close co-operation with the North Atlantic Treaty Organisation', and recognised the 'undesirability of duplicating the military staffs of NATO'. Thus, the military functions had largely been seceded to NATO from the start.

98. Helmut Schmidt, *A Grand Strategy for the West* (New Haven: Yale University Press, 1985), p. 61.

99. With the repeal of the constraints upon the manufacture of certain conventional arms in 1985, the FRG became more enthusiastic about the WEU.

100. G. Wyn Rees, *The Western European Union at the Crossroads: Between Trans-Atlantic Solidarity and European Integration* (Boulder, Colorado: Westview Press, 1998), p. 22.

101. Alfred Cahen, in Michael Clarke and Rod Hague (eds), *European Defence Co-operation: America, Britain, and NATO* (Manchester: Manchester University Press, 1990), p. 56.

102. Full text of the Rome Declaration 26–7 October 1984 quoted in, Alfred Cahen, *The Western European Union and NATO*, pp. 83–90.

103. Alfred Cahen, *The Western European Union and NATO*, p. 38.

104. Quoted in Stephen George, *An Awkward Partner: Britain in the European Community* (Oxford: Oxford University Press, 1990), p. 202.

105. Margaret Thatcher, *The Downing Street Years* (London: Harper Collins, 1993), p. 745.

106. Garnham, *The Politics of European Defence Cooperation*, p. 118.

107. Quoted in Alfred Cahen, *The Western European Union and NATO*, p. 15 (emphasis added).

108. *European Yearbook*, Vol. 35, 1987, WEU 4–5.

109. *Platform on European Security Interests*, The Hague, 27 October 1987, Section III (a).

110. See *Question No. 2106/87 by Mr. Vandemeulebroucke, Concerning the Platform on European Security and the Single European Act*, 28 April 1988, Strasbourg, Doc. 88/107.

111. Unlike the Washington treaty's Article 6, the WEU has no geographical restrictions imposed on it by treaty.

112. Germany provided replacement minesweeping forces elsewhere and Luxembourg made a financial contribution.

113. Germany's constitutional sensitivities were to provide a significant impediment to the development of a truly European security identity in the practical, military sense, until the Federal Constitutional Court in Karlsruhe delivered an official interpretation of the relevant articles of the constitution on 12 July 1994.

114. Willem van Eekelen, *Debating European Security*, p. 49.

115. For further details see, Timothy J. Birch and John H. Crotts, 'European Defence Integration: National Interests, National Sensitivities', in Alan W. Cafruny and Glenda G. Rosenthal (eds), *The State of the European*

Community: The Maastricht Debates and Beyond (Vol. 2) (Harlow, Essex: Longman, 1993), pp. 265–81.

116. Quoted in Charles Krupnik, 'Not What they wanted: American Policy and the European Security and Defence Identity', in Alexander Moens and Christopher Anstis, *Disconcerted Europe: The Search for a New Security Architecture* (Boulder: Westview Press, 1994), pp. 117–8.
117. Full text, see *Europe Documents*, No.1608, 29 March 1990.
118. For the full text see *Agence Europe*, No. 5238, 20 April 1990.
119. European Parliament, *Session Document* (B–3–1167/90, 7 June 1990).
120. Presidency Conclusions, European Council, Dublin 25–6 June 1990, in *Europe Documents*, No.1632/1633, 29 June 1990.
121. Hans van den Broek, 'The Common Foreign and Security Policy in the Context of the 1996 Intergovernmental Conference', Speech at the Royal Institute for International Relations, Brussels, 4 July 1995, *Studia Diplomatique*, Vol. 48 (4), 1995, p. 32.
122. Secretary James Baker III had also encouraged Germany's federalist tendencies when, in response to Kohl's agitating for a unified Germany, Baker offered support including the hope that not only should Germany remain in NATO, but that it should become part of an 'increasingly integrated European Community'. Thatcher, *The Downing Street Years*, p. 795.
123. The unification of Germany had, as Prime Minister Margaret Thatcher observed, 'strengthened the hand of Chancellor Kohl and fuelled the desire of President Mitterrand and Jacques Delors for a federal Europe which would "bind in" a new Germany to a structure within which its preponderance would be checked'. Thatcher, *The Downing Street Years*, pp. 759–760.

3   From Political Community to Uncommon Security

1. For an account of the EC/WEU action in the Gulf War see, Pia Christa Wood, 'European Political Cooperation: Lessons from the Gulf War and Yugoslavia', in Alan W. Cafruny and Glenda G. Rosenthal, *The State of the European Community: The Maastricht Debates and Beyond*, Vol. 2 (Harlow, Essex: Lynne Rienner Publishers, 1993), pp. 227–44.
2. Ibid., p. 229.
3. Bregor Schöllgen, 'Putting Germany's Post-Unification Foreign Policy to the Test', *NATO Review*, Vol. 41 (2) April 1993, p. 17.
4. Ibid., p. 18.
5. The WEU's condemnation of Iraq's invasion of Kuwait followed the example set by the United Nations, which in Security Council Resolution 660 called for full and unconditional withdrawal.
6. Trevor C. Salmon, 'Testing times for European Political Cooperation: The Gulf and Yugoslavia, 1990–92', *International Affairs*, Vol. 68, No. 2 (1992), p. 244.
7. Again, Germany did not participate on constitutional grounds and Luxembourg, with no navy, made financial contributions.
8. See especially, Report of the Assembly of the WEU, *Consequences of the Invasion of Kuwait: Continuing Operations in the Gulf Region*, Doc. 1248, Paris, 7 November 1990.

9. Quoted in Finn Laursen and Sophie Vanhoonacker (eds), *The Inter-governmental Conference on Political Union: Institutional Reforms, New Policies and International Identity of the European Community* (Maastricht: European Institute of Public Administration, 1992), p. 315.

10. Ibid., p. 314.

11. For full text see Laursen and Vanhoonacker, pp. 318–21.

12. These were, to recap. The Italian proposals on CFSP of 18 September 1990, The Commission's proposal of 21 October 1990, the Franco-German Proposals of 6 December 1990, those made in a speech by Douglas Hurd (based on a speech in Berlin) of 10 December 1990, and the President of the European Council's conclusions, 14–15 December 1990.

13. Laursen and Vanhoonacker, p. 324.

14. The pillar approach consisted of a number of inter-linked policy areas of which foreign and security policy would be but one; the first or 'community' pillar (based on the Treaties of Paris and Rome, as modified in the 1986 SEA); the second or 'foreign and security' sphere; and the third or 'criminal law and home affairs' policy domain.

15. *Europe Documents*, No. 1690, 21 February 1991.

16. Steven Philip Kramer, *Does France Still Count? The French Role in the New Europe* (Westport, Connecticut: Praeger, 1994), p. 35.

17. The latter was essential for Germany to play a role in out-of-area activities. The constitutional issue was a delicate one since it had to be addressed in order for Germany to play a significant role in Europe's evolving security environment. The alternative, as Roger Palin has noted, 'was a renationalisation of Germany's force structure as part of a more independently minded nation – a Germany within Europe, as opposed to a European Germany'. See Roger H. Palin, 'Multinational Military Forces: Problems and Prospects', *Adelphi Paper 294* (London: IISS/Oxford University Press, 1994), p. 10.

18. *Rapport d'Information déposé par la Délégation de L'Assemblée Nationale pour les Communautés Européennes, L'Europe et sa sécurité: bilan et avenir de la politique étrangère et de sécurité commune (PESC) de L'Union européenne* (France: Assemblée Nationale, 31 mai 1994), p. 19.

19. *Europe Documents*, No. 1706, 16 April 1991.

20. 'Luxembourg Presidency's Concept of Political Union', June 1991, in *Agence Europe*, No. 5524, 30 June 1991, pp. 5–7.

21. Ibid., loc.cit.

22. The proposal called for the European parliament to be given veto power over any EC law which was subject to majority voting in the Council of Ministers and to accord it equal decision power with the Council in matters pertaining to the environment, research and overseas development assistance.

23. *Atlantic News*, No. 2357, 9 October 1991

24. Ibid.,

25. *Atlantic Document*, No. 74, 18 October 1991.

26. Ibid., *Treaty on Political Union: Common Foreign and Security Policy*, Article II.

27. Ibid., Section IV, Article 3, 'WEU–NATO Cooperation'.

28. NATO's June 1991 Copenhagen summit had encountered difficulties over this very issue.

29. Panos Tsakaloyannis, *The European Union as a Security Community: Problems and Prospects* (Baden-Baden: Nomos Verlagsgesellschaft, 1996), p. 130.

30. *Atlantic News*, No. 2360, 18 October 1991.
31. *Agence Europe*, No. 1746/7, 20 November 1991.
32. Address by President George Bush, Oklahoma State University, 4 May 1990, excerpted in – Adam Daniel Rotfeld and Walther Stützle (eds), *Germany and Europe in Transition* (Oxford: SIPRI/Oxford University Press, 1991), p. 97.
33. Address by James A. Baker III, U.S. Secretary of State, to the Berlin Press Club, 12 December 1989, quoted in Rotfeld and Stützle (eds), p. 96.
34. Margaret Thatcher, *The Downing Street Years* (New York: HarperCollins, 1993), p. 796.
35. *London Declaration on a Transformed North Atlantic Alliance*, Issued by the Heads of State and Government participating in the Meeting of the North Atlantic Alliance, 5–6 July 1990 (Brussels: NATO Press Office).
36. On Franco-German defence integration see, Simon Duke, *The New European Security Disorder* (London: Macmillan/St Antony's, 1996), pp. 215–54.
37. *The Alliance's New Strategic Concept*, agreed upon by Heads of State and Government participating in the meeting of the North Atlantic Council, Rome 7–8 November 1991, Part II, Paras. 17,21,22.
38. Ibid., Article 52.
39. *Defending Our Future*, Statement on Defence Estimates 1993, Cm.2270 (London: HMSO, July 1993), p. 16.
40. The Bartholomew Memorandum was attributed to the US Under Secretary of State, Reginald Bartholomew. Exactly who wrote the memorandum remains unclear and speculation has involved not only Bartholomew but also European Bureau Deputy Assistant Secretary, James Dobbins; National Security Advisor, Brent Scowcroft and State Department Counsellor, Robert Zoellick.
41. Willem van Eekelen, *Debating European Security, 1948–98* (The Hague: Sdu Publishers, 1998). For full text of the Bartholomew Memorandum see Annex II, pp. 340–44.
42. Ibid., p. 342.
43. *Agence Europe*, No. 1746/7, 20 November 1991.
44. Stephen Philip Kramer, *Does France Still Count?*, p. 37.
45. Quoted in Charles Krupnik, p. 126.
46. *The Alliance's New Strategic Concept*, agreed upon by the Heads of State and Government participating in the meeting of the North Atlantic Council, Rome, 7–8 November 1991, Part II, para. 52.
47. In addition to the British command of ARRC, NATO multinational forces consist of seven corps-strength units (around 50000–70000 troops). Six of the corps are based in Europe. All are multinational, two commanded by Germany, one by Belgium and one by a German–Danish staff. The seventh corps, based in the former DDR, is German commanded and German in composition, in compliance with agreements forbidding NATO to deploy in this area.
48. *The Alliance's New Strategic Concept*, agreed upon by the Heads of State and Government participating in the meeting of the North Atlantic Council, Rome, 7–8 November 1991, Para. 52.
49. The United Kingdom contributes roughly 60 percent of the headquarters staff and the remainder are international. ARRC was created by the NATO Defence Planning Committee and it is partly headquartered in the United

Kingdom and based in Germany. Troops from Germany, the Netherlands, Italy, Greece, Spain, Turkey and Britain are included in the corps with some ground forces from the US, along with logistical support. The force is designed to respond in five to seven days and would include a British heavy armoured division.

50. Desmond Dinan, *Ever Closer Union? An Introduction to the European Community* (London: Macmillan, 1994), p. 182.
51. See below, footnote 60.
52. Mazzuchelli, *France and Germany at Maastricht: Politics and Negotiations to create the European Union* (New York: Garland Publishing Inc., 1997), p. 191.
53. For an authoritative account of the various national positions in the lead up to, during, and after the negotiations, see Finn Laursen and Sophie Vanhoonacker, *The Ratification of the Maastricht Treaty: Issues, Debates, and Future Implications* (Dordrecht: Martinus Nijhoff Publishers, 1994).
54. *Report of the Assembly of the WEU: The Future of European Security and the Preparation of Maastricht II – Reply to the fortieth annual report of the Council*, 16 May 1995, Doc. 1458, p. 10.
55. On 8 March 1995 Klaus Kinkel spoke in favour of a merger between the EU and WEU. Reported in *Die Zeit*, 10 March 1995. In an interview with *Le Figaro* on 16 March Kinkel reiterated his position and also spoke of the need for a European foreign affairs ministry. See *WEU Assembly Report*, Doc. 1458, 16 May 1995, pp. 11–12.
56. Ambassador Giovanni Jannuzzi, 'Europe and a Security Dimension', *NATO Review*, Vol. 39 (2), April 1991 (Web edition at ⟨www.nato.int/docu/review/articles/9102.htm⟩.
57. TEU, Article P 2.
58. TEU, Article J 4.3.
59. TEU, Article J 1.1.
60. For example TEU, Article J 1.3.
61. TEU, Article J 4.2.
62. On this issue see C.W.A. Timmermans, 'The Uneasy Relationship between the Communities and the Second Pillar: Back to the 'Plan Fouchet?', *Legal Issues of European Integration*, No. 1, 1996, pp. 61–70.
63. This contrasts with Pillar 1 (the existing European Communities) which is marked by Community competence and not intergovernmentalism.
64. Treaty establishing the European Community, Article 3b. Some have disputed the extent to which the principle of subsidiarity can be applied to the second pillar. For instance, Nanette Neuwahl argues that Title V of the TEU, unlike Title VI on Co-operation in the fields of Justice and Home Affairs, does not contain explicit reference to the principle. In another example David O'Keefe and Patrick Twomey argue that, 'The principle of subsidiarity is intended to govern the relations between the Community and its Member States. Therefore, it cannot, *prima facie*, be used in relations between the pillars'. In David O'Keefe and Patrick M. Twomey (eds), *Legal Issues of the Maastricht Treaty* (Chichester: Chancery Law Publishing, 1994), p. 236–7.
65. TEU, Article F1.
66. TEU, Article D.

67. TEU, Article J.8.1.
68. TEU, Article J.3.6.
69. TEU, Article J.3.7.
70. The non-jurisdiction of the Court of Justice in the second pillar is a matter of dispute amongst legal experts since some of the organs of the first pillar also operate in the second pillar, albeit with different roles and powers (for instance, the European Council is integrated into the legal framework of the community via Article 103 of the Treaty establishing the European Community) which may then imply that they are subject to the indirect scrutiny of the Court of Justice. See Christian Tietje, 'The Concept of Coherence in the Treaty on European Union and the Common Foreign and Security Policy', *European Foreign Affairs Review*, No. 2, 1997, p. 232.
71. TEU, Article J.8.2
72. Article J 3.2 (the article also refers to Article 148(2) of the Treaty Establishing the European Community which specifies the weighted voting procedure for qualified majority votes.
73. Fraser Cameron, 'Where the European Commission Comes In: From the Single European Act to Maastricht', in Elfriede Regelsberger, Philippe de Schoutheete de Tervarent, Wolfgang Wessels (eds), *Foreign Policy of the European Union: From EPC to CFSP and Beyond* (Colorado: Lynne Rienner Publishers, 1997), p. 100.
74. TEU Article J 8.5.
75. Mathias Jopp, 'The Defense Dimension of the European Union: The Role and Performance of the WEU', Ibid., p. 166.
76. TEU Article J 4.4.
77. TEU Article J 4.1 (Emphasis added).
78. Willem van Eekelen, p. 118.
79. For text of document see, Auke Venema and Henriette Romijn, *Documents on International Security Policy*, May 1989–December 1991 (Brussels: Netherlands Atlantic Commission, NATO Office of Information and Press, February 1992).
80. *NATO's Core Security Functions in a New Europe*, statement issued by the North Atlantic Council meeting in ministerial session, Copenhagen, 6–7 June 1991, Para. 7.
81. NATO Press Communiqué M–NAC–(92)51, 4 June 1992, para. 11.
82. The tasks are defined in *Petersberg Declaration*, Western European Union, Council of Ministers, Bonn, 19 June 1992, as including, 'humanitarian and rescue tasks; peacekeeping tasks; tasks of combat forces in crisis management, including peacemaking', (Section II: On Strengthening WEU's Operational Role, Para. 4).
83. 'Preliminary Conclusions on the Formulation of a Common European Defence Policy', Noordwijk, 14 November 1994, in *Europe Documents*, No. 1911, 22 November 1994.
84. Ibid., Para. 160.
85. Ibid., Para. 164.
86. Ibid., Para. 172
87. Final Text of the Ministerial Council of the WEU, Madrid, 14 November 1995, Para. 5, in *Atlantic Document*, No. 92, 17 November 1995.
88. Named after the town near Venice where EC Ministers held informal talks on security-related issues on 6 October 1990.

89. 'Report to the European Council in Lisbon on the Likely Development of the Common Foreign and Security Policy with a view to Identifying Areas Open to Joint Action *vis-à-vis* Particular Countries or Groups of Countries', *Europe* No. 5761, 29–30 June 1992 (Hereafter, *Lisbon Report*).
90. Lisbon Report, Para. 2.
91. Lisbon Report, Para. 3.
92. Lisbon Report, Paras. 9–10.
93. Lisbon Report, Para. 10.
94. Lisbon Report, Para. 12.
95. Lisbon Report, Para. 35. This list was added to, with the possibility of more being added in future, at the European Council's Edinburgh summit of 11–12 December 1992.
96. In the case of South Africa the Nine found a course of action very difficult to agree upon in spite of the underlying condemnation of apartheid. The outcome was the adoption of a Code of Conduct applying to EC companies conducting business with South Africa. But the Code was voluntary and there were no mechanisms for penalties in case of violation. For a detailed assessment of the effectiveness of the sanctions against South Africa, see Martin Holland, *European Union Common Foreign Policy: From EPC to CFSP Joint Action and South Africa* (New York: Macmillan/St Martin's Press, 1995).
97. Jacques Santer, 'The European Union's Security and Defense Policy: How To Avoid Missing the 1996 Rendez-Vous', *NATO Review*, Vol. 43 (6), November 1995, Web edition at ⟨www.nato.int/docu/review/articles/9506-1.htm⟩.
98. Lisbon Report, Para. 38.
99. European Council of Edinburgh, Presidential Conclusions, Part 1, Annex, *Agence Europe*, No. 5878, 13–14 December 1992.
100. *Report on Joint Action and the Development of the CFSP in the Field of Security*, Ad Hoc Working Group on Security, 7 December 1992.
101. Ibid., Section IV 'Wider Issues', Para. 9.
102. The five subcommittees were: Evaluation of Risks and Threats (Chair: Michael Sturmer); EU–WEU–NATO Institutional Coherence (Chair: Henri Froment-Meurice); Economic Aspects (Chair: Herman Mulder); Values (Chair: Revd. Edourd Herr); and The Decision-Making Process (Chair: Edmond Wallenstein).
103. High-level group of experts on the CFSP, First Report, *European Security Policy towards 2000: ways and means to establish genuine credibility* (Brussels: Commission of the European Union, 19 December 1994), p. 3.
104. Ibid., p. 4.
105. Article V of the Brussels Treaty reads: If any of the High Contracting Parties should be the object of an armed attack in Europe, the other High Contracting Parties will, in accordance with the provisions of Article 51 of the Charter of the United Nations, afford the Party so attacked all the military and other aid and assistance in their power.
106. *European Security Policy towards 2000*, p. 4.
107. Ibid., p. 7.
108. Ibid., p. 10.
109. Ibid., p. 16.
110. 'Relations with Western Partners', *Report to the European Parliament on Progress towards European Union*, Brussels, Doc. 91/419, 27 November 1991.

111. Vlad Sobell, 'NATO, Russia and the Yugoslav war', *The World Today*, No. 11, November 1995, p. 211.
112. For a detailed discussion of 'permissive consensus' and policy legitimacy within the EU, see Daniela Obradovic, 'Policy Legitimacy and the European Union', *Journal of Common Market Studies*, Vol. 34(2), June 1996, pp. 191–221.
113. Simon Nuttall, *European Political Co-operation* (Oxford: Clarendon Press, 1992), p. 11.
114. Edouard Balladur, *French Proposals for a Pact on Stability in Europe*, Copenhagen, 22 June 1993.
115. These were, Albania, Austria, Belarus, Cyprus, Finland, FYROM, Holy See, Iceland, Malta, Moldova, Norway, Russia, Sweden, Switzerland, Turkey and Ukraine.
116. In 1987 the WEU established a Working Group on security in the Mediterranean. The EU also produced a report on the implications of developments in the region for European security. The CFSP Working Group concluded that security in the Mediterranean region, which is fundamental to European security, is a responsibility for the EU as a whole. The WEU concurred, in its Kirchberg Declaration, and as a result expanded its existing agreement with the Maghreb countries to Egypt and other non-WEU Mediterranean states.
117. *Preliminary Conclusions on the Formulation of a Common European Defence Policy*, Permanent Council Report, 10 November 1994.
118. Ibid., Part II 'Definition and Scope', Para. 2.
119. Ibid., Para. 4.
120. Ibid., Para. 6.
121. Ibid., Section V, 'The Relationship between WEU and NATO', Para. 17.
122. Ibid., loc. cit.
123. Ibid., Part B: 'The Construction of a Common European Defence Policy', Para. 24. (Emphasis added).
124. These might include 'joint actions' on the following issues: provision of humanitarian assistance in the former Yugoslavia; administration of Mostar; support for the extension of the NPT; support for the Middle East peace process; agreement on export controls for dual use goods; and promotion of the 'Stability Pact' (the Balladur Plan) as a means of addressing minority and border issues in central and eastern Europe.
125. Hans van den Broek, 'The Common Foreign and Security Policy', pp. 33–4.
126. *Report on the Functioning of the Treaty on European Union*, 10 May 1995, Doc. IP/95/465.

4   Expanding Europe, Decreasing Security

1. Article N.2 of the TEU provides that, 'A conference of representatives of the government of the Member States shall be convened in 1996 to examine those provisions of this Treaty for which revision is provided.'
2. Full text of 'Reflections on European Policy', in *Agence Europe*, No. 1895/6, 7 September 1994.
3. *WEU's Contribution to the European Union Intergovernmental Conference of 1996*, WEU Council of Ministers, 14 November 1995 (Brussels: Press and Information Service, 1995).

4. See interview with Prime Minister Edouard Balladur from *Le Figaro* reproduced in *Agence Europe*, No. 1891, 3 September 1994.

5. Since the document emanated from a parliamentary group (headed by Wolfgang Schäuble) it was not a document that necessarily expressed the position of the government or the Chancellor (although he was aware of its contents) and it therefore left Germany's position in the IGC relatively unconstrained.

6. *WEU's Contribution to the European Union Intergovernmental Conference of 1996*, WEU Council of Ministers, 14 November 1995, Para. 99 (Brussels: Press and Information Service, 1995).

7. Peter Norman, 'Franco-German Defence Strains', *Financial Times*, 5 March 1996, p. 5.

8. The other two were making the Union 'more relevant to its citizens in the field of human rights, internal security, employment and the environment', and 'improving the Union's efficiency and democracy'.

9. UNSC Resolution 1011, 2 March 1997.

10. Press Conference by the Foreign Secretary, Mr. Robin Cook, Luxembourg, 2 June 1997, at http://britain-info.org/bis/fordom/eu/97602fs.htm.

11. *Treaty of Amsterdam amending the Treaty on European Union, the Treaties establishing the European Communities and certain related acts* (Luxembourg: Office for Official Publications of the European Communities, 1997).

12. For the text of the Treaty of Amsterdam see, *Treaty of Amsterdam amending the Treaty on European Union, the Treaties establishing the European Communities and certain related acts* (Luxembourg: Office for Official Publications of the European Communities, 1997); the Consolidated Version of the Treaty on European Union, appears in *European Union: Consolidated Treaties* (Luxembourg: Office for Official Publications of the European Communities, 1997). Care should be taken since the Consolidated Treaties comprise both the *Consolidated Version of the Treaty on European Union* and the *Consolidated Version of the Treaty Establishing the European Community*. The relevant CFSP sections appear in Title V, Articles 11–29 of the former although there are things of relevance to the CFSP in the second treaty.

13. CTEU, Article 3.

14. Christian Tietje notes that the English language version of the TEU refers to 'consistency' while the French and German versions refer to 'cohérence' and 'Kohärenz' respectively. He noted that 'one of the first tasks of the Review Conference in 1996 should be to clarify the language of the English version of the treaty.' As is indicated in the main text, this was not done. See Christian Tietje, 'The Concept of Coherence in the Treaty on European Union and the Common Foreign and Security Policy', *European Foreign Affairs Review*, No. 2, 1997, pp. 211–33.

15. CTEU, Article 17.1 (former Article J 4 .5 of the TEU).

16. CTEU, Article 17.2.

17. CTEU, Article 24.

18. Boutros Boutros-Ghali, *An Agenda for Peace: Preventive diplomacy, peacemaking and peace-keeping*, 17 June 1992, UN Doc, A/47/277.

19. CTEU, Article 18.1–5.

20. CTEU, Article 18.3.

21. The idea of a High Representative had in fact been broached at least three years earlier but the post remained unfilled due to differences over the mandate that should be attached to the post and the highly sensitive question of who should be appointed. See Bulletin EU6-1966, Annexes to the Conclusions of the Presidency (98/108).
22. *Treaty of Amsterdam*, Declarations adopted by the Conference, Declaration 6 on the establishment of a poliby planning and early warning unit, 2 October 1997.
23. Details in *Agence Europe*, No. 7257, 6/7 July 1998, p. 4.
24. CTEU, Article 14.4.
25. CTEU, Article 18.5
26. Mark Turner, 'CFSP Gets New Marching Orders', *European Voice*, 5–11 February 1998, p. 6.
27. CTEU, Article 23.2.
28. Under Article 205 (ex Article 148.2 of the Treaty Establishing the European Community) of the *Consolidated Version of the Treaty Establishing the European Community*, the votes for a qualified majority vote in the Council are weighted as follows:

Belgium	5	France	10	Austria	4
Denmark	3	Ireland	3	Portugal	5
Germany	10	Italy	10	Finland	3
Greece	5	Luxembourg	2	Sweden	4
Spain	8	Netherlands	5	United Kingdom	10

29. CTEU, Article 17.1.
30. CTEU, loc. cit.
31. CTEU, Article 17.3.
32. CTEU, loc. cit.
33. 'Declaration of Western European Union on the Role of Western European Union and its relations with the European Union and with the Atlantic Alliance', Text in *Treaty of Amsterdam* (Luxembourg: Office for Official Publications of the European Communities, 1997), pp. 125–31.
34. Ibid., p. 129 (emphasis added).
35. Ibid., loc. cit.
36. CTEU, Article 19.2.
37. *The Draft Treaty of Amsterdam, Inter Institutional Agreement between the European Parliament, the Council and the European Commission on provisions regarding financing of the Common Foreign and Security Policy* Doc. CONF/4001/97, June 1997.
38. 'Interinstitutional Agreement on the financing of the common foreign and security policy', *Bulletin EU*, 7/8–1997.
39. CTEU, Article 28.3.
40. David Allen, 'The European Rescue of National Foreign Policy', in Christopher Hill, *The Actors in Europe's Foreign Policy* (London: Routledge, 1997), p. 298.
41. Applications for membership have been addressed to the Council from Turkey (14 April 1987 – rejected 20 December 1989 by the Commission), Cyprus (12 July 1990), Malta (16 July 1990) and Switzerland (20 May 1992 – a public

referendum in December 1992 voted against membership). The ten associated CEE countries addressed applications to the Council in the following order: Hungary (31 March 1994), Poland (5 April 1994), Romania (22 June 1995), Slovakia (27 June 1995), Latvia (13 October 1995), Estonia (24 November 1995), Lithuania (8 December 1995), Bulgaria (14 December 1995), Czech Republic (17 January 1996) and Slovenia (10 June 1996).

42. The list appears in *Enlargement: Questions and Answers* (Brussels: European Commission, 30 July 1996) See ⟨http://europe.eu.int/comm/dg1a/enlargement⟩. The Madrid European Council meeting in December 1995 confirmed the criteria and added that there was a need to 'create the conditions for the gradual, harmonious integration of the candidate countries' through the development of the market economy, the adjustment of their administrative structures and the creation of a stable economic and monetary environment.

43. Communication of the Commission, *Agenda 2000*, Part One 'The Policies of the Union', Section iv. 'The Union and the World', Strasbourg, 15 July 1997, Doc.97/6.

44. Ibid., loc. cit.

45. Ibid., loc. cit.

46. Ibid., loc. cit.

47. Ibid., loc. cit.

48. 'The Effects on the Union's Policies of Enlargement to the Applicant Countries of Central and Eastern Europe', Part II Analysis, 1. The External Dimension, *Agenda 2000*, Part 1.1.

49. Ibid., loc. cit.

50. Gediminius Vitkus, 'Lithuania and the European Union: Membership Conditions – the Security Dimension', in Klaudijus Maniokas and Gediminas Vitkus (eds), *Lithuania's Integration into the European Union* (Vilnius: European Integration Studies Centre, 1997), p. 29.

51. 'The Effects on the Union's Policies of Enlargement to the Applicant Countries of Central and Eastern Europe', Part II Analysis, 1. The External Dimension, *Agenda 2000*, Part 1.1.

52. *Enlargement: Questions and Answers* (Brussels, European Commission, DG1A, 30 July 1996).

53. Ibid., Chapter 1, Para. 4 (emphasis added).

54. The Effects on the Union's Policies of Enlargement to the Applicant Countries of Central and Eastern Europe', Part II Analysis, 1. The External Dimension, *Agenda 2000*, Part 1.1.

55. *Madrid Declaration on Euro-Atlantic Security and Co-operation*, Issued by the Heads of State and Government meeting in Madrid, 8 July 1997, NATO Press release M–1(97)81, para. 1.

56. Ibid., para. 2.

57. Ibid., para. 8.

58. Ibid., para. 13.

59. For further details of the MCG see, Jette Nordam, 'The Mediterranean Dialogue: Dispelling misconceptions and building confidence', *NATO Review*, Vol. 45(4), July–August 1997, pp. 26–9.

60. Madrid Declaration, para. 16.

61. Ibid., para.18.

62. *The Economist*, 12–18 July 1997, p. 17.
63. *Statement by President Clinton on NATO Enlargement*, 12 June 1997. ⟨http://dns.usis.if/publish/armscontrol/archive/1997/june/nat0612b.html⟩
64. 'A Bigger NATO: Europe Takes Shape', *The Economist*, 12–18 July 1997, p. 17.
65. *Report to the Congress on the Enlargement of the North Atlantic Treaty Organization: Rationale, Benefits, Costs and Implications* (Washington DC: Bureau of European and Canadian Affairs, U.S. Department of State, 24 February 1997), p. 2.
66. Ibid., loc. cit.
67. Jonathan Dean, 'The NATO Mistake: Expansion for all the wrong reasons', *The Washington Monthly*, Vol. 29 (7), July/August 1997, p. 36.
68. Ibid., loc. cit.
69. Ibid., p. 37.
70. *Speech by NATO Secretary-General Javier Solana*, NATO Summit meeting, Madrid, 8 July 1997, available on the Web at http://www.nato.int/docu/speech/1997/s970708d.htm.
71. Patrick Worsnip, 'Albright Tells Russia Baltics can join NATO', *Reuters*, 13 July 1997.
72. Remarks by His Excellency Lennart Meri, President of Estonia, Madrid, 9 July 1997, available on the Web at http://www.nato.int/docu/speech/1997/s970709l.htm.
73. *The Economist*, 12–18 July 1997, p. 17.
74. Statement by Mr Victor Sheiman, Official Representative of President A. Lukashenko, State Secretary of the Security Council of the Republic of Belarus, at the inaugural meeting of the EAPC, Madrid, 9 July 1997, available on the Web at ⟨http://www.nato.int/docu/speech/1997/s970709j.htm⟩.
75. William Drozdiak, 'Growing Pains at a New NATO: Will Alliance's Popularity Diminish its Efficiency', *International Herald Tribune*, 11 July 1997, p. 1.
76. They are respectively, *Founding Act on Mutual Relations, Cooperation and Security between NATO and the Russian Federation*, Paris, 27 May 1997, and the *Charter on a Distinctive Partnership between the North Atlantic Treaty Organisation and Ukraine*, Madrid, 9 July 1997.
77. *Founding Act on Mutual Relations*, Part 1, Principles.
78. Ibid., loc. cit.
79. *Charter on a Distinctive Partnership between the North Atlantic Treaty Organization and Ukraine*, Madrid, 9 July 1997. Text in *NATO Review*, Vol. 45 (4), July–August 1997, p. 5–6.
80. *Charter on a Distinctive Partnership between the North Atlantic Treaty Organisation and Ukraine*, Madrid, 9 July 1997, paras. 6–7.
81. Ibid., paras. 14–15.
82. *NATO Study on Enlargement*, September 1995, Chapter 1, Para. 5.
83. Ibid., Chapter 4, Para. 45(g).
84. Ibid., Chapter 4, Para. 59.
85. Ibid., Chapter 4, Para. 65.
86. Ibid., Chapter 4. Paras. 66–7.
87. Ibid., Chapter 5. Para. 76.
88. The first widely available figures were those supplied by Ronald D. Asmus, Richard L. Kugler and F. Stephen Larrabee, 'Adapting NATO: What Will NATO Enlargement Cost?', *Survival*, Autumn 1996, Vol. 38(3), pp. 5–27.

89. The figures represent the total of incremental costs plus the cost of measures to improve modernization and restructuring incurred between the years 1997–2009 (two/three years prior to accession and ten years thereafter). For full details see *Report to Congress on NATO Enlargement*, pp. 12–22.
90. Ibid., p. 18.
91. This estimate does not include the financial costs of U.S. assistance programmes to Central and Eastern Europe to modernise their militaries and to prepare them for possible NATO membership. Since FY 1995 these various programmes, including the Warsaw Initiative, have totalled $200 million.
92. *NATO Enlargement: Costs Estimates Developed to Date are Notional*, 18 August 1997, GAO/NSIAD–97–209 (Washington DC: General Accounting Office, 1997), p. 2.
93. Ibid., loc cit.
94. *NATO Enlargement and International Law*, Critical Memorandum July 1997, www.ddh.nl/org/ialana/nato.html.
95. *Report to Congress on NATO Enlargement*, p. 20.
96. Calculations are based on SIPRI Military Expenditure data, *SIPRI Yearbook 1996* (Oxford: Oxford University Press/SIPRI, 1996), p. 366. If the latest reported military expenditure figures are taken, expressed in 1990 prices and exchange rates, the combined military expenditure for the Czech Republic, Hungary and Poland is $ 2.3 billion dollars (using 1995 figures for all except Hungary which uses a 1994 figure). The estimated DoD new member costs represent between 10.02–15.24 percent of their combined defence expenditure.
97. *Report to Congress on NATO Enlargement*, p. 18.
98. Paul Taylor, 'U.S., Europeans Clash Over NATO Enlargement', *Reuters*, 9 July 1997.
99. Ibid.
100. William Drozdiak, 'Snag in NATO Expansion', *International Herald Tribune*, 3 October 1997, p. 1.
101. 'NATO enlargement cost debate begins in earnest', *Jane's Defence Weekly*, 11 June 1997, at
    ⟨www.janes.com./public/defence/editors/nato/dw970611-nato.html⟩.
102. Tasos Kokkinides, 'NATO's U-Turn on Cost Study', *Basic Reports*, No. 62, 15 December 1997, pp. 1–2.
103. Amos Perlmutter and Ted Galen Carpenter, 'NATO's Expensive Trip East: The Folly of Enlargement', *Foreign Affairs*, January/February 1998, p. 5.
104. For a particularly good examination of the methodological pitfalls of public opinion data in the European security area, see Richard Sinnott, 'European Public Opinion and Security Policy', *Chaillot Papers*, (28) July 1997, (Paris: Institute for Security Studies WEU, 1997).
105. Ibid., Table 1, p. 50.
106. Ibid., Table 3, p. 52.
107. Ibid., Tables 7–8, p. 55.
108. Ibid., Table 5, p. 53.
109. See *Standard Eurobarometer* 47, Tables and Questions, Table 2.2 (Support for Current Issues), (Brussels: EU Commission, 1997).
110. *Standard Eurobarometer*, 47 (Brussels: EU Commission, 1997), p. B.18.

111. Ibid., Table 2.1 (Support for Current Issues), p. B.16.
112. Ibid., Tables and Questions, Table 2.1 (Support for Current Issues), p. B.16.
113. Ibid., Fig.5.1 (Fieldwork March–April 1997), p. 56.
114. Ibid., loc. cit.
115. *Standard Eurobarometer* 46, Fig. 4.1 (Fieldwork October–November 1996), p. 40.
116. Scores are based on means calculated by applying the coefficients 4,3,2 and 1 respectively to the categories lot of trust, some trust, not very much trust and no trust at all, which respondents chose. The mid-point is 2.50; below this negative answers predominate and above, positive ones. For full data see *Standard Eurobarometer* 46, Tables and Questions, Table 4.4 (Trust Among Nationalities), (Brussels: EU Commission, 1996), p. B.46.

5   Transatlantic Relations and European Security

1. Francis Fukuyama, 'The End of History', *The National Interest* (Summer 1989), No. 16, pp. 3–19.
2. Samuel P. Huntington, 'The Clash of Civilizations?' *Foreign Affairs*, Vol. 72 (3), Summer 1993, pp. 22–49.
3. It should be noted that a debate was already established on declinism amongst economists, IPE scholars, and economic historians. Paul Kennedy's work acted as a catalyst for the more general debate. For earlier work in the 'declinist' genre see, Charles P. Kindleberger, *The World in Depression, 1929–39* (Berkeley: University of California Press, 1973); Stephen Krasner, 'State Power and the Structure of International Trade', *World Politics*, 28 (3) (April 1976), pp. 317–47; George Modelski, 'The Long Cycle of Global Politics and the Nation-State', *Comparative Studies in Society and History*, Vol. 20 (2) (April 1978), pp. 214–35; and Mancur Olson, *The Rise and Decline of Nations* (New Haven: Yale University Press, 1982).
4. Paul Kennedy, *The Rise and Fall of the Great Powers: Economic Change and Military Conflict from 1500 to 2000* (New York: Random House, 1987), p. xxiii.
5. David P. Calleo, *Beyond American Hegemony: The Future of the Western Alliance* (New York: Basic Books, 1987). For a more recent argument in the 'declinist' tradition, see Donald W. White, *The American Century: The Rise and Decline of the United States as a World Power* (New Haven: Yale University Press, 1996).
6. Calleo, *Beyond Hegemony*, pp. 3–4.
7. See, for instance, Henry R. Nau, *The Myth of America's Decline* (New York: Oxford University Press, 1990); and Samuel P. Huntington, 'The U.S. – Decline or Renewal?', *Foreign Affairs*, Vol. 67 (2) (Winter 1988/89), pp. 76–96.
8. Joseph S. Nye, Jr., *Bound to Lead: The Change in the Nature of American Power* (New York: Basic Books, 1990), p. 261.
9. Joint Chiefs of Staff 1769/1 'United States Assistance to Other Countries from the Standpoint of National Security', 29 April 1947, quoted in John Lewis Gaddis, *The Long Peace: Inquiries into the History of the Cold War* (New York: Oxford University Press, 1987), p. 40.
10. See Samuel P. Huntington, *Foreign Affairs*, November/December 1996, p. 44 for an overview of the differences.

11. Address by President Clinton to the people of Detroit, *The Legacy of America's Leadership as We Enter the 21st Century*, 22 October 1996 (Washington DC: Department of State, 1996).
12. Ibid., (emphasis added).
13. Warren Christopher, 'America's Leadership, America's Opportunity', *Foreign Policy*, No. 98, Spring 1995, p. 8.
14. Strobe Talbott, 'Democracy and National Interest', *Foreign Affairs*, Vol. 75(6), November/December 1996, p. 63.
15. Barry M. Blechman, William J. Durch, David F. Gordon and Catherine Gwin with Todd Moss and Jolie M.F. Wood, *The Partnership Imperative: Maintaining American Leadership in a New Era* (Washington DC: Henry L. Stimson Center and the Overseas Development Council, 1997), p. 1.
16. Douglas Brinkley, 'Democratic Enlargement: The Clinton Doctrine', *Foreign Policy*, No. 106, Spring 1997, pp. 114–16. For an examination of the same theme see, Vincent A. Auger, 'Seeking "Simplicity of Statement": The Search for a New U.S. Foreign Policy Doctrine', *National Security Studies Quarterly*, Spring 1997, Vol. III (2), pp. 1–21.
17. Jacob Heilbrunn, 'Clothed Ambition: Warren Christopher', *The New Republic*, Vol. 208 (5) p. 25. See also Jurek Martin, 'Clinton's Foreign Policy', *The Financial Times*, 18 August 1994, p. 5; and 'William Jefferson Bonaparte', *The Economist*, 17 September 1994, p. 25.
18. *Strategic Assessment 1996: Instruments of U.S. Power* (Washington DC: National Defense University), pp. 96–9.
19. John M. Goshko, 'Reduced U.S. Role Outlined: But Soon Altered', *Washington Post*, 26 May 1993.
20. Executive summary text of PDD–25 may be found in *U.S. Department of State Dispatch*, Vol. 5 (20), 16 May 1994, pp. 318–21.
21. Arthur Schlesinger Jr., 'Back to the Womb?', *Foreign Affairs*, Vol. 74(4), July/August 1995, p. 7.
22. Strobe Talbott has made the interesting point that the criticism of the Clinton administration's emphasis on enhancing democracy overseas comes not only from isolationists but also from some internationalists who warn that 'a "crusade" on behalf of democracy will overstretch American resources and mire the United States in endless, debilitating brawls, often on the side of undeserving clients'. See 'Democracy and the National Interest', *Foreign Affairs*, Vol. 75(6), November/December 1996, pp. 47–64.
23. Ibid.
24. *United States Security Strategy for Europe and NATO*, (1996), p. 5.
25. See NATO Press Communiqué M–1 (91)44, 7 June 1991.
26. Philip H. Gordon, 'Does the WEU Have a Role?', *The Washington Quarterly*, Vol. 20 (1), Winter 1997, p. 131.
27. USECOM has deployed forces 51 times to 30 countries since the end of the Gulf War. The six operations referred to are PROVIDE COMFORT (N.Iraq, 1991–), SHARP GUARD (Adriatic, April-1993), DENY FLIGHT (Bosnia, April 1993–...), ABLE SENTRY (Former Yugoslav Republic of Macedonia, Spring 1993–), SUPPORT HOPE (Rwanda, June–September 1994).
28. See Raymond Seitz, 'America's Foreign Policy: From the Jaws of Victory', *The Economist*, 25 May 1995, pp. 21–3.

29. Ibid., loc. cit.
30. Martin Walker, 'China Preys on American Minds', *Guardian Weekly*, 6 April 1997, p. 6.
31. 'U.S. Census 1990', extracts in *United States Security Strategy for Europe and NATO* (Washington DC: Department of Defense, Office of International Security Affairs, 1996).
32. William Branigin, 'One in 10 Americans is Foreign-Born', *Guardian Weekly*, Vol. 156 (16), 20 April 1997, p. 15. The report also points out that the racial and ethnic make-up of the foreign born population has also changed strikingly. Nearly 85.8 percent of the foreign born who arrived before the 1970s were whites, that proportion dropped to 62.1 percent for the first six years of the 1990s. During the same period, the percentage of African-Americans more than doubled, to 8.7 percent, and the proportion of Asians and Pacific Islanders tripled to 28.6 percent. Hispanics (who may be of any race) accounted for 43 percent of newcomers since 1990 and 32.2 percent before 1970. The Census Bureau lists the current U.S. population as 84.2 percent white, 13.3 percent black, 1.6 percent Asian–Pacific Islander, and 7.4 percent classified as Hispanic.
33. For a contrasting view on this issue see Philip Gordon, 'Recasting the Alliance', *Survival*, Vol. 38(1), Spring 1996, pp. 32–58.
34. Ibid., p. 39.
35. Richard Halloran, 'The Rising East', *Foreign Policy*, No. 102, Spring 1996, p. 21.
36. Samuel P. Huntington, 'The West: Unique, Not Divided', *Foreign Affairs*, Vol. 75 (6), November/December 1996, p. 44.
37. Office of European Union and Regional Affairs, Bureau for European and Canadian Affairs, *US–European Union Relations*, 3 December 1996.
38. Ibid., loc. cit.
39. 'Strategic Assessment 1995' (INSS) quoted in *United States Security Strategy for Europe and NATO* (Washington DC: Department of Defense, Office of International Security Affairs, 1996).
40. Christoph Bertram, *Europe in the Balance: Securing the Peace Won in the Cold War* (Washington DC: Carnegie Endowment for International Peace, 1995) p. 3.
41. Sir Leon Brittan commented, 'It comes as no surprise to me that the first meeting you are holding should be with the representatives of the European Union. It comes as no surprise, but a great pleasure'. In Remarks by the Secretary of State Madeleine Albright, Dutch Foreign Minister Hans von Mierlo, and the Vice President of the European Commission, Sir Leon Brittan, *The U.S.–EU Ministerial*, Remarks to the Press, 28 January 1997 (Washington DC: Department of State, 1997).
42. *United States Security Strategy for Europe and NATO*, (1996) p. 15.
43. Ibid., p. 18.
44. James B. Steinberg, Director, Policy Planning Staff, U.S. Department of State, *Advancing NATO's Adaptation*, Remarks before the Atlantic Council of the United States, 13 June 1996 (Washington DC: Department of State, 1996).
45. *United States Security Strategy for Europe and NATO* (1996), p. 1.
46. Ibid., loc. cit.
47. Ibid., p. 2.
48. See, for instance, Charles Kupchan, 'Reviving the West', *Foreign Affairs*, May/June 1996, Vol. 75 (3), pp. 92–105; and Simon Serfaty, 'America and

Europe Beyond Bosnia', *Washington Quarterly*, Vol. 19(3), Summer 1996, pp. 31–44.

49. Charles Kupchan, 'Reviving the West', *Foreign Affairs*, Vol. 75, No. 3, May/June 1996, p. 94.

50. Margaret Ball, *NATO and the European Union Movement* (London: Stevens and Sons Ltd., 1959), p. 402.

51. For a full discussion of the Helms-Burton legislation from a European perspective, see Kinka Gerke, 'The Transatlantic Rift over Cuba, The Damage is Done', *The International Spectator*, Vol. XXXII(2), April–June 1997, pp. 27–52.

52. Office of the Spokesman, U.S. Department of State, *US–European Union Cooperation*, Remarks by Secretary of State Christopher, Italian Foreign Minister Susanna Agnelli, and Vice President of the European Commission, Sir Leon Brittan. 11 April 1996.

53. *Joint U.S./EU Action Plan*, 3 December 1995, (Washington DC: U.S. Department of State, 1996).

54. *The New Transatlantic Agenda: Update*, Prepared by the Bureau of European and Canadian Affairs (Washington DC: U.S. Department of State, 4 February 1997).

55. See Simon Duke, *The Burdensharing Debate: A Reassessment* (London: Macmillan, 1993).

56. Mark M. Nelson, 'Joint Foreign Policy Remains Distant Dream for European Union', *The Wall Street Journal*, 26 September 1996.

57. Ibid., loc. cit.

58. Stuart Eizenstat, 'Why Europe Must Forge Stronger Security Links', *Financial Times*, 2 December 1995, quoted in Terrence R. Guay, 'The European Union's Intergovernmental Conference: Pressures for a Common Defence Policy', *National Security Studies Quarterly*, Spring 1997, Vol. III (2), p. 51.

59. Lionel Barber, 'Europe Urged to End Reliance on U.S'., *Financial Times*, 25 May 1993, quoted in Terrence R. Guay, p. 52.

60. Roy Denman, 'A Common European Foreign Policy? Not Yet, But In Time', *International Herald Tribune*, 6 November 1996.

61. *Communiqué of the North Atlantic Council*, Brussels, 18 December 1990, Para. 5.

62. NATO Press Communiqué M–1 (94)3, *Declaration of the Heads of State and Government Participating in the Meeting of the North Atlantic Council*, Brussels, 11 January 1994.

63. Ibid.

64. Ibid., Para. 6.

65. Ibid., Para. 9 (emphasis added).

66. *Statement of the President* (Washington DC: The White House, Office of the Press Secretary), 6 September 1996 (emphasis added).

67. *United States Security Strategy for Europe and NATO*, (1996), p. 35.

68. Ibid., loc. cit.

69. *United States Security Strategy for Europe and NATO*, (1996), p. 26.

70. Press Briefing by National Security Advisor, Anthony Lake and Director for Strategic Plans and Policy for the Joint Chiefs of Staff, Lieutenant General Wesley Clark, 5 May 1994, *U.S. Department of State Dispatch*, 16 May 1994, Vol. 5(20), p. 319.

71. Lionel Barber, 'Reinvigorating the Transatlantic Alliance', *Agence Europe*, February 1996, pp. 21–2.

72. Special Meeting of the North Atlantic Council, Brussels, 10 January 1994 (Brussels: NATO Information Service), Opening Statement.
73. 'A Russian–German Axis?', *Foreign Report*, 20 January 1994.
74. Arguably this happened in May 1994 with the passage of President Clinton's PDD–25 which emphasised that U.S. participation in peacekeeping would henceforth be more 'selective and effective' and that one of the main criteria for involvement would be whether issues of vital national interest were involved.
75. WEU Kirchberg Declaration, 9 May 1994, *Atlantic Document* No. 85, Para. 3.
76. Ibid., loc. cit.
77. North Atlantic Council, Istanbul, Ministerial Meeting of the NAC, *Final Communiqué*, 9 June 1994, Para. 2.
78. WEU Council of Ministers, *Noordwijk Declaration*, 14 November 1994, Para. 20.
79. *Western European Union, The Future of European Security and Preparations for Maastricht II*, Doc. 1458, Report submitted on behalf of the Political Committee by Mrs. Aguiar, Rapporteur, to the Assembly of the WEU, 16 May 1995, p. 25.
80. *Atlantic News*, No. 2772, 6 December 1995.
81. G. Wyn Rees, *The Western European Union at the Crossroads: Between Trans-Atlantic Solidarity and European Integration* (Boulder, Colorado: Westview, 1998), p. 83.
82. *Final Communiqué, Ministerial Meeting of the North Atlantic Council, Berlin*, 3 June 1996, Press Communiqué M–NAC–1 (96) 63.
83. *Fact Sheet: NATO Adaptation/Enlargement*, Bureau of European and Canadian Affairs, 12 February 1997 (Washington DC: Department of State, 1997) (Emphasis added).
84. *Fact Sheet: NATO Adaptation/Enlargement.*
85. *Ministerial Meeting of the North Atlantic Council, Berlin*, 3 June 1996, Para. 7.
86. *Fact Sheet: NATO Adaptation/Enlargement*, (Emphasis added).
87. *Ministerial Meeting of the North Atlantic Council, Berlin*, 3 June 1996, Para. 8.
88. James B. Steinberg, *Advancing NATO's Adaptation*, Remarks by the Director, Policy Planning Staff, U.S. Department of State, before the Atlantic Council of the US, 13 June 1996 (Washington DC: U.S. Department of State, 1996).
89. David S. Huntington, 'A Peacekeeping Role for the Western European Union', in Abram Chayes and Antonia Handler Chayes (eds), *Preventing Conflict in the Post-Communist World: Mobilizing International and Regional Organizations* (Washington DC: The Brookings Institution, 1996), p. 437.
90. On this topic see, Jim Eberle, 'NATO's higher command', in Lawrence Freedman (ed.), *Military Power in Europe* (London: Macmillan, 1990).
91. Yves Boyer, 'WEU: A French Perspective', in Anne Deighton (ed.), *Western European Union 1954–1997: Defence, Security, Integration* (Oxford: St Antony's College, 1997), p. 68.
92. Anthony Cragg, 'Internal Adaptation: Reshaping NATO for the challenges of tomorrow', *NATO Review*, Vol. 45 (4) July–August 1997, p. 33.
93. 'War over Naples', *The Economist*, Vol. 341 (7994), 30 November 1996, p. 34.
94. Jospeh Fitchett, 'U.S. Tried to Fend Off Paris on a NATO Post', *International Herald Tribune*, 4 December 1996, p. 8.
95. Pauline Neville-Jones, 'Dayton, IFOR and Alliance Relations in Bosnia', *Survival*, Vol. 38(4), p. 50.

96. U.S. non-combat forces served under a Turkish commander in Somalia, a Swede in Macedonia, and a Canadian in Bosnia.
97. *United States Security Strategy for Europe and NATO*, (1996), p. 20 (emphasis added).
98. For details of the respective command positions and attached responsibilities see *NATO Handbook* (Brussels: NATO Office of Information and Press, 1995), pp. 168–87.
99. Stanley Sloan, 'Combined Joint Task Force and New Missions for NATO', *CRS Report for Congress*, 94–249S, 17 March 1994, pp. CRS–5–6.
100. For an excellent overview of America's post-cold war use of military force see Thomas Halverson, 'Disengagement by Stealth: The Emerging Gap Between America's Rhetoric and the Reality of Future European Conflicts', Lawrence Freedman (ed.), *Military Intervention in European Conflicts* (Oxford: Blackwells Publishers, 1994), pp. 76–94.

6 Transatlantic and 'Euro' options – Yugoslavia

1. Article 2(7) of the UN Charter which states, 'Nothing contained in the present Charter shall authorize the United Nations to intervene in matters which are essentially within the domestic jurisdiction of any state or shall require the Members to submit such matters to settlement under the present Charter'.
2. Quoted in David Buchan, *Europe: The Strange Superpower* (Brookfield: Dartmouth, 1993), p. 67.
3. In the preceding month a majority of the *Bundestag* had supported recognition of Croatia and Slovenia.
4. David Buchan, *Europe: The Strange Superpower*, p. 68.
5. Catherine McArdle Kelleher, *The Future of European Security: An Interim Assessment* (Washington DC: Brookings Institution, 1995), p. 117.
6. Laura Silber and Allan Little, *The Death of Yugoslavia* (New York: Penguin Books, 1995), p. 221.
7. Ibid., p. 222.
8. David Schoenbaum and Elizabeth Pond, *The German Question and Other German Questions* (New York: St Martin's Press in association with St Antony's College, Oxford, 1996), p. 190.
9. Peter Viggo Jakobsen, 'Myth-making and Germany's Unilateral Recognition of Croatia and Slovenia', *European Security*, Vol. 4(3), Autumn 1995, p. 404.
10. Wolfgang Krieger, 'Towards a Gaullist Germany? Some lessons from the Yugoslav Crisis', *World Policy Journal*, Spring 1994, p. 32.
11. George Ross, 'After Maastricht: Hard Choices for Europe', *World Policy Journal*, Vol. 9(3), Summer 1992, p. 497.
12. Andreas G. Kintis, 'The EU's Foreign Policy and War in Former Yugoslavia', in Martin Holland (ed.), *Common Foreign and Security Policy: The Record and Reforms* (London: Pinter, 1997), p. 155.
13. WEU Council of Ministers, *Ostend Declaration*, 19 November 1996, Section III, Para. 21.
14. The operations grew in scope and were renamed Operations Maritime Guard and Sharp Fence in November 1992.

15. Quoted in Brigitte Sauerwein, 'WEU Closing in on NATO', *International Defense Review*, Vol. 26 (3), 1993, p. 187.
16. Maynard Glitman, 'US Policy in Bosnia: Rethinking a Flawed Approach', *Survival*, Vol. 38, no. 4, p. 73.
17. The WEU Ministers noted 'with regret' the U.S. measures to modify its participation with respect to the enforcement of the arms control embargo in the combined WEU/NATO Operation Sharp Guard.
18. Reuter, *Agence Europe*, 'EC President Scalfaro stresses the need for "Direct and Effective" links between EC and NATO', 6 March 1993.
19. Willem van Eeklen, *Debating European Security 1948–98* (The Hague: Sdu Pubishers, 1998), p. 169.
20. For a comprehensive examination of this issue see, Panos Tsakaloyannis and Dimitris Bourantonis, 'The European Union's Common Foreign and Security Policy and the Reform of the Security Council', *European Foreign Affairs Review*, (2) 1997, pp. 197–209.
21. Bhaskar Menon, 'Making and Keeping the Peace', in John Tessitore and Susan Woolfson (eds), *A Global Agenda: Issues Before the 51st General Assembly of the United Nations* (New York: Rowman and Littlefield Publishers, Inc.), pp. 15–16.
22. NATO Press release (98)18, *Statement by the North Atlantic Council on the Continuation of a NATO-led Multinational Military Presence in Bosnia and Herzegovina*, 20 February 1998.
23. For an overview of SFOR's responsibilities see, General Wesley Clark, 'Building a lasting peace in Bosnia and Herzegovina, *NATO Review*, Vol. 46(1), Spring 1998, pp. 19–22.
24. *Agence Europe*, 27 February 1998, No. 7169, p. 2.
25. Ibid., loc. cit.
26. Ibid., loc. cit (emphasis added).
27. Quoted in G. Wyn Rees, *The Western European Union at the Crossroads: Between Trans-Atlantic Solidarity and European Integration* (Boulder, Colorado: Westview Press, 1998), p. 84.
28. *Crisis News Centre '97*, Direct from Tirana, 9 March 1997, Available on the Web at ⟨http://www.albania.co.uk/crisis⟩.
29. Hanspeter Neuhold, 'The Common Foreign and Security Policy: A Poor Record and Meagre Prospects', *CFSP Forum*, 3/97, p. 4.
30. Ibid., loc. cit.
31. *Agence Europe*, 13 May 1998, No. 7220, p. 3.
32. *Agence Europe*, 9 May 1998, No. 7218, p. 2.
33. Carl Bildt, 'Déjà vu in Kosovo', *Financial Times*, 9 June 1998, p. 12.
34. Bosnia-Herzegovina, Croatia, Macedonia, Montenegro, Serbia and Slovenia.
35. Roughly 1.8 million Albanians live in Kosovo.
36. For instance, on 28 September 1998 diplomats were shown the bodies of 15 ethnic Albanian men, women and children who were shot in the back of the head and mutilated at a makeshift camp in a heavily wooded section of the Drenica region, west of Pristina. Serbs claimed that at least 39 Serbs were tortured, mutilated and killed in early September near Glodjane.
37. Aleska Djilas, 'Imagining Kosovo', *Foreign Affairs*, Vol. 77(5), September/October 1998, p. 127.
38. Statement by US Ambassador to the United Nations, Bill Richardson, to the UN Security Council on Kosovo Resolution, 31 March 1998.

39. S/RES/1160, 31 March 1998.
40. The Office of the Prosecutor of the International Tribunal was established by resolution 827 of 25 May 1993 to address war crimes in Bosnia-Herzegovina as well as Rwanda at a later date.
41. *Determined Falcon* was assembled at four days' notice and involved 85 aircraft from 13 air forces.
42. Alexander Nicoll, 'NATO Breaks its chains', *Financial Times*, 18 June 1998, p. 14.
43. The comments also applied to the former Yugoslav Republic of Macedonia and Cyprus. See *Agence Europe*, 19 March 1998, No. 7183, p. 2.
44. UNPREDEP is the UN prevention force in Skopje.
45. S/RES/1199, 23 September 1998.
46. Resoftlinks, 7 October 1998, http:///news.resoftlinks.com/981007.
47. Associated Press, 8 October 1998.
48. NATO Press statement, 'Statement by the Secretary General following the ACTWARN decision', 24 September 1998, Vilamoura, Portugal.
49. Press Conference, Secretary of Defense William Cohen and U.S. Chairman of the Joint Chiefs of Staff General Henry S. Shelton, NATO Defence Ministers Meeting, Vilamoura, Portugal, 24 September 1998.
50. The Russian Foreign Minister, Igor Ivanov, told the press on 6 October 1998 that Russia would veto any move to approve NATO strikes on Yugoslavia by the Security Council.
51. As note 47.
52. *Resoftlinks*, 23 September 1998, http://news.resoftlinks.com.
53. Russia voted in favour of resolution 1199 but this was based on the understanding that the Security Council was introducing no measures of force.
54. *Financial Times*, 8 October 1998, p. 8.
55. *The Economist*, 17 October 1998, p. 33.
56. *The Economist*, 24 October 1998, p. 39.
57. *Financial Times*, 19 November 1998, p. 2.
58. According to *The Economist*, 1 October 1998, radical elements of the KLA were behind the September murder of the 'defence minister' in Ibrahim Rugova's unrecognised ' government', p. 33.
59. For instance, the bodies of two Serb policemen were found by U.S. observers in Malisevo on 9 November 1998 in what was apparently a retaliatory killing for the earlier deaths of five KLA members.
60. North Atlantic Council, Press Release (98)130, 19 November 1998.
61. Carl Bildt, *Financial Times*, 9 June 1998, p.12.
62. For a good overview of the EU and conflict prevention see Reinhardt Rummel, 'The CFSP's Conflict Prevention Policy', in Martin Holland (ed.), *Common Foreign and Security Policy: The Record and Reforms* (London: Pinter, 1997), pp. 105–20.

7 Progress towards Defining the Common Defence Policy

1. *Agence Europe*, No. 7216, 7 May 1998, p. 1.
2. WEU Declaration I, *The Role of the WEU and its relations with the European Union and the Atlantic Alliance*, annexed to the Treaty on European Union

(Luxembourg: Office for Official Publications of the European Communities, 1992), Section A&B.

3. *Petersberg Declaration*, Section I, 'On WEU and European Security', 19 June 1992, Paras. 1–3.
4. From 1999 the WEU and EU Presidencies will be held by the same country for the first six months of the year.
5. Ibid., Section II, Para. 3.
6. Michael O'Hanlon, 'Transforming NATO: The Role of European Forces', *Survival*, Vol. 39(3), Autumn 1997, p. 5.
7. Ibid., loc. cit.
8. Ibid., p. 13.
9. *Petersberg Declaration*, Section II, Para. 8.
10. Ibid., Section II, Para. 9.
11. Under an agreement signed in January 1993 between France, Germany and NATO, French contributions to the Eurocorps could come under NATO *operational command* in a crisis. Certain specific conditions applied however to the control arrangements, such as the need for Franco-German agreement on the release of forces to the Eurocorps only after France had agreed to a mission plan.
12. *North Atlantic Council, Declaration of the Heads of State and Government participating in the Meeting of the North Atlantic Council held at NATO Headquarters, Brussels,* 10–11 January 1994 (Brussels: North Atlantic Treaty Organization, Press Communiqué, M–1 (94(3)), Para. 3.
13. WEU Council of Ministers, *Lisbon Declaration*, 15 May 1995, Para. 5.
14. WEU Council of Ministers, *Ostend Declaration*, 19 November 1996, p. 1.
15. Roger Palin, *Adelphi Paper 294*, p. 55 (emphasis added).
16. 'Jane's Defence Weekly Interview: José Cutileiro, Secretary-General of WEU', *Jane's Defence Weekly*, Vol. 27 (18), 7 May 1997, available on the Web at ⟨http://www.janes.com/public/defence/interviews⟩.
17. Colonel Bernard Vezinhet, Head of Logistic/Movements and Finance Section of the WEU Planning Cell, *Symposium on European cooperation on the procurement of defence equipment*, Munich 1–2 October 1997 (Paris: Assembly of the Western European Union, 1997). Colonel Vezinhet notes that the Plans section has a staff of eight whose tasks are to monitor FAWEU, joint defence planning with NATO and liaison with Eurolongterm (evaluation of military requirements over a 10 year span) and WEAG, p. 62.
18. *NATO Brief*, No. 6 (1990), p. 6, quoted in Werner J. Feld, *The Future of European Security and Defense Policy* (Boulder: Lynne Rienner Publishers, 1993), p. 9.
19. WEU Council of Ministers, *Ostend Declaration*, 19 November 1996, p. 1.
20. *Agence Europe*, No. 7193, 2 April 1998, p. 2.
21. General Pierre Forterre, Commander of the European Corps, at a symposium on *European cooperation on the procurement of defence equipment*, Munich 1–2 October 1997 (Paris: Assembly of the Western European Union, 1997), p. 59.
22. Simon Duke, *The New European Security Disorder*, p. 223.
23. For details of the December compromise see, Robert J. Art, 'Why Western Europe Needs the United States and NATO', *Political Science Quarterly*, Volume 111 (1), Spring 1996, p. 29.
24. 'US, Bonn Clash over Pact with France', *Wall Street Journal*, 27 May 1992, p. A9.

25. Belgium and Spain signed the SACEUR Agreement of January 1993 and Luxembourg announced its intention to do so shortly thereafter in May 1994.
26. General Pierre Forterre, p. 59.
27. Ibid., p. 58.
28. Quoted in Andreas Kintis, 'The EU and the War in Former Yugoslavia', in Martin Holland (ed.), *Common Foreign and Security Policy: The Record and Reforms* (London: Pinter, 1997), p. 161.
29. Michael O'Hanlon, p. 9.
30. *A European Intelligence Policy*, Assembly of the Western European Union, Doc. 1517, 13 May 1996, submitted on behalf of the Defence Committee by Mr Baumel, Chairman and Rapporteur, para. xxvii.
31. François de Rose, 'A Future Perspective for the Alliance', *NATO Review*, Vol. 43(4), July 1995, Web edition at ⟨www.nato.int/docu/review/articles/9504-2.htm⟩.
32. *A European Intelligence Policy*, para. xxviii.
33. Ibid., Part III 'Is the CJTF concept the ultimate solution for Europe's intelligence deficiencies?', Paras. liv–lv.
34. Ibid., para. xxxix.
35. Helios 1 imagery was used from 17 April 1993 following the signature of a Memorandum of Understanding between the WEU and the three operating countries, France, Italy and Spain.
36. *A European Intelligence Policy*, Section IV. 'Towards a European observation satellite system', para. lxi.
37. The Secretary-General currently employs 101 personnel while the Satellite Centre accounts for 64. In terms of the 1998 budget they account, respectively, for 322.8 million Belgian francs and 356.3 million Belgian francs respectively, out of a total budget of 1319.9 million.
38. *Preliminary Conclusions on the Formulation of a Common European Defence Policy*, WEU 1994, Part II, 'WEU's Operational Role', Para. 32, at com94–184 at marvin.nc3a.nato.int
39. François Heisbourg, 'La politique de défense à l'aube d'un nouveau mandat présidentiel', *Politique Étrangère*, No. 1, 1995, p. 74.
40. 'Rühe stirs weapons controversy', *Financial Times*, 26 November 1996, p. 3.
41. Ralph Atkins and David Owen, 'France drops satellite project', *Financial Times*, 11–12 April 1998, p. 2.
42. 'Britain withdraws from military satellite project', *Financial Times*, 13 August 1998, p. 1.
43. *A European Intelligence Policy*, para. xlv.
44. Ibid., para. lvii.
45. Ibid., para. lxxxv.
46. Ibid., para. lxxxvi.
47. *Agence Europe*, No. 7195, 4 April 1998, p. 2.
48. WEU Council of Ministers, *Ostend Declaration*, p. 1.
49. Ibid., para. xcii.
50. Ibid., para. xcvii.
51. The 1996 budget was in the region of $40 million. Salaries and allowances for attached military personnel are paid by the core group outside the WEU budget. Figures in, 'Jane's Defence Weekly Interview: José Cutileiro, Secretary-General of WEU', *Jane's Defence Weekly*, Vol. 27(18), 7 May 1997.

52. For a detailed discussions of this theme see Jörg Monar, 'The Financial Dimensions of the CFSP', in Martin Holland (ed.), *Common Foreign and Security Policy: The Record and the Reforms* (London: Pinter, 1997), pp. 34–52; and Thomas Hagleitner, 'Financing the CFSP: A Step towards Communitarisation or Institutional Deadlock?', *CFSP Forum*, 2.95, pp. 6–7.

53. Thomas Hagleitner, *CFSP Forum*, 2.95, p. 7.

54. See Simon Duke, *The Burdensharing Debate: A Reassessment* (London: Macmillan, 1993).

55. Center for Strategic and International Studies, ed., *Defense in the late 1990s: avoiding the train wreck* (Washington DC: CSIS, 1995), p. 12.

56. Ethan Kapstein, 'Towards an American arms trade monopoly', *Foreign Affairs*, Vol. 73(3), May/June 1994, pp. 13–19.

57. FINABEL'S principal task was to promote interoperability amongst the land forces of the participant countries. See Willem van Eekelen, *Debating European Security 1948–1998* (The Hague: Sdu Publishers, 1998), p. 282.

58. Alessandro Politi, 'Western European Union and Europe's Defence Industry', in Anne Deighton (ed.), *Western European Union 1954–1997: Defence, Security, Integration* (Oxford: St Antony's College, 1997), p. 135.

59. See *SIPRI Annual 1996: World Armaments and Disarmament* (Oxford: Oxford University Press/SIPRI, 1996).

60. Peter Van Ham, 'The Prospects for a European Security and Defence Identity', *European Security*, Vol. 4(4), Winter 1995, p. 539.

61. In fact the situation is more absurd than Van Ham indicates since there are *ten* combat tank manufacturers in Europe, compared to *two* in the U.S.

62. 'Raytheon's Rise', *The Economist*, January 18–24, 1997, p. 69.

63. Ibid., loc. cit.

64. Airbus currently involves Aerospatiale, BAe, Dasa and Casa.

65. A more realistic comparison though would consider not just the size of combined defence budgets but the amounts spent on research and development and the proportion of expenditure which may be recovered through arms sales. In general, the European NATO members tend to spend more on costs associated directly or indirectly with personnel and not as much on research and development. The procurement sector of the US budget is approximately twice that of combined European budgets. This would logically suggest that changes not just to, but also within, defence budgets should be considered.

66. Deputy Director-General of Aerospatiale, Jean-Louis Fache, *Symposium on European Cooperation on the Procurement of Defence Equipment*, Munich, 1–2 October 1997, p. 74.

67. For a brief but detailed overview of the developments in the US arms industry and their implications for European security, see Jens van Scherpenberg, 'Transatlantic competition and European defence industries: a new look at the trade–defence linkage', *International Affairs*, Vol. 73 (1), 1997, pp. 99–122.

68. Lord Levene, Former Head of Defence Procurement, UK Ministry of Defence, *Symposium on European Cooperation on the Procurement of Defence Equipment*, Munich, 1–2 October 1997, p. 35.

69. Luís María de Puig, President of the WEU Assembly, Ibid., p. 15.

70. Jacques Santer, 'The European Union and the world in 1998', The Inaugural City Europe Lecture – Guildhall, London, 29 January 1998, at

⟨http://europa.eu.int/comm/dg 1a/01-98/speech⟩⟩. The Commission had, as Santer observed, previously outlined in detail the challenges facing the European defence industries and reached the conclusions mentioned above. See, *The Challenges facing the European defence-related industry – a contribution for action at European level*, COM (96) Final, 24 January (Brussels: European Commission, 1996).

71. 'Conclusions of the Presidency', 31/31, *Bulletin* EU 6–1997.
72. *The Economist*, 'Global Defence Industry Survey: Divided continent', June 14–20, 1997, p. 11.
73. Ibid., loc. cit.
74. Graham Woodcock, Secretary-General, EDIG, *Symposium on European Cooperation on the Procurement of Defence Equipment*, p. 43.
75. Ibid., General Schlieper, Chairman WEAG National Armaments Directors, p. 51.
76. Article 223 (b) reads: 'Any Member State may take such measures as it considers necessary for the protection of the essential interests of its security which are connected with the production of or trade in arms, munitions and war material; such measures shall not adversely affect the conditions of competition in the common market regarding products which are not intended for specifically military purposes'.
77. Article 223 was modified thus, 'The progressive framing of a common defence policy will be supported, as Member States consider appropriate, by cooperation between them in the field of armaments', *Treaty of Amsterdam*, Article J.7(1).
78. *The Economist*, 'Global Defence Industry Survey', 14–20 June 1997, p. 13.
79. Wolfgang Piller, Member of the Board of Management, External Relations and Governmental and Political Affairs, Daimler-Benz Aerospace AG, Germany, in *Symposium on European Cooperation on the Procurement of Defence Equipment*, Munich, 1–2 October 1997 (Paris: Assembly of the WEU), p. 79.
80. Information from Alexander Nicoll, 'Eurofighter missile bids start in UK', *Financial Times*, 29 May 1998, p. 6.
81. Alexander Nicoll, 'Eurofighter project may unite military aircraft sector', *Financial Times*, 7 July 1998, p. 1.
82. EADC, as envisaged at the time of the July meeting, would ring together BAe (UK), Dasa (Germany), Aerospatiale and Dassault (France), and interests of Finmeccanica (Italy), Casa (Spain) and Saab (Sweden).
83. Alexander Nicoll, 'Eurofighter tempts Norway in bid to win key contract', *Financial Times*, 23 July 1998, p. 6.
84. 'Britain opts out of Europe', *The Economist*, 23 January 1999, pp. 72–4.
85. See Timothy J. Birch and John H. Crotts, 'European Defense Integration: National Interests, National Sensitivities', in Alan W. Cafruny and Glenda G. Rosenthal, *The State of the European Community: The Maastricht Debates and Beyond*, Vol. 2 (Harlow, Essex: Lynne Rienner Publishers, 1993), pp. 265–81.
86. Quoted by Colonel Bernard Vezinhet, in *Symposium on European Cooperation on the Procurement of Defence Equipment*, pp. 63–4.
87. Ibid., p. 64.
88. Rear Admiral Guillermo Leira, NATO Director of Armaments Planning, Programmes and Policy, in *Symposium on European Cooperation on the Procurement of Defence Equipment*, p. 66.

89. Report published June 1998.
90. The future tense is used since the conditions for incorporating the WEAO under the WEAG are not present yet. In recognition of this France, Germany, Italy and the United Kingdom established a quadrilateral development and procurement structure (OCCAR) in November 1996 as a step towards the eventual formation of a European Armaments Agency.
91. Mr de Puig, (President of the Assembly of the WEU) in, *Symposium on European Cooperation on the Procurement of Defence Equipment*, Munich, 1–2 October 1997 (Paris: Assembly of the WEU), p. 14.
92. All thirteen European NATO members are WEAO members.
93. WEU Council of Ministers, *Ostend Declaration*, 19 November 1996, Section VI, Para. 32.
94. The European Defence Industries Group consists of representatives of all member states of the WEAG, plus Sweden and Finland, who have observer status.
95. Alexander Nicoll and David Owen, 'European defence consolidation accelerates', *Financial Times*, 21 April 1998, p. 1.
96. EFTA was founded, with Britain as a founder member, as a less restrictive version of the EEC. It appealed to the minimalist free-trade principles of the Member States. The other members were Austria, Denmark, Norway, Portugal, Sweden and Switzerland.
97. Report of the European Commission, 'The Challenge of Enlargement', *Europe Documents*, No. 1790, 3 July 1992.
98. See, for example, M.Rosch, 'Switzerland's Security Policy in Transition', *NATO Review*, No. 6, 1993; and A. Mock, 'Austria's Role in the New Europe', *NATO Review*, 1995.
99. Kaj Sundberg, Former Ambassador of Sweden to Belgium, 'The New European Security Architecture: A Swedish Perspective', *NATO Review*, Vol. 39(3), June 1991, Web edition at ⟨www.nato.int/docu/review/articles/9103-3.htm⟩.
100. Surya P. Subedi, 'The Common Foreign and Security Policy of the European Union and Neutrality: Towards Co-Existence?', *Netherlands International Law Review*, XLII, 1995, pp. 408, 411.
101. *WEU Council of Ministers, Preliminary Conclusions on the Formulation of a Common European Defence Policy*, Noordwijk, 14 November 1994, p. Section II, Para. 6.
102. 'Europe and the Challenge of Enlargement', Commission Report, Supplement to the Conclusions of the European Council in Lisbon, *Europe Documents*, No. 1790, 3 July 1992, p. 2.
103. It was also agreed at Corfu that expansion should include Malta and Cyprus.
104. Petersberg Declaration, June 1992, Section II, Para. 3.
105. Ibid., Section 7.
106. Kirchberg Declaration, 9 May 1994, *Document on a Status of Association with WEU*. The category 'associate partnership' should not be confused with 'associate membership' which applies generally to all of those who are members of NATO but not of the WEU (Iceland, Norway and Turkey). Under the Maastricht Declaration of 10 December 1991, 'other European member States of NATO were invited to become members of WEU in a way which would give them the possibility to participate fully in the activities

of WEU'. See, 'Document on Associate Membership' agreed to at the Ministerial Council in Rome on 20 November 1992.

107. WEU Council of Ministers, *Madrid Declaration*, 14 November 1995, Para. 21.
108. Ibid., Section III, Paras. A–B.
109. Kirchberg Declaration, Part III, Declaration following from the 'Documents of Associate Membership' of 20 November 1992, 9 May 1994 (Paris: Western European Union, 1994).
110. It should though be noted that in the event of either/and observers or associate partners participating in a WEU operation, they would be asked to contribute to its costs.
111. *Communiqué of the Meeting of the North Atlantic Council, Berlin*, 3 June 1996, M–NACC–1(96)64.
112. WEU Council of Ministers, *WEU Contribution to the European Union Intergovernmental Conference of 1996*, Madrid, 14 November 1995, Section 1.A Para. 28.
113. Western European Union, Declaration II, Annexed to the Treaty on European Union, 11 December 1991 (Luxembourg: Office for the Official Publications of the European Communities, 1992).
114. Ibid., Para. 18.
115. North Atlantic Council, Brussels, January 1994. Annex.
116. North Atlantic Council, Communiqué issued by the Ministerial Meeting of the North Atlantic Council, NATO Headquarters, Brussels, 1 December 1994, Para. 5. Text may be found in *NATO Review*, No. 1, January 1995, pp. 26–8.
117. Dmitri Trenin, 'Avoiding a New Confrontation with NATO', *NATO Review*, Vol. 44, No. 3, May 1996, p. 17.
118. *Agence Europe*, No. 7267, 20/21 July 1998, p. 6.
119. *The Economist*, 1 August 1998, p. 14.
120. *Agence Europe*, No. 7267, 20/21 July 1998, p. 7.
121. *Agence Europe*, No. 7271, 27/28 July 1998, p. 2.
122. *Agence Europe*, No. 7220, 13 May 1998, p. 3.
123. Willem van Eekelen, 'WEU Prepares Way for New Mission', *NATO Review*, Vol. 41. No. 5, October 1993, p. 20.
124. *Livre Blanc sur la Défense*, Ministère de la Défense (Paris, Service d'Information et de Relations Publiques des Armées, février 1994), p. 40.
125. Robert Graham, 'French Armed Forces face shake-up', *Financial Times*, 8 July 1998, p. 3.
126. *Statement on Defence Estimates*, Secretary of State for Defence, Cmnd. 2550 (London: HMSO, 1994), pp. 2–9.
127. *White Paper on the Security of the Federal Republic of Germany and the situation and future of the Bundeswehr* (Bonn: Federal Ministry of Defence, 1994), p. 40.
128. Klaus Kinkel, 'Peacekeeping Missions: Germany can now play its part', *NATO Review*, Vol. 42, No. 5, October 1994, p. 7.
129. For an in-depth examination of this theme see Roberta Haar, *Explaining Germany's and Japan's Reticence to Assume Regional Security and Political Leadership Roles Befitting their Economic Status in the Post-Cold War Era*, August 1998 (Unpublished Ph.D dissertation, The Pennsylvania State University).
130. Quoted in Robert P. Grant, 'France's New Relationship with NATO', *Survival*, Vol. 38 (1), Spring 1996, p. 58.

131. Charles Millon, 'France and the Renewal of the Atlantic Alliance', *NATO Review*, Vol. 44, No. 3, May 1996, pp. 13–14.
132. For instance, Peter Tarnoff, Under Secretary of State for Political Affairs in the State Department, made a controversial speech to reporters in 1993 announcing that the US no longer has the leverage, the influence or the inclination to use force in every crisis. In spite of hasty contradictions by Warren Christopher, what became known as the 'Tarnoff Doctrine' was seen by European capitals as a retreat by the US from active leadership and underscored the need for a coherent European foreign and security policy identity.
133. WEU Council of Ministers, *WEU Contribution to the European Union Intergovernmental Conference of 1996*, Madrid, 19 November 1995, Section C Para. 39.
134. WEU Council of Ministers, *Madrid Declaration*, 14 November 1995, Section VI Para. 27.
135. Since Iceland has no indigenous military forces it is discounted.
136. Jonathan Eyal, 'Defence on the Cheap', *Financial Times*, 9 July 1998, p. 9.

8   Conclusion

1. Robin Niblett, 'The European Disunion: Competing Visions of Integration', *The Washington Quarterly*, Winter 1997, Vol. 20(1), p. 107.
2. Anne Deighton (ed.), *Western European Union 1954–97: Defence, Security, Integration* (Oxford: St Antony's College, 1997), p. 169.
3. Philip Gordon, 'Does Western European Union have a Role?', in Deighton (ed.), p. 109.
4. The new agencies, which were designed to assist the Council and were operationalised in January 1986, are the Agency for the Study of Arms Control and Disarmament Questions, the Agency for the Study of Security and Defence questions and the Agency for the development of co-operation in the field of armaments.
5. John Gerard Ruggie, 'Consolidating the European Pillar: The Key to NATO's Future', *The Washington Quarterly*, Vol. 20(1), Winter 1997, p. 115.
6. Ibid., loc. cit.
7. Philip Gordon, 'Does the WEU Have a Role?', *The Washington Quarterly*, Vol. 20(1), Winter 1997, p. 126.
8. *Report of the Assembly of the WEU: The Future of European Security and the preparation of Maastricht II* – reply to the fortieth annual report of the Council, 16 May 1995, Doc. 1458, p. 2.
9. Deighton, p. 174.
10. 'Introduction: Actors and actions', Christopher Hill and William Wallace, in Christopher Hill (ed.), *The Actors in Europe's Foreign Policy* (London: Routledge, 1996), p. 5. The capability-expectations gap is explored more fully in Christopher Hill, 'The Capabilty-Expectations Gap, or Conceptualizing Europe's Inernational Role', *Journal of Common Market Studies*, No. 3, September 1993, pp. 305–28.
11. Christopher Hill, 'Closing the capabilities-expectations gap?', in John Peterson and Helene Sjursen (eds), *A Common Policy for Europe?* (London: Routledge, 1998), p. 29.

12. *Treaty of Amsterdam Amending the Treaty on European Union, The Treaties Establishing the European Communities and Certain Related Acts* (Luxembourg: Office for Official Publications of the European Communities, 1997), Art. J.1.

13. Alan Osborn, 'UK assumed EU presidency', *Europe*, December/January 1997, p. 11.

14. *UK Presidency: Half Time Report*, ⟨http://presid.fco.uk/achievements/⟩.

15. A measure of how divisive was to emerge after the expiry of Britain's presidency when the Conservative leader, William Hague, decided to put the question of British membership of EMU to a ballot, having failed to find any internal consensus.

16. Robert Peston, 'Premier tiptoes through EU defence minefield', *The Financial Times*, 1 October 1998, p. 5.

17. Charles Grant, *Can Britain lead in Europe?* (London: Centre for European Reform, 1998).

18. *The Economist*, 10 October 1998, p. 40.

19. Charles Grant, *Can Britain lead in Europe?* p. 44.

20. Ibid., p. 45.

21. Ibid., p. 46.

22. Ibid., pp. 48–9.

23. *The Times*, 21 October 1998, p. 1.

24. Ibid.

25. *Agence Europe*, 26–7 October 1998, p. 5.

26. *Agence Europe*, 5 November 1998, p. 3.

27. Ibid., loc. cit.

28. Ibid., loc. cit.

29. *Agence Europe*, 6 November 1998, p. 5.

30. Ibid., p. 6.

31. Ibid., loc cit.

32. Ibid., p. 5.

33. *Agence Europe*, 9–10 November 1998, p. 5.

34. *Agence Europe*, 16–17 November 1998, p. 6.

35. Franco-British summit – *Joint Declaration on European Defence*, 4 December 1998, at http://www.ambafrance.org.uk.

36. Ibid., Para. 2.

37. Ibid., Para. 3.

38. The situation of Canada remains somewhat ambiguous but approaches to the WEU suggest that Canada may be willing to collaborate in certain activities with the full members.

39. See *FT Com*, 2 February 1999 and 10 February 1999, at ⟨http://www.ft.com/hippocampus⟩.

40. Alexander Nicoll and Ralph Atkins, 'Aerospace: European Defence Unity Urged', *Financial Times*, 2 February 1999.

Index